PANEPIPHANAL WORLD

The Florida James Joyce Series

UNIVERSITY PRESS OF FLORIDA

Florida A&M University, Tallahassee
Florida Atlantic University, Boca Raton
Florida Gulf Coast University, Ft. Myers
Florida International University, Miami
Florida State University, Tallahassee
New College of Florida, Sarasota
University of Central Florida, Orlando
University of Florida, Gainesville
University of North Florida, Jacksonville
University of South Florida, Tampa
University of West Florida, Pensacola

Panepiphanal World

James Joyce's Epiphanies

Sangam MacDuff

Foreword by Sebastian D. G. Knowles

University Press of Florida
Gainesville · Tallahassee · Tampa · Boca Raton
Pensacola · Orlando · Miami · Jacksonville · Ft. Myers · Sarasota

Published with the support of the Swiss National Science Foundation.

Copyright 2020 by Sangam MacDuff
All rights reserved.
Published in the United States of America

25 24 23 22 21 20   6 5 4 3 2 1

ISBN 978-0-8130-6632-5 (cloth)
ISBN 978-0-8130-6813-8 (pbk.)
ISBN 978-0-8130-5743-9 (ePDF)

The Library of Congress has cataloged the printed edition as follows
Names: MacDuff, Sangam, author. | Knowles, Sebastian D. G. (Sebastian David
    Guy), author of foreword.
Title: Panepiphanal world : James Joyce's epiphanies / by Sangam MacDuff ;
    foreword by Sebastian D. G. Knowles.
Other titles: James Joyce's epiphanies | Florida James Joyce series.
Description: Gainesville : University Press of Florida, 2020. | Series: The
    Florida James Joyce series | Includes bibliographical references and
    index.
Identifiers: LCCN 2019032962 (print) | LCCN 2019032963 (ebook) | ISBN
    9780813066325 (hardback) | ISBN 9780813057439 (pdf)
Subjects: LCSH: Joyce, James, 1882–1941—Criticism and interpretation.
Classification: LCC PR6019.O9 Z7183 2020 (print) | LCC PR6019.O9 (ebook)
    | DDC 823/.912—dc23
LC record available at https://lccn.loc.gov/2019032962
LC ebook record available at https://lccn.loc.gov/2019032963

The University Press of Florida is the scholarly publishing agency for the State University System of Florida, comprising Florida A&M University, Florida Atlantic University, Florida Gulf Coast University, Florida International University, Florida State University, New College of Florida, University of Central Florida, University of Florida, University of North Florida, University of South Florida, and University of West Florida.

University Press of Florida
2046 NE Waldo Road
Suite 2100
Gainesville, FL 32609
http://upress.ufl.edu

For Sabrina, Sofia, and Lilly

CONTENTS

List of Figures   ix

List of Tables   xi

Foreword   xiii

Acknowledgments   xv

Abbreviations   xvii

1. Introduction   1
2. From Genesis to Joyce: A Brief History of Epiphany   23
3. "Remember your epiphanies . . . deeply deep"   51
4. Silence and Repetition in *Dubliners*   76
5. "A day of dappled seaborne clouds": *A Portrait of the Artist*'s Epiphany   102
6. Permutations of Epiphany in *Ulysses*   145
7. The Panepiphanal World of *Finnegans Wake*   181
8. Conclusion   225

Appendix: Epiphanies in Joyce's Work   233

Notes   237

Bibliography   263

Index   279

FIGURES

1. César Abin, "Caricature of James Joyce" 60
2. Euclidian Gnomon 95
3. "Position of a Child in the Womb" 173
4. "Form of a Child in the Womb" 173

TABLES

1. Epiphanies in *Portrait*   103
2. Epiphanies in *Ulysses*   146

FOREWORD

What is actually celebrated on the Feast of the Epiphany? The appearance of the magi? Christ's Nativity, or the baptism? The manifestation of a bright star, possibly Halley's Comet, visible over Palestine a decade earlier than any of these? The Feast of the Epiphany is an open-ended signifier in the Christian calendar and so is a rich and appropriate site for MacDuff to begin. MacDuff points out that pre-Christian manifestations of the divine were generally nonnegotiable: if an angel or a god showed up in the Old Testament or in classical literature, you just had to deal with it. The key with the Christian epiphanies is that the revelations must be interpreted to be understood, a move from ontology to epistemology. As MacDuff says, following Morris Beja in this argument, an epiphany puts the responsibility on the viewer, insisting on the subjective truth of the experience.

Joyce is a palimpsest: every bit of writing is a rewriting, and his early epiphanies return in his work again and again. Three of them, in particular, show up like ghosts at every party: the one about injustice ("Apologise / Pull out his eyes"), the one about abjection ("The hole we all have"), and the one about a mother's love ("Years and years I loved you when you lay in my womb"). MacDuff's analysis of the "hole" epiphany is brilliant: MacDuff neatly connects the navel with the anus, with the navelcord of "Proteus," a church nave, and the original sense of "nave" as a central hub into which radial spokes are inserted. The reading of this epiphany displays MacDuff's maieutic art, uncoiling significance from small things, giving an embryonic image a chance to breathe and take up the space it demands. The same skill is in play with MacDuff's reading of Joyce's manuscript copy of "The Apocalypse of St. John," which is a revelation. Building from the small to the great, MacDuff constructs a compelling case not just for the importance of the document but also for the persuasiveness of his own method.

MacDuff moves from hole to whole, from vacuum to plenum. For MacDuff, silence and repetition are the anode and cathode of Joyce's art and the twin poles of the modernist mind. Each epiphany is what Bergotte, in Proust's *The Captive*, would call a "little patch of yellow wall": in the painter's dying appreciation of Vermeer's *View of Delft*, Proust captures the idea of art as a tiny part of a larger image, a precious substance in itself that also participates in a greater whole. The same happens in *Swann's Way*, as Marcel admires the twin steeples of Martinville, with the steeple of Vieuxvicq dancing behind it. His resulting creation, a page of description that celebrates the play between art and life, fills him with happiness. So it was for Joyce, who kept a manuscript of his epiphanies with him until the end of his writing life, leaving them only when he fled occupied France in December 1940. MacDuff tells us why and reintroduces us to a world we thought we knew, showing us how much more there is to see.

Sebastian D. G. Knowles
Series Editor

ACKNOWLEDGMENTS

Parts of this book have previously appeared as "Joyce's Revelation: 'The Apocalypse of Saint John' at Cornell," in *Genesic Fields: James Joyce and Genetic Criticism,* edited by Genevieve Sartor (Leiden and Boston: Brill, 2018), 118–26, and "Death and the limits of epiphany: Wordsworth's 'spots of time' and Joyce's epiphanies of death," in *James Joyce Quarterly* 53.1–2 (Fall/Winter 2015): 61–74. I am grateful to the publishers for permission to include revised versions in the present work, and to Betsy Jolas for permission to reproduce César Abin's caricature of James Joyce from *transition* 21 (March, 1932): 256.

Research grants from the European Society for the Study of English and the Swiss Association of University Teachers of English enabled me to visit the Universities of Buffalo, Cornell, and Yale in 2015, and I am grateful to the Swiss National Science Foundation, who supported an Open Access edition of this publication.

In addition to institutional support, I have benefited from the assistance of more people than I can hope to acknowledge, including the many colleagues, students, and friends who helped to shape these ideas. I thank them all, though I can but name a few: David Spurr guided me throughout the project, helping to improve it in every way; Deborah Madsen, Maud Ellmann, Fritz Senn, Finn Fordham, Simon Swift, Angus McFadzean, Sebastian Knowles, Jean-Michel Rabaté, and Morris Beja read earlier drafts, offering perceptive criticism and encouragement; Eleanor Deumens masterminded the project at the University Press of Florida; Penelope Cray edited the manuscript meticulously; and Stephanye Hunter has been instrumental in bringing it to press.

Having always lived in communities, I am blessed with many friends and a large, extended family. It would be impossible to thank them all individually, but I am particularly grateful to Mike Wilding, Rosemary Summers, David Wyllie, Sally Wyllie, John Lennard, Tom Raymont, Rory O'Bryen, and Tristram Stuart for their unfailing friendship and support. Finally, and most importantly, I thank my parents, my children, and Sabrina, without whom I could never have written this book.

ABBREVIATIONS

CW	Joyce, James. *The Critical Writings*. Ed. Ellsworth Mason and Richard Ellmann. New York: Viking, 1973.
D	———. *Dubliners*. London: Penguin, 2000.
E	———. *Exiles: A Play in Three Acts*. London: J. Cape, 1972.
FW	———. *Finnegans Wake*. London: Penguin, 1992.
JJA	———. *The James Joyce Archive*. Ed. Michael Groden et al. 63 vols. New York: Garland, 1977.
LI–LIII	———. *Letters of James Joyce*. 3 vols. Ed. Stuart Gilbert and Richard Ellmann. New York: Viking, 1957–66.
P	———. *A Portrait of the Artist as a Young Man*. London: Penguin, 1992.
PSW	———. *Poems and Shorter Writings*. Ed. Richard Ellmann, A. Walton Litz, and John Whittier-Ferguson. London: Faber and Faber, 1991.
SH	———. *Stephen Hero*. Ed. Theodore Spencer, rev. John J. Slocum and Herbert Cahoon. London: J. Cape, 1975.
U	———. *Ulysses: The Corrected Text*. Ed. Hans Walter Gabler. Harmondsworth: Penguin, 1986.
OE	Beckett, Samuel, et al. *Our Exagmination Round His Factification for Incamination of "Work in Progress."* London: Faber and Faber, 1972.
JJ	Ellmann, Richard. *James Joyce*. New York: Oxford University Press, 1959.
MBK	Joyce, Stanislaus. *My Brother's Keeper*. New York: Viking, 1958.
WD	Scholes, Robert, and Richard M. Kain. *The Workshop of Daedalus: James Joyce and the Raw Materials for* A Portrait of the Artist as a Young Man. Evanston, Ill.: Northwestern University Press, 1965.

1

Introduction

> He desired not to be a man of letters but a spirit expressing itself through language.
>
> James Joyce

In Joyce's early novel, *Stephen Hero*, Stephen Daedalus famously defines an "epiphany" as

> a sudden spiritual manifestation, whether in the vulgarity of speech or of gesture or in a memorable phase of the mind itself. He believed that it was for the man of letters to record these epiphanies with extreme care, seeing that they themselves are the most delicate and evanescent of moments. (*SH* 216)

This definition introduced the term "epiphany" to literary studies, shaping all subsequent debates. Indeed, the passage has been interpreted so extensively that one might wonder whether there is anything left to add, but the quotation I have chosen for my epigraph, which Joyce recorded under "Dedalus" in his alphabetical notebook (*WD* 96), indicates how much remains to be analyzed, for there has not yet been a study of Joyce's *linguistic* epiphanies.

In this book, I argue that language is the site of the Joycean epiphany: unlike classical, biblical, and Romantic epiphanies, the "spiritual manifestation" is not a divine apparition or an immanent revelation but "spirit expressing itself through language" (*WD* 96). Stephen's aesthetics of epiphany, the manuscript epiphanies themselves, their role in the genesis of Joyce's works, and the lifelong investigation of language he conducted through them all point to a single conclusion: for Joyce, an epiphany is not a revelation of God, nature, or the mind but of the human spirit embodied in language.

But if Joyce's epiphanies are simply linguistic phenomena, why has their significance been overlooked for so long? From the publication of *Stephen Hero* in 1944 until Morris Beja's *Epiphany in the Modern Novel* (1971), the concept of epiphany was central to Joyce studies;[1] indeed, it became so widespread that some critics believed the term had become a worn-out cliché or meaningless catch-all. Ironically, the most virulent attack came from Robert Scholes,[2] who edited the first complete edition of Joyce's epiphanies in 1965.[3] Having coauthored *The Workshop of Daedalus*, Scholes's objection to "epiphany hunters" was naturally influential, and since the 1970s, the epiphanies have largely been neglected in Joyce studies.

While Scholes's demand for greater precision was warranted, the reaction against the epiphanies was misguided, particularly because there has been so much confusion about Joyce's early texts. In 1941, Harry Levin, one of the earliest and best of Joyce's readers, believed that the "book of epiphanies" Stephen thinks of writing in *Stephen Hero* was *Dubliners* (Levin 1941, 29). With the publication of the manuscript "epiphanies" in Buffalo (1956) and Cornell (1965), Levin's mistake became apparent: by 1904, Joyce had written at least forty short texts he called "epiphanies." Even when these were identified, there was still confusion about their genre: several critics referred to them as prose pieces, despite the fact that Joyce's brief, enigmatic texts alternate between dramatic sketches and prose-poetic vignettes. The latter are highly lyrical but obscure, while the elliptical dialogue of the dramaticules is frequently puzzling; there is rarely, if ever, a "sudden spiritual manifestation." Indeed, Joyce's epiphanies often seem trivial, or even insignificant, rather than revelatory, making it difficult to reconcile them with Daedalus's epiphanic theory. To many commentators, this obscurity and banality seemed to undermine the claims of early critics like Irene Hendry that "Joyce's work is a tissue of epiphanies" (1946, 461), but one could equally argue that it is their "vulgarity of speech"—or ordinariness of language—that substantiates her intuition. Not recognizing the fundamentally *textual* nature of the epiphanies, in the 1970s and 1980s post-structural critics concentrated on *Ulysses* and *Finnegans Wake*, with some critics regarding the epiphanies as juvenilia— a notion conclusively disproved by the fact that three-quarters of Joyce's epiphanies are reused in his later works.

These misunderstandings concerning the nature and function of the epiphanies are partly explained by the uncertainty surrounding the texts.

Their date of composition is unknown: the most likely interval is 1901–1903, but Joyce may have begun earlier and continued later.[4] Their number is uncertain: since an autograph manuscript of twenty-two epiphanies in Buffalo is numbered discontinuously to seventy-one, it has long been thought that more than thirty are missing, and critics have tried to identify the "lost" epiphanies in Joyce's works; but a typescript of the epiphanies I discovered in 2015 raises doubts about the authenticity of the verso numbering.[5] The sequence of the Yale typescript and the uncertainty of the Buffalo numbering also call into question the order of the epiphanies: it has been assumed, for instance, that Joyce progressed from dramatic to lyrical epiphanies in his prose works, but close study of the extant manuscripts, including the Yale typescript, shows that this claim rests on false grounds, and that little, in fact, can be said with any confidence about the order of the epiphanies.

Given the uncertainty surrounding the date, number, and order of the epiphanies, I believe it is high time to reassess their significance. In this book, I offer fresh readings of Joyce's epiphanies, both as distinctive individual texts that question the nature of epiphany as an event and as a genre, and also as an ordered collection or "book of epiphanies." Since Joyce reused thirty of the forty extant epiphanies, I examine them in the context of his subsequent works, returning to the earliest surviving manuscripts to consider the role of the epiphanies in shaping Joyce's oeuvre, their relation to other modernist epiphanies, and what this might teach us about modernism as a whole.

The Crucible

The earliest critical commentary on Joyce's epiphanies is Stanislaus Joyce's Dublin Diary, begun in September 1903. The diary, which Stanislaus called "My Crucible," is a key, and familiar, source of information about Joyce's earliest work, but its crucial, alchemical role as a repository of those works has rarely been recognized. The diary opens with a memorable account of James Joyce's developing character, lamenting his preference for "the sampling of liqueurs, the devising of dinners, the care of dress, and whoring" over serious artistic endeavor, for Stanislaus recognized his brother's literary talent to be "very great indeed" (1971, 14). Writing before Joyce had drafted any of the works that were to make his reputation, and with only a handful of poems and epiphanies to go by, Stanislaus proved an astute judge of his elder brother, and his preference for Joyce's epiphanies over his lyrics was equally prescient (1971, 14). The finely wrought poems, put into sequence by Stanislaus, yielded Joyce's first publication, *Chamber Music* (1907), but the formal innovations of the epiphanies initiated an extraordinary literary experiment that led to *Dubliners*, *A Portrait of the Artist as a Young Man*, *Ulysses*, and *Finnegans Wake*.

When Stanislaus Joyce copied twenty-four of his brother's epiphanies into his "Selections in Prose from Various Authors" (begun in October 1903), alongside quotations from Tolstoy, Goethe, and Rousseau, the comparison must have seemed almost as precocious as Joyce's comment to his parents, aged thirteen, on Hermann Sudermann's *Heimat*: "The subject of the play is genius breaking out in the home and against the home. You needn't have gone to see it. It's going to happen in your own house" (*MBK* 87). Despite Joyce's monumental hubris, however, in hindsight he was vindicated, just as Stanislaus's "Selections" now appears to be an accurate assessment of Joyce's stature. Copied no later than 1904, the collection indicates the crucial role of the epiphanies in shaping Joyce's oeuvre: A. Walton Litz rightly judges them Joyce's "earliest important literary compositions" (157), and to the extent that Joyce's work is "one great work" (Tindall 1959, ix), the epiphanies are a point of origin.[6]

In addition to his notebook "Selections," which contains the only extant copy of seventeen epiphanies, Stanislaus made two fair copies (Cornell 4609 Bd Ms 3). These epiphanies are preserved, along with nine of Joyce's earliest manuscripts, on paper that Stanislaus Joyce reused for his diary, showing the extent to which Stanislaus was already his brother's keeper in Dublin. In December 1904, Stanislaus decided to call the diary "My Crucible" (1971, 99), but the literary miscellany he used to "refine [him]self" (1971, 99), including five early essays, Joyce's holograph copy of Revelation, two poems, and three epiphanies, constitutes the crucible of Joyce's art.

In the first of these essays, a review of "Ecce Homo" at the Royal Hibernian Academy (1899), Joyce's response to Munkácsy's Passion trilogy tells us much about his attitude toward divine revelation. *Ecce Homo*: "Behold the Man," Joyce translates Pilate's words, praising the humanity of Munkácsy's Christ not as a remote instrument of "Divine Law," the "Incarnate Son of God," but as a simple "Man of Sorrows." Likewise, he approves the artist's choice "to make Mary a mother and John a man" (*CW* 36): his figures are not symbols of higher spiritual truths but dramatic representations of the human spirit, just as the "sudden spiritual manifestation" of Joyce's epiphanies is an immanent, humanist revelation rather than a transcendental theophany.

In "Ecce Homo," Joyce calls this "drama," an expression of "the everlasting hopes, desires and hates of humanity" in any form of art (*CW* 32), echoing the same definition in his first paper for the Literary and Historical Society of University College Dublin (*CW* 41). In that paper, "Drama and Life" (1900), Joyce claims that "drama arises spontaneously out of life and is coeval with it" (43); more radically still, he argues that drama exists even "before it takes form, independently" of the work of art (41): "It might be said fantastically that as soon as men and women began life in the world there was above them and about them, a spirit, of which they were dimly conscious, which they would have had sojourn in their midst in deeper intimacy and for whose truth they became seekers in after times, longing to lay hands upon it" (41). At first, this spirit, above and about us, is an "elfish . . . Aerial" thing, yet "in after times," we seek to lay hands on it through a "deeper intimacy" with the "truth" of our own experience (41). Drama seeks to manifest this spirit, and since it is "coeval" with life, Joyce concludes that "life we must accept as we see it before our eyes, men and women as we meet them in the real world, not as we apprehend them in the world of faery" (45). This fundamental acceptance of life, however we encounter it, is the attitude of Joyce's mature art; yet here, at least, it grows out of a "longing to lay hands upon" spirit. As it happens, Joyce's adverb, "fantastically," derives from the same root as "epiphany," and it might be said epiphanically that in the "Crucible" essays Joyce conceives of drama, encompassing all arts and all of life, as the revelation of an animating spirit.

The most zealous statement of this youthful credo occurs in the next paper Joyce read to the Literary and Historical Society, "James Clarence Mangan" (1902), where he writes of a "serene spirit which enters . . . the hearts of men." This spirit is beauty, or "the splendour of truth,"[7] "a gracious presence when the imagination contemplates intensely the truth of its own being or the visible world, and the spirit which proceeds out of truth and beauty is the holy spirit of joy" (83). While Joyce came to distrust those big words like "beauty" and "truth," recoiling from Platonic forms and theosophical beliefs into the empirical, "the holy spirit of joy" remains, from bathers whooping a raucous "call of life" in *Portrait* (184) and the hockey players celebrating joyfully in "Nestor" (prompting

Stephen's famous definition of God as "a shout in the street" [*U* 2.386]) to the "joysis crisis" of *Finnegans Wake* (395.32; see Spurr 2015). These spontaneous outbursts of powerful emotion are highly dramatic, in Joyce's sense, but also Romantic, whereas his epiphanies frequently appear trivial and enigmatic; yet Joyce's conception of an immanent, ubiquitous epiphany "you damn well have to see" (*U* 9.86) is already contained in the manifestation of "the visible world." Unlike the vision of the Romantics, there is nothing beyond this revelation, just as there is no hidden significance in Joyce's epiphanies; everything is given, however prosaic it may appear. Yet this does not entail the reduction of the world, or the text, to meaningless matter; rather, the world as we see it comes into being through imaginative contemplation, just as for Joyce the materiality of language reveals "the continual affirmation of the spirit" (*CW* 83).

Joyce echoes this conclusion in *Ulysses*, where Bloom dissents "tacitly from Stephen's views on the eternal affirmation of man in literature" (*U* 17.29–30), suggesting a certain distance from the author's early theory. Yet the substitution of "man" for "spirit" is wholly in keeping with Joyce's earlier view, as *Stephen Hero* makes clear: "The spirit of man makes a continual affirmation" (*SH* 85). Although Daedalus, the "heaven-ascending essayist," is undoubtedly mocked for his epiphanic vision of literature and poetry ("the poetic phenomenon is signalled in the heavens"), it is important to realize that the paper he delivers to the University's Literary and Historical Society—an essay first titled "Drama and Life," though it takes its conclusion from "James Clarence Mangan"—is a tissue of Joyce's early aesthetics and criticism (44–85). Whatever irony there may be, these are Joyce's poetics, and after being refined in the crucible of his art, they culminate in a powerful conclusion: that language is itself an epiphany, the continuous manifestation of the human spirit.

The Language of Revelation and the Revelation of Language

One word stands out in Stephen's "*revelation* of the beautiful" (*SH* 85). The only word in italics, it emphasizes the revelatory quality of Stephen's aesthetics. This is not simply a manner of speaking; Stephen's aesthetics are literally drawn from Revelation. "[T]he holy spirit of joy" that continually affirms the human spirit is announced in Apocalyptic terms: after the "treacherous order" is destroyed, "a host of voices is heard singing, a little faintly at first, of a serene spirit which enters . . . the hearts of men"

(*CW* 83; Rev. 5:11–13). Likewise, the primeval spirit of "Drama and Life," that "roaming air" that "has never left our vision, [and] shall never leave it, till the firmament is as a scroll rolled away," proceeds to and from the Apocalypse (*CW* 41; Rev. 6:14; *P* 121). These allusions are explained by a surprising document in Stanislaus's "Crucible": a handwritten copy of Revelation, made by the young James Joyce.

This manuscript, titled "The Apocalypse of St. John," has not received the attention it deserves. It was discovered by Scholes and Kain, who cite it as evidence of Joyce's familiarity with the King James Bible, the version he copied (despite the Douay title [*WD* 264]). Virginia Moseley repeats this point in her preface to *Joyce and the Bible* (viii), but, surprisingly, she doesn't mention the manuscript again. Roy Gottfried elaborates on the same point, providing a fuller account of the Bibles Joyce quotes from, but his account of the manuscript itself adds little to Robert Scholes's catalog of the Joyce Collection at Cornell. Although Michael Groden's *Index* also lists the manuscript, it was not reproduced in the *James Joyce Archive* and remains unpublished. This may explain why Joyce's autograph copy has not been studied in detail, but scrutiny of the "Apocalypse" reveals a tantalizing glimpse of Joyce's early attitude toward religion and aesthetics.

On sixty-four loose sheets, Joyce copied the entire book of Revelation, through to chapter 18, verse 3; an additional leaf contains Revelation 19:11–17, suggesting that Joyce may have completed the copy on pages now lost, rather than having deliberately broken off. The manuscript must predate epiphany 1904, since the first date Stanislaus records on the recto used for his diary is January 6, 1904 (f.71), but it may have been made considerably earlier.[8] An unusually fair copy, the extant pages contain no marginalia or annotations, and aside from the lacuna (18.3–19.11), there are very few omissions, errors, or repetitions. This fidelity is interesting in itself: I can think of no other text Joyce copies with such careful and sustained attention, which raises the question why he did so and why he chose the King James Version rather than the Douay-Rheims translation he was brought up with.

Notwithstanding its accuracy, there are several significant changes to the source text that shed light on Joyce's procedure. In addition to minor punctuation changes, there are six corrections, thirty-six substantive variations, and hundreds of marked letter s's. Many of these are trivial, but in three cases they are revealing. First, Joyce occasionally seeks to clarify the sense through parenthetical insertions, suggesting an interest in the literal meaning of the text: for instance, in 4.3 he adds, "And he that sat **(on the throne)** was to look" (Joyce's alterations in bold), and in 4.7, "the second **living being (was)** like a calf." In the Authorized Version Joyce owned,[9] the latter verse reads "And the first beast was like a lion, and the second beast like a calf, and the third beast had a face as a man, and the fourth beast was like a flying eagle"; Joyce substitutes "living being" for "beast" throughout, as he does through most of the book, suggesting an alternative interpretation of the beasts of Apocalypse.[10] Likewise, his version of 2.4, which changes "thy first love" to "my first love," and 11.3, where "peace" replaces "power," may provide clues to Joyce's reading of Revelation; in these cases, variation implies interpretation. The third type of change concerns the letter s, which Joyce strikes through more than three hundred times, as in 5.1: "And I S̸aw in the right hand of him that S̸at on the throne a book written within and on the backside, S̸ealed with S̸even S̸eals." At first, he marked only soft initial s's, as in this verse, suggesting that he was interested in the frequent sibilance of the Authorized Version, but later he also slashed Z, ʃ and ʒ sounds, in initial, medial, and terminal positions (while never striking through a soft c), indicating that he became focused more on the letter than on the sound.

This characteristically Joycean focus on the meanderings of a single letter indicates an interest in the language of Revelation, lending support to the obvious explanation that Joyce chose the King James Version for its celebrated style, perhaps copying it as an exercise in literary apprenticeship. But if so, this doesn't explain why Joyce chose the book of Revelation in particular. He would have found "the rhythmic rise and fall" of "lucid supple periodic prose" (*P* 180–81) throughout the Authorized Version; and even the most characteristic qualities of Revelation—its geometrical structure, its rich, concatenating imagery, and its lyrical language—can be found in Daniel, Ezekiel, or Psalms. Nevertheless, the formal structure of Revelation, organized around sequentially unfolding symbolic patterns like the seven churches, seals, trumpets, figures, and vials of chapters 1–16, rather than linear plotlines, may have attracted Joyce as a model of narrative order. Similarly, the Apocalyptic proliferation of images and symbolic associations, whose ultimate significance remains obscure, can be compared to the gnomonic principles of absence and reiteration that govern Joyce's art, from the epiphanies to the *Wake*.

Joyce's changes, whether clarifying the sense or altering the meaning, show his interest in interpreting Revelation; how he did so can be inferred from the extensive use he made of it subsequently. Each of Joyce's works can be considered as a revelation: the thwarted hopes and dreams of *Dubliners*, the artist's soul in *Portrait*, the extraordinariness of the ordinary in *Ulysses*, the revelation of language in the *Wake*; and each of Joyce's books alludes frequently to the book of Revelation. In *Portrait*, Father Arnall draws on the imagery of Apocalypse to convey the dread of final judgment:

> Doomsday was at hand. The stars of heaven were falling upon the earth like the figs cast by the figtree which the wind has shaken. The sun, the great luminary of the universe, had become as sackcloth of hair. The moon was bloodred. The firmament was as a scroll rolled away. (*P* 121)

Compare Revelation 6:12–14:

> And I beheld when he had opened the sixth seal, and, lo, there was a great earthquake; and the sun became black as sackcloth of hair, and the moon became as blood;
> And the stars of heaven fell unto the earth, even as a fig tree casteth her untimely figs, when she is shaken of a mighty wind.
> And the heaven departed as a scroll when it is rolled together; and every mountain and island were moved out of their places.

The preacher goes on to cite Revelation 10:1–6, and after the sermon, Stephen feels the sinful "beast" in his soul blasted by "the angel's trumpet," and the "wind of the last day" scourging the "jewel-eyed harlots of his imagination" (*P* 123–24; Rev. 8–11, 17). His contrition leads to repentance, confession, absolution, and a new communion with church and God, but this traditional journey of the soul is only a passage in the artist's apprenticeship, so that the language of Revelation prepares the ground for Joyce's *Künstlerroman*.

Ulysses also contains numerous allusions to Revelation, including Bloom's throwaway, "Blood of the Lamb" (*U* 8.9; Rev. 7:14–15), Ann Hathaway, "whore of Babylon" (*U* 9.339; Rev. 17:5), "the new Jerusalem" (*U* 12.1473; Rev. 21–22), the Alpha and the Omega (*U* 3.39, 13.1258, 1264; Rev. 1:8, 1:11, 21:6, 22:13), and the traditional iconography of the evangelists (*U* 12.1443–46; Rev. 4.7–8). The densest concentration is found in "Circe," leading Virginia Moseley to claim that "Joyce's technique of hallucination in the Nighttown scene points directly to the last book of the New Testament" (65). This probably overstates the case, but the episode is certainly branded with the "Mark of the beast" (*U* 15.209): the phrase is repeated at 15.844–45; another firebrand preacher, Alexander J. Dowie, denounces Bloom as "the white bull mentioned in the Apocalypse" (15.1757–58; cf. Rev. 13, 16–17); and soon after, news of the "Antichrist" is in the papers (15.2135), with a Nessian "Sea serpent" announcing his "Safe arrival" (2140; cf. 2135 and Rev. 12:19). On the one hand, these examples support Moseley's reading of the book of Revelation as the nightmare of history; on the other, they attest to Joyce's continuing fascination with the beasts of Apocalypse, whether evangelical or anti-Christian. Setting aside problems of tone, in both cases Joyce tends to bring symbolic beasts back down to earthly creatures: the "living beings" representing Matthew, Mark, Luke, and John are brought closer to home as the four Annalists of Irish history, symbolized by a "bogoak sceptre" (lance), an American puma (in place of the British lion), "a Kerry calf and a golden eagle from Carrantuohill" (12.1443–46). Similarly, "Mark of the beast" (15.209) refers to Bloom's close brush with a "dragon sandstrewer" (185), or street-cleaning vehicle, and more immediately to "lost cattle" (208), which in light of the preceding chapter, "Oxen of the Sun," can be read as both real cattle lost to foot-and-mouth disease and the semen Bloom expended through autostimulation in "Nausicaa," a mark of his crime against fecundity.

Finnegans Wake pursues this interest in beasts of burden and beasts of revelation: at the end of 3.3, the four old men who represent, among other things, the four evangelists and the four Masters, metamorphose into the ass: "Mattahah! Marahah! Luahah! Joahanahanahana!" (554.10); in 3.4, they become the "four hoarsemen on their apolkaloops" (557.1–2; Rev. 7). Unlike in *Ulysses*, though, this beast is less humanized or animalized than made literal: according to the four, "there are fully six hundred and six ragwords" in Shaun's "Magis landeguage," tainting the language of the *Wake* (cf. 478.17–18) with the number of the beast (Rev. 13:8), here reduced to Salvarsan 606, a remedy for syphilis. Beginning with "a bockalips" (6.26), the *Wake* is frequently figured as "Revelation!" (242.21): Shaun the Post, circulator of language, declares "Johannisburg's a revelation" (453.33–34); as "Walker John Referent," he is an avatar of John of Patmos, exhorted by the Four (analysts as well as Annalists and evangelists) to "Play us your patmost! And unpackyoulloups!" (526), thereby revealing the book's unconscious. Indeed, one of the most strikingly self-reflexive images in the *Wake* is that of the sealed book of life (Rev. 5–6, 20:12; cf. *FW* 22.28, 212.23,

245.20, 264.06), a closed scroll that finally unfurls in book 4, when "A hand from the cloud emerges, holding a chart expanded" (593.18; cf. Rev. 6:14). As these examples indicate, *Finnegans Wake* rewrites the book of revelation as the revelation of the book, an epiphany of language.

The origins of this revelation can be traced back to "The Study of Languages" (1898–1899), held in Stanislaus's "Crucible." Joyce's matriculation essay, composed when he was sixteen or seventeen, lacks the sophistication of his mature reflections on language, but it provides a brilliant insight into his early theory. Shaped by pedagogical influences and the prevailing intellectual climate, Joyce's essay gives the first sign of his lifelong fascination with etymology, noting that "in the history of words there is much that indicates the history of men" (28). Echoing Ruskin (1864, §27), Joyce recommends studying the classics because they allow us to access "the feelings of great writers, to enter into their hearts and spirits, to be admitted, by privilege, into the privacy of their proper thoughts" (*CW* 29). This spiritual conception of literature may sound naive, particularly when Joyce idealizes the purity of language, which the "masters of English" keep "inviolate," but later he was to see the same epiphany constantly manifest in the continuous "transition" of language (*CW* 29), whether through its written history or through the protean speech he heard around him. As Joyce saw, language is constantly being created in its continuous affirmation of the spirit, and each of his works presents this linguistic epiphany. The result of this experiment was Joyce's discovery, "I can do anything with language I want" (*JJ* 702). His practice of turning words over and around, breaking old languages down letter by letter to piece together a new one, prompted *transition* to hail the "Revolution of the Word,"[11] but really Joyce was engaged in the *revelation* of the word, or better still, its "revolations" (*FW* 350.32). The origins of this practice go back to the epiphanies.

"Epiphany" and the "book of epiphanies"

Alongside critical and theological texts, "My Crucible" contains Joyce's most formative literary material: drafts of two poems for *Chamber Music* and three epiphanies. Stanislaus Joyce copied these epiphanies twice in the same order (*JJA* 7.46–49), suggesting they may have been intended for circulation, which correlates with Joyce's reference to a collection titled "'Epiphany'" (Joyce's quotation marks: February 8, 1903, *LII* 28) that he seems to have shown George Russell and W. B. Yeats, who praised Joyce's "delicate spiritual writing" (S. Joyce 1971, 14). Writing from Paris a month later, Joyce told Stanislaus he had "written fifteen epiphanies—of which twelve are insertions and three additions" (*LII* 35), which indicates that Joyce thought of his "epiphanies" as an ordered collection. Although he chose not to publish the ensemble in an independent volume, he clearly held his early work in high esteem, apparently keeping a copy with him, through all his peregrinations, until the last months of his life, when he fled Saint-Gérand-le-Puy in the winter of 1940.[12] With the exception of *Dubliners*, Joyce recycled epiphanies in every major work, including *Pomes Penyeach*, *Stephen Hero*, *Exiles*, and *Giacomo Joyce*, as well as *Portrait*, *Ulysses*, and *Finnegans Wake*, so that Joyce's "earliest important literary compositions" can also be regarded as a point of origin for his oeuvre.

In total, forty epiphanies survive, although there may originally have been more. Twenty-three are in Joyce's hand (including one draft), while seventeen are preserved by Stanislaus. Never more than a page long, they are roughly divided between dramatic sketches and lyrical prose poems, recording two types of manifestation, "in the vulgarity of speech or of gesture" and those from "a memorable phase of the mind" (*SH* 216). Daedalus thinks of "collecting many such moments together in a book of epiphanies" (216); within the surviving pages of *Stephen Hero*, he never does so, but the fourteen epiphanies Joyce reused form key points in the novel (cf. *WD* 6). Similarly, Joyce (who signed his first short stories Stephen Daedalus), never published a single volume of "Epiphany"; instead, he wrote *several* books of epiphanies, constantly recycling his earliest work.

Before examining how he did so, it will be useful to consider an example of each type of epiphany. "The Hole in Georgie's Stomach," a dramatic epiphany, opens a hiatus in the text, a hole that leads to the death of Joyce's brother George and to the navel, as the source of life and oracular knowledge:

[Dublin: in the house in
Glengariff Parade: evening]

Mrs Joyce —(*crimson, trembling, appears at the parlour door*) . . . Jim!
Joyce —(*at the piano*) . . . Yes?
Mrs Joyce —Do you know anything about the body?. . What ought I do? . . . There's

	some matter coming away from the hole in Georgie's stomach. . . . Did you ever hear of that happening?
Joyce	—(*surprised*) . . . I don't know. . . .
Mrs Joyce	—Ought I send for the doctor, do you think?
Joyce	—I don't know. . . . . . What hole?
Mrs Joyce	—(*impatient*) . . . The hole we all have . . . . . here (*points*)
Joyce	—(*stands up*)¹³

As with the other dramatic epiphanies, stage directions, speech headings, and precise lineation evince Joyce's careful composition, while the use of contractions, Hiberno-English, timed pauses, and prosodic features give the impression of authentic speech. The most important of these features is certainly ellipsis, both in the gaps and silences that riddle the text and in the unspoken hole "we all have /. . . . .here."¹⁴ This epiphany is surely the most striking example of Stephen's "vulgarity of speech or of gesture," and it is shocking, at least on a virginal reading, precisely because of its uncertainty: which hole? Clearly Joyce is confused, since he has to ask, and the dramatic stage direction, "stands up," immediately after Mrs Joyce's deictic indication, mischievously plays on the reader's principal doubt, the anus.

When we know that Georgie Joyce contracted typhoid fever, developed peritonitis, and died of a perforated intestine on March 9, 1902 (*JJ* 97–98), then we can be sure the hole is the navel. It would be implausible to assume that Mrs. Joyce doesn't know the word, and even if she considers it indelicate, it seems strange that she doesn't use it. Perhaps, like Mr. Kernan, who cannot remember the correct word for the body of a church in "Grace"—that is, the nave—she is simply unable to recall it. In fact, "navel" is derived from "nave," which originally means a central hub, and like the hub of a wheel, into which radial spokes are inserted, this central hole supports a number of possibilities. A textual hole itself, we may be tempted to think that if this is one of the little slips Stanislaus said Joyce was trying to capture, those "little errors and gestures . . . by which people betrayed the very things they were most careful to conceal," then perhaps May (Mary) Joyce betrays her fear of the body, or mortality, or alternatively perhaps Joyce, under the shadow of Ibsen, wants to reveal the social mores that prevent people from speaking openly, even in the face of death.

Stanislaus tells us how deeply Georgie's death affected James (*MBK* 134–36)—after all, he called his own son Giorgio, and by a strange coincidence, Joyce himself died of peritonitis (*JJ* 98)—yet the power of this epiphany lies less in the shock of the experience than in its associations. This is apparent in the word "hole," repeated three times, which is not only a semantic hole, holding the space open for a number of possible referents, but also, when fixed to the navel, a linguistic cord linking back to the body of language. Indeed, the navel has a central place in Joyce's corpus: Maud Ellmann contends that Stephen's "strandentwining cable of all flesh" (*U* 3.37) can be traced back to the word "foetus" in *Portrait* (89), and that the "irrepressible Greek e" in *Ulysses* betrays a Holmesian clue to the omphalos, for at the navel of the world is inscribed a capital epsilon; she even suggests that this capital E may be related to Earwicker's lateral symbols in the *Wake* (1984, 96–103). Be that as it may, it is worth remembering that in both the Gilbert and the Linati schemata, the art of "Proteus," in which Stephen thinks of a navelcord leading to "Edenville," is philology. Thus, as Hugh Kenner argues, the strandentwining cables are not only of flesh but also of language, cords of all words linking back through the great philological tree (94–120).

In *Stephen Hero*, we learn that Daedalus reads Skeats's etymological dictionary "by the hour" (*SH* 32), and it is a fair bet that Joyce did the same. The power of the epiphany comes from the fact that "the hole we all have here" is never named, so that its very absence exerts a pressure of meaning, asking the reader to supply the missing reference. Throughout the epiphany, words are put under pressure, and this pressure comes from within—that is, from the pressure of meaning they bear within themselves. For instance, "hole," meaning hollow, is cognate with "hold," as in the hold of a ship, and both may be derived from the Teutonic base *hal*, meaning to cover or hide. Thus, in Joyce's epiphanies, apparently hollow words cover their own hidden meanings. A good example is the word "matter," which, according to Skeat, is etymologically related to "pus" and "mother," so that the word itself threatens to secrete its subcutaneous content. In a similar vein, Skeat defines "body," related to the Sanskrit *bandlia* (meaning "bondage" or "fetter") as "that which confines the soul," while "stomach" is derived from a Greek word στομάχος, meaning a mouth, an opening, or the gullet, probably connected with στένω, to groan or sigh, and Sanskrit *stan*, to sound, so that we can read the epiphany in a new light: despite his absence, Georgie's specter seems to speak through the confines of the "body" in the text,[15] as his "stomach" becomes a kind of mouth giving voice to its own meanings through the "matter" that exudes from its unspoken "hole."

In a quite literal sense, spoken language issues from an oracular hole, but if Lacan is right that language arises from desire and that desire is founded on an imaginary lack at the heart of subjectivity, then language itself is predicated on a central nave, an absence at its origin.[16] Attempting to pin down the meanings of a word like "matter" through dictionary definitions or etymological derivations leads to endless threads of receding meaning that support unlimited webs of linguistic association. Even when diligent detective work uncovers definite referential content, as is the case in this epiphany, there is always an element of uncertainty in Joyce's language. Philip Herring traces Joyce's uncertainty principle back to the word "gnomon" in *Dubliners* (xii), but I would argue that it is already at work in the epiphanies, for, as Jean-Michel Rabaté has argued, Joyce's work, like Stephen's world, micro- and macro-cosm, is founded "upon the void. Upon incertitude, upon unlikelihood" (1991, chap. 1; *U* 9.842).

That void, I have suggested, lies at the heart of language, but Rabaté contends that for Joyce as much as Stephen, there is one tenet of faith: *amor matris*, the love of a mother, in both its senses (viii–xxiii, 39–40). We see this in one of Joyce's lyrical epiphanies, "She Comes at Night":

> She comes at night when the city is still;
> invisible, inaudible, all unsummoned. She
> comes from her ancient seat to visit the
> least of her children, mother most venerable,
> as though he had never been alien to her.
> She knows the inmost heart; therefore
> she is gentle, nothing exacting; saying,
> I am susceptible of change, an imaginative
> influence in the hearts of my children.
> Who has pity for you when you are sad
> among the strangers? Years and years I
> loved you when you lay in my womb.

Stanislaus tells us that this is the record of a dream Joyce had in Paris, probably in early 1903, in which Mary Joyce is "confused in his sleeping brain with the image of the Virgin Mother" (*MBK* 229–30). "[M]other most venerable" seems to support Stanislaus's interpretation, but it is not the only one. As she says, her image is "susceptible of change": "ancient seat" evokes a pagan figure of power, while "the least of her children" suggests female fertility, so that she is as much matriarchal goddess as mother of God. In dreamlike fashion, her image changes from phrase to phrase, exerting a potentially unlimited "imaginative influence" on the mind of the reader. Yet the reason this epiphany evokes so many associations is precisely that at its heart there is a gap, an absence, like "The Hole in Georgie's Stomach." "She knows the inmost heart," but she never reveals its truth, even in "Circe" when Stephen asks the ghost of his mother, "Tell me the word, mother, . . . The word known to all men" (*U* 15.4192–93). Gabler's restoration at 9.429–30 strongly suggests that word is "love," but its power, surely, lies in the fact that it is not given, because the very absence of an answer summons up any number of possibilities.[17]

This paradoxical nexus in which meaning seems to proliferate from its absence characterizes Joyce's lyrical epiphanies, pointing to a constituent paradox at the nucleus of the signifier itself. There are various ways one might theorize this gnomic condition; here I draw on psychoanalysis. As the record of a real dream, epiphany #34 confirms Freud's remarks on the nature of condensation: "It is in fact impossible to be sure that a dream has been fully interpreted. Even if the solution seems satisfactory and without gaps, the possibility always remains that the dream may have yet another meaning," because "[t]here is at least one spot in every dream at which it is unplumbable—a navel, as it were, that is its point of contact with the unknown" (1977, 383, 186). Analogous to the unspoken umbilicus of the "Hole" epiphany, in "She Comes at Night" this navel that connects to the unknown is the "inmost heart" the mother never names.

Although Stephen hedges his bets in saying that "*amor matris . . . may* be the only true thing in life" (*U* 9.843; my emphasis), Rabaté is more definite: he posits love as Joyce's central tenet of faith, for love is "[w]hat resists, or ought to resist, doubt" (xviii). As I have shown, though, it is not clear what the mother knows in epiphany #34; her knowledge of the "inmost heart" is passed over in silence, so that love is only one possibility. Through resonant hiatuses like the hole in epiphany #19 and the heart in epiphany #34, Joyce seems to show that the only thing definite in language is its lack of definite meaning, while paradoxically, uncertainty produces a potentially infinite number of possibilities.

This certainty in the void, coupled with the endless deferral and proliferation of meaning, characterizes Joyce's elegiac epiphanies, four of which deal with the death of his brother Georgie and three with the loss of his mother. Like Wordsworth's "spots of time," each of which is an encounter with mortality, death is a central theme in Joyce's epiphanies and their only certainty. Another epiphany, which relates to Georgie's death, ends: "I am very sorry he died. I cannot pray for him as the others do. . . . . Poor little fellow! Everything else is so uncertain!" Given the narrator's inability to pray, and Joyce's refusal to do so at his mother's wake (*JJ* 141; *MBK* 234), this certainty can hardly be faith; the only thing certain is death, as *Exiles* confirms when Richard hears Beatrice make the same remark: "And does death not move you, Mr. Rowan? It is an end. Everything else is so uncertain!" (*E* 23; Beja 1971, 101).

Death, then, is "an end," "the end," and the one thing of which we can be certain (*E* 23; *P* 122–23). Yet this certitude cannot be grasped empirically: as Wittgenstein says, we can never experience death, for it lies at the boundary of nonbeing (6.4311). Joyce's epiphanies manifest this finitude through the emptiness at the heart of language, an absence that is revealed through the textual hole in epiphany #19, or the lacuna of the inner heart in "She Comes at Night." These resonant hiatuses become charged with all the uncertainty of the poetic words and images that surround them, and the imaginative associations of Joyce's poetic language are apt to proliferate endlessly. Thus, we see in the epiphanies two fundamental principles of Joyce's mature art: the art of silence and cunning concealment, where the world and the word are founded on resonant lacunae; and the endlessly proliferating profusion of polysemous and polyphonic signifiers, echoing across languages, texts, speakers, and time to animate the *Wake*. These techniques are both epiphanic, but in two quite different ways: the first manifests an absolute certainty in the revelation of absence; the second manifests a continuously changing presence in the act of being created. They come to light in Joyce's epiphanies of death because death is the natural limit of experience, a limit that simultaneously reveals the universal truth of our mortality, opens onto the void beyond experience, and puts pressure on the finite present.

Protean Epiphanies

In the "Proteus" episode of *Ulysses*, Stephen reflects ironically on his early work: "Remember your epiphanies written on green oval leaves, deeply deep, copies to be sent if you died to all the great libraries of the world, including Alexandria?" (*U* 3.141–43). Many critics assume that Joyce shared Dedalus's ironic attitude, losing interest in the epiphanies after *Portrait*, if not *Stephen Hero*, but in fact he continued to use them until the final pages of *Finnegans Wake* (see appendix). Indeed, one of the earliest sketches for *Finnegans Wake*, the contest between Berkeley and St. Patrick, which Joyce drafted in 1923 and returned to in 1938, includes a striking vision of the "hueful panepiphanal world" (611.22). Archdruid Berkeley's theory of color, in which the all-manifest world of reflected light blinds us to the "true inwardness of reality," invites imaginative contemplation of the "truth" of the "visible world," sending a ray back to "Mangan" (*CW* 83); at the same time, like Martha Clifford's substitution of "world" for "word" (*U* 5.244), it reflects on the panepiphanal wor(l)d of Joyce's text.

Subsequent chapters will trace the emergence of this linguistic epiphany through *Dubliners*, *Portrait*, *Ulysses*, and *Finnegans Wake*, arguing that, in addition to the structural importance of the epiphanies Joyce reuses and the stylistic poles they define, there is a natural de-velopment, or unfolding, from the language of the epiphanies to the "panepiphanal" language of the *Wake*. As his neologism suggests, for Joyce, like Wordsworth, epiphany is manifest everywhere. Naturally, therefore, it is manifest in language, so it seems evident that language should be the site of the literary epiphany, but as I will show in the next chapter, traditional epiphanies record the apparition of a deity, while Romantic epiphanies show forth the sublimity of nature and/or the mind; Joyce's epiphanies are unique in making language the vehicle of its own revelation.

For almost forty years, Joyce conducted an ongoing literary experiment into the nature of his medium; the importance of the epiphanies is that they pose the central problem he investigates. As A. Walton Litz observes, the two types of epiphany, dramatic and lyrical, represent "the twin poles of Joyce's art," which Litz terms "dramatic irony and lyric sentiment" (*PSW* 158). One might quibble with these terms (there is little or no dramatic irony in the epiphanies, for instance), but Litz's thesis provides a powerful model for the structural significance of the epiphanies in Joyce's later work. By adapting this stylistic model to its underlying principles, I argue that these poles operate like anode and cathode: the "negative" charge of ellipses, gaps, and silences in the dramatic epiphanies create resonant lacunae for the imagination to fill, while in the lyrical epiphanies complex patterns of repetition and variation give a "positive," accretive charge to symbolic associations, which is nevertheless riddled with indeterminacy.

In chapters 3 and 4, I develop this model through the epiphanies and *Dubliners*, redefining Joyce's twin poles as ironic realism and lyrical symbolism before refining them into the principles of silence and repetition. Exploring the resonant hiatuses of the dramatic epiphanies and their subsequent reworkings, I show that the "negative" pole is associated with absence and the void: in the domain of writing, it is represented by the blank page before inscription, the space between words, and the referential gap they contain; in the realm of speech, it is the silence before, between, and after every utterance. In Derrida's terms, this pole represents the play of difference in the chain of signification; following Rabaté, I call it silence, or "the void element which ensures displacement" (1984, 45). Conversely, the prose poetry of Joyce's lyrical epiphanies typifies his art of repetition and variation: the "positive" pole represents the generative impulse underlying Joyce's interlacing patterns, from overarching symbolic structures to recurrent imagery or leitmotifs, from endless inter- and intra-textual chains of quotation to the repetitive patternings of sound and letter that weave each phrase together.

For the sake of clarity, I refer to these poles as silence and repetition, but they are never wholly separate; as in an electrolytic circuit, linguistic current flows between. The frequent silences and ellipses of the dramatic epiphanies always occur before, between, or after vocal utterances, and it goes without saying that the words Joyce records are both different and repeated. Likewise, the frequent repetition of words, images, phonemes, and graphemes in the lyrical epiphanies *always* contains a difference, if only in the intervening text. Even when an identical phrase is reused, its context varies, so that the repetition *necessarily* differs from the original, an insight Joyce has fun with: in "Eumaeus," Bloom thinks comically of "history repeating itself with a difference" (16.1525–26), while *Finnegans Wake* traces innumerable permutations of the "same renew[ed]" (e.g., 18.5, 134.17, 226.17, 277.22–28). Derrida's term "iteration" "(*iterum*, anew, does it not come from Sanskrit *itara*, other?)" shows how repetition enfolds difference, even when a text is copied identically (1976, 209); indeed, difference is a condition of repetition because there must be a gap (whether temporal, spatial, or contextual) between the element that repeats and that which is repeated.

This gap, or difference, emanates from the pole of silence, in the broad sense I have defined it. Since repetition includes difference, and difference is a name for silence, repetition must include silence, demonstrating one way that Joyce's poles interact. Following J. Hillis Miller, I argue that this gap between repetitions opens the space for imaginative association, revealing the generative, cornucopian impulse of language. This generative notion of repetition as difference, or reiteration, can be related to a third term, "reproduction." "[W]hen we come to the phenomena of artistic conception, artistic gestation and artistic reproduction I require a new terminology," Stephen tells Lynch (*P* 227), and at least one critic has proposed that the term he is looking for is epiphany (Harrison 149). Stephen's triad figures art as a natural process, emphasizing the artist's progeny, but the third term is also a synonym of repetition as reduplication, implying that every copy is different, just as every offspring is a mutation. This notion of reproduction as mutation (rather than the organic unity of art) is crucial to Joyce's developing aesthetics, particularly in "Oxen of the Sun," where Joyce's *difference* from his source texts reveals the originality of his own linguistic creation. These devious reproductions invite comparison with another of Stephen's triads, whose last term, "cunning," may be derived from the Aryan root *gen-*, to bring forth or produce (Skeat), while the first of Stephen's "arms" is "silence."

On this correlation, silence corresponds to "artistic conception," tracing the biological metaphor back to the moment of creation. Stephen is fond of this trope, echoing Shelley and D'Annunzio as he declares: "In the virgin womb of the imagination the word was made flesh" (236). Stephen's ejaculation of the villanelle is laced with irony (a point I will return to), but at the same time, the physical nature of Stephen's jouissance underscores the materiality of his poem (scribbled on the back of a cigarette box), just as his ambition "to recreate life out of life" (186) grounds his epiphanic aesthetics in biological reproduction. Throughout *Portrait*, language, fantasy, and sexuality are constantly intertwined, suggesting that language manifests desire, and each of Joyce's works brings the materiality of language to the fore. These are key aspects of Joyce's linguistic epiphany, but Stephen's maieutic conception of the artist is particularly interesting because, if the analogy holds, it suggests that repetition (as reproduction) issues from a silent conception. Speech obviously issues from silence, and I have already shown that silence, as difference, is a condition for repetition; but in Joyce's triad, the reverse is also true—reproduction is a condition for conception, posing the analogous question: is repetition a condition of silence?

As John Cage realized when he stepped into an anechoic chamber, we can never experience silence;[18] it can only be imagined as the absence of sound, a property of the void. Conceptually, too, silence, as absence, can only be imagined in opposition to presence; a transcendental signified, its referent can never be given. Like the Real in Lacanian theory, silence cannot be attained through Symbolic representation, and yet the gap it represents is the condition for language. For Lacan, the Symbolic order of language arises from the desire to fill a fundamental gap or *béance*; yet this desire itself originates in the mirror stage, at the moment the subject recognizes itself as other and thereby enters the Symbolic order. Rodolphe Gasché proposes a similar movement in his "General Theory of Doubling," arguing that "[t]o give oneself a presence entails relating to oneself" through "spacing" or self-difference; subjectivity emerges through an act of "originary doubling," where doubled and double come into being simultaneously through self-reflection (225–39). According to these theories, identity and difference, like silence and repetition, emerge together, so that the manifestation of silence necessarily depends upon repetition. Again, silence is exemplary here because it has no empirical referent; it can be posited only in relation to other signifiers (absence, quiet, snow, space, and so forth). In Derrida's words, "there is no repetition possible without the *graphics of supplementarity*" (1981, 168), where the supplement, in both its senses (as replacement and addition), depends upon a gap, a space of silence. Another term for this "infrastructural" space is *différance*, which simply reunites two words with a common root: difference and deferral, a repetitive movement or *play* in the chain of signifiers. As Derrida's terms reveal, the relation is commutative: difference implies repetition, just as repetition implies difference, because repetition, derived from *re* (back, again) + *petere* (to make for or pursue), is not only a restatement but also a turning (back or again) toward a repeated or repeating element.

For Joyce, like Heidegger, language is an epiphany, but whereas Heidegger sees the world becoming manifest through language, Joyce's epiphanies focus on the moment language comes into being. The paradox of this moment is that language issues from silence in a referential act, yet this "originary doubling," a self-differing reduplication, actually brings silence into being. All of Joyce's works issue from this paradox; indeed, it is constantly reproduced in them. The same could be said of all writing, but the remarkable thing about Joyce's texts is that they become increasingly conscious of this condition, from the "perfectly silent" ending of "A Painful Case" to the "thought-enchanted silence" of *A Portrait*, from the "universal language" of gesture in *Ulysses* to "silence speak[ing] the scene" in *Finnegans Wake*. Likewise, Joyce's work manifests a growing awareness of its repetitive structures, from Farrington's absent-minded scribal error, writing "*Bernard Bernard* instead of *Bernard Bodley*" in "Counterparts" and Father Arnall's vision of hell, with its "ceaseless repetition of the words: ever, never" ticking in the silence, to *Ulysses* "constantly repeating itself with a difference" and the *Wake*'s endless variations on the "seim anew" (215.23). At the same time, each of Joyce's works insists more stringently than the last on the materiality of its own text, from the strange-sounding words on the opening page of *Dubliners* to the peregrinations of the letter in *Finnegans Wake*. This increasingly self-reflexive awareness of *both* the materiality of the text *and* its signifying function are Joyce's vehicles of revelation. Both can be traced back to the epiphanies, where they always appear together, because in the nucleus of the linguistic epiphany, the two poles fuse together, suggesting that materiality and reflexivity are two sides of the same sign, like silence and repetition.

2

From Genesis to Joyce
A Brief History of Epiphany

When Joyce called his early prose poems and "fragment[s] of colloquy" (*SH* 216) "epiphanies" (*LII* 35), he gave new meaning to an ancient theological term. Originally restricted to illumination in its literal sense, *epiphaineia* means a "manifestation" or "striking appearance," especially the apparition of a divinity (*OED*). Greek literature records many such manifestations, often using the verbs *phaino* or *epiphaino* to do so, and the New Testament uses the same words to refer to the first and second comings of Christ.[1] The oldest canonical gospels, those of Mark and John, begin with Jesus's baptism, while Matthew and Luke commence with the Nativity; in each case Jesus's birth and spiritual rebirth are presented as epiphanies. No wonder the Eastern Church, which teaches that Jesus was born and baptized on January 6, adopted the Greek term for the Feast of the Epiphany. There was considerable controversy over what to designate as Epiphany among early theologians, however, which is reflected in the range of manifestations celebrated, including the baptism, the miracle at Cana, the Nativity, and the visit of the magi. In his sermons on Epiphany, Augustine focuses primarily on the Matthean account, strengthening the Catholic association with the spiritual illumination that led the magi to Christ. These sermons form part of the liturgy of the Epiphany cycle, which runs from January 6 to Joyce's birthday on February 2, celebrating four major manifestations: the apparition of the star, Christ's baptism, Cana, and Candlemas, when Jesus is presented in the Temple as a "light" and "revelation."[2]

The *OED* distinguishes two meanings of "epiphany": the first refers to the Catholic festival; the second to divine manifestations. References to the Feast of the Epiphany are found in Middle English texts, while the first recorded use in a non-Christian context is Gale's *Court of Gentiles*

(1677). Both meanings can be used in figurative senses: Crashaw's dedicatory poem "To the Queen's Majesty, On Twelfth Day," in which he consoles the exiled queen, Henrietta Maria, that "all the Yeare is your Epiphany" employs the former; De Quincey extends the second meaning in *Style*, describing the "revelations" of Attic literature as "two manifestations or bright epiphanies of the Grecian intellect" (Brewster 1905, 129). This citation is dated 1859 in the *OED*, although De Quincey's essay was serialized in *Blackstone's* from 1840 to 1841 (Brewster 1905, 27), and in 1838 Emerson had already written: to the "aroused intellect . . . a fact is an Epiphany of God" (qtd. in Abrams 1971, 413). Nichols notes that a draft version of Emerson's December 19, 1838, lecture expands on the journal to show how these "dull, strange despised" facts "have no value until they take their order from conscious intelligence," while to the seeing soul, "the least fact . . . is full of meaning" (1959, 3.47–49; Nichols 8–9). There is no evidence that Joyce knew Emerson's lecture, but several critics have noted the similarity between Emerson's use of the term and Joyce's: "By an epiphany he meant a sudden spiritual manifestation, whether in the vulgarity of speech or of gesture or in a memorable phase of the mind itself" (*SH* 216).

While Emerson's journal provides a first citation for the figurative application of "epiphany," Joyce's definition gives us its contemporary meaning:

> 3 a (1): a usually sudden manifestation or perception of the essential nature or meaning of something (2): an intuitive grasp of reality through something (as an event) usually simple and striking (3): an illuminating discovery, realization, or disclosure
> b: a revealing scene or moment. (Merriam-Webster)

Internet searches confirm that 3a, which corresponds to Stephen's definition, is now the dominant contemporary sense, while 3b, corresponding to the genre Joyce called "Epiphany" (*LII* 28), has become a common literary term.[3] Since *Stephen Hero* wasn't published until 1944 and the first epiphanies until 1956, Joyce could not have known how widely his neologism would be adopted, but even in Stephen's seminal definition, his novel use of "epiphany" epitomizes the view that language is constantly being created through every act of communication in its "continuous affirmation of the spirit" (*CW* 83).

As a "complex coherent organism" that both "remember[s]" and "mutate[s]" (Kenner 1972, 96), language evolves in time, and it is striking that the origins of Joyce's coinage contain the seed of his linguistic epiphany. According to Walter Skeat, whose *Etymological Dictionary* Stephen Daedalus reads "by the hour" (*SH* 32), "epiphany" is derived from the Greek *epi* ("upon, to, besides") and *phainein* ("to show"). Thus, the "appearance" or "manifestation" (*epiphaneia*) may be shown forth *upon* the site of epiphany or *beside* it. The former suggests both traditional, transcendental apparitions *above* the site of revelation, such as the star of the magi, and the immanent epiphanies of the Romantics, which appear *in* nature and/or the mind. The latter reveal something hitherto unrecognized, but when the transcendental is figured above and beyond, there is a displacement, and this gap in the epiphany is made clearer by the horizontal axis of "besides." Although Joyce's epiphanies occur in language, they stem from the same roots, revealing both the silences that give rise to signification and the extraordinary nature of the most ordinary signs.

The next chapter analyzes Joyce's early aesthetics and epiphanies in detail, showing how he developed this notion of the linguistic epiphany. Despite its novelty, however, Joyce's use of the word "epiphany" makes it clear that his concept is founded on a tradition dating back to the Greeks. Critics have underestimated the significance of this history, declaring that Joyce's "secular" epiphanies have little in common with classical and biblical evocations while overestimating their similarity to Wordsworth's "spots of time";[4] but the tale of Joyce's epiphanies is "the same told of all" (*FW* 18.19–20): "history repeating itself with a difference" (*U* 16.1525–26).

Classical and Biblical Epiphanies

Critical opinion is divided over the nature and significance of epiphanies in classical literature. Nichols notes that "Greek literature and religion commonly recorded appearances of gods and goddesses, which were described as 'epiphanies,'" claiming that divine visitations can be traced back to the earliest Greek myths, such as Dionysius's "manifestation" in Magnesia (5–6). Beja, on the other hand, contends that the tradition of epiphany begins with Paul on the road to Damascus: "the moment of vision is a Christian phenomenon, with only a few real antecedents in Classical and Hebraic literature" (1971, 24). In a sense both are right, for there is no doubt that Greek literature is replete with epiphanies, but it is also true, as Beja argues, that these moments of divine intervention are different from Christian visions.

The *Iliad* begins with the descent of Apollo and Athena (1.47, 1.195), while Hera and Zeus send thoughts and dreams to the Greeks. Gods frequently intervene on both sides of the battle for Troy, interspersing the epic with a series of epiphanic intercessions. Likewise, the *Odyssey* begins with Pallas Athena pleading Odysseus's case before the gods. She frequently appears in human form, as a young girl, a shepherd, a maiden, or mentor to guide Telemachus, and Joyce incorporates this apparition into his schemata for *Ulysses*, where Pallas Athena (as Mentor) corresponds to the milkwoman in the opening episode. Joyce's charts, which introduce the customary titles assigned to his chapters, continue this Homeric interchange between gods and mortals: Nestor appears as Deasy; Proteus is manifest as primal matter; and later episodes claim correspondences with Jove, Hermes, and Orpheus.

Euripides was also fond of presenting gods on stage. Like the *Iliad*, *Alcestis* begins with an apparition of Apollo, who predicts the eponymous heroine's return, and the play ends with Heracles bringing her back from the dead. Similarly, *Electra* concludes with the deified Dioscuri, Castor and Pollux, appearing from the deus ex machina to counsel Electra and Orestes on the libations they must perform to atone for their matricide. In *Finnegans Wake*, "castor and porridge" (*FW* 489.16), the "heavenlaid twin[s]" (177.21), are recast as the eternally warring brothers, Shem and Shaun, while "Dyas [a Vedic equivalent of Zeus] in his machine" (55.34) reappears as the "god of all machineries" (253.33).

If Aristotle is right that the deus ex machina is rather a contrived way to resolve the plot, its relatively common occurrence in the extant tragedies bears testimony to the frequency and importance of divine apparitions in Greek literature. Indeed, Phylarcus's *On the Appearance of Zeus* and two lost works on the epiphanies of Apollo and Heracles by the Alexandrian author Istros indicate that the manifestations of a single god could fill a treatise. Unfortunately, these works have not survived, but there is evidence that both were composed around 200 BCE, roughly the same time that Syriskos recorded "the *epiphaneiai* of the Parthenos" (Platt 148–49).[5]

Divine manifestations were common in Greek literature, but it is rarer to find examples of personal revelation. Birgit Neuhold suggests Plato lays the groundwork for the Romantic moment in the *Symposium*, where Diotima instructs Socrates in the ascent of *erotomachia*, from love of the body to beauty in general, thence virtue, and finally knowledge. "[W]hen a man has reached this point in his education in love," Diotima says, "[t]hen suddenly he will see a beauty of a breathtaking nature" (Plato 210; see Neuhold, *Measuring the Sadness*, 18–20). Neuhold argues that this passage is "transitory, intense, privileged and replete with rhetorical markers" (21), all features she identifies with epiphany, but Diotima's vision is "eternal" and absolute, not transitory (210–11). Moreover, Plato describes an abstract ideal through the mouthpiece of a mouthpiece, rather than giving a record of personal experience, which is quite different from Emerson's dull facts or Joyce's vulgarities of speech and gesture.

The same point can be made about revelations in Hebraic literature. Although there is no exact equivalent of the word "epiphany" in Hebrew,[6] there are literally hundreds of examples of God appearing in the Pentateuch, often in a dream or in the guise of an angel. In Genesis alone, God appears to Abram (12:7, 17:1), Abraham (18:1), Isaac (26:2–4), and Jacob. In Jacob's dream, a visitant angel is revealed as God (31:11–13). In honor of the manifestation, God instructs Jacob to build an altar at Bethel, before blessing him (35.1–9). Indeed, it is possible to read the first chapter of Genesis as God's original epiphany, so that the world itself becomes a divine manifestation, a sacred text celebrated throughout the scriptures.[7] This association between the Word and the world is explicit in the Gospel According to Saint John: "In the beginning was the Word, and the Word was with God, and the Word was God" (1:1), a text that haunts the imagination of Stephen Dedalus. The reason it does so, I shall argue, is that when "the Word became flesh and dwelt among us, full of grace and truth" (1:14), John provides the prototype for a literal epiphany in which language embodies spirit.

Christians view the Incarnation as "the glorious Epiphany of God our Saviour" (Irving 342), which "derives its full force" from the contrast between "God and man, lowly and sublime, *humilis and sublimis*" (Auerbach 1973, 65). Epiphanies are often considered as paragons of the sublime, and the archetypal Christian epiphany, manifesting the divine in the ordinary, provides a prototype for Romantic revelations, but Joyce's epiphanies are quite different, for he makes no distinction between "lowly and sublime." There is no room for the sublime (< sub + limis: below the limit) in Joyce, because in his epiphanies the ordinary *is* the limit of experience. Put differently, the Romantics venerate the extraordinariness of the ordinary, whereas Joyce never veers from its ordinariness. As textual manifestations, his epiphanies don't reach for anything beyond themselves; they are fully materialized in literary form.

Returning to the Old Testament theophanies, it is notable that in each case the patriarchs hear the voice of God; Yahweh may appear as an angel or in dreams, but there is rarely any doubt about the significance of the message. In Ezekiel's grand "visions of God" (1:1) fire unfolds in the clouds of a whirlwind, taking on the form of four living creatures that become lions, oxen, and eagles before morphing into wheels within wheels (1:4–16). The profusion of imagery makes it almost impossible to imagine the intertwined wings of the creatures or their multifaceted heads, but when the prophet returns to their appearance in the cloud as "burning coals of fire, . . . lamps" and the "flash of lightning" (1:13–14), the nature of the illumination is clear. Again, it is difficult to envisage how the wheels of beryl and crystal contain the living spirit of the creature and the simulacrum of the firmament as they rise up into the sky (20, 22), but when Ezekiel hears "the voice of the Almighty" and sees a throne surrounded by the brightness of rainbows, he knows that he has seen "the likeness of the glory of the Lord" (24, 28). Immediately after, he hears God's voice, is converted, and becomes a prophet (2:1–3).

Revelation 4–5 recalls Ezekiel's imagery in the throne surrounded by rainbows, where lamps of fire burn and flash lightning before "a sea of glass like unto crystal" (4:2–6). In the midst of the throne, four beasts (or "living beings" in Joyce's holograph copy), "full of eyes within," are likened to lion, calf, man, and eagle (4:7). But where Ezekiel hears the one voice of God, John hears "the voice of many angels"—a chorus of "ten thousand times ten thousand" praising the "Lamb that was slain" (5:11). Like the multiplying angels, the symbols of Revelation concatenate continuously, adding layer upon layer of imagery, so that the whole book becomes one grand vision of Apocalypse (< apokalypsis, "revelation"). But just as Ezekiel's vision begins and ends with the voice of God, so too the book of Revelation is framed as "[t]he Revelation of Jesus Christ," God-given and sent by an angel to John (1:1). At the very end of Revelation, Jesus returns: "I Jesus have sent mine angel to testify unto you these things" (22:16). Thus, the truth of Apocalypse is guaranteed by Christ, in the same way that Hebraic visions, even those as recondite as Ezekiel's, were given absolute, determinate meaning by Yahweh. It is evident from these examples that biblical epiphanies, whether in the Old or New Testament, record transcendental experiences in which God is manifest directly.

However, the way that John of the Apocalypse develops and expands upon Ezekiel also demonstrates how the first Christian scribes reinterpreted

Hebraic Scripture. In some of the last words of the Bible, immediately following the verse quoted above, Jesus says, "I am the root and the offspring of David, [and] the bright and morning star" (22:16), establishing his royal Jewish lineage while looking back to Matthew.

The New Testament begins with the most famous of all epiphanies: the star of the magi.[8] Preparing for the apparition, Matthew recounts a typical Old Testament genealogy, tracing the fourteen generations from Abraham to David and thence the royal line of descent to Joseph (Matt. 1:1–17). This is of course key to establishing Jesus as "King of the Jews" (Mark 2:2), assuring continuity with Hebraic Scripture. Both Brown and Beare suggest that Matthew was a Greek-speaking scribe with knowledge of Hebrew living in an area of Judeo-Christian conflict or interchange (Brown 46; Beare 10); it is natural therefore that Matthew draws heavily on Old Testament visions and prophecies to narrate the coming of Christ. In addition to the five formula citations that structure chapters 1–2,[9] there are obvious parallels between Moses escaping the Pharaoh in Egypt (Ex. 2) and Herod's massacre of the innocents, just as Joseph, dreamer of dreams and sojourner in Egypt, can be seen as a "reapplication of the patriarch Joseph" (Brown 72). But to indicate the full significance of Jesus's coming, the evangelist turns to Old Testament epiphanies, reinterpreting them as prophecies of the Christian epiphany. For instance, when Joseph discovers that Mary is pregnant and considers how she might be delivered in private, "behold, the angel of the Lord appeared (*ephánī*) unto him" (1:20), telling him of the immaculate conception. This dream visitation, the first epiphany in the New Testament, is frequently compared to Judges 13:3: "And the angel of the Lord appeared unto the woman, and said unto her, Behold now, thou [art] barren, and bearest not: but thou shalt conceive, and bear a son," just as Jesus's birth is seen as a fulfillment of the prophecy of Emmanuel (Mark 1:23). In Judges, this son of the Holy Ghost is Samson, and in the Lucan account, Jesus, like Samson, is a Nazarene, although in Matthew Jesus is born in Bethlehem. Even the star that leads the magi to their Davidic Messiah echoes Balaam, an eastern magus, who saw "a vision of the Almighty" and foretold that "there shall come a Star out of Jacob, and a Sceptre shall rise out of Israel" (Num. 24.16–17; Trench 34; Brown 190–96).

These parallels illustrate why the Matthean narrative needs to be read in relation to its scriptural forbears, both in the hermeneutic tradition of typological interpretation and as a dialogical text. Indeed, there is good evidence of Matthew rewriting and reinterpreting Mark, as well as the Torah, suggesting that literal, typological, anagogical, and allegorical exegeses are written into the gospel. For example, Balaam provides an Old Testament type of the magus, but since he is frequently seen as a false prophet, anagogical readings quickly arise, particularly in relation to the parable of the ass (Num. 22), which has led several interpreters to view the magi as sorcerers (Trench 8–9). The magi are more commonly represented as the three kings or wise men from Babylonia, and allegorical interpretations of their gifts are widespread, although Matthew tells us neither how many they were nor where they came from. Recent scholarship favors the more literal interpretation that they were astrologers, arguing that astrology was practiced extensively in the ancient world and often regarded as a kind of science. The exact time of a star rising was of critical importance to the accuracy of astrological predictions, hence Herod's concern for precise information to ascertain the location of the newborn king (2.7). Christian apologists go further, suggesting that Matthew refers to a new star, such as the nova said to herald the birth of Mithridates, or perhaps to Halley's Comet, which was visible from Palestine in 12 BCE (Beare 75).

Thus, over and above the textual difficulties of the Greek, or the relationship between the gospels and other apocryphal sources, there are significant hurdles in the way of interpreting the epiphany. I have indicated these in terms of the fourfold medieval exegesis: literal, typological, anagogical, and allegorical interpretations. Modern Bible studies show that the Bible is open to critical interpretation in the same way as any other text, but what makes it such a powerful test case is the Catholic doctrine of inerrancy, which states that the sacred texts "have God for their author" (Second Vatican Council, 3.2; 2 Tim. 3:16–17). Biblical epiphanies explicitly claim this status as a revelation of God, no matter how ordinary the manifestation. In Matthew, the magi rejoice the moment they see the star, as though they know its portent (2.10). They follow it directly to the infant Jesus and bow down before him, though there is nothing extraordinary about the "house" of Mary and Joseph, and they have been led to expect a king (11).[10] This direct access to God's revelation links the epiphany to the Old Testament theophanies where God spoke to the patriarchs. Indeed, immediately after delivering their gifts, God warns the magi not to return via Jerusalem, and in the following verse, "the angel of the Lord appeareth [*phainetai*] to Joseph," bidding him flee to Egypt (2.12–13).

Interpreting the Epiphany

Post-Enlightenment evocations of epiphany are usually opposed to the divine manifestations of the Bible, but it is clear that biblical revelations are subject to the same problems of interpretation as any other text, while Romantic epiphanies make similar truth claims as their scriptural counterparts. With the exception of Hopkins's "theophanies" and Eliot's later poetry, modern literary epiphanies are usually regarded as secular. In *Epiphany in the Modern Novel*, Morris Beja observes that, despite a "general disillusion with religion" in the late nineteenth and early twentieth centuries, there is "a continuing need . . . for meaningful, unifying, 'spiritual' emotions or experiences" (21). This leads to a shift "from divine revelations, purely religious experiences, to epiphanies, for the most part regarded as secular" (46), as modernist writers, no longer confident of receiving God's truth, search for their own answers.[11] For Beja, this accounts for modernists' fascination with highly charged but ephemeral moments: "Doubtful of immortality, they turned against it and cherished mortality; afraid of death, they worshipped life" (50). Beja suggests that as well as a loss of faith in orthodox religion, a concomitant loss of confidence in rational enlightenment provides further impetus toward the "instantaneous, intuitive illumination" that epiphany idealizes (21).

Ashton Nichols develops a similar argument in *The Poetics of Epiphany*, tracing a change of emphasis from the inspired seer of biblical revelations to the Romantic interpreter of oracular epiphanies. Whereas the Old Testament prophets are literally inspired with the spirit of God, as in the coal that touches Isaiah's lips and makes him an agent of truth, ensuring that "the total meaning of the event is contained in its telling" (13), "the epiphanies that begin with Wordsworth leave their ultimate meaning unstated" (16), and therefore demand interpretation. As I have shown, though, biblical epiphanies require interpretation like any other text. The only qualitative difference is the source of meaning: whereas for Matthew God was the author of the word and the world, Wordsworth describes a phenomenological experience governed by "the language of the sense," a world we half perceive and "half-create" (1986, 149).

This transference of authority from the Logos that self-evidently manifests its own truth to the witness of revelation who must interpret its significance leads to an increased focus on subjective experience and opens the door to doubt. Beja cites St. Paul's vision on the road to Damascus—"and suddenly there shined round about him a light from heaven" (Acts 9:3)—as the first Christian conversion, but he doesn't note its variants. Neuhold argues convincingly that there is a distinct difference between the biographical narratives in The Acts of the Apostles (probably written by Luke), which present the epiphany as a "light from heaven" (9:3, 22:6, 26:13), and the autobiographical accounts in the Pauline Epistles (Neuhold, *Measuring the Sadness*, 22–25). For instance, 1 Corinthians 9 begins: "Am I not an Apostle? am I not free? have I not seen Jesus Christ our Lord?" Paul's rhetorical questions are probably intended to assert authority, but they open up the possibility of doubt and self-questioning, particularly in light of his repeated claim that he is "the least of the apostles, unfit to be called an apostle" (24).

In the same way, Augustine's account can be read as "the archetypal pattern of the conversion" (Beja 1971, 26)—a long search for truth, frequently beset by doubts despite moments of illumination like the "flash of one trembling glance" that reveals "THAT WHICH IS" (7.22), until finally, after hearing of two soldiers who find faith in the life of St. Anthony, Augustine despairs and rushes out to the garden, where he hears a voice chanting "*Tolle lege*" ("Take up and read": 8.28).[12] Here Augustine opens the Bible at Romans, and "instantly at the end of this sentence [13.13–14], by a light as it were of serenity infused into my heart, all the darkness of doubt vanished away" (8.28).

This would seem to indicate that Augustine's conversion lies in a sudden illumination that dissolves doubt, but when he first heard the commandment to read, Augustine's "countenance altered" and he "began to think most intently, whether children were wont in any kind of play to sing such words." Unable to recall them, Augustine tells us: "I arose, interpreting them to be no other than a command from God to open the book, and read the first chapter I should find" (8.28).

Thus even at the moment of revelation, Augustine is filled with doubts and it is only after exhausting the explanations his intellect supplies that he concludes he is hearing the word of God. Unlike Ezekiel's absolute conviction in divine revelation, for Augustine "the perceptual experience" of hearing the children chanting "is merely the raw material for an interpretation" (Nichols 16). Comparing himself to Anthony, who heard God speaking to him in the words of the gospel, Augustine interprets a potentially everyday experience as a divine revelation.

It is significant that the mysterious voice Augustine hears, even if it is a transcendental theophany, has to be interpreted as such, because this heralds a shift toward the immanent experience of the Romantic epiphany. At the center of this shift is the locus of truth. Both biblical and classical epiphanies typically make an absolute claim to truth through the manifestation of a divine being, but whereas for the Old Testament prophets, the epiphany is ontological, for the evangelists, epiphany must be interpreted in relation to Scripture. This means that the epiphany becomes an epistemological experience, even when the illumination is as dazzling as St. Paul's conversion (Acts 9.3–9). Far from being blinded by the light, Augustine's initial doubts and his focus on ordinary sensory experience as the trigger of revelation suggest that the truth of the epiphany is to be sought in the individual who perceives it, or in everyday events themselves—characteristic sites of the Romantic epiphany. Indeed, Augustine, a professor of rhetoric, has a remarkably modern approach to Scripture. Reflecting on the multitude of interpretations of Genesis that already existed in the late fourth century, he concludes that "the truth which those words contain appear to different enquiries in a different light" (12.24). Although Augustine never doubts that Genesis is the word of God, his willingness to sanction innumerable interpretations as potentially true marks an important step toward the modern literary epiphany.

Phillip Cary goes so far as to claim that Augustine "originates medieval and modern semiotics" (143; see Neuhold, *Measuring the Sadness*, 25–36). I can find no evidence of Joyce using Augustine's "semiotics" directly, but "the ruah of . . . Hippo" (*FW* 38.30–31)—or spirit of Augustine—certainly shapes the vision and language of the *Wake*. In May 1927, Joyce wrote to Weaver, explaining a passage from the first chapter of *Work in Progress*, glossing the opening phrase, "O foenix culprit!" (23.16), as follows: "*O felix culpa!* S. Augustine's famous phrase in praise of Adam's sin. Fortunate fault! Without it the Redeemer wd not have been born. Hence also the antecedent sin of Lucifer without which Adam wd not have been created or able to fall" (*SL* 321). Of course, "foenix" is also "Phoenix park" (*SL* 321), the "culprit" is HCE (or Humphrey Chimpden Earwicker, in one of his avatars), and without his crime, the book would not exist as we know it. This motif runs right through the *Wake:* "O fortunous casualitas!," "O happy fault!," "O felicitous culpability" (175.19, 202.34, 263.29), and given that the fall is also the fall of Babel, this "Fortunate fault" is the sin that brings the plurality of languages into being.

Another famous phrase of Augustine's, "*Securus iudicat orbis terrarium*" ("the verdict of the world is secure"),[13] also echoes through the *Wake*. In 1.4, it is quoted verbatim in defence of "our hagious curious encestor," HCE, whose original sin is compared to Adam and Eve "uncover[ing] the nakedness of an unknown body," and the fall of Babel, since when "the sibspeeches of all mankind have foliated"; in each case, the "framing up of such figments . . . bring[s] the truth to light" of our happy fall into postlapsarian history (96.26–36). In fact, Augustine's phrase "is not too high a motto for all human artwork," Joyce states in "Drama and Life" (*CW* 42), and his last work includes two dozen variations on it, bringing the very notion of sin into question, as *Finnegans Wake* offers its all-redeeming vision of the world. Although the *Wake* is riddled with uncertainty, Joyce's language rests secure in its indeterminacy, celebrating the endless foliations of a happy fall into babelian polyglossia.

Medieval Manifestations

The origins of Wakese can be traced back to the epiphanies, but the interwoven text that constitutes his "chaosmos of Alle" (*FW* 118.21) is in important respects a medieval illumination. Unfurling this scroll to its beginnings, we find that Daedalus's theory of epiphany in *Stephen Hero* is ultimately derived from a series of aesthetic reflections that Joyce recorded between January 1903 and November 1904.[14] Initially, these were prompted by his reading of Aristotle in Paris (*LII* 28, 38), which proved influential enough for him to proclaim himself an "Aristotelian" (S. Joyce 1971, 53). In "The Holy Office" (1904), Joyce names his persona "Katharsis-Purgative," bringing the "mind of witty Aristotle" to tavern and brothel, before affirming the medieval mettle of his soul, "[s]teeled in the school of old Aquinas" (1–6, 81–82). Following this scholastic tradition, both *Stephen Hero* (77) and *Portrait* (209) characterize Stephen's theory as "applied Aquinas," even though the "lore" Stephen relies on is "only a garner of slender sentences from Aristotle's poetics and psychology and a *Synopsis Philosophiae Scholasticae ad mentem divi Thomae*" (*P* 176). These are often slighted as textbook selections, but Stephen tells the Dean of Studies he "can work on at present by the light of one or two ideas of Aristotle and Aquinas," since they illuminate his thinking with "the lightnings of intuition" (176). As Fran O'Rourke has shown, Joyce too based his aesthetics on a few isolated quotations from Aristotle's *Nicomachean Ethics*, translated from the French, and Aquinas's *Summa Theologiae*, probably quoted from memory; consequently, his aesthetics bear little relation to Aristotelian or Thomist doctrine, but the ideas Joyce garnered from the angelic doctor (along with another medieval theologian, Duns Scotus) provided the springboard for his definition of epiphany.

Stephen's definition undoubtedly has roots in Romanticism, but Umberto Eco argues convincingly that "Joyce remained medievally minded from youth through maturity," seeking to re-create "the universal rules of cosmic order" in his microcosmic works, where "[e]very word embodies every other because language is a self-reflecting world" (1989, 6–7). For Eco, this "Order . . . is the mechanism which permits epiphanies," and although his definition of epiphany as "the living symbol of something" (7) is vague, when Eco's axiom is applied to language, it leads to a brilliant insight: that Joyce's "medieval mind" creates a linguistic epiphany through the semiotic web of the *Wake*.

The paradigm for Joyce is Dante, whom he loved "almost as much as the Bible" (*JJ* 226). Mary Reynolds argues that the complex poetic structure of the *Commedia* with its subtle patterns of interweaving imagery "became a central poetic principle in Joyce's own work" (175). For instance, Reynolds shows how Dante's imagery of light, first announced by the reflected sunrise in *Inferno* 1.17, continues through to the final cantos of the *Commedia* (119–48). This luminous epiphany seems to have dazzled Joyce: reading "Dante tires one quickly," he said; "it is as if one were to look at the sun" (*JJ* 430). Of course, Dante's divine apparition is never presented directly; "*l'amor che move il sole e l'altre stele*" invites us to imagine the primum mobile manifest as love—but love, like light, is a metaphor with an unspoken tenor. Lucia Boldrini contrasts this mystical silence of the unsayable with Joyce's linguistic void, distinguishing Dante's leaps from Joyce's gaps (149–62), but the underlying structure remains the same. Similarly, as Reynolds argues, Joyce's patterns of repetition and variation are structurally equivalent to Dante's *entrelace*, and in both cases they are employed to create epiphanies, whether in Dante's heavenly rose or Joyce's "immense system of . . . correspondences" (*CW* 221).

In fact, there are close correspondences between Dante's "*candida rosa*" (*Paradiso* 31.1), whose "*trina luce*" (trinal light, 31.28) splits the white light of heaven into three colored circles reflecting each other like rainbows—a vision words are inadequate to describe (33.115–23)—and Joyce's "prism of a language manycoloured," refracting Dantean rhymes into three distinct hues (*P* 181; *U* 7.713–24), before figuring language in the *Wake* as an infinite spectrum of light, reflected in Issy and the rainbow girls. For Dante, words can never express this conception of "l'alto lume," just as the circle can never be squared (33.116–38), which is why God is never named; likewise, Archdruid Berkeley's "hueful panepiphanal world" is merely a "photoreflection," for the "true inwardness of reality," the "gloria of light actually retained," is invisible (611.13–24). Yet, in both the *Commedia* and the *Wake*, figures of negation combine with interlacing motifs such as light, extraordinary verbal innovation, and complex literary structures to make language a vehicle of revelation, revealing both poets' underlying reverence for language.

Lucia Boldrini shows how Dante gives ordinary language the same status as sacred Scripture by extending traditional biblical exegesis to *literary* texts in his *Convivio* and *Epistle to Can Grande* (Boldrini 27–37). This fourfold interpretation implies polysemy, and Boldrini argues that Joyce's polysemia can be compared to Dante's, but whereas for Dante it offers a means of adding and ordering multiple levels of meaning, for Joyce it becomes a means of including and distorting all possible meaning. Boldrini pursues this analogy in *De Vulgari Eloquentia*, where Dante sifts through Italian vernaculars to combine the best of each into a "*vulgare illustre*," or radiant language (103), just as Joyce combines seventy-plus idioms into the hybrid form of the *Wake* (102–16). In this context, the synthetic language of the *Divine Comedy*, grafting a dozen dialects, as well as Latin and Provençal, onto a Florentine base, provides a compelling model for the multilingualism of the *Wake*. Moreover, Boldrini's argument for the origins of Dante's polysemy and polyglossia in scriptural revelation may apply to Joyce. Estimates vary as to the number of languages in the *Wake*, but Laurent Milesi points out that the text hints at seventy, a doubly significant figure: "It is the traditional number of peoples said to have inhabited the earth, and the Talmud states that each commandment which issued from God's mouth in the gift of the Law on Mount Sinai was divided into 70 languages, so that each people could hear the divine revelation" (Milesi 2004, 153).

Dante. . . . Rousseau. Wordsworth. Joyce

"In Dante dwells the whole spirit of the Renaissance," Joyce told Francini Bruni (*JJ* 226). He also said he would take Shakespeare over Dante as his desert island book (Budgen 183), so we shouldn't read too much into these pronouncements, but when it comes to the development of Joyce's epiphanies, it makes sense to pass directly to the Romantics. This is not to deny the importance of Renaissance writers for Joyce, but he was not primarily interested in those authors for moments of epiphany.[15] As Beja, Langbaum, and Nichols have argued, for a direct literary model we must look to Wordsworth, but before turning to Wordsworth's "spots of time," I want to show how the key developments I have outlined were extended by Rousseau. To recapitulate, there are three key developments in the history of the literary epiphany from Genesis to Joyce: first, a gradual process of internalization as literary epiphanies move from object to subject, transcendence to immanence, ontology to epistemology; second, as epiphanies become experiences requiring interpretation, they are increasingly susceptible to doubt; and third, as writers begin to scrutize both the experience of epiphany and its literary representation, the focus of epiphany turns to language.

Birgit Neuhold demonstrates this growing skepticism from Augustine's *Confessions* to Rousseau's. As she shows, there are striking parallels between Augustine's conversion and Rousseau's "illumination de Vincennes": in both revelations the context is the visit of/to a friend (Alypius; Diderot); both are triggered by reading a fragment of text (Romans 13; the *Mercure de France*); and both writers exhibit intense physical reactions: Augustine casts himself down under "a certain fig-tree, giving full vent to [his] tears" (8.12.28), while Rousseau collapses under a tree to find his shirt wet with his tears.[16] These similarities indicate that Rousseau is consciously reworking Augustine's seminal moment in his account to Malesherbes, and when Rousseau rewrites this scene in Book 8 of his *Confessions*, the parallel to Augustine's conversion (*Confessions* 8) is unmistakable.

Both writers also draw on St. Paul for their road and prison motifs, and, like Paul's conversion, Rousseau's epiphany is recounted twice. Although the situation in Rousseau's *Confessions* (1769–70) is almost identical to the letter of 1762, the moment of revelation is transformed. In his letter to Malesherbes, Rousseau described the incident as a revelation that led him to his vocation as a writer, for "[a]ll that I was able to retain from the flood of great truths which . . . engulfed me in light as I lay beneath that tree, is scattered all too sparsely through my three principal works" (6–7). By contrast, looking back on the same experience seven years later, Rousseau describes his state as an agitation approaching delirium (476); and whereas the central insight of Rousseau's 1762 illumination is the natural goodness of man, in the *Confessions*, Rousseau is surprised by his naive enthusiasm for truth, liberty, and virtue (477).

I am not sure whether Stanislaus Joyce was thinking of the young idealist or the mature skeptic when he hoped his brother would "become the Rousseau of Ireland" (1971, 3); in either case, Rousseau's progression from epiphanic ideals to retrospective skepticism bears comparison with Stephen's aesthetics of epiphany, developed through *Stephen Hero*, *Portrait*, and *Ulysses*. Doubt, confession, and revelation are central to both writers, but Joyce goes far beyond Rousseau, for his epiphanies are never flashes of light or moments of vision; rather, they offer mundane snapshots of ordinary life, voicing a fundamental skepticism toward the notion of truth.

This growing doubt gradually permeates the text, until language itself becomes the site of epiphany. Paul de Man's reading of the Romantic moment illustrates this shift. In "Intentional Structure of the Romantic Image," de Man compares three passages from Rousseau, Wordsworth, and Hölderlin, each describing a journey through the Alps that culminates in "a moment of spiritual revelation" (de Man 1984, 10). For de Man, these texts represent more than an ascent from earthly, material nature to a mental and celestial world; in them, he traces a shift from the objective world to the imagination, from the pure language of nouns in Hölderlin's "Brot und Wein" to "Heimkunft," where "the poetic word has become an offspring of the sky" (14, 15). This poetic revolution leads de Man to claim that the Romantics "put into question, in the language of poetry, the ontological priority of the sensory object" (14, 15), a radical claim that might lead to false conclusions.[17] Yet with the emphasis on questioning rather than negation, and on poetic language rather than imagination, this process of self-reflexive interrogation leads from Romanticism to Modernism.

Untethered from referential objects, language itself becomes an object of scrutiny (in its material form and its signification), opening the door to doubt and revelation. There are glimmers of this linguistic reflection in the Romantics, but broadly speaking, Rousseau's doubts concern the veracity of his epiphanic *experience*, whereas Joyce's epiphanies put language itself into question. Likewise, Wordsworth's revelations are imaginative experiences, whereas Joyce's are linguistic. There can be no doubt about the connection, though, particularly when we compare Wordsworth's Apocalyptic imagery and aesthetics of the sublime with Joyce's.

Both the sublime and revelatory aspects of Wordsworth's epiphanies are evident in his celebrated description of the descent to Gondo:

> The unfettered clouds and region of the Heavens,
> Tumult and peace, the darkness and the light—
> Were all like workings of one mind, the features
> Of the same face, blossoms upon one tree;
> Characters of the great Apocalypse,
> The types and symbols of Eternity,
> Of first, and last, and midst, and without end. (6.566–72)

Wordsworth creates a sublime vision of rock and sky, woods and waterfalls, through a series of striking antitheses: "woods decaying, never to be decayed, . . . Winds thwarting winds," "torrents shooting from the clear blue sky" [556–61]), culminating in "Tumult and peace, the darkness and the light" (567). But Wordsworth also draws on Revelation for the imagery of clouds and heavens, darkness and light, the first and last end,[18] likening these contradictory aspects of nature to "Characters of the great Apocalypse, / The types and symbols of Eternity." While explicitly invoking typological and allegorical hermeneutics ("types and symbols"), Wordsworth goes beyond the traditional Enlightenment metaphor of nature as God's book, for the revelation he represents is a phenomenological experience, "half create[d]" (1986, 116) by the subject, and re-created by the poet in his epiphany. When these contradictory images, simultaneously describing an extraordinary sight and the overwhelming effect it has upon the speaker—"Tumult and peace"—are finally resolved into "the workings of one mind," Wordsworth creates an exquisite ambiguity between the mind of God and the mind of the poet.[19] Indeed, this ambiguity is central to Wordsworth's epiphanies, where the godlike infinitude of *both* nature *and* the mind are manifest through a Kantian revelation, in which the pure idea of unity is awoken by the sublime, affording a transcendental glimpse of the infinite (*Critique of Judgement* §§25–26).

Arguably, the most important study of the literary epiphany is *Natural Supernaturalism*, where M. H. Abrams shows how two key metaphors from Apocalypse—the New Jerusalem as heaven on earth and the marriage of Christ with humanity—profoundly shaped Christian thought. Since the biblical narrative is composed of a few key events with a definite beginning, middle, and end, and given the strong exegetical tendency to read the Bible either typologically, as prefigurations and postfigurations of the defining moments, or allegorically and anagogically, as symbols of an esoteric truth, biblical eschatology is readily extended from the day of reckoning for the human race to the individual's final judgment. This leads to the tradition of spiritual autobiography heralded by St. Paul and Augustine, a mode of interpretation carried much further by Inner Light Protestants, such as Jacob Boehme and radical Puritans such as Gerrard Winstanley. For Winstanley, "*Adam* is within every man and woman," while the spirit "is the light and life of Christ within the heart" (176, 214, qtd. in Abrams 1971, 53). Blake develops the same theme in *Jerusalem* when he asks, "Is the Holy Ghost any other than an Intellectual Fountain?" and "What are the Pains of Hell but Ignorance, Bodily Lust, Idleness and devastation?" (77). Joyce in turn saw a "glorified humanity" stamped in Blake's work, suggesting that "the visionary ecstasy of the seer" in "a poor London room" marked "the first time in the history of the world that the Eternal spoke though the mouth of the humble" (*CW* 218–21). Joyce's emphasis on the humble medium is significant, for his "sudden spiritual manifestation" in "the vulgarity of speech or of gesture" follows in the same tradition, carrying the process of internalization into language by conceiving of literature as "the continual affirmation of the human spirit" (*CW* 83).

In *The Prelude*, too, divinity is found within:

> Of Genius, Power,
> Creation and Divinity itself
> I have been speaking, for my theme has been
> What passed within me. . . .
> This is, in truth, heroic argument. (3.171–74)

Indeed, in the "Prospectus" to *The Recluse* (to which *The Prelude* was to form the "ante-chapel"), Wordworth announces that

> the discerning intellect of Man,
> When wedded to this goodly universe
> In love and holy passion, shall find [heaven]
> A simple produce of the common day. (52–55)

Wordworth's metaphor recalls the nuptial imagery at the end of Revelation where Jerusalem, as the new heaven on earth, is "prepared as a bride for her husband" (21.2), for "the marriage of the Lamb is come"

(19.6–7)—although in Wordsworth's version, "the Lamb and New Jerusalem are replaced by man's mind as the bridegroom and nature as the bride" (Abrams 1971, 56), so that the "great consummation" is transposed from the indefinite future to the present moment. Wordsworth's "high argument," then, is that paradise is no "mere fiction" or "history only of departed things"; through our "discerning intellect," we can experience it here and now through "the simple produce of the common day," because "Mind" and "World" are divinely and "exquisitely . . . fitted" (Prospectus 63–68).[20]

As a young man, Joyce copied the entire Book of Apocalypse by hand, frequently echoing its imagery in his subsequent works. He, too, internalized Revelation; but whereas Wordsworth uses Apocalyptic metaphors to chart the growth of the poet's soul, Joyce constantly returned to the language of Revelation in his search for the revelation of language.

There is a similar transposition between Wordsworth's neo-Kantian aesthetics of the sublime and Joyce's aesthetics of epiphany. In the *Prelude*, privileged moments evoke sublime experiences, such as the climactic view from Mount Snowdon: "The perfect image of a mighty Mind, / Of one that feeds upon infinity" (13.69–70). Indeed, by the end of *The Prelude*, all things have "an underpresence, / The sense of God," for nature is filled with "sublime and lovely forms," giving rise to "the one thought / By which we live, Infinity and God" (72–76, 183–84). This sublime "Power" of nature "Thrusts forth upon the senses"—"a genuine Counterpart . . . of the glorious faculty / Which higher minds bear with them as their own" (85–90). For Wordsworth, this "glorious faculty" that sees and partakes of "the mighty unity / In all which we behold" (254–55) allows us to see the infinite power of nature in every experience: "This is the very spirit in which [higher minds] deal / With all the objects of the universe" (91–92). With its biblical origins, sublime aesthetics, panoramic scope, and everyday language, this "rapture of the Hallelujah sent / From all that breathes and is" (1805, 13.262–63) has much in common with the Joycean epiphany. But as I show in the next chapter, while Joyce followed Wordsworth in viewing all experience as potentially sublime, his aesthetics of epiphany embody their own theory, revealing the sublimity of language.

A final correspondence worth commenting on is the connection between Wordsworth's "spots of time" (1799, 1.288) and Joyce's elegiac epiphanies.[21] Both deal with death, although in each case, loss is figured differently. In each of Wordsworth's "spots" of time, death is elided, but this absence becomes the nodal point for a complex emotional and perceptual experience that transforms the narrator, and these heightened moments provide key scenes for the two-part *Prelude* of 1798–99, whose epiphanic structure Wordsworth expands upon in the later versions. The first of these moments is occasioned by a drowned man dredged from Esthwaite lake, where the "breathless stillness" of the "beauteous scene" is shattered by the shocking image of his "ghastly face" as his body rises "bolt upright" from the water (258–79). The second is an early memory, from "the twilight of rememberable life," when the young poet "through fear / Dismounting" led his horse down a steep descent to discover the remains of a gibbet where a man was hung for murdering his wife (296–313). Here, Wordsworth's description of the "long green ridge of turf. . . . Whose shape was like a grave" bears comparison to "The Thorn," and just as the stonelike thorn and grave-like moss of the lyric are invested with mystery by the tale of Martha Ray, Wordsworth's spot of time is given epiphanic significance not by the horror of the gallows but by the mysterious girl he sees as he climbs back to the summit of the beacon, "A girl who bore a pitcher on her head / And seemed with difficult steps to force her way / Against the blowing wind" (317–19). Looking back, the mature poet recognizes that "It was in truth / An ordinary sight"; and yet, he says, it invested the whole scene with a "visionary dreariness" (319–22).

This ability to color ordinary events with visionary significance is the essence of the modern epiphany, allowing revelation to be found in, or ascribed to, the most commonplace experiences. This point seems contradicted by the dramatic encounters with death Wordsworth describes, especially the last, dealing with the death of John Wordsworth when William was thirteen. However, the significance of this event is expressed not in the death itself, which is narrated matter-of-factly ("he died, / And I and my two Brothers, orphans then, / Followed his body to the grave" [351–53]), but by the excursion that precedes it and the reflections that follow.

Shortly before their father's death, the speaker and his brothers, Richard and John, had climbed a crag above a crossroads, seeking an early sign of the horses that would bear them home. Perched on the highest vantage point, on a "Stormy, . . . rough, and wild" December day, when the wind whistled through a hawthorn and they had only a solitary sheep for company, the speaker peers through the gaps in the mist at the "intermitting prospects of the wood / And plain beneath" (348–49). This sublime vision is juxtaposed with the bare account of John Wordsworth's death, which appears to the poet as a "chastisement" (355) when he thinks back to the "anxiety of hope" and "trite reflections of morality" he recently felt on the crag, causing him to bow down "[t]o God, who . . . corrected [his] desires" (360). Thus, the moment of death is retrospectively reconfigured as a manifestation of divine judgment,

> And afterwards the wind, and sleety rain,
> And all the business of the elements,
> The single sheep, and the one blasted tree,
> . . . and the mist . . .
> All these were spectacles and sounds to which
> I often would repair, and thence would drink
> As at a fountain. (361–70)

As this passage makes clear, the "spot of time" is not an isolated moment; the death of the father is intimately bound up with the elements and experiences that precede it, just as the sight of the gibbet is associated with the difficult descent and the girl with the pitcher, or the vision of the drowned man is connected to the boy's confusion upon seeing a "heap of garments" by the lake. To the speaker, these memories gain in power each time they are recalled, transforming the shock of the initial experience into a source of strength, for they "impressed [his] mind / With images, to which in following years / Far other feelings were attached" (283–85). Indeed, Wordsworth's "spots of time . . . retain / A fructifying"—or "renovating" (1805)—"virtue, whence, . . . our minds / (Especially the imaginative power) / Are nourished, and invisibly repaired" (288–94), just as his memory of the wind and rain, the "single sheep and the one, blasted tree," soothes his pain and refreshes his spirit.

As I have shown, death is also the most important theme in Joyce's epiphanies, and the structure of the epiphanies bears close comparison to Wordsworth's "spots of time." This is as true at the microscopic level, where Wordsworth's spots confront death as a temporal and existential limit while Joyce's epiphanies encounter the limits of language, as it is at the macroscopic, for Joyce's works, like Wordsworth's, are structured around a series of epiphanies. There are numerous similarities between their respective moments of revelation, from the formative role of the book of Revelation to neo-Kantian aesthetics of the sublime and a deistic vision of the all-manifest epiphany. But there are also significant differences between Wordsworth's epiphanies and Joyce's: for Wordsworth, any experience may occasion a "spot of time," but such incidents always lead to privileged moments, revealing the extraordinary in the ordinary, whereas Joyce's epiphanies manifest the ordinariness of the ordinary and therefore seem banal. Consequently, there is rarely any doubt in Wordsworth's moments of insight, which typically present a triumphant revelation, whereas incertitude is central to Joyce's manifestations. Epistemological differences have tonal reverberations: Joyce's epiphanies are characterized by irony, with occasional flashes of humor, both of which are sorely missing in Wordsworth. And finally, while for both writers the epiphany is a literary artifact, Wordsworth emphasizes the referential experience of epiphany, whereas Joyce shows forth the epiphany of language.

Joyce's Epiphanies "in a Wordworth's"

Ashton Nichols's *The Poetics of Epiphany* traces Joyce's aesthetics back to Wordsworth and Shelley. As Nichols shows, there are striking parallels between Daedalus's definition:

> By an epiphany he meant a sudden spiritual manifestation, whether in the vulgarity of speech or of gesture or in a memorable phase of the mind itself. He believed that it was for the man of letters to record these epiphanies with extreme care, seeing that they themselves are the most delicate and evanescent of moments. (*SH* 216)

and Shelley's "Defence of Poetry," where in "the best and happiest of moments,"

> We are aware of evanescent visitations of thought and feeling sometimes associated with place or person, sometimes regarding our own mind alone, and always arising unforeseen and departing unbidden, but elevating and delightful beyond all expression. (532)

Stephen's "most delicate and evanescent of moments" are remarkably similar to Shelley's "evanescent visitations": both arise unexpectedly from ordinary places, conversations, or moments of reflection, affecting "those of the most delicate sensibility" and leading us back to "the wonder of our being" when poetry touches "the enchanted chord" (532), "a spiritual state" that "Luigi Galvani, using a phrase almost as beautiful as Shelley's, called the enchantment of the heart" (*P* 231). Nichols demonstrates how these parallels run through Stephen's aesthetics, suggesting that "Joyce imported Shelley's ideas directly into his own theory of epiphany" (104). Although Nichols ascribes Stephen's theory to Joyce and makes no distinction between the theory in *Stephen Hero* and the aesthetics in *Portrait* (where the word "epiphany" does not occur), the similarities are undeniable, showing the extent to which Joyce drew on Romantic poetics both for his theory of epiphany in *Stephen Hero* and his conception of the artist in *Portrait*.

This Romantic influence goes beyond "The Defence of Poetry." Nichols argues that Shelley's and Joyce's theories "derive ultimately from Wordsworth," specifically the 1802 preface to *Lyrical Ballads* (104–5), where the poet's "lively sensibility" is affected by "absent things as if they were present," throwing over "incidents and situations from common life" a "colouring of imagination, whereby ordinary things should be presented to the mind in an unusual aspect" (244; see Nichols 104–5). There can be little doubt about the importance of the "Preface" to both Shelley and Joyce, but Nichols's focus is too narrow. As Abrams has shown, Wordsworth's poetics of epiphany are expressed most powerfully not in the preface to *Lyrical Ballads* but in the "Prospectus" that concludes the preface to *The Excursion*, a poem Joyce cites as an example of Wordsworth's genius. In a letter of May 1905, Joyce's "history of literature" awards "the highest palms to Shakespeare, Wordsworth and Shelley" (*LII* 90); his next letter, dated June 6, 1905, judges between them: "I think W[ordsworth] of all English men of letters best deserves your word 'genius.' Read his poem to his lost son in 'Excursion'" (2.91).

Wordsworth is frequently regarded as the founder of the modern literary epiphany. In *Natural Supernaturalism*, Abrams notes striking similarities between Wordsworth's "spots of time" and the "Modern Moment," especially Hopkins's theophanies and Joyce's epiphanies (1971, 418–22). Robert Langbaum is more explicit: "The epiphanic mode," derived from Wordsworth, "is to a large extent the Romantic and modern mode—a dominant modern convention" (336). Ashton Nichols develops this thesis in *The Poetics of Epiphany* (1987): "Wordsworth's spots of time bear comparison not only to Joyce's epiphanies but to Coleridge's 'flashes,' Shelley's 'best and happiest moments,' Keats's 'fine isolated verisimilitude,' Browning's 'infinite moment,' Arnold's 'gleaming' moments, and Tennyson's 'little things . . . that strike on a sharper sense'" (5). Nichols convincingly demonstrates that epiphany is characteristic of nineteenth-century poetry and that it continues to play a crucial role in the poetry of Yeats, Eliot, Stevens, and Heaney. In Nichols's account, Browning "becomes a central transitional figure, in whose increasingly narrative monologues the new epiphany begins the movement from lyric poem to novel" (5). However, I believe Baudelaire's *Petits Poèmes en Prose* had a much greater effect on Joyce's formal experiments in the epiphanies (more than half of which are prose poems), while Pater's hedonistic atomism, memorably expounded in the conclusion to *The Renaissance*, provides perhaps the strongest link to the modern narrative epiphany.

According to Stanislaus Joyce, "Jim's... ambition in life is to burn with a hard and gem-like ecstasy" (1971, 43), a phrase that deliberately echoes Pater's conclusion,[22] and in *Epiphany in the Modern Novel*, Morris Beja points out striking similarities between the little vignettes Marius records in his notebook (Pater 1873, 284–86) and Joyce's early epiphanies (Beja 1971, 39–40). More recently, Jay Losey has shown that there are important similarities between Pater's "imaginary portraits" and the epiphanies, while John McGowan demonstrates how Pater's emphasis on maximally charged moments of experience leads to a tension between the traditional concept of the "soulful self" and the "dispersed, transient" subjectivity of the modernist epiphany.

In his seminal study, Morris Beja leaves little doubt about the relevance of Romantic notions of epiphany to twentieth-century fiction. Beja emphasizes not only the frequency of epiphanic moments in modernist fiction but also the importance of epiphany as an aesthetic ideal to the artistic aims of its novelists. For instance, Henry James spoke of converting "the very pulses of the air into revelations" (1962, 31–32); Virginia Woolf describes "moments of being"—"little daily miracles, illuminations, matches struck unexpectedly in the dark" when "a whole vision, an entire conception, seemed contained in [a] moment" (1935, 259–60); Thomas Wolfe tries to "fix eternally in the patterns of an indestructible form a single moment of man's living" (551); and Joseph Conrad stresses that the task of the writer is "to make you hear, to make you feel... before all, to make you see" an epiphany so complete that "behold!—all the truth of life is there: a moment of vision, a sigh, a smile—and the return to an eternal rest" (xv–xvi).[23]

Clearly epiphanies do not begin and end with modernist fiction. Wim Tigges's *Moments of Moment* collects essays on writers as diverse as Ann

Radcliffe, Ralph Waldo Emerson, Walt Whitman, George Moore, Elizabeth Bowen, Samuel Beckett, Philip Larkin, Seamus Heaney, and Thomas Pynchon. Elsewhere, critics have discerned epiphanies in the work of Shakespeare, Sterne, Eliot, Wetherell, Dickens, Hardy, Dostoyevsky, Tolstoy, Wharton, Proust, Mann, and Pasternak, to name a few.[24] In the same way, Joyceans have often been tempted to apply the term to Joyce's work as a whole. In an influential early study, Irene Hendry proclaims that "Joyce's work is a tissue of epiphanies . . . from the briefest revelation in his lyrics to the epiphany that occupies one gigantic, enduring 'moment' in *Finnegans Wake*" (1946, 461). William Tindall calls *Dubliners* "an epiphany of epiphanies," taking the same approach to Joyce's other works, each of which he portrays as a series of epiphanic moments, including an epiphany of Dublin itself (1951, 11, 34). Maurice Beebe, Hugh Kenner, and William T. Noon also made epiphany central to their analyses of Joyce, so that by 1965 Florence Walzl could write, "It has long been recognised that Joyce's writing is a texture of epiphanies" (436).

Yet this very profusion provoked a reaction against the term. In "Joyce and the Epiphany: The Key to the Labyrinth?" (1964), Robert Scholes regards "Epiphany-hunting" as "a harmless pastime" that "ought probably to be condoned, like symbol-hunting, archetype-hunting, Scrabble, and other intellectual recreations" (66), although as a critical term he is adamant that the phrase should be used only to designate "those little bits of prose which Joyce himself gave the name to" (76). Riled by Walzl's failure to heed his proscription, Scholes set out a ten-point corrective, asserting that "the term 'Epiphany' as all too commonly used in discussion of *Dubliners* and Joyce's other fiction has nothing to do with the term 'Epiphany' as Joyce himself used it" (1967, 152). Although contentious, Scholes's view was naturally influential, since he had edited the epiphanies in *The Workshop of Daedalus* (1965). His sideswipe at epiphany-hunters in general, and Walzl in particular, for using Joyce's term "to gain a spurious authority for many a tenuous aperçu, which might seem much less impressive if not cloaked in the borrowed raiment of Joyce's phraseology" (1967, 152) provoked a heated correspondence in *Proceedings of the Modern Language Association*. Scholes continued to maintain that "epiphany" had become a "cliché" in Joyce criticism, "an arid formula for cranking out unnecessary interpretations," while Walzl rightly pointed out that the notion of epiphany is central to Daedalus's aesthetic theory and that Joyce was familiar with epiphany in the liturgy, legitimating a broader use of the term that "tends to illuminate, rather than obscure, his definitions and to clarify his own later practices in fiction" (1967, 154).

If Scholes was justified in querying the overenthusiastic use of "epiphany" in early Joyce studies, where it is often applied indiscriminately to Joyce's use of symbols, leitmotifs, the revelations of character or reader, and virtually any climactic moment, it is nevertheless the case, as Feshbach and Beja (1972) have argued, that epiphany remains central to Joyce's work.[25] Scholes's admonition that the term should only be applied to the manuscript epiphanies is too stringent, but he was right that it needs to be circumscribed. At the same time, given its rich literary, theological, and philosophical tradition, it is difficult to arrive at a strict definition. Beja attempts to do so in *Epiphany in the Modern Novel*, provisionally defining epiphany as "a sudden spiritual manifestation, whether from some object, event, or memorable phase of the mind—the manifestation being out of proportion to the significance or strictly logical relevance of whatever produces it" (18). While Beja's emphasis on suddenness, triviality, and irrelevance is helpful, his definition is caught between the demands of generality and specificity. The first phrase is drawn from *Stephen Hero*, but because Beja also wants to account for epiphanies in Proust, Woolf, Faulkner, and modernist fiction as a whole, he first broadens the scope of epiphany (to "some object, event or memorable phase of the mind") and then limits its effect (to the disproportionality between the significance or logical relevance and origin of the manifestation). Subsequent theorists have been led down the same path, attempting to identify further criteria of epiphany, such as Langbaum's "psychological association, momentaneousness, suddenness and fragmentation" (in Tigges 1999, 44) or to classify them according to type. For instance, Nichols distinguishes between the "proleptic" epiphany, "in which the mind, in response to a present predisposition, transforms a past experience to produce a new sense of significance" (74), and the "adeolonic" epiphany, which "refers to a nonperceptual manifestation produced immediately by a powerful perceptual experience" (75). Wim Tigges adopts this distinction, identifying three subcategories of proleptic epiphanies (those in which a past event is later seen in a new light; moments when the past is recaptured, as in Proust; déjà vu) and five types of adeolonic epiphanies, triggered by place, person, language, an object, and the "ultimate moment," death (27–30).

While these taxonomies encourage reflection on the variety of moments we may wish to call epiphanies, as definitions they are unsatisfying because each category or subcategory is open to interpretation: in Tigges's scheme virtually any literary event or encounter could be interpreted as an epiphany. This highlights important questions about the locus of epiphany: Are objects (or events) epiphanized, or do subjects experience epiphany; and if the latter, are they perceived by literary characters or by the reader? These questions, which continue to inspire lively debate among Joyce scholars, arise directly from Stephen's theory of epiphany; unless they can be answered, it will be impossible to arrive at a comprehensive and tenable definition.

Therefore, I will begin with Joyce's definition in *Stephen Hero*, arguing that Stephen's "sudden spiritual manifestation" is a *significant* act, "whether in the vulgarity of speech or of gesture or in a memorable phase of the mind" (*SH* 216). Focusing on the language of the epiphanies and the way they are reused in Joyce's later works, I will endeavor to bring Joyce's epiphanies to light as purely linguistic phenomena.

As such, they are quite different from classico-biblical and Romantic evocations of epiphany, albeit with important similarities. Despite a gradual shift from traditional, transcendental apparitions to the immanent revelations of the Romantic period, Joyce's epiphanies, like Wordsworth's, are steeped in the language of Revelation. Indeed, for Joyce, language itself becomes the revelation, sublating distinctions between transcendence and immanence, objectivity and subjectivity, ontology and epistemology. By relocating the epiphany in the word, Joyce departs significantly from its earlier loci: divine apparitions, the universal book of God, or the perceiver. At the same time, his move follows a historical trajectory of interpreting the logos, continuing the overall trend toward internalizing experiences of epiphany (increasingly subject to doubt) from biblical prophets to Romantic poets. Since the epiphanies come into being through, and exist wholly within, the Symbolic order of language, a Lacanian reading might track this internalization back to the origins of the subject in the recognition of self as other. For Lacan, the insatiable desire to bridge that schism promulgates the Symbolic order, providing an apt analogy for Joyce's epiphany of language, whereby a "deep wound of doubt" or "void" of "incertitude" (*E* 144; *U* 9.842) leads to an absence of determinate meaning in the epiphanies and their endless capacity to signify, inscribing "absence

[as] the highest form of presence" (*WD* 144). This central absence, or silence, is the major difference between Joyce's epiphanies and those of his precursors, which are manifestations of *presence*, whether transcendental or immanent; yet Joyce's representation of absence also connects his epiphanies to the literary tradition I have outlined, because when language is figured as a cornucopian void, it becomes the site of revelation.

3

"Remember your epiphanies . . . deeply deep"

In comparison to the classical, biblical, and Romantic traditions of epiphany outlined in the previous chapter, Joyce's epiphanies seem trivial, even meaningless. Where classical and biblical epiphanies present a direct manifestation of a deity and Romantic epiphanies offer sublime visions of the infinitude of nature and/or the mind, Joyce's consist of baffling snatches of dialogue and opaque paragraphs of poetic prose. Their significance is difficult, and sometimes impossible, to determine, which has led some critics to dismiss them as the immature productions of a "piping poet" (*MBK* 247).[1] Failure to inspire revelation is usually accounted for by lack of context: "Narrative context is everything, for without it, the epiphany remains a mere fragment" (Beja 1984, 715). Since the dramatic sketches record real events, and more than half the extant epiphanies are reused in Joyce's later works, the majority of critical discussions rely on biographical evidence or surrounding narratives to elucidate their significance.[2] Yet, while factual and fictional contexts help us understand their import, there is nothing in the form that requires a narrative setting; Robert Scholes argues, "It was the essence of epiphany in Joyce's youthful theory and practise that it had no context. Each was a little independent gem" (1964, 76). M. H. Abrams, Robert Langbaum, Morris Beja, Ashton Nichols, Wim Tigges, and Paul Maltby all emphasize the momentary nature of epiphany, and many of the most famous Romantic epiphanies are brief lyrics. Thus, the failure of Joyce's epiphanies to instill revelation in the manner of their biblical or Romantic precedents is not caused by lack of context; rather, it is the result of their radically different aesthetics.

In this chapter I argue that, in contrast to biblical or Romantic revelations, Joyce's epiphanies reveal nothing beyond themselves. For all the contextual background we can supply, their significance remains fundamentally obscure. This opacity draws attention to linguistic form, revealing the nature of language through its own textual presence. The two types of epiphany, dramatic and lyrical, manifest two fundamental features: a void at the heart of language, caused by an absence of determinate meaning, and teeming presence in the unlimited profusion of signification.

As A. Walton Litz has observed, the dramatic and lyrical epiphanies form the "twin poles of Joyce's art" (*PSW* 158). Litz defines these poles as "dramatic irony and lyric sentiment," although there is little or no dramatic irony in the epiphanies, and "lyric" suggests a connection to poetry. In place of these terms, I prefer "ironic realism" and "lyrical symbolism," which apply more directly to Joyce's narrative modes. Using these labels, I show that in the dramatic epiphanies Joyce develops a range of stylistic techniques that lead to the realism and irony of his mature works and that in the narrative epiphanies he hones the poetic techniques that create the lyricism and symbolism of his fiction.

Beyond these stylistic tendencies, I hold that the indeterminate nature of Joyce's later work is already present in the epiphanies, because at the heart of all the interpretations they suggest, there is a fundamental absence of referential meaning: we find Phillip Herring's "uncertainty principle" in the epiphanies, along with the void of Pyrrhonic skepticism Rabaté identifies in *Joyce Upon the Void*. In contrast to Rabaté, though, I question whether love is the central tenet of Joyce's faith; in the epiphanies, death is a stronger certitude, while both are subordinate to language.

The Manuscript Epiphanies

Joyce's epiphanies were probably written between 1901 and 1904,[3] the same time as *Chamber Music*. They have been seen as counterparts to Joyce's lyrics and are frequently described as prose poems, although this is somewhat misleading since sixteen of the forty extant epiphanies are in dramatic form and three of the lyrical epiphanies include dialogue. Verso numbering on Joyce's manuscript suggests that originally there may have been more than seventy. Twenty-three are in Joyce's hand (Buffalo 1.A, Cornell 18), while Stanislaus Joyce's "Selections in Prose and Verse" (Cornell 4.10) contains twenty-four epiphanies, seventeen of which are not included in the Buffalo manuscript.[4] Joyce's holograph epiphanies at Buffalo are copied with unusual care, each on a single page, though they are never more than twenty lines long, suggesting the value Joyce gave them, while one epiphany exists in draft form (Cornell 18), evincing Joyce's meticulous composition. Their importance can be judged from Joyce's correspondence: he refers to the epiphanies in seven letters written between 1903 and 1907. The first, dated February 8, 1903, indicates that his work on "Epiphany" was well under way, for he had given a manuscript copy to George Russell, mentioning to Stanislaus that "my latest additions to 'Epiphany' might not be to his liking" (*LII* 28), while just over a month later, Joyce tells his brother: "I have written fifteen epiphanies—of which twelve are insertions and three additions" (*LII* 35). This clearly suggests that Joyce thought of the epiphanies as an ordered collection; he may even have considered publishing them in a slim volume akin to Baudelaire's *Petits Poèmes en Prose* before deciding that he could reuse them in *Stephen Hero* (*JJ* 89).[5]

In *The Workshop of Daedalus*, Robert Scholes uses internal biographical evidence and the verso numbering on the holograph leaves to establish an order for the epiphanies, suggesting that "[w]hen Joyce had arranged his seventy-some Epiphanies, he had before him an excellent supplement to the outline for *Stephen Hero*" (6). Scholes's order is far from certain, but Joyce's plans for *Stephen Hero* support the contention that "[t]hese Epiphanies became [Joyce's] principal building blocks for the novel" (*WD* 6). After copying out his 1904 essay, "A Portrait of the Artist," Joyce recorded a series of notes for *Stephen Hero*, including "Epiphany of Thornton," "Epiphany of Hell," and "Epiphany of Mr Tate" (Buffalo 2.A.16, 20). These notes speak to *Portrait*'s complex genesis, from *Stephen Hero*, his 1904 essay, and ultimately, the epiphanies. Scholes may be right in stating that the epiphanies provide cornerstones for *Stephen Hero*, but since half the original manuscript is lost, his claim is problematic, whereas there is a strong case for regarding them as the key moments in *A Portrait of the Artist as a Young Man*.

In all, at least fourteen epiphanies are reused in *Stephen Hero* and twelve in *Portrait*, with a number of additional echoes. Morris Beja identifies twelve epiphanies in *Ulysses* and three notable similarities in *Finnegans Wake* (1984, 712–13), a list that could well be expanded (see appendix). In addition to these, several critics have attempted to identify lost epiphanies.[6] Although speculative, their putative epiphanies illustrate the extent to which the modes of ironic realism and lyrical symbolism that Joyce developed in the epiphanies shape the dialogue, narrative, and poetics of his mature work, allowing one to read all of Joyce as epiphanic.

The Theory of Epiphany

The best guide to Joyce's epiphanies is Daedalus's theory in *Stephen Hero*. Toward the end of chapter 24,[7] Stephen is walking through Eccles Street (Bloom's street) with Cranly one evening "when a trivial incident set him composing some ardent verses which he entitled a 'Vilanelle [sic] of the Temptress'" (216):

> The Young Lady—(drawling discreetly) . . . O, yes . . . I was . . . at the . . . cha . . . pel. . . .
> The Young Gentleman—(inaudibly) . . . I . . . (again inaudibly) . . . I . . .
> The Young Lady—(softly) . . . O . . . but you're . . . ve . . . ry . . . wick . . . ed. . . . (*SH* 216)

This "fragment of colloquy" produces a keen effect on Stephen's "sensitiveness," apparently because, through the embodiment of its elided words, it reveals a hidden content of desire. The words are "trivial," but the effect they produce is not; by hinting toward some undisclosed sin enacted at the moment the woman is praying, they seem to give voice to Stephen's fantasy, as though his cloudy reflections on religion, femininity, and masculinity had suddenly precipitated into the real world, projecting desire onto the words he overhears. The associations evoked by the dialogue are as vague as Stephen's ruminations before the incident, and they can never finally be pinned down because a) there is a hiatus in the text (we are not told what the young man says); and b) we can imagine any number of possibilities in its place. This basic nexus provides the seminal structure of Joyce's epiphanies, where textual lacunae propel speculation into the hermeneutic void.

In theory, any hiatus shares these properties, but the power of Joyce's epiphanies depends on the extent to which he is able to create *resonant* gaps and silences, just as the effect of this incident depends upon the fact that there is no limit to the thoughts we can imagine "dancing the dance of unrest" in Stephen's brain. Like Flo feeling "the rings" as *Come and Go* closes in silence (Beckett 2006, 355), Joyce's epiphanic gaps train readers to hear the ringing silence of textuality; in doing so, the theoretical properties of the lacuna are shown to have been actual all along, a play of difference in the chain of signification. In the next section, I show that silence (including any hiatus in the text) and repetition (a relation that encompasses difference) characterize Joyce's two types of epiphany. To the extent that these are fundamental properties of language, they characterize all literary texts, but the epiphanies are paradigmatic because they explicitly manifest these conditions.

Dramatic and Lyrical Epiphanies

The structure of Stephen's triviality suggests that Joyce's epiphanies are very different from his Romantic forebears,' but he may have drawn on Shelley for his two types of epiphany. Where Shelley distinguishes between poetic moments inspired by "people or places" and those arising in "our own mind" (532), Joyce makes a distinction between spiritual manifestations in "the vulgarity of speech or of gesture" and in a "memorable phase of the mind itself" (*SH* 216). But whereas Shelley's dyad is theoretical, Joyce put it into practice, creating a formal difference between dramatic and lyrical epiphanies.

Stanislaus Joyce tells us that Joyce's earliest epiphanies were dramatic: "In the beginning . . . Epiphanies were always brief sketches, hardly ever more than some dozen lines in length, but always very accurately observed and noted, the matter being so slight" (*MBK* 124–25). Stanislaus refers to the early epiphanies as "notes," records of authentic conversation, which is borne out by Oliver St. John Gogarty's quip in *As I Was Going Down Sackville Street*: "Which one of us had endowed him with an 'Epiphany' and sent him to the lavatory to take it down?" (294). Gogarty must have known that he figured in an epiphany, for he complains that "to be an unwilling contributor to one of his 'Epiphanies' is irritating" (294). Gogarty had a right to feel aggrieved, but the epiphany he inspired is of particular interest because it is the only surviving draft:

in O'Connell St:

        [Dublin:ˬin Hamilton, Long's, the chemist's,]

    Gogarty —Is that for Gogarty?   pay
    The Assistant —(looks)—Yes, sir . . . Will you ˬtake it with you? for it now?
    Gogarty —No, send it put it in the

	account; send it on. You know the address.
	(takes a pen)
The Assistant	—~~Yes.~~ ₐYe . . . es.
Gogarty	—5 Rutland Square.
	while
The Assistant	—(half to himself ~~as~~ he writes)
	. .5 . . . Rutland . . . Square.⁸

It is apparent from this draft that Joyce did not simply transcribe a real conversation: the use of stage directions, speech headings, and lineation create a dramatic sketch, and revisions such as "while" for "as" (presumably for assonance) and the phonetic extension of "Ye-es" reveal the pains Joyce took to construct its effects. These details play a crucial role in creating the tone, for the piece seems to depend upon the contrast between the assistant's hesitant deference and Gogarty's crisp imperatives. In this context, the long-drawn "Ye-es" begins to look uncertain, making Gogarty's assertion "You know the address" seem presumptuous; the result is to give the address a prominence it would not otherwise have, especially when it is repeated in the final line with emphasis, as if to underline that this is a solid, middle-class address,⁹ one from which payment can be expected (*WD* 50). Thus, the subtle irony with which Gogarty's pretensions are unveiled, in contrast to the servility of the assistant, suggests another contrast, with the artist paring his fingernails above or behind the epiphany, just as Joyce himself was presumably beside or behind Gogarty at the chemist's during this brief exchange.

The extent to which this piece has been composed raises questions about the authenticity of the dialogue, but there can be little doubt that the epiphanies record real events. "Poor Little Fellow" is a direct response to the death of Joyce's brother Georgie in March 1902; the "Two Mourners" were observed by Stanislaus and James at their mother's funeral in August 1903 (*MBK* 235); the party described in "She Dances with Them in the Round" was given by the Sheehys (Joyce, not having a suit of his own, went in a baggy dress suit borrowed from Gogarty [*MBK* 256–57]). The dramatic epiphanies situate these events precisely because their location is specified at the head of the text, like the opening stage directions in a play. Five epiphanies are set at the Sheehys' house in Belvedere Place, which Joyce frequented from 1897 to 1901 (#11–14, #17); two are records of his trip to Mullingar in July 1900 (#9, #15); "His Dancing" is another response to Georgie's death; "Fred Leslie's My Brother" must have occurred on Joyce's return from Paris around Christmas 1902; and the Bray address given in "Apologise" dates the scene to 1891.

The fact that these epiphanies record real persons, places, and events does not necessarily mean that the dialogue is authentic, although each of these sketches employs a range of features designed to create the impression of real speech. To this end, Joyce employs contractions, ellipsis, timed pauses (marked by a variable number of dots), exclamations, false starts, repetition, incomplete utterances, Hiberno-English, deixis, and colloquial language to mimic natural speech, as well as a range of paralinguistic and prosodic features indicating the tone and manner of delivery. In comparison with nineteenth-century fiction, or even the naturalistic drama Joyce admired, these techniques make Joyce's dialogue seem extremely realistic, giving the impression that the "fragment of colloquy" he constructs transcribes spontaneous conversation.

To the extent that speech is the verbal manifestation of our thoughts and feelings, this is an epiphanic aim, but Joyce's purpose appears to have been more precise. According to Stanislaus, the epiphanies "were in the beginning ironical observations of slips, and little errors and gestures—mere straws in the wind—by which people betrayed the very things they were most careful to conceal" (*MBK* 126). There is no guarantee that Joyce would have shared his brother's judgment, but Stanislaus's account is telling. His verbal "slips" and "gestures" probably recall *Stephen Hero*'s "vulgarity of speech and of gesture," and many of the epiphanies can be read as ironically observed parapraxes. For instance, this scene seems opaque in isolation:

[Dublin: at Sheehy's, Belvedere Place]

Joyce —I knew you meant him. But you're wrong about his age.
Maggie Sheehy—(*leans forward to speak seriously*) Why, how old is he?
Joyce —Seventy-two.
Maggie Sheehy—Is he?

But when reused for a guessing game in *Stephen Hero* (51), where the subject is Ibsen, it reveals Miss Daniel's ignorance in contrast to Stephen.

"Your Favorite Poet" works in the same way, with Hannah Sheehy, after a dramatic pause and hush, answering that her favorite German poet is ". .I think. . . . . Goethe. . . . .," implying a limited frame of reference. The effect of these pieces is surely ironic, revealing the ignorance and conventional assumptions of the speakers in contrast to the sensitivity and intelligence of the artist capable of recording them (compare #9, #10, #13).

In this sense, the dramatic epiphanies appear to betray the ignorance of others through the vulgarity (or ordinariness) of their words and gestures, in contrast to Joyce's memorable phases of the mind, which are shown forth in the lyrical epiphanies. But on several occasions, Joyce seems the subject of irony: if the epiphanies record "any showing forth of the mind by which he considered one gave oneself away" (Gogarty, 294–95), then Joyce was not averse to giving himself away. Skeffington and Maggie Sheehy's mockery of "our friend Jocax" in "The Day of the Rabblement" is a good example, as is "The Stars on Joyce's Nose," where Dick Sheehy pokes fun at Joyce's literary snobbishness (playing on the conventional license of the artist) by asking if he has read a mildly salacious anti-Catholic novel, *The Escaped Nun*.

	[Dublin, on the North Circular Road: Christmas]
Miss O'Callaghan	—(*lisps*)—I told you the name, *The Escaped Nun*.
Dick Sheehy	—(*loudly*)—O, I wouldn't read a book like that . . . I must ask Joyce. I say, Joyce, did you ever read *The Escaped Nun?*
Joyce	—I observe that a certain phenomenon happens about this hour.
Dick Sheehy	—What phenomenon?
Joyce	—O . . . the stars come out.
Dick Sheehy	—(*to Miss O'Callaghan*). . Did you ever observe how . . . the stars come out on the end of Joyce's nose about this

hour? . . . (*she smiles*). . Because
I observe that phenomenon.

If Sheehy's joke is rather lame, it exposes Joyce's ruse as lamer still, while Joyce's obvious evasion of the question draws attention to the peculiarly evasive nature of Sheehy's observation. The apparition of the stars is the epiphanic phenomenon par excellence, recalling Matthew and Luke, and their appearance at the end of Joyce's nose creates an image at once comic, undercutting Joyce's studied ignorance with a pinocchioesque outgrowth, and gnomic, in the sense that the very absence of meaning attributed to such meaningful symbols seems to imbue the stars on Joyce's nose with an absurd but ineradicable significance.

Morris Beja points out that this epiphany may explain the curious star on Joyce's nose in the portrait he commissioned from César Abin for his fiftieth birthday (715–16; Figure 1).[10] It is of course impossible to verify the connection, but Joyce's meticulous instructions for the drawing, figuring himself as a question mark hanging above the point of the world (occupied entirely by Ireland, with Dublin in black) suggest both the mystery and the mysterious significance of his work, a point that is nowhere more evident than at the point of his nose.

While every other symbol has a stated significance,[11] the illumination of the star is gnomic, in both its ordinary, sententious sense (associated with the star of the magi) and the obsolete, jocular meaning of "gnomon" as the nose (*OED*). Joyce plays on this meaning in his first short story, "The Sisters," where Father Flynn's cavernous nostrils, filled with the snuff of simony, loom large. At the key moment in the story, when Eliza confides that "there was something queer coming over him latterly" and seems about to reveal the mystery of her late brother, the priest, she suddenly breaks off and lays a finger against her nose, as though to conceal a secret (*D* 9). It is this sense of a concealed truth, a hidden meaning, that Joyce's epiphanies tease us with. Like the star on the end of Joyce's nose, they hint toward an epiphanic revelation, but when we search for it, we find only an absence of meaning, like the complete non sequitur of Joyce's answer, or the gaps and silences that pervade "The Sisters."

Phillip Herring has argued that Joyce's texts are fundamentally indeterminate because they introduce "a range of interpretive possibilities" while "an essential piece of evidence is missing that would allow us a measure of security in interpretation" so that "readers are invited to fill the gap by

Figure 1. César Abin, "Caricature of James Joyce." *transition* 21 (1932): 265. ©Betsy Jolas. Reprinted with permission.

speculating about what is missing" (xxii). Herring traces the uncertainty principle back to the word "gnomon," showing that Joyce's short stories are as riddled with gaps as his later works, but he could equally have begun with the epiphanies.

"Forty Thousand Pounds" provides a good example of the uncertainty principle at work:

[Dublin: on Mountjoy Square]

Joyce —(*concludes*). . . . That'll be forty thousand pounds.
Aunt Lillie —(*titters*)—O, laus!. . . . I was like that too. . . . . .
. . . When I was a girl I was <u>sure</u> I'd marry a
lord . . . or something . . .
Joyce —(*thinks*)—Is it possible she's comparing
herself with me?

Here, as in the other dramatic epiphanies, deixis, contractions, exclamations, hesitations, emphasis, and vague language create the impression that we are breaking in on a real conversation, but this epiphany is unique because the stage directions indicate that Joyce's final line is thought, not said. As a literal representation of Joyce's mental response, the question is pellucid, yet its significance remains unclear: Is it supposed to show Aunt Lillie's solipsism in comparing herself to Joyce, or Joyce's arrogance in rejecting the very possibility? Ultimately, it is not possible to decide whether Aunt Lillie betrays herself or Joyce gives himself away, and in either case, what they reveal. If we identify with the Joyce character as implied author, then the epiphany appears to reveal Aunt Lillie's vulgarity,[12] in contrast to Joyce; if, on the other hand, we identify with Lillie, or adopt an "objective" position outside the characters, then the omniscient perspective of the dramatist whose stage directions afford access to Joyce's thought allows us to read the epiphany as a revelation of his narcissism. Joyce creates similar ambiguities in many of the epiphanies and in his subsequent works, but irrespective of the interpretative stance readers adopt, there is further uncertainty about what exactly is being compared (vain, self-aggrandizing fantasies? ego? self-worth?). This inscrutability of reference is central to the dramatic epiphanies, which betray "the very things they [are] most careful to conceal" (*MBK* 126) through their own slips and lapses.

If the dramatic epiphanies are objective, presenting characters directly through their own words, "Forty Thousand Pounds," with its representation of unspoken thought, provides a bridge toward the subjective mode of the lyrical epiphanies, which record "memorable phases of the mind." Stanislaus Joyce tells us that as they progressed, "[t]he epiphanies became more frequently subjective and included dreams which [Joyce] considered in some way revelatory" (*MBK* 125). According to Stanislaus, he himself figured as "An Arctic Beast" in one of the earliest dream pieces, while in another he appears as "The Big Dog" (135–36). "His Dancing," "She Comes at Night," and "Two Sisters" record dreams in which George Joyce, May Joyce, and Henrik Ibsen appear. "The dreams are genuine," Stanislaus says, although "they have undergone literary treatment . . . to reproduce dream impressions" (127). He explains that "[t]he revelation and importance of the subconscious had caught [Joyce's] interest," and "he may have hoped [dreams] would reveal things our controlled thoughts unconsciously conceal" (126–27). In this sense, they are subjective counterparts to the dramatic epiphanies, for both seek to reveal "the significance of unreflecting admissions and unregarded trifles" (127), whether through verbal slips or memorable phases of the mind.

There is no way to corroborate Stanislaus's claims, but editors have noted the dreamlike quality of many of the later epiphanies. Whether dreams or not, these lyrical epiphanies create memorable images and impressions through carefully wrought poetic language. Written at the same time as *Chamber Music*, they have the rhythmical and musical qualities of Joyce's lyrics; they can be compared to prose poems that make use of alliteration, assonance, rhyme, rhythm, and the techniques of repetition and variation Joyce was perfecting in his poetry to irradiate symbolic and imagistic associations. For example, in "The Race":

> The human crowd swarms in the enclosure,
> moving through the slush. A fat woman passes,
> her dress lifted boldly, her face nozzling in
> an orange. A pale young man with a Cockney
> accent does tricks in his shirtsleeves and
> drinks out of a bottle. A little old man has
> mice on an umbrella; a policeman in
> heavy boots charges down and seizes the
> umbrella: the little old man disappears.
> Bookies are bawling out names and prices;
> one of them screams with the voice of a
> child—"Bonny Boy!" "Bonny Boy!" . . . Human

creatures are swarming in the enclosure,
moving backwards and forwards through
the thick ooze. Some ask if the race is going
on; they are answered "Yes" and "No." A
band begins to play. . . . . . A beautiful brown
horse, with a yellow rider upon him, flashes
far away in the sunlight.

The opening words create an odd, dreamlike effect, as though the crowd might not be human, an impression accentuated by the bestial connotations of "swarms" and "enclosure," which make it difficult to situate the scene. Apparently set at a racetrack, there is a deliberate blurring of the animal and the human, an imprecision that enhances the magical realist effect of the woman "nozzling in an orange" and the "little old man" with "mice on an umbrella." Joyce's use of alliteration, assonance, and anaphora make the figures almost as indefinite as the articles that introduce them, and in dreamlike fashion, the little old man disappears, after which we get two and a half lines of pure poetry:

Bóokies are báwling out námes and príces;
Óne of them scréams with the vóice of a chíld—
Bónny Bóy! Bónny Bóy!

The first two lines have a marked dactylic rhythm, which contrasts nicely with the amphimacers in the horse's name. The alliteration at the beginning and end of the sentence also undergoes a pleasing transformation as the long stressed vowels of "bookies" and "bawling" are shortened in "bonny" and wrenched up into the diphthong "boy." The effect of these lines is one of great realism, as though the voice comes to life through its rhythmic precision, and the clarity of the bookie's call, in contrast to the haziness of the preceding images, sets up the final juxtaposition. Between the ellipses, Joyce recalls the opening, offsetting the flat realism of the dialogue ("'Yes' and 'No'") with the band, and this musical association, like the bookie's poetic cry, helps to ensure that the animalized crowd of "[h]uman creatures . . . swarming in the enclosure" is both opposed to, and mirrored in, the beautiful racehorse "with a yellow rider upon him, flash[ing] far away in the sunlight."

Joyce's techniques of repetition and variation can be compared to musical variations on a theme, employing counterpoint to set one melody off against another, or creating harmonies and overtones through careful arrangement of the parts. These subtle effects can be heard in the following epiphany:

> The spell of arms and voices—the white arms of roads, their promise of close embraces and the black arms of tall ships that stand against the moon, their tale of distant nations. They are held out to say: We are alone,—come. And the voices say with them: We are your people. And the air is thick with their company as they call to me their kinsman, making ready to go, shaking the wings of their exultant and terrible youth.

The opening states the theme in a musical phrase whose alternating stresses emphasize three nouns. The phrase could hardly be simpler, but just as the genitive can be read both ways (as the spell whose ingredients are arms and voices, or the spell cast by them), so too each noun phrase rings with overtones, even the first time it is sounded: the spell is both objective and subjective (a mood or affect); the arms are literal and figurative (a military synecdoche); the voices seem heard and imagined. Through contrasting adjectives (white, black) and complementary metaphors (roads, ships), a complex series of correspondences is constructed in which the arms are both enticing and forbidding. In the "tale" they tell, the arms morph into the voices, commingling as "they are held out to say," but just as their words are paradoxical ("We are alone"), they never fully merge, because the balanced offset structure of the sentences ("We/And/We/And") serves to keep them apart. This marked structural divide, at the very moment the bodily symbols unite, mirrors the position of the dreamer, who is at once alone and among his kin ("We are your people"). At the same time, this balanced movement carries the reader forward with assurance as the symbols accrue associations of homecoming and belonging, creating the impression that their significance is understood. Recapitulating the theme, Joyce unites his keynotes in the final sentence, where the initial dreamlike indeterminacy of "the spell" becomes as charged as the air is thick with "their company" calling (in both the literal and figurative senses) to the narrator, "their kinsman" (which recalls "your people," "nations," and "the promise of close embraces"). And in the final verb phrases, a magical reversal is effected, for the pronouns make it seem almost as though it is the narrator making ready to go.

Reused in both *Stephen Hero* and *Portrait*, this is one of Joyce's most significant epiphanies. The surviving pages of *Stephen Hero* begin in its midst, the sketch transposed to fit the third-person, past-tense narrative, but otherwise little changed. Immediately after the epiphany, across the paragraph break, Joyce has written "Departure for Paris" (*SH* 240). Marked in blue crayon, this note refers to Joyce's revisions for *Portrait*, where the same epiphany is returned from the third to the first person, forming the antepenultimate entry in Stephen's diary, headed "16 *April*: Away! Away!" In these final brief entries, the epiphany is linked to three crucial themes: Mrs. Dedalus's hopes that her son may learn "away from home and friends what the heart is and what it feels" (275); Stephen's poetic affirmation, "to forge in the smithy of my soul the uncreated conscience of my race"; and the final invocation to Daedalus. As Robert Scholes points out, in "The Spell of Arms and Voices," "we see Joyce beginning to clothe himself in the Daedalian myth" (*W* 40); in fact, he creates a double image, for when Stephen cries "[o]ld father, old artificer," he seems to create himself anew, as both the namesake of Daedalus and his son, Icarus, preserving a powerful tension between prophecies of Stephen's escape through flights of the poetic imagination and a hubristic fall, as he stands on the brink of the future, "shaking the wings of his exultant and terrible youth."

This epiphany is as important for its linguistic qualities as for its thematic content, revealing the power of poetic language to create epiphanic effects through aural, imagistic, and semantic associations. These poetic effects become central to Joyce's fiction: throughout *Dubliners*, *Portrait*, *Ulysses*, and *Finnegans Wake*, musical and symbolic associations are used to create not only lyrical prose but also radiant and epiphanic moments, like the poetic language of "Araby" or the famous ending to *Portrait*, chapter IV. At the same time, in the midst of all the proliferating associations Joyce generates, meaning is impossible to pin down, creating both indeterminacy and a superabundance of signification.

The Aesthetics of Epiphany

To recognize Joyce's epiphanies as moments of revelation, we need a new aesthetics of epiphany, and this is exactly what Joyce set out to define in the Commonplace notebook he kept in Paris and Pola from January 1903 to November 1904—a period during which he composed at least fifteen epiphanies (*LII* 35). Extracts from the Paris-Pola notebooks are reused widely in *Stephen Hero*: Aquinas's statement, *"Pulchra sunt quae visa placent"* ("beauty is that which pleases when seen") and his criteria of beauty—*integritas, consonantia, claritas*—are introduced during Stephen's interview with the President of the College at the end of chapter 18 (100–101); in chapter 22, Stephen discusses the relationship between the beautiful and the good with Father Artifoni (175–76), who encourages his student to write a treatise on aesthetics; and this impulse is recalled several times before Stephen finally expounds his theory to Cranly in chapter 24, culminating in Stephen's famous definition of epiphany: "By an epiphany he meant a sudden spiritual manifestation, whether in the vulgarity of speech or of gesture or in a memorable phase of the mind itself" (*SH* 216). For all the attention this sentence has received, no one, to my knowledge, has noted that Daedalus's epiphany is a *significant* act, pointing the way to Joyce's linguistic epiphany.[13] The signs here are subtle, their significance not readily apparent, but by carefully unpacking Daedalus's key terms, the emphasis on language becomes clear. Like the restless thoughts that precipitate his theory, "spiritual" suggests a number of possible interpretations, beginning with Emma's soul "manifest[ing] itself" in "every stray image of the streets" and the "theory of dualism" Stephen toys with, in which "the twin eternities of spirit and nature" are manifest in "the twin eternities of male and female" (215). This openness to interpretation may explain why the term "epiphany" has become so widespread (Harrison 143), but there is a common anthropological thread. "[S]pirit" is derived from *spiritus* (breath), as Stephen recalls in "the poor breath, the poor helpless human spirit, sobbing and sighing" (*P* 120). The critical writings that inform *Stephen Hero*, such as "Ecce Homo," "Drama and Life," and "James Clarence Mangan," clearly conceive of the spirit in human terms, and there can be no doubt that Stephen's "spiritual manifestation" is a natural experience, occurring through language, mind, or body.

For Stephen, epiphanies are always significant, because they are conveyed through a signifying system: the vulgarity of "*speech* or of *gesture*, or in a *memorable phase of the mind.*" Here "vulgarity" refers primarily to *ordinary* speech or gesture, rather than indelicacy (*OED*), but Stephen is clearly responding to hints of vulgar eroticism in the dialogue he overhears (*SH* 216). In the preceding chapter, Stephen is also provoked by a group of young students (including Emma), whose postural "affectations" and phatic "babble" irritate him with their "vulgarity" (188), suggesting a connection between desire and the charged language or gestures that occasion an epiphany. In fact, the retreating rain clouds that brighten Stephen's mood after this show of "vulgarity" are copied with very few changes from "The Girls, The Boys" (epiphany #25), and immediately afterward Stephen tells Cranly, "There should be an art of gesture" (*SH* 188). On the following page, Stephen repeats the word six times, linking gesture to rhythm and music, even that of a single word (189). Naturally, words and gestures go together: the boy in "Araby" compares his body to a harp and his beloved's "words and gestures" to "fingers running upon the wires" (*D* 23); in *Portrait*, Stephen is drawn to the theatrical "voices and gestures" priests assume rather than their "awful power" (171; cf. 153, 198, 251); and in *Ulysses*, he is wooed by J. J. O'Molloy's "grace of language and gesture" (7.776). Indeed, in "Circe" Stephen thinks that "gesture . . . would be a universal language" (15.105–07), and in *Finnegans Wake* Joyce plays on the work of Marcel Jousse, who studied the gestural origins of language: "In the beginning was the gest he jousstly says" (*FW* 465.05).[14]

Joyce's interest in gesture suggests that he regarded it as a semiotic system structurally equivalent to speech, and the same premise underlies Stephen's definition, where ordinary speech and gesture provide two manifestations of the linguistic epiphany. Moreover, when Dedalus reads the flight of birds as script (*P* 243–45), he traces the origins of writing back to movement, a gestural expression derived from the ibis-headed Thoth, "god of writers" (244), so that "speech" or "gesture" can be taken to imply any act of communication. The reference to Thoth indicates Dedalus's reverence for language, but he is equally amused by "the god's image for it made him think of a bottlenosed judge in a wig, putting commas into a document" (244), demonstrating again that the "sudden spiritual manifestation" is always a revelation of *human* spirit through language, whether through speech, gesture, writing, or "a memorable phase of the mind."

"Memorable," meaning both "worthy of remembrance" and "able to be remembered," is derived from Latin *memorāre*, "to say, mention, recall to mind" (*OED*). According to Daedalus's definition, then, epiphanies encompass not only striking, unforgettable moments but *any* experience capable of being remembered, where recall depends on the possibility of relating an event verbally or summoning it in the mind through symbolic representation. For something to be memorable, it must leave a trace, and these traces constitute the Symbolic order (Ansermet and Magistretti 2015), which means that a "memorable phase of the mind" is predicated on our perceptual capacity for language.

But for Joyce the significance of "phase" is more specific. Skeat defines the word as "an appearance," tracing it back to the same root as "epiphany," the Indo-European BHA, meaning to shine, speak, or show. As Skeat explains, "*phasis* not only means 'appearance,' . . . but also 'a saying, declaration'" (as in *emphasis*), pointing once more to the connection between epiphany and language. This is also borne out by its original meaning, the appearance of the moon or planet at a given time, for, as we shall see, Joyce extends the traditional association between epiphany and the apparition of luminous bodies in the heavens to language (e.g., "the signature of [W. Shakespeare's] initial" Stephen reads in Cassiopeia, or Bloom's "interstellar . . . writing" [*U* 9.931, 14.1106–09]). This emphasis on speech and writing as shining brings to light Joyce's conception of the epiphanic origins of language, whose clearest precedent is the Gospel According to St. John. John associates the Word with God, and God with the source of life and light (1:1–9), incarnated as Jesus Christ (1:13). The evangelist's avowed role is "to bear witness of the Light" (1:7) of Christ's revelation, so the words John sets down represent the manifestation of divine light. However hubristic it might appear, this is remarkably similar to Joyce's "countergospel," *Finnegans Wake* (Spurr 2015), where language is figured as light, all-manifest in the "hueful panepiphanal world" (*FW* 611.22). Likewise, Professor MacHugh associates language and radiance in "Aeolus," recounting the epiphanic origins of writing: having "spoken with the Eternal amid lightnings," Moses brings the tablets of the law down from Sinai "with the light of inspiration shining in his countenance" (*U* 7.866–69; cf. Ex. 24:12, 31:15–16, 34:1–29).

The connection between light and language is present from Joyce's first published story, "The Sisters," which opens with a boy looking for the reflected candlelight that would provide a sign of death while repeating the memorable words "gnomon," "paralysis," and "simony." This theme, presented on Joyce's first leaf of prose and numerous subsequent foliations, can be traced back to Stephen's definition, where the word "phase," like "epiphany," has roots in an Indo-European base meaning to speak, show, or shine. These senses are all at play in the original aesthetics of *Stephen Hero*, but *Portrait* develops them further. It will be recalled that Stephen's theory of beauty involves three "phases of apprehension": Aquinas's "*integritas, consonantia, claritas*" translated as "wholeness, harmony and radiance" (*P* 229). The "first phase of apprehension is a bounding line drawn about the object," either in space or time, allowing "the esthetic image" to be "luminously apprehended" (230). In the second phase, *consonantia*, an object is analyzed as "complex, multiple, divisible, . . . the result of its parts and their sum, harmonious" (230). Initially, Stephen thinks *claritas* refers to "a light from some other world" (230), but this Platonic enlightenment is rejected in favor of Duns Scotus's *haeccitas*: "You see that [the object] is that thing which it is and no other thing. The radiance of which he speaks is the scholastic *quidditas*, the *whatness* of a thing" (231). This third "phase of apprehension" (*P* 229) corresponds to the moment of epiphany in *Stephen Hero*, when Stephen first states that "*Claritas* is *quidditas*," declaring that when "we recognise that it is *that* thing which it is . . . the commonest object . . . seems to us radiant" (*SH* 218). Developing the aesthetics of *Stephen Hero*, these "phases of apprehension" illuminate the connection between light, language, and epiphany: "The instant wherein that supreme quality of beauty, the clear radiance of the aesthetic image, is apprehended luminously by the mind which has been arrested by its wholeness and fascinated by its harmony is the luminous silent stasis of esthetic pleasure, a spiritual state" (*P* 231). This shift in emphasis from "epiphany," suggesting a singular event, to the cognate "phase," implying change, indicates a broader development in Joyce's epiphanies. As the partial apparition of a cyclical process, revolving planetary phases are much closer to the poetics of *Finnegans Wake* than are singular apparitions of being. This may explain why Joyce revised the theory of epiphany in *Stephen Hero*; indeed, the failure of Daedalus's ideal points to Joyce's changing conception of epiphany, especially his turn to language.

Having defined "epiphany" in the passage analyzed above, Stephen gives Cranly an example: the Ballast Office clock. "I will pass it time after time, allude to it, refer to it," he says, with no special significance; "[t]hen all at once I see it and I know at once what it is: epiphany" (216). The revelation is sudden and unexpected, but the underlying experience is repetitive ("time after time"), suggesting that one of the functions of verbal repetition in Joyce's epiphanies is to facilitate such moments, particularly when they are developed into leitmotifs in his prose works. Appearing as a single moment in a repetitive cycle, the epiphany marks a phase on the face of a clock, indicating the double nature of Joyce's temporality, particularly in *Ulysses* and the *Wake*, whose time is both cyclical and punctual, allowing epiphanies to become both universal and arbitrary.

Stephen explains the revelation by asking Cranly to imagine a "spiritual eye" adjusting its vision to "[t]he soul of the commonest object"; at the moment it is brought into focus, "[t]he object achieves its epiphany" (218). This slippage between the observer and the observed has led to disagreement about whether the manifestation of spirit occurs in the subject or the object,[15] propagating a wide range of critical interpretations. For instance, Beja compares Stephen's aesthetics to Schopenhauer's Romantic rereading of Kant, which "does away with the dualism between subject and object" (1971, 30). Caufield explores the connection to Schopenhauer in greater detail, arguing that "Stephen's use of Schopenhauer's aesthetics" can be explained by the fact that "Post-Kantian German Idealism and its Romantic reverberations in *fin de siècle* letters . . . were a part of the critical medium in which Joyce's aesthetic sense developed" (714). In the same vein, Scholes and Corcoran derive Stephen's aesthetics "from the tradition that includes Lessing, August and Friedrich von Schlegel, Kant, Schelling and Hegel" (691). However, the Schopenhauerian parallels that Caufield provides are tenuous, while Scholes and Corcoran provide no textual evidence for their claim that Stephen's aesthetics are "explicitly indebted" to Hegel.

In fact, Joyce seems to have regarded the aesthetics in the Paris-Pola notebook not as "applied Aquinas" or Aristotle, neither as Kantian nor Hegelian, but as his own, for he signed and dated each entry with a flourish.[16] In *Stephen Hero*, Daedalus tells Cranly, "No esthetic theory . . . is of any value which investigates with the aid of the lantern of tradition" (217). Stephen's point here is that beauty is relative ("Greek beauty laughs at Coptic beauty and the American Indian derides them both" [217]), but it also justifies his desire to formulate a new aesthetic theory with a universal criterion for beauty. This is a recurring theme in the Commonplace book of 1903–1904, where Joyce draws on the Greek roots of "aesthetic" (of or relating to sensory perception) to equate beauty with apprehension: "Every sensible object that has been apprehended can be said in the first place to have been and to be beautiful in a measure beautiful; and even the most hideous object can be said to have been and to be beautiful insofar as it has been apprehended" (*WD* 81; cf. 82–83). Daedalus makes the same equation between beauty and apprehension in *Stephen Hero*: "It is almost impossible to reconcile all tradition whereas it is by no means impossible to find the justification of every form of beauty which has been adored on the earth by an examination into the mechanism of esthetic apprehension.... The apprehensive faculty must be scrutinised in action" (*SH* 217). Thus Daedalus's aesthetics, like Joyce's, are founded on "the mechanism of esthetic apprehension." This original sense of "esthetic" as sensory perception is particularly associated with Kant,[17] and although Stephen analyzes the "apprehensive faculty" in relation to Aquinas's criteria of beauty, his theory shares several similarities with Kantian aesthetics.

First, Stephen says to Cranly: "Consider the performance of your own mind when confronted with any object, hypothetically beautiful.... To apprehend it you must lift it away from everything else: and then you perceive that it is one integral thing, that is *a* thing. You recognise its integrity. Isn't that so?... That is the first quality of beauty: it is declared in a simple sudden synthesis of the faculty which apprehends" (217). This "simple sudden synthesis" is similar to Kant's "synthesis of apprehension" in the *Critique of Pure Reason*, where a manifold of empirical data is "gathered together" in a single "moment" (A99). Of course, for Kant, this intuition of an object, such as a house, is never a conception of "a thing in itself at all but only an appearance, i.e., a representation, the transcendental object of which remains utterly unknown" (A190). Indeed, the fundamental premise of Kant's first *Critique* is that we can never have access to the transcendental object, the noumenon; what the synthesis of apprehension reveals is the a priori idea of unity that structures spatiotemporal experience (A100). But the culmination of Stephen's theory, in which "the object achieves its epiphany," suggests that when the focus of the perceiver's "spiritual eye" is perfectly adjusted, "the object is epiphanised" (*SH* 216–17), letting its noumenal reality shine forth.

In Stephen's aesthetics, this occurs after the second phase, analysis, where "[t]he mind considers the object in whole and in part, in relation to itself and to other objects," examining its form and structure in detail (217). This second stage of apprehension corresponds quite closely to Kant's "synthesis of reproduction in the imagination," where the mind comprehends a given object by comparing a series of sensory presentations, past and present (A101–2). The processes are not identical, since Kant emphasizes the temporal sequence of apperception and the role of memory in facilitating our imaginative recognition of the unity of the phenomenal representation, while Stephen focuses on the formal "symmetry" of the object, "travers[ing] every cranny of its structure" to recognize its integrity (217), but there is nevertheless a marked similarity between Stephen's analytical procedure and Kant's synthesis of reproduction.

However, Stephen's third phase, in which the object is epiphanized, seems to have nothing in common with Kantian aesthetics. After recognizing the object as "*one* integral thing" and then, through analysis, as "an organised composite structure, a *thing* in fact," he says that the mind makes "the only logical possible synthesis," discovering "that it is *that* thing which it is" (218). This is the moment Stephen calls epiphany, when the soul of the object, "its whatness, leaps to us from the vestment of its appearance" and seems "radiant." Ostensibly, Stephen is reinterpreting Aquinas's *claritas* as quidditas, but Stephen's "whatness" sounds suspiciously like Kant's noumenon shining forth from the vestments of its appearance. On this reading, Stephen's third phase amounts to a revelation of the noumenal object, which is unequivocally barred in Kant's doctrine, so it is no surprise when Stephen concedes that the Ballast Office clock "has not epiphanised yet" (218). Kant's proscription implies that Stephen will wait forever for an epiphany of the clock, a rejection emphasized by Cranly's "hostility" (218) toward the theory.

Stephen's failure to demonstrate epiphany is significant, because nothing in Joyce's epiphanies or any of their subsequent reworkings suggests that Joyce ever deviated from Cranly's skepticism toward the possibility of epiphany as an absolute or noumenal revelation. Nevertheless, Stephen's "yet" implies a vestige of hope. So long as epiphany depends on the object, they will wait in vain, but in Stephen's theory *any* object is capable of epiphany at any moment, if only we have eyes to see it, for every object offers an epiphany in its quidditas. And this is precisely the kind of revelation Joyce's epiphanies offer: not the flash of insight from beyond but "whatness" manifest to the reader as a textual object shown forth for subjective contemplation.

One might object that this makes the epiphanies into the Emperor's New Clothes, dressing the bare manifestation of textuality in theological raiment, but the discourse of the sublime Joyce appropriates in his aesthetics shows that language is itself the epiphany. Just as Joyce's autograph "Apocalypse" sheds light on his revelation of language, its sublimity is illuminated by Kant. Like Wordsworth, Joyce interprets the Kantian sublime as potentially present in any empirical experience, but Joyce goes beyond Wordsworth to include language in the realm of sensory experience. In doing so, Joyce was far ahead of his time, for we are only just beginning to recognize the relevance of Kant's "Analytic of the Sublime" to the philosophy of language.

It is well known that Kant follows Burke in distinguishing between the beautiful and the sublime. For Kant, "[t]he beautiful in nature is a question of the form of an object, and this consists in limitation, whereas the sublime is to be found in an object even devoid of form, so far as it immediately involves, or else by its presence provokes, a representation of *limitlessness*, yet with a super-added thought of its totality" (2009, 245). While beauty is a formal quality, consisting in limitation, the sublime is not necessarily formless: a more literal translation of "*das Erhabene ist dagegen auch an einem formlosen Gegenstande zu finden*" is "the sublime can *also* be found in a formless object" (Pillow 2000, 69). Although the sublime is frequently found in objects that appear formless, such as a storm or the heavens, it also refers to objects that are too large to perceive in their totality. When confronted by objects such as these, "our imagination, even in its greatest effort to do what is demanded of it and comprehend a given object in a whole of intuition (and thereby to exhibit the idea of reason), proves its own limits and inadequacy, and yet at the same time proves . . . itself adequate to that Idea" (257). This applies most obviously to the "mathematical sublime" (248–50), where the mind submits vast or formless objects to the idea of totality. Since space and past time are infinite, Kant reasons, this totality "does not even exempt the infinite," and our "ability even to think the given infinite without contradiction, is something that requires the presence in the human mind of something supersensible" (254).

Kant argues that nature "is sublime in such of its phenomena as in their intuition convey the idea of their infinity," and these phenomena reveal not only our ideas of totality but also our own freedom (see 260–64 on the "dynamical sublime"). While Kant's examples are typical of eighteenth-century aesthetics—cliffs, thunder, lightning, the Milky Way, and so on—suggesting vast, powerful, or formless natural phenomena, there is nothing to prevent smaller objects, including works of art, from being sublime. As Kirk Pillow explains, in addition to the mind's regress to infinity in the mathematical sublime, Kant reasons that "[t]he power of imagination is limited by a maximum of comprehension which it cannot exceed" (Pillow 2000, 74). This limitation applies not only to phenomena of great magnitude but also to our inability to comprehend all the parts of a sufficiently complex object as a whole: "Imagination runs into difficulty in trying to comprehend an object as a unity . . . whenever it faces something vast, elaborate, or *complex* enough to overwhelm its powers" (Pillow 2000, 74). That this complexity applies not only to physical structures but also to the ideas of reason is evident from the fact that Kant links the sublime to God, freedom, immortality, eternity, and even "aesthetic ideas" that "evoke much thought, yet without the possibility of any definite thought whatever . . . and which language, consequently, can never fully capture or render completely intelligible," such as "death, envy and all vices, as also love, fame, and the like" (314). These examples, empirical but "transgressing the limits of experience" (314), just as their concepts defy the bounds of language, indicate that sublime reflection, as Kirk Pillow calls it, is also to be found in literary texts.

In the last chapter, I argued that the Kantian sublime is central to Wordsworth, epitomizing the Romantic epiphany as a whole, with its focus on the infinitude of time, space, and the human mind. Based on Stephen's disquisition in *Stephen Hero*, it is tempting to apply Kant's dictum to the theory of epiphany, seeing Stephen's aesthetics as a failed attempt to reach the noumenal. But the aesthetics in *Stephen Hero* apply to language as much as any other experience, with a special, self-reflexive relevance to their own text, so that the Kantian parallels point to the sublimity of language. Just as Kant's transcendental aesthetic is a theory of experience per se, in which the awe and majesty of the sublime is potentially available in any experience (assuming that at a microscopic level all experience is sufficiently complex to overwhelm our apprehensive faculties), for Joyce the sublime is not a rhetorical mode but a basic property of language.

Toward the end of his "Analytic of the Sublime," Kant concludes that poetic "genius" is none other than the ability to awaken the sublimity of the mind through language (313–16). His account of the faculties "which constitute genius," including "spirit" ("the animating principle in the mind") and "the soul" (313–14), are reminiscent of Daedalus's aesthetics, and Kant's "Analytic" helps to explain how the complex symbolic and linguistic associations of Joyce's later texts, can, at times, evoke a feeling of the sublime: since we are unable to assimilate the full assembly of symbolic associations in a work like *Finnegans Wake*, while recognizing its unity as a work of art, Joyce's texts awaken a pure idea of totality. Yet these glimpses are fleeting and can never be attained as a present totality, because Joyce's semantic voids ensure that complete assimilation of the text is no more attainable than the noumenal; the revelation, if there is one, is not of absolute, determinate meaning but of the limitlessness of language. Whereas the Kantian sublime is a transcendental intimation of totality, Joyce preempts Derrida in presenting the infinitude of language as an endless system of differences, where meaning is always deferred. Pervading this system is a referential void, an abyss of meaning that is itself sublime, explaining why, in place of traditional revelation, Joyce's epiphanies manifest absence as the highest form of presence. And yet, as we have seen, the epiphanies *present* this revelation in literary form, bringing silence into language and constantly repeating it to create a series of linguistic epiphanies from *Dubliners* to the *Wake*.

4

Silence and Repetition in *Dubliners*

The notion of epiphany in *Dubliners* has proved controversial. While *Portrait*, *Ulysses*, and *Finnegans Wake* reuse a total of thirty epiphanies, none of the forty surviving sketches recur in *Dubliners*. The most plausible explanation is that Joyce was working on the early versions of *Portrait* concurrently with the first stories he wrote for *Dubliners*, and as Walzl puts it, Joyce "had reserved the central experiences of his own life from childhood on for his 'autobiographical' novel" (1984, 168). Given the autobiographical nature of the epiphanies, along with the fact that fourteen are reused in *Stephen Hero* and twelve in *Portrait*, it seems natural to consider the epiphanies as manuscript material for *Portrait*, as Scholes and Kain did in *The Workshop of Daedalus*, rather than ur-texts for *Dubliners*.

However, this doesn't negate the role of the epiphanies in *Dubliners*. Numerous early commentators noted a similarity between Joyce's supposed neologism *epicleti* and his earlier adoption of the theological term "epiphany."[1] In August 1904, Joyce told his friend Constantine Curran, "I am writing a series of epicleti"—or perhaps "epiclets"—"I call the series *Dubliners* to betray the soul of that hemiplegia or paralysis which many consider a city" (*LI* 55). According to Ellmann, *epicleti* is a mistake for *epikleseis* (*JJ* 169), the moment of transubstantiation in the Orthodox Mass when the Holy Ghost transforms bread and wine into the body and blood of Christ. This account is disputed by Wolfhard Steppe, who claims Joyce wrote "epiclets," as in mini-epics, but his own reading is by no means certain,[2] and even if "epicleti" should be abandoned, the underlying analogy holds. Extrapolating from the host, there is a natural similarity between Joyce's invocation (*epiklesis*: to call upon or invoke) for *Dubliners*, and Daedalus's definition of epiphany as "a sudden spiritual manifestation" (*SH* 218). In Joyce's words, the little *tranches de vies* he depicts in his stories "betray the soul . . . of the city," just as the epiphanies "betrayed the very things [their speakers] were most careful to conceal" (*MBK* 126), while, at the moment of epiphany, "[t]he soul of the commonest object . . . seems to us radiant" (*SH* 218).

It is not surprising, then, that many critics have agreed with Beck's appraisal that "*Dubliners* exemplifies Joyce's specific aesthetic theory of epiphany" (21). Indeed, upon publication of *Stephen Hero* in 1944, Harry Levin believed that *Dubliners* was the "book of epiphanies" Daedalus thinks of writing (Levin 1941, 29; *SH* 216). His mistake became apparent when O. A. Silverman published the Buffalo epiphanies in 1956, but Levin's reading influenced a generation of Joyceans, including Florence Walzl, who remains one of *Dubliners*' most perceptive critics. Her essay on "The Liturgy of the Epiphany Season" (1965) offers a sustained defence of *Dubliners*' epiphanic structure, arguing that "the narratives resemble the liturgical epiphanies," with each story "leading directly to an epiphany" (443). Few readers have pursued Walzl's theological parallels, but fewer still have challenged her basic premise; for more than sixty years, undergraduates have been taught to read *Dubliners* as "an epiphany of epiphanies" (Tindall 1959, 11).

Nevertheless, this is the kind of overenthusiastic proclamation Scholes railed against, and while critical introductions continue to discuss the importance of epiphany to *Dubliners*,[3] since the late 1970s focus has shifted from the revelatory aspect of the stories to their silences and obscurity. Hugh Kenner, dubbed "the man in the gap" (Benstock 1976, 434), brought many of these puzzles and omissions to light. His influential reading of "Eveline" in *Joyce's Voices* (1978), which hinges on the fact that there were no ships bound directly from Dublin to Buenos Aires, provides the best known example of this form of negative inference, while his earlier article "The Rhetoric of Silence" (1977) laid the template for "gnomonic criticism" (Benstock 1976, 428). Marilyn French developed this approach to *Dubliners* more fully in her widely cited article, "Missing Pieces in Joyce's *Dubliners*" (1978), while her paper at the 9th Joyce Symposium on the "discontinuities, gaps in logic and memory, and distortions of reality" that characterize Joyce's women paved the way for feminist accounts of incompleteness (1988, 271). Around the same time, Jean-Michel Rabaté pursued Kenner's focus on lacunae in his well-known essay, "Silence in *Dubliners*," which helped open up a new field of post-structuralist readings. Subsequently, Stephen Heath, Colin McCabe, Hélène Cixous, and Derek Attridge contributed important deconstructivist accounts of *Dubliners* that subvert traditional wisdom by overturning apparent structures of meaning in favor of hidden or neglected details,[4] while Rabaté's psychoanalytical interpretation of the unsaid is explored in greater depth by Garry Leonard's Lacanian study of hidden and repressed narratives (1993). More recently, Margot Norris's *Suspicious Readings of Joyce's* Dubliners (2003) offers an illuminating insight into the gnomonic depths of Joyce's stories.

Taken together, these studies accumulate an overwhelming body of evidence that Joyce's early narratives resist interpretation as steadfastly as his later works, which would seem to preclude the possibility of epiphany, since its traditional associations with revelation or illumination are attendant upon definite manifestation. Faced with these difficulties, critics have naturally tried to fill the gaps in Joyce's texts: from Gifford's seminal *Notes* (1967) to Donald Torchiana's impressively detailed *Backgrounds for Joyce's Dubliners* (1987), editors and commentators have sought to supply the missing pieces to the puzzle; but as Herring shows, many of Joyce's cruxes cannot be solved because they are fundamentally indeterminate (xx).

Nevertheless, as countless readers have verified, the texts produce striking effects, particularly in their endings, even if these moments are typically elusive. Even the most lucid attempts to interpret the stories as epiphanies, such as Harry Levin's groundbreaking work or Warren Beck's perceptive readings, always leave something unaccounted for, because their underlying hermeneutic is to discover determinate meaning through careful scrutiny. "Epiphany-hunters" approach the stories as though Joyce had constructed a series of elaborate riddles we might solve by carefully following the clues hidden in the text; what they ignore is that the stories themselves are riddled with holes, many of which can never be repaired because there is not enough information to make a determinate judgment. To cite one example, we are not in a position to know the nature of the priest's infirmity in "The Sisters," just as we cannot be sure of the circumstances in which he appears to have been relieved of his priestly duties; consequently, there is no way to be sure that we understand the significance of his laughter in the confessional. But the power of the ending lies precisely in its marriage of mystery and revelation, hinting toward something profound whose significance evades the reader. And herein lies the essence of Joyce's epiphanies, charging the emptiness and openness of an unbridgeable abyss with rings of resonant association.

Styles of Epiphany

The epiphanic nature of *Dubliners* is apparent in the stylistic modes Joyce employs: the dialogue is characterized by the ironic realism of the dramatic epiphanies, while at their moments of greatest intensity, the poetic tenor of Joyce's narratives closely resembles the lyrical symbolism of the dream epiphanies. Examples of each can be found throughout, but I will illustrate their roles in "Araby."

To create the illusion of authentic speech, Joyce employs contractions, Hiberno-English, slang, deixis, ellipsis, pauses, repetition, and all the techniques of verisimilitude he perfected in the dramatic epiphanies. Take, for instance, the conversation between the stallholder and two young gentlemen at the end of "Araby":

—O, I never said such a thing!
—O, but you did!
—O, but I didn't!
—Didn't she say that?
—Yes. I heard her.
—O, there's a . . . fib! (27)

Repetition, phatic exclamations, colloquial vocabulary, rapid turn-taking and contractions create the illusion that we are breaking in on a real conversation, while the punctuation and dramatic pause, marked by ellipsis, suggest its playful, flirtatious tenor. Although the ellipsis could plausibly be filled in with a stronger reproach, such as "lie," whatever it is she is supposed to have said can never be ascertained. Hovering around this statement that she did or didn't make, the text points provocatively toward something unspoken, inviting the reader to fill in the blanks. This strategy of charging silences with association is familiar from the dramatic epiphanies; here, the romantic purpose of the visit encourages the reader to see an implicit eroticism in the exchange, unmasking the boy's sentimental longings. Just as he "luxuriate[s]" in the "enchantment" of the word *Araby*, all week he fantasizes about the name and image of the girl, though he barely exchanges a word with her, and this reticence allows him to escape from the painful reality of desire into the fantasy he imagines will complete his lack. By contrast, the youths appear driven by desire to such an extent that what was or wasn't said becomes irrelevant, because the real subject of conversation is immediate and libidinal. Indeed, this structure of desire, as both lack and surplus, is identical to the "fragment of colloquy" that precipitates Daedalus's theory of epiphany:

> The Young Lady—(drawling discreetly) . . . O, yes . . . I was . . . at the . . . cha . . . pel. . . .
> The Young Gentleman—(inaudibly) . . . I . . . (again inaudibly) . . . I . . .
> The Young Lady—(softly) . . . O . . . but you're . . . ve . . . ry . . . wick . . . ed. . . . (*SH* 216)

In both cases, there is a hiatus: we are not privy to the words of the Young Gentleman in *Stephen Hero* or of the stallholder in "Araby," inciting readers to speculate on what is missing; at the same time, the women's protestations ("fib," "wick . . . ed") imply a level of false modesty, or even jouissance, which is surplus to the text. Thus, Joyce teases the reader with desire for knowledge of these lost words that form the kernel of desire for the interlocutors. In doing so, he creates resonant hiatuses: gaps in the text that are simultaneously empty and overflowing.

In the same way, Joyce's narratives invite endless speculation by creating poetic passages whose symbolic significance is overdetermined but whose referential content remains indeterminate. There are many examples, including the opening paragraph of "Araby," where the narrator creates a self-consciously poetic tone. Six times in seven lines, the setting is personified—North Richmond Street is literally and metaphorically "blind"; the houses are "conscious," gazing at one another with their "imperturbable faces"; even the Christian Brothers' School "set[s] the boys free" (21). This poetic tenor continues: in the third paragraph, the houses "had grown sombre," the streetlamps "lifted their feeble lanterns," and the boys' shouts "echoed in the silent street," picking up on the personification of the opening to develop motifs that run through the story. The imagery of light and darkness, sound and silence, continues in the angelic descriptions of Mangan's sister standing in the light of the door, with the narrator likening his body to a harp, "her words and gestures . . . like fingers running upon the wires" (22–24). These leitmotifs accrue symbolic overtones through layers of association, just as the variations on a theme Joyce develops in the lyrical epiphanies make possible unlimited semantic proliferation. Indeed, the harp simile concludes a paragraph reminiscent of "The

Race." In the epiphany, the bookie's cries of "Bonny Boy!" ring out amid the noise and bustle of the racetrack, contrasting the named horses with "human creatures," and, in the same way, the name of the boy's beloved springs to his lips at the moment "the curses of labourers, the shrill litanies of shop-boys," and "the nasal chanting of street-singers" converge "in a single sensation of life," so that her idealized image, figured in the grail-like chalice, is raised above the crowd of "drunken men and bargaining women," like the distant and unattainable racehorse "flashing far away in the sunlight." Both passages describe an extraordinary moment of vision in an ordinary setting, but the similarity goes beyond their shared subject; in each case, Joyce achieves striking, magical-realist effects by employing literal language to describe concrete details while simultaneously employing densely patterned figurative language to transform these urban commonplaces into polyvalent symbols like the chalice and the harp.

Set pieces such as this occur throughout *Dubliners*, employing the intricate imagery and poetic prose of the lyrical epiphanies, but "Araby" is particularly lyrical because Joyce attempts to re-create the intoxicating ardor of the boy's infatuation through the musicality of its narrative. First and foremost, this music depends on delicate runs of assonance and alliteration, heard in even the most prosaic sentences: "The career of our play brought us through the dark muddy lanes behind the houses where we ran the gauntlet of the rough tribes from the cottages, to the back doors of the dark dripping gardens where odours arose from the ashpits, to the dark odorous stables where a coachman smoothed and combed the horse or shook music from the buckled harness" (21–22). This passage, with its elaborate runs of plosives and fricatives, interweaving with the long open vowels of "odours arose" / "coachman . . . combed," and all their subtle modulations, transforms the mundane reality of muddy lanes and ashpits into the poetic memories of the narrator. Indeed, Joyce seems to recall this scene in a letter to Grant Richards: "It is not my fault that the odour of ashpits and old weeds and offal hangs round my stories. I seriously believe that you will retard the course of civilization in Ireland by preventing the Irish people from having one good look at themselves in my nicely polished looking-glass" (*LII* 64).[5] Recalling his explanation that "I am trying . . . to give people some kind of intellectual pleasure or spiritual enjoyment by converting the bread of everyday life into something that has a permanent artistic life of its own for their mental, moral, and spiritual uplift" (*MBK* 103–4), Joyce suggests that the purpose of lyrical symbolism is to effect such a conversion, immortalizing ordinary objects and events through literature, and that his ultimate aims in doing so were aesthetic, intellectual, ethical, spiritual, and political.

At the most basic level, Joyce's art is one of repetition and variation. Here, as in the lyrical epiphanies, he uses harmonies of sound to enhance poetic sense, converting unremarkable memories into a memorable evocation of childhood. Epiphany #37 provides a useful comparison: "I lie along the deck, against the engine-house, from which the smell of lukewarm grease exhales." From these unromantic beginnings, the narrator imagines "[g]igantic mists ... marching under the French cliffs," and "[b]eyond the misty walls," in a dark cathedral, he hears "the bright, even voices of boys singing before the altar." While the personified and figurative repetitions of the mist, enhanced by the half-rhyme with "cliffs," provide the element for this imaginative transformation, between and beneath them, "[t]he sea moves with the sound of many scales." Alternating sibilants and murmurs, Joyce emphasizes both the sound of the sea and its movement before uniting them in "scales," which is at once musical, visual, and kinesthetic, since the sea's music is produced by ranks of scalar waves in movement.

These subtle modulations of sound and rhythm play a crucial role in creating Joyce's epiphanic effects, harnessing the musical and poetic aspects of language to transmute everyday referents like ashpits and the sea into evocative symbols. In the first epiphany, young Joyce hides beneath the table, turning painful reality into art as he transforms Mr. Vance's threats into poetry: "Pull out his eyes, / Apologise, / Apologise, / Pull out his eyes" (1). The principal elements of Joyce's poem are rhyme, rhythm, and chiasmus, and the same techniques are instrumental in "Araby," allowing the narrator to transcend the humdrum details of daily life into the intoxicating ardor of first love. For example, immediately after the last-quoted sentence, a chiastic effect is created through the figures of light and darkness ("light/shadow/shadow/shadow/light" [22]) that define Mangan's sister. Two lines later, a repetitive, swaying rhythm re-creates the hypnotic effect she has on the boy: "[h]er dress swúng as she móved her bódy and the sóft rópe of her háir tóssed from síde to síde" (22), and the next sentence begins with a perfect couplet, showing that Joyce was as conscious of the rhyme and rhythm of phrase and period in *Dubliners* as he was in *Chamber Music*:

Évery ¦ mórning I ¦ láy on the ¦ flóor
ín the front ¦ pár-lour ¦ wátching her ¦ dóor. (*D* 22)

These effects are not confined to "Araby." Throughout *Dubliners*, Joyce makes judicious use of carefully patterned prose to create passages of rich lyricism, and these stylistic peaks often coincide with an emotional climax, leading to a moment of recognition. For instance, in the last part of "The Dead," as Gabriel watches his wife walk ahead with Bartell D'Arcy, the narrator switches gear, employing rhyme, rhythm, and alliteration to convey Gabriel's mood:

The blóod went bóunding alóng his véins;
and the thóughts went ríoting thróugh his bráin,
próud, jóyful, ténder, válorous. (214)

As a small instance of Joyce's skill, note how the strong iambic pulse skips a beat as the blood goes "bounding along," and the way the rioting thoughts break out into triple meter, mimicking Gabriel's excitement. These riotous fantasies spill into the narrative as the free indirect discourse seizes upon an epi(cleti)c simile—"[m]oments of their secret life together burst like stars upon his memory"—and in the following pages Gabriel's memories and desire burst out in a series of elaborate variations: "Like the tender fires of stars moments of their life together that no one knew of or would ever know of, broke upon and illumined his memory" (215). Imagery of the heart, blood, stars, and memory echoes through to the end of the story, creating a vital counterpoint to Gretta's revelation and Gabriel's final reflections. Indeed, the richly poetic tone of the final passage would hardly be possible were it not for the subtly poetic prose that precedes it, and the same point holds true of all the epiphanies in *Dubliners*.[6]

As these examples show, the dialogue and narrative of *Dubliners* are strikingly similar to the dramatic and lyrical epiphanies. In the first pairing, Joyce utilizes a wide range of spoken language features to create a style of "scrupulous meanness" (*LII* 134) that combines realism and irony; the second pair are replete with poetic techniques, creating highly lyrical prose, full of musical and symbolic overtones. These formal similarities are close and frequent enough to suggest that the style of *Dubliners* is based on the stylistic poles of the epiphanies, but I would argue that *Dubliners* is a *doubly* epiphanic text, informed not only by the stylistic innovations of the epiphanies but also by their aesthetic principles. In the case of "Araby," this is evident in the conversations that start and finish the boy's quest and the lyrical symbolism of the beginning and ending.

The boy's sole dialogue with Mangan's sister leaves him "so confused that [he does] not know what to answer," even forgetting whether he said he was going to the bazaar (23). Vague and conditional, his parting line ("—If I go, I said, I will bring you something" [24]) contrasts with the precise details of the porcelain vases and flowered tea sets at the stall, where the narrator records every word (27). As noted, the stallholders' conversation is truncated, so that the implicit mode of seduction assumes a central place in the text, despite the fact that it is unspoken. Shrouding and revealing the mystery of desire, their conversation exposes a world of mature sexuality that reveals the narrator's infatuation as mere fantasy, vain as his projections about the bazaar.

Like the conversations that introduce and terminate the boy's quest, the beginning and end of the story provide mirrored counterparts. Initially the boy is as blind as North Richmond Street, occupying the empty, detached house at the end of the cul-de-sac. He seems ignorant of the yellowed books he finds in the late priest's garden and blind to the phallic signifier of the bicycle pump, while we, like the conscious houses of the street, see his ignorance. Almost without knowing it, we are placed in the position of the ghost of the late priest whose house the boy inhabits, interpreting his remains. Just as the boy "could interpret [the] signs" of his uncle's inebriation, we are invited to interpret the signs of the boy's romantic intoxication in order to disclose the reality of his unconscious desire. By the end of the story, he seems to catch a glimpse of his condition, but at the same time, the veracity of his insight is undermined by a perspectival inversion: whereas early on, the boy hides in the darkness and security of the parlor, with the blind lowered almost to the sash, gazing down at Mangan's sister, whose figure is "defined by the light" (22), in the final lines, as he gazes "up into the darkness," he sees himself in a new light. The complete darkness of the hall, now empty, mirrors the blind, "uninhabited house" the boy moves into at the beginning, suggesting that the boy is no more aware of himself than he was at the beginning. Yet this impression is at odds with the clarity of the boy's vision: "Gazing up into the darkness I saw myself as a creature driven and derided by vanity; and my eyes burned with anguish and anger" (28). The darkness of the surroundings now seems ambiguous, questioning the validity of his insight, even as it serves to accentuate his lucidity. And the revelation is lucid, if only because the prose is lucid, combining lexical precision with density of meaning and aural echoes. Juxtaposing cause and effect through the alliteration and assonance, the sentence achieves the poise and balance of Joyce's "lucid supple periodic prose" (*P* 181); even the falling cadence of the final phrase, descending into trochees, describes "the curve of an emotion" (*PSW* 211). What makes this ending remarkable, though, is that while the emotion is clearly named, the precise nature and cause of the boy's "anguish and anger" are difficult to determine. In characteristically Joycean fashion, the story authorizes innumerable interpretations, from the naive reading of the boy's disappointment at arriving late, wasting a shilling and being unable to buy a present, to a recognition that his love was no more than fantasy, a solipsistic projection that reveals the vanity of his self-love, and broader reflections on the futility of desire.

Like all of Joyce's epiphanies, the ending of "Araby" combines aphoristic clarity with gnomic significance, as in the exemplary phrase "driven and derided by vanity." Read as an allegorical figure, vanity derides the boy, but if vanity forms part of his self-image, then the boy derides himself. Assuming the role of vanity, he is literally nothing (< Latin vānus, empty, void); split between "creature" and "vanity," he is doubled. Again, this emptying out and doubling of significance is characteristic of Joyce's epiphanies.

Structures of Epiphany

In addition to shaping the style of the epiphanies, *Dubliners* builds on their structure. There is an obvious similarity between the discrete, but ordered and interconnected stories of *Dubliners* and Joyce's numbered epiphanies, originally designed for a unified collection. It has often been remarked that the titles of the first and last stories, "The Sisters" and "The Dead," could be exchanged, and the circular structure of beginning and ending is more striking still: *Dubliners* begins with a boy looking up at a lighted window for a sign that the old priest had died, and ends with an aging man looking out of a darkened window thinking of a dead youth. This formal unity is less marked in the epiphanies, but Joyce's reference to "insertions" and "additions" suggests an ordered collection, while several epiphanies combine dialogue with lyrical prose to provide generic cohesion. Close thematic links between pieces dealing with death, love, propriety, dreams, or voyages, as well as recurrent topoi (e.g., sticks and animals) help to unify the epiphanies, just as *Dubliners* is unified by recurrent characters (Kathleen Kearney), themes (death, marriage, nationalism, art, politics, religion), motifs (lamps, coins, absent fathers, priests), and words (e.g., "grace").

Yet *Dubliners* is also a collection of separate stories, just as the epiphanies are a series of autonomous texts, each on a separate page. At the thematic level, breaks between Joyce's narratives are emphasized by breaks in circulation, from the specter of Father Flynn, whose circulation has literally stopped, to the paralysis of the transportation system with snow lying "general all over Ireland" (225). Joyce's death epiphanies emphasize an analogous moment of rupture, and this shared focus on death as an experiential void ("the hole we all have"), coupled with the life-in-death of memory ("the memory of those dead and gone" [D 204]), points to an underlying pattern of rupture and recollection.

Besides shaping the collection, this structure is evident within individual stories, most dramatically in the unexpected changes of perspective that close (and open) Joyce's stories, like the switch in focalization at the end of "Eveline." In "Araby," a first-person narrative, it was the boy's angle of vision that changed; in "Eveline," we are faced with a radical switch of focalization, from the free indirect discourse that invites us into Eveline's memories, hopes and fears, to the final image of her, objectivized and dehumanized, "like a helpless animal" (34). "Eveline" is typically held up as a model of free indirect style, but in the final section there is a gradual shift of focus toward Frank, evinced by the pronouns. The final paragraph begins: "He rushed beyond the barrier. [. . .] He was shouted at to go on." Frank is clearly the grammatical subject, yet the earlier focalization still tempts us to read these lines from Eveline's point of view. But in the final line of the story, "[h]er eyes gave him no sign of love or farewell or recognition," so the reader is as excluded from her consciousness—and her motives—as Frank. Whether we focalize the final line through Eveline or Frank, this gap between them leaves an interpretive space in the text, even as it multiplies perspectives.

The power of the ending is achieved by bridging Joyce's stylistic poles. From the first word, "She," the story is focused on the eponymous heroine, but in the final lines Frank punctuates the narrative with increasingly frantic cries ("Come! . . . Come! . . . Eveline! Evvy!"). Breaking in on

Eveline's reveries, there is an urgent realism in these cries, opposing Frank's dramatic irony[7] with Eveline's lyrical symbolism. The story opens with Eveline "watching the evening invade the avenue," and her propensity to see things poetically continues through to the ending, where the literal significance of the bell that "clanged upon her heart"—presumably a final call to board the ship—is colored by Eveline's "silent fervent prayer" immediately before, so that its churchgoing associations bring into play thoughts of marriage (cf. 30–31) or death (recalling Eveline's promise to her mother, 33). In the same way, the daunting voyage that lies ahead, so plainly figured in the prospect of the sea, becomes transfigured into metaphorical ballast to bolster Eveline's decision through sentences like "[a]ll the seas of the world tumbled about her heart" and "he would drown her." Thus, at the heart of the dialogue lies her silent, incomprehensible refusal—a powerful and unaccountable hiatus that begs for interpretation—while the very fabric of Eveline's reality is prone to symbolic transfiguration. This bridging of the poles discharges the power of the ending, for the final sentence brings both points of view into a single circuit, centered equally on Eveline's gaze and Frank's, as it offers both absence of meaning ("no sign") and a profusion of possibilities: "Her eyes gave him no sign of love or farewell or recognition" (34).

Virtually all the stories in *Dubliners* exploit Joyce's modes of ironic realism and lyrical symbolism to create epiphanic effects. The final revelation is typically the result of a new perspective, opening a gap on what has gone before, even as the viewpoints multiply. For example, the first three stories depict moments of insight for their child protagonists: the dramatic change of perspective for the boy in "Araby" can be seen at the end of "The Sisters," where Eliza's revelations alter the boy's view of Father Flynn, just as the narrator of "An Encounter" sees Mahoney in a new light in the closing lines. The third-person stories of adolescence rely largely on the change of narrative focalization seen in "Eveline" to create new perspectives for the reader: the switch to Villona announcing daybreak at the end of "After the Race" affords an ironic perspective on the previous night's antics; "The Boarding House" cleverly alternates Mrs. Mooney's, Mr. Doran's, and Polly's points of view, allowing us to judge both their complicity and their collusion; and the unexpected switch to Lenehan creates a blind spot in "Two Gallants," leaving the nature of Corley's exchange with the slavey in the dark, so that the apparition of the coin assumes a mysterious, unexpected significance. In each case, the change of perspective offers a structural implementation of the core principles that emerge from the epiphanies: difference and proliferation.

Silence and Repetition

Both the structure of *Dubliners* and its style are informed by these principles, as *Dubliners* refines them to the quintessential forms of silence and repetition. As Jean-Michel Rabaté points out, silence has many functions in *Dubliners*: "Silence can mean the inversion of speech, its mirror, that which structures its resonance, since without silence, speech becomes a mere noise, a meaningless clatter; silence can reveal a gap, a blank space in the text, that can be accounted for in terms of the characters who betray themselves by slips, lapses, omissions; or in terms of the general economy of the texts, silence being the void element which ensures displacement, hence circulation. Silence can finally appear as the end, the limit, the death of speech, its paralysis" (45). Rabaté interprets Joyce's "silent ruses" psychoanalytically (45–71), but their revelations are also a form of epiphany. Both the gaps by which characters "betray themselves" and the "void element which ensures displacement" are epiphanic, for the former is the mechanism of the dramatic epiphanies, while the latter applies its principle to narrative. Examples are not difficult to find: Old Cotter's unfinished sentences, heavy with implication, typify *Dubliners*'s elliptical dialogue, while the silence that reigns over Father Flynn's house in "The Sisters" (first in the "dead-room" and then in the whispered euphemisms downstairs, where "a silence took possession of the little room" [6–9]) soon extends its grip to the collection, providing a pervasive but inaudible backdrop whose traces are felt all the way through to the great silence that closes "The Dead."

While the texts of *Dubliners* arise from a void of silence, in each story the epiphanic ending depends on repetition. These encompass straightforward verbal repetitions, like the word "paroxysm" at the end of "A Little Cloud" or "grace," which closes out its eponymous tale; the musical phrasing of Joyce's poetic language; and subtler echoes of imagery, ideas, and perspectives that structure the narratives. Some of Joyce's most memorable characterization is produced by repeated traits, like Maria's caricatured laugh ("Maria laughed again till the tip of her nose nearly met the tip of her chin" [97; cf. 95, 101]) or Freddy Malin's queer gesture, "rubbing the knuckles of his left fist backwards and forwards into his left eye" (185, cf. 186). Repetition helps create realistic dialogue, as in the extraordinary leave-taking scene after the Misses Morkans' annual dance, "where goodnight was said" eleven times in as many lines (213–14). Perhaps Joyce, like Eliot, was echoing *Hamlet* (4.5.72–73; cf. *The Waste Land*, 2.170–72), in which case there is a poignant note to the repetition, but its immediate effect is to combine realism with the minimalist beauty of the chiming phrase, making the inanity and redundancy of speech pleasing. Similarly, while much has been made of Mrs. Malin's empty speech as a paragon of scrupulous meanness, there is a certain beauty in the simplicity of her repetition, because, like Chandler's poetic imaginings, we can read her reported dialogue as the work of a master ventriloquist.

If the repetitions were all identical, they would become monotonous, but as with the lyrical epiphanies, Joyce plays variations on a theme. Aural effects are created principally through rhyme, rhythm, assonance, and alliteration, while semantic echoes are produced by the figurative play of imagery; both are the result of modulated repetition, and the mutations can be as subtle as a single word (e.g., from "rubbing" to "rub"), or as clearly demarcated as the chiastic ending of "The Dead." At first sight, these lyrical transformations seem a natural continuation of the dream epiphanies, charging resonant words and images with layers of symbolic significance, but the repetitive dialogue of *Dubliners* owes much to the dramatic epiphanies: by employing their ironic realism, even in moments as mundane as Freddy's eye-rubbing or the peal of good nights, Joyce exposes the verbal tics and gestures by which his characters reveal themselves.

Perhaps the clearest example is "A Painful Case." The resonant silence of the ending creates one of the most powerful epiphanies in the collection. Its immediate impact is caused by the repetition of the "perfectly silent" night in the penultimate and antepenultimate sentences, but these are only the final terms in an extended series. Every sentence in the final paragraph is "a short sentence about [Duffy] containing a subject in the third person and a predicate in the past tense" ("He turned . . . He began . . . He halted . . ."), as though the text has caught Mr. Duffy's "odd autobiographical habit" (104, 113–14). This sense of Duffy's self-awareness being manifest in the text goes a long way toward explaining the ending, because as Duffy becomes conscious of his intransigent isolation, it takes on a new significance. Duffy's solitude can be traced back to the monk-like austerity of his lodgings and his daily routine, described in the opening paragraphs and confirmed when the reader is informed that "he had neither companions nor friends, church nor creed, . . . visiting his relatives only at Christmas and . . . when they died" (105). Yet despite the daily reminders of his routine, and despite the fact that the protagonist repeatedly enunciates his own loneliness, Duffy seems unaware of his isolation until the final silence, and it is this situation of only just having realized the significance of something that has always already been known that creates its revelatory quality, for it captures an apparently eternal truth in the moment it comes to light, generalizing a universal human condition from a particularly painful case.

At key points in the story, Duffy's unconscious seems to speak through the language of the text, either through his own revealing writings or the free indirect discourse that exposes him. One example has already been noted: his odd autobiographical habit, with its objective, retrospective aspect (resembling nothing so much as an obituary), obliquely suggests his desire to be seen, remembered, loved; but, like his visits to his relatives' funerals, to be loved in his absence, revealing his "disappointed" longing (104). The form of these self-reflections applies not only to the ending but also to the entire third-person, past-tense narrative, including the report of Mrs. Sinico's death.

Just as Duffy reads between the lines to uncover the concealed details of her apparent suicide, we are invited to read the symptoms of Duffy's loneliness in the narrative. The clearest evidence is furnished by the occasional notes he inscribes on his "little sheaf of papers" (*D* 103).[8] Magalaner suggests these notes are akin to Joyce's epiphanies (96), a surprising comparison, for at first sight, the genres seem distinct. Originally, aphorisms were definitions or concise statements of scientific principle; in literature, they usually refer to short, pithy sentences containing general truths or maxims (*OED*). As such, they appear quite different from Joyce's obscure, enigmatic epiphanies, which, though short, are never less than five lines. But Richard T. Gray shows that literary aphorisms are frequently obscure and enigmatic, characterized by gaps, indeterminacies, and self-reflexivity, despite their everyday language (46–63). He even identifies a sub-genre, the "Aphorism of Epiphany," where "everyday language functions" as a "commonplace object which is infused with a profound significance" (93). To understand this significance, readers "must perform a hermeneutical task," deciphering "cryptic" texts to "'create' for themselves the meaning" (94–95).

Duffy's aphorism, written two months after his estrangement from Mrs. Sinico, is presented as an epiphany of this kind, in which he, too, "undergoes an epiphanic experience in uncovering the meaning hidden deep within the text" (Gray 1987, 95). That is not to say that Duffy's views on love and friendship are general truths, but rather that they are framed as Duffy's revelation, an insight that allows him to rationalize his isolation. Even if Duffy were right that "Love between man and man is impossible because there must not be sexual intercourse and friendship between man and woman is impossible because there must be sexual intercourse" (108), there is nothing in his theory to prevent heterosexual love or homosocial friendship; what he unwittingly reveals is that his isolation is as self-imposed as the barrier he imagines between himself and Mrs. Sinico.

Duffy's recent acquisitions include *Thus Spake Zarathustra*, a possible source for the aphorism (Magalaner 1953), though if so, then Duffy's addition is telling, for there is no mention of sex in Zarathustra's sermon on friendship. Not that Duffy's desire is purely sexual, but the terms in which the relationship is narrated hint at barely hidden undercurrents: the phallic implications of Joyce's lush imagery in "[h]er companionship was like a warm soil about an exotic" are surely deliberate, as is the "union" they feel as darkness falls upon them with the music still vibrating in their ears, creating an ironic double entendre when "[t]hey agreed to break off their intercourse" (107–8). These veiled allusions add a certain frisson to the narrative of Duffy's repressed desire, but beyond its prurient interest, the hint that they may become lovers is primarily of significance insofar as sexual union stands for union with the other. Joyce is careful to preserve the ambiguity in "they spent their evenings alone" and although "[l]ittle by little . . . their thoughts entangled," it is significant that they are "united" in "their isolation": Duffy feels "exalted" by the "union," but even as they sit together, he catches himself "listening to the sound of his own voice." Indeed, just when he feels closest to Mrs. Sinico, he hears "the strange impersonal voice which he recognised as his own, insisting on the soul's incurable loneliness. We cannot give ourselves, it said: we are our own" (107). The mysterious origin and power of Duffy's insight is signaled by "the strange impersonal voice which he recognised as his own." The discourse it formulates is equally strange, both singular and plural, as though to insist on the plurality of the self, even at the moment Duffy comes to stand for everyman. Like the strange disembodied voices that call out "We are alone" in "The Spell of Arms and Voices," the grammatical structure of Duffy's thought implies that he is both alone and together, but his interpretation of the sentence as "insisting on the soul's incurable loneliness" shows that he has lost faith in communion. Having lost Mrs. Sinico, a "lonely road" leads him home from Parkgate to Chapelizod, and when he seeks the company of the public house, he hears the trams swishing along the "lonely road" outside (109, 112). "Living over his life with her . . . , he realised that she was dead, that she had ceased to exist, that she had become a memory," adumbrating Gabriel's speech and the ending of "The Dead" (204–5, 224–25), but it is only now that she is gone that "he understood how lonely her life must have been, sitting night after night alone in that room. His life would be lonely too until he, too, died, ceased to exist, became a memory—if anyone remembered him" (112–13).

"Lonely . . . alone . . . lonely" and in the final line, "He felt that he was alone": the alternation sets up a correspondence between solitude, loneliness, and death that finally breaks down Duffy's belief in his emotional autonomy, just as his rigid moral nature falls to pieces when he melodramatically assumes the guilt for Mrs. Sinico's suicide. Significantly, both breakdowns occur as a result of reliving the past, first in his memory, as he sits in the pub, and then as he walks through the bleak alleys of Phoenix Park, where they walked four years before. There, even the trees are "gaunt," spectral; he feels her "near him in the darkness. At moments he seem[s] to feel her voice touch his ear," and as he pauses to listen, he hears "the laborious drone of the [goods train] reiterating the syllables of her name": Émily Sínico, Émily Sínico . . . After the dactylic rhythm of the engine dies away, he listens again, but "he could hear nothing," only the perfect silence of the ending.

This dead silence has been a long time coming; like the memories of Mrs. Sinico, it comes back to haunt the ending, and its repetition, along with that of "alone," creates the sense of epiphany. These repetitions allow the final silence to be identified with Duffy's solitude, so as the night becomes "perfectly silent," his solitude becomes absolute. In the wake of Emily Sinico's death, as his memories of her peter out like the fading of her name, Duffy is confronted with his own intransigent isolation, and this recognition mirrors the strange impersonal voice insisting on the soul's incurable loneliness. His final revelation has already been prefigured as the repressed truth of his unconscious, which enables us to reread the story as the tale of Duffy's desire. And although we have heard this discourse echoing throughout the story, when Duffy finally becomes conscious of it, the fact that he no longer recoils from his alterity, but seems to accept that there is nothing inside, just as he can hear nothing outside, means that the final silence is truly resonant, resounding not only with its earlier echoes but with a newfound peace, for the night was perfectly silent.

* * *

Virtually all the moments that have been likened to epiphanies depend on this conjunction of silence and repetition. Eleven of the fifteen stories in *Dubliners* contain "silence," and those where the word does not occur include significant silences, such as Eveline's frozen cry or the unnamed substance in "Clay." Likewise, every story in *Dubliners* includes noteworthy repetitions, particularly in the final lines: as each story trails off into silence, it is left ringing with the echoes of its limitless significance. This play of silence and repetition helps to explain even the most intractable of *Dubliners*'s epiphanies—those gnomic bookends, "The Sisters" and "The Dead."

We have encountered many of the silences in "The Sisters," but they are worth repeating: Old Cotter's ellipses, the euphemistic dialogue, Eliza's nose-tapping, the dead-room, and the strange silence on the other side of the confessional. Some are easy to interpret, like the aunt's elliptical question, "Did he . . . peacefully?" and Nannie's silent gestures toward the corpse (7, 6), but they still have to be interpreted, just as the reader has to infer the signs of Nannie's deafness (6).[9] Eliza is an expert at such interpretation, throwing a cloak of euphemistic silence over the priest's death ("You couldn't tell when the breath went out of him . . ." [7]) and deftly deflecting the aunt's tentative enquiry "And everything . . . ?" with her matter-of-fact account of Father O'Rourke anointing him and preparing him for death (7). Yet the unsettling implications of the aunt's unfinished question remain, for the sense of social decorum she exhibits implies that she wouldn't ask if there were no grounds for concern. Of course, Father Flynn may have been innocent, but in the absence of explanation, a sense of repressed secrecy haunts the conversation, so that one can even interpret the aunt's conventional phrases of consolation as a sinister form of interrogation, inviting Eliza to unburden herself by sharing her grief ("It's when it's all over that you'll miss him"). On this "suspicious" reading (cf. Norris 2003, 16–29), Eliza appears too canny for the aunt: after the pitch-perfect reflection that she won't be bringing her brother his beef-tea any more, she turns the tables: "nor you, ma'am, sending him his snuff" (8).

For all that it adheres to unspoken codes of propriety, dutifully marking Eliza's respect for the aunt's social station and including her in the orbit of grief, this remark comes to sound like an insinuation, because at just this point Eliza stops "as if communing with the past" and says "shrewdly": "Mind you, I noticed there was something queer coming over him latterly. Whenever I'd bring in his soup to him there I'd find him with his breviary fallen to the floor, lying back in the chair with his mouth open" (9). Echoing Old Cotter's remarks, the first in the story, that there was "something queer . . . something uncanny about him" (1), this statement seems to offer a clue, particularly when Eliza lays her finger against her nose and frowns. There are many ways to interpret her gesture: an unconscious act (the joke of a mischievous narrator?); an obscure hint at a secret known only to Eliza; that the aunt and Eliza know something they are wary of revealing before the boy. The list can never be exhaustive, because when Eliza touches the gnomon, she creates a rupture in the text.

Eliza's act is a key moment in the story, the moment we come closest to discovering the mystery of her brother's death. Yet her sign, if it is one, is as mysterious as Old Cotter's ellipses: the promises to reveal his theory all trail off into silence, just as Eliza's pointed hints are left hanging in the air. In both cases, by the withholding of this information, the reader is incited to speculate upon it, just as when the boy tastes his sherry (but refuses the crackers) "under cover" of the silence that "took possession" of the priest's room, we are invited to interpret the act as a partial communion. This symbolism is of course strengthened by the no less mysterious (and repeated) imputation that it was the chalice Father Flynn broke "[t]hat affected his mind" (9–10), which allows the boy's act to be read as absolution.[10] But in fact, we never find out how the chalice broke or in what way it affected the priest's mind: the meaning of the symbol is as empty as its contents. If it were really the cause of the priest's decline, Nannie and Eliza would hardly bury him with it; instead, it functions as a cover-up, another silence masking the truth about Father Flynn. Naturally, the aunt is not duped: "And was that it? . . . I heard something" (10). Once again, her ellipsis hints at the continuing mystery, which Eliza acknowledges with a nod, and the tale of "poor James" wandering alone and talking to himself. Yet her final revelation is as mysterious as anything in the story: alone in the darkened confessional, is it Father Flynn giving confession, is he confessing, or is his laughter the chuckling of a senile old man? The latter seems most likely, but his priestly duties and the symbolism of the confession-box make it hard to resist other readings. Like everything else in the story, it encompasses an extraordinary range of interpretations, from the "maleficent and sinful" pleasure of a pedophile enjoying his own perversion to the sagacity of a wise fool laughing in the face of death.[11] The significance of the ending is repeatedly hinted toward but never spoken; like Eliza and the boy, who strain to hear the laughter, we are left searching for meaning in a veiled silence.

This silence resonates through a series of verbal echoes. The story begins with the third stroke, and this repetition comes with its own silent shadow, because on a first reading we are primed by the word "time" to connect the three strokes to the tolling of a bell, suggesting a death knell, before the priest's oft-repeated words, "I am not long for this world" (cf. John 8.23), and the boy's repetition of the word "paralysis" makes us reread the strokes as seizures. Indeed, the opening is structured by a series of repetitions: "night" occurs five times, while "lighted," "candles," and "window" are repeated in the first few sentences, beginning a chain of associations that continues throughout the collection.[12] These textual patterns allow us to hear the silent reverberations of the words the boy repeats to himself: *paralysis, gnomon, simony*. Although only paralysis and simony recur in the story, the gnomon is an infinitely reiterable figure, since the missing corner is an exact replica of the original parallelogram:[13]

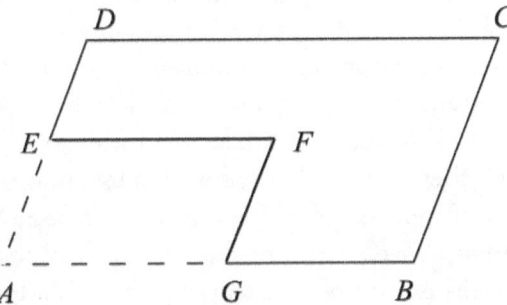

Figure 2. Euclidian Gnomon. Adapted by the author from *The Elements of Euclid*, ed. Isaac Todhunter (London: Macmillan, 1869), II, def. 2.

This figure, like an arrowhead, points toward something absent. Like the gnomon of a sundial, it can reveal hidden truths as profound and intangible as time, but it does so through its shadow, for it is only by tracing back the lines of the gnomon that we can fill in the missing piece. Shaped like the carpenter's square, this sets the rule for the gnomonic repetitions of *Dubliners*: each one points to a gap, a silence, a missing piece at its origin, yet upon inspection, this missing piece turns out to be a shadow of the whole, supplementing the original figure even as it is the lack that generates it. Boxed into Joyce's silences and repetitions, this gnomonic structure provides a geometrical figure for the linguistic epiphany.

Like the dramatic epiphanies, the dialogue in "The Sisters" is full of pauses and ellipses. "Silence" is among the most frequently repeated words in *Dubliners*, a word that shadows the text even in its absence. In this regard, it is analogous to the gnomon. But speech in "The Sisters" is also gnomonic in its repetition, as in Eliza's last line, "wide-awake and laughing-like to himself." Her speech is full of repetitive saws ("there's no friends like the old friends . . . no friends that a body can trust"), phrases ("poor James!"), and conjunctions ("So one night . . . and . . . So then . . . So then . . . And . . ." [8–10]). Eliza echoes the boy's aunt ("quite peacefully" [7]) and Old Cotter ("something queer" [1, 9]), while the aunt echoes Eliza (7) and repeats her own phrase, "have mercy on his soul" (2, 9). Like the gnomon, these phrases hint at something missing, an absent presence, that describes much of the dialogue. For instance, Old Cotter keeps announcing his theory ("I'll tell you my opinion . . . I have my own theory about it . . . I think it was one of those . . . My idea is . . ." [1–2]), but never actually spells it out, so that we, like the boy, are left puzzling "to extract meaning from his unfinished sentences" (3). An unwitting Iago, each time he repeats his veiled insinuations, the monstrous suspicions grow, but his hints are so vague and fragmentary that we are left chasing shadows (there is even a red-spotted handkerchief, blackened with snuff). "Give me the oracular proof!" cries Othello, but there are only mirages and duplicity, like Joyce's hall of mirrors, where each image is reflected in an endless series of repetitions. We can never be sure which, if any, to trust, but all of them reflect on the process of representation, revealing both sides of the mirror: the image reflected and the tain of silence.

To illustrate this, let us return to the echoes that close "The Sisters." At the end of Eliza's polysyndetic tale comes the remarkable image of the priest, sitting in the dark "confession-box, wide-awake and laughing-like softly to himself." At this point, Eliza stops suddenly "as if to listen" and the boy listens too. There is "no sound in the house," but the silence is full of echoes: "The old priest was lying still in his coffin as we had seen him, solemn and truculent in death, an idle chalice on his breast" (10).

Virtually every word here is taken from the description in the dead-room (cf. 6–9), weaving a series of repetitions into a rhythmical incantation that ends on a near rhyme, so that in the silence each word teems with meaning. Strangely, the symbolic weight of the chalice, so frequently alluded to, becomes "idle" in the ending, like the old man's words; yet, on reflection, it was the boy who thought his words idle, when they turned out to be prophetic (1), and in the same way, the silence they listen to is filled with implication, like a gnomon boxed into the corner. It is noticeable that this pause has a structural similarity to the pause when Eliza taps her nose: there she continued as though nothing had happened, and here too, she resumes where she left off, "Wide-awake and laughing-like to himself." Like the word she drops, "softly," the pregnant silence of the gnomon is both cut away from and added to her musical phrase, imbuing it with indecipherable but inexhaustible significance.

These structures create the epiphanic effect, for silence riddles the text, in both senses: the discourse is punctuated by ellipses, but it also resonates with them, because the gaps are riddling, allowing unspoken suggestions to sift into the text. Seen from the other side, Joyce's gnomonic repetition generates endless reiterations, but all of them reproduce the same gaps and silences that riddle the original figure. Again, there is a coincidence of opposites at the moment of epiphany because the two poles are charged by the same structure. At its nucleus lies a core of silence that can only be negatively exposed; each time this silence is summoned, the very signifiers that invoke it are charged with a mysterious added significance, and it is these implications (simultaneously ringing around and teeming from the empty signifier) that are apt to proliferate. In this way, the gnomonic repetitions all point to a central lacuna embedded in the structure of the signifier, while it is this lacuna itself that gives rise to the endless play of signification. This could be termed rich ambiguity, but Joyce goes beyond conventional accounts of uncertainty and polysemy to expose a general paradox of meaning embedded in every signifier. Like the missing piece of the gnomon, Joyce's narratives point toward a significance forever beyond reach, and this structure is repeated right through to the final story.

I mentioned earlier that the interchangeable titles of "The Sisters" and "The Dead" suggest the circular nature of the collection. "The Dead" repeats words, motifs, themes, and characters from virtually all the stories: Gabriel's meditations on the past, memory, and mortality echo Mr. Duffy's reflections to develop a central theme, the interrelationship between the living and the dead; recalling Kathleen Kearney and the Antient Concert Rooms (from "A Mother"), Miss Ivors's interrogation develops themes of nationalism and identity that recur throughout; the six repetitions of the word "grace" in "The Dead" are only the most obvious of Joyce's verbal echoes. Other links are subtler but no less evident—for instance, the pound coin that Freddy Malins repays Gabriel unexpectedly returns the gold sovereign from "Two Gallants," while Mr. Brown's "gallantry" (183, 193) continues the ironic exposé of its theme. Indeed, in the subtle repetition of motifs such as absent fathers, overbearing mothers, priests, pierglasses, lighted windows, pictures, musical allusions, and debt, or the themes of art, music, marriage, religion, class, politics, paralysis, and death, it is possible to detect links to all the stories.

As well as repeating features that are present in the text, "The Dead" repeats the silence, absence, and indeterminacy of *Dubliners*. Notable among these are the hush that precedes Gabriel's speech, that which descends on the hotel room before Gretta's revelation, and the silent snow falling softly through the ending. But there are other silences too, such as the silence that buries Mr. Browne's excessive discourse (185, 202), and the silent procession through the corridors of the Gresham, in which Gabriel hears the sound of molten wax falling from the candle and the thumping of his own heart (217). The first of these reminds us that silence always shadows speech, even in its most voluble excesses (from logorrhoea to jouissance), while the latter reiterates the significance that silence bestows through negative relief. In this case, the isolated sound of drips falling on the tray and Gabriel's heartbeat alert us to the significance of these details: the candle recalls the opening of "The Sisters," bringing into play the topoi of light and darkness, the tapping sound provides a pre-echo of the ending, and Gabriel's thumping heart emphasizes his lifeblood and his lust. These functions are central to the Joycean epiphany, because they figure as gnomonic complements to the text: the former indicates an absence *within* discourse, as well as the absence *of* discourse; the latter summons up the silence from which speech rises and into which it returns, a stillness in which each word resonates. These gnomonic signifiers, pointing toward (and away from) an absence that cannot be presented, both define and are defined by a "void element which ensures displacement" (Rabaté 1984, 45).

It follows that the gnomonic structure of the epiphanies is everpresent in Joyce's texts, because everpresent in language. As we shall see, this is the revelation of *Finnegans Wake*, but as a first approach to the linguistic epiphany, I will try to pinpoint the epiphanic nature of *Dubliners* more precisely, through the very gaps and indeterminacies that pin holes in the text and thereby point beyond it.

As a fitting conclusion, "The Dead" contains the same central lacunae we find elsewhere in the collection: the forgotten Parkinson; the mystery of Lily's bitter retort; the absence of Gabriel's father; and wider problems of interpretation, such as Gabriel's mood at the end of the story or his feelings for his wife. There is a distinction between indeterminacies of absence, like Gabriel's father, where gaps and silences reveal something missing, and those where information is uncertain, such as the identity of Aunt Kate's prize tenor. The question of Parkinson's existence is trivial, but it shows how Joyce compounds uncertainties through repetition, first when Bartell D'Arcy comments on the strange fact that the name is unknown to him, and then when Browne tries to save her blushes (200). Like the dramatic epiphanies, this fragment of dialogue reveals something about all three characters, and perhaps middle-class dinner conversation among the opera aficionados of late Victorian Dublin, but it also demonstrates how repetition increases indeterminacy. In this case, the uncertainties involve the purity of Parkinson's voice, his existence, and whether Browne has heard of him; in each case, the uncertainty doubles, bringing into play other questions—about the reliability of memory, for example.

None of these questions is of great importance, but the same structure applies in more significant examples of indeterminacy, such as the snow. At the beginning of the story, the snow is introduced in wonderfully poetic terms: "A light fringe of snow lay like a cape on the shoulders of his overcoat and like toecaps on the toes of his galoshes; and, as the buttons of his overcoat slipped with a squeaking noise through the snow-stiffened frieze, a cold, fragrant air from out-of-doors escaped from crevices and folds" (177). Here rhyme and rhythm, assonance and alliteration, create the air of pure, pristine beauty the snow ushers in, and in characteristically Joycean fashion, this atmosphere is translated into the lyrical symbolism of the narrative. Immediately afterward, we have the ironic realism of the dramatic epiphanies compressed into two lines of dialogue:

—Is it snowing again, Mr Conroy? . . .
—Yes, Lily, . . . and I think we're in for a night of it. (177)

Despite its simplicity, the realism of Lily's redundant question can suggest many things—respect, deference, naivety—while Gabriel's unspoken response (smiling at the three syllables he gives her name) can be interpreted as both condescension and affection, just as his appraisal of her figure suggests both fatherly feelings and desire (177). Like the dialogue in "A Little Cloud," we are invited to speculate both on what is said and how it is heard; in both cases, multiple interpretations are possible, and the double perspective ensures that no summation is complete. This is itself a form of irony, given that irony always depends upon a gap between what is said and what it is taken to mean, but there is a much more obvious example of dramatic irony in Gabriel's reply, for even on a first reading, his answer sounds prophetic.

From the beginning of the story, snow carries positive associations of freedom, beauty, and purity, which are created through passages of lyrical symbolism, and negative connotations of cold, confinement, sickness, and death, which are typically voiced through ironic realist dialogue. For instance, the aunts greet Gretta by saying she must be "perished alive," compressing the major themes of the story into a conventional idiom that contains a brilliant oxymoron (177). Soon after, Gabriel remembers the "dreadful cold" Gretta caught the previous year, and toward the end of the story, when the snow is slushy underfoot and the air is bitter, Aunt Kate warns that "Mrs Malins will catch her death of cold" (207). By contrast, when Gabriel finds a moment alone, he goes to the embrasure and taps the windowpane, thinking "how cool it must be outside!" and "How pleasant it would be to walk out alone," along the river and through the park, with the snow "lying on the branches of the trees and forming a bright cap on the top of the Wellington Monument" (192). Just as he is about to begin his speech, he raises his eyes from the row of upturned faces to the light of the chandelier and thinks of people standing outside on the quay looking up at the lighted window. This thought opens a contrast between the imagined gaze of the other envying the gaiety within and Gabriel's own discomfort at the stuffy atmosphere as he dreams of fresh air and the snow-laden trees in the park. This chain of thought returns him again to his image of the gleaming cap of snow on the Wellington Monument, which he now imagines "flash[ing] westward over the white field of Fifteen Acres" (203), allowing the vast white field to symbolize freedom. This reflection is picked up in the final paragraph as Gabriel thinks of "his journey westward" and in his omniscient vision of the snow lying "general all over Ireland," falling on "the dark central plain, . . . and farther westward" (225).

It has been noted before that this imaginary journey westward can be seen as a journey toward death, a return to the Gaelic heartland, or Gabriel's search for a new freedom. Likewise, Walzl and others have argued that the snow can be seen as a symbol of both life and mortality (1969, 431–43; cf. *JJ* 252–63). Indeed, the lines have been analyzed so extensively that there is little left to add; my point is simply to show that the reason Joyce's symbol is so indeterminate, encompassing diametrically opposed readings, is that throughout the story it has accrued layers of meaning that are all remembered and reactivated in the final echoes. All but one of the last nine sentences describe the snow, picking up on the taps on the window, the lamplight, the connotations of the West, the snow lying general all over Ireland, and the lonely churchyard in Oughterard. Yet these echoes are not simply repetitive; like the falling snow (repeated seven times), the earlier echoes die away, giving place first to the chiastic inversions that weave the paragraph together and then to new reflections, incorporating the imagery of Calvary in the crooked crosses and headstones, the barren thorns, and ultimately the universal symbol of the final descent. Thus, the structure of repetition and mutation allows a constant proliferation of meaning, with each new association reflecting back on those that prefigure it, massively overdetermining the symbol even as its indeterminacy increases. These gnomonic iterations create the conditions for what Kirk Pillow calls "sublime reflection," when a single poetic symbol becomes sufficiently complex that it indicates a network of associations too great to be unraveled and assimilated in their totality. Following Kant's analytic of the sublime, this manifests both the finitude of our perception in the face of potentially infinite complexity and a transcendental glimpse of its totality. And this, I think, is exactly what the ending of "The Dead" gives us as Gabriel's thoughts wander from desire to death, love to identity, and the solid world dissolving and dwindling into a state of final rest. Asking us to follow all these threads at once, with all their interwoven echoes and repetitions, going right back to the opening of "The Sisters," the final epiphany grants a powerful intuition of the unity of *Dubliners* as a whole, but since we are unable to synthesize every part of the structure, this intuition is itself transcendental, revealing a unity we can neither doubt nor comprehend.

5

"A day of dappled seaborne clouds"

A Portrait of the Artist's Epiphany

Joyce reuses fourteen epiphanies in *Stephen Hero* and twelve in *Portrait*, with many further echoes and similarities. Phrasing from several epiphanies can also be discerned in Joyce's 1904 essay, "A Portrait of the Artist," suggesting that Scholes's claim that *Stephen Hero* is structured around the epiphanies (*WD* 6) holds good for each version of *A Portrait of the Artist as a Young Man*. In fact, the case is much stronger for *Portrait* than *Stephen Hero*, since less than half the latter survives, with neither the beginning nor the end of the manuscript,[1] whereas the relevance of the epiphanies to *Portrait* is immediately apparent from their use in the novel (table 1).

As the table illustrates, *Portrait* begins and ends with an epiphany. There are epiphanies in every chapter, often occurring before a climactic moment, like the end of chapter 2, and the central epiphany occurs near the center of the novel, just after the moment Kenneth Burke calls "the point of farthest internality" (324). The importance of these epiphanies at the beginning, middle, and end is self-evident, but all twelve play key roles in the narrative.

Although a good deal of work has been done on the epiphanies, no one has yet shown how the structure of *A Portrait* grows from them.[2] In the following analysis, I will demonstrate their role in *Portrait*, both as climactic moments in the narrative and as exemplary passages that shed light on its organization. By focusing on the differences between Joyce's *Portrait* epiphanies and their earlier versions, I argue that the genesis of the novel reveals its fundamental structural principle: the difference between repetitions creates the possibility for endless proliferation. Walter Benjamin associates this echoing gap with Proust (201–16), but it is equally characteristic of Joyce, because difference-in-similitude constitutes the underlying structure of Joyce's epiphanies and the genitive principle of *A Portrait of*

Table 1. Epiphanies in *A Portrait of the Artist as a Young Man*

Portrait	Epiphany
P.4– 1.1 (Prelude)	1. "Apologise"[a]
P.25–1.2 (Clongowes)	28. "The Ship"
Pp.70–71–2.2 (Dublin)	5. "Is That Mary-Ellen?"
P.72–2.2 (Dublin)	3. "The Last Tram"
P.106–2.4 (Cork)	31. "Upon Me from the Darkness"
Pp.148–49–3.3 (Confession)	6. "Half-Men, Half-Goats"
P.164–4.1 (Spiritual Discipline)	24. "Her Arm on My Knees"
Pp.234–35–5.1 (The University)	25. "The Girls, the Boys"
P.238–5.2 (Villanelle)	26. "She Dances with Them in the Round"
P.272–5.4 (Journal)	29. "Images of Fabulous Kings"
P.274–5.4 (Journal)	27. "Hoofs upon the Dublin Road"
P.275–5.4 (Journal)	30. "The Spell of Arms and Voices"

Note: a. Numbers refer to those given in *WD* and *PSW*; the titles are taken from Beja (in Bowen and Carens, 712–13). Page numbers are keyed to the Penguin edition used throughout this book; the part and section designations are taken from John Paul Riquelme's edition (New York: Norton, 2007), 307–308.

the Artist as a Young Man. Borrowing Derrida's term, the recycling of the former in the latter can be regarded as Joyce's "signature" (1992, 33–75), an ever-varying repetition of the same epiphanic structure. Just as every signature is different, though each guarantees authorship, Joyce's signature epiphanies differ in every iteration ("A Portrait," *Stephen Hero*, *Portrait*) while providing a mark of identification across each of Joyce's works.

Patterns of repetition and variation are evident from the first epiphany:

                    [Bray: in the parlour of the
                    house in Martello Terrace]

Mr Vance   —(*comes in with a stick*) . . . O, you know,
              he'll have to apologise, Mrs Joyce.
Mrs Joyce   —O yes . . . Do you hear that, Jim?
Mr Vance   —Or else—if he doesn't—the eagles'll
              come and pull out his eyes.
Mrs Joyce   —O, but I'm sure he will apologise.
  Joyce   —(*under the table, to himself*)

> —Pull out his eyes,
> Apologise,
> Apologise,
> Pull out his eyes.
>
> Apologise,
> Pull out his eyes,
> Pull out his eyes,
> Apologise.

Kenner proclaimed that "every theme in the entire life-work of James Joyce is stated on the first two pages of the *Portrait*" (1948, 365)—something of an overstatement, perhaps, but there is no doubt that the opening section adumbrates the central concerns of the novel, particularly in the epiphany that concludes the overture. Mr. Vance represents the first in a sequence of fearful male authority figures, such as Fathers Dolan and Arnall; the unnamed transgression suggests the burden of sin and guilt Stephen struggles against; Joyce's refusal to apologize foreshadows Stephen's rebellion; and the retreat into language, turning Vance's threats of blindness into chiastic verse (a paradigm of varied repetition), becomes prophetic of Stephen's vocation as an artist.[3]

At first sight there is little difference between the original epiphany and the scene as it appears in *Portrait*, but the changes Joyce introduces are significant:

> He hid under the table. His mother said:
> —O, Stephen will apologise.
> Dante said:
> —O, if not, the eagles will come and pull out his eyes.
>
> *Pull out his eyes,*
> *Apologise,*
> *Apologise,*
> *Pull out his eyes.*
>
> *Apologise,*
> *Pull out his eyes,*
> *Pull out his eyes,*
> *Apologise.* (4)

The most obvious alteration is that Vance's role is transferred to Dante. This makes good sense, since Dante plays a more significant role in the novel, and the combination of biblical threats with strict moral instruction introduces her character; but the change of speaker also affects the portrayal of gender and authority: Dante's threat, following Mrs. Dedalus's insistent declarative, ensures that female figures become the center of power and punishment in *Portrait* (Henke 1982).

Isolating the threat of punishment from the crime, Joyce creates an oppressive atmosphere in which Stephen is threatened with terrifying consequences for reasons unknown, and this generalized fear is strongly reinforced by the second change from epiphany to novel: eliding the second half of the original stage direction "(*to himself*)," we never know who says the famous lines. Indented and italicized, the verses float freely; we can imagine Stephen repeating them to himself (an early example of interior monologue) or that he overhears them. With no speech heading or quotation marks, there is no reason to suppose that the words are spoken at all, and this lack of deictic reference leaves space for other sources of textual quotation. For instance, Gifford notes that Dante's threat is derived from Isaac Watts's *Divine Songs Attempted in the Easy Language of Children*, where in "Obedience to Parents," Watts warns the child that "breaks his father's law, / Or mocks his mother's word":

What heavy Guilt upon him lies!
   How cursed is his Name!
The Ravens shall pick out his Eyes,
   And Eagles eat the same. (8–12; 1761, 33)

In the original epiphany, Stephen has crossed Mr. Vance, and in *Portrait* he is threatened with the consequences of defying his mother's word, so Stephen's "heavy guilt" and the punishment he faces can be traced to Watts, who alludes to Proverbs: "The eye that mocketh at his father, and that despiseth the labour of his mother in bearing him, let the ravens of the brooks pick it out, and the young eagles eat it" (30.17). Thus, the lines in *Portrait* can be seen as a palimpsest of quotations: the scriptural text, Watts's didactic song, Joyce's epiphany, and the published stanzas.

The novel begins with an epigraph from Ovid and ends by quoting Stephen's diary; in between, there are quotations on virtually every page. In Bakhtin's terms, the density of intertextual allusion makes *Portrait* a supremely dialogical novel, constantly interacting with the texts it repeats, while the contextual difference between "original" and quotation, including Joyce's recycling of his epiphanies, is an example of heteroglossia, the principle that each utterance, even a single word, is dependent on context for meaning, and therefore unique (Bakhtin 1987, 41–68). Bakhtin's terms help show how *Portrait*'s dialogism opens lines of communication with other literary texts, and earlier versions of the novel, allowing for endless chains of connection, while each quotation differs in context and is therefore heteroglot. But quotation is a form of repetition, while heteroglossia generalizes difference, pointing back to Joyce's fundamental mechanism of repetition and variation.

Originating in the epiphanies, this structure shapes the novel. Organized around a series of striking incidents separated by considerable intervals of time and space, there are numerous gaps in the narrative; since these incidents are frequently repeated, the series is both elliptical and iterative. For instance, the novel's opening words follow a fairy tale formula; the "Baby Tuckoo" story is often retold; Stephen has wet the bed and smelled the oilsheet daily, sung his green rose song and danced to the sailor's hornpipe before. In their (re)telling, these events initiate new series—Simon Dedalus's storytelling, the queer smell of the oilsheet, the rose motif—creating the leitmotivistic structure. Of course, repetition is never identical: if nothing else, the context changes, and rereading is never the same. The gap between repetitions is charged by difference, and this gap opens the space for what Benjamin calls the "image" (201–16). As J. Hillis Miller explains, "The image is the meaning generated by the echoing of two dissimilar things. . . . It is neither in the first nor in the second nor in some ground which preceded both, but in between, in the empty space" (9). Benjamin compares a large sock in the laundry, which, to an imaginative child, might recall a Christmas stocking; in the absence of the real thing, this pairing allows the sock to become a sack, filled with imaginary presents (Benjamin 1999, 204–5). In the same way, patterns of repetition and variation in Joyce's epiphanies allow us to perceive both similarities between iterations and their differences; the charged gaps that emerge provide openings for Benjamin's image.

Returning to the epiphany, this process is enacted in the change from Vance to Dante, or from Proverbs to Watts to the chiastic verse in *Portrait*, because the difference between quotations (including the genesis of the text from its earlier iterations) opens a space for reflection. In the change from masculine to feminine, Protestant to Catholic figures of authority, we are invited to speculate on broader questions of gender, religion, and power in the novel. Since Vance, a Protestant, quotes "Obedience to Parents," a didactic song by the English churchman, Isaac Watts, while the second epiphany identifies Stephen with Parnell (a point I will return to), Vance could be associated with the tyrannical father of the Anglo-Irish Ascendancy, while the switch to Dante, as a kind of wicked stepmother, shows the punishing control of the Catholic Church in Ireland. These images become more complex still because the difference between Watts's song and its scriptural source opens a textual space that invites readers to speculate on questions as diverse as obedience and disobedience, guilt, blindness, punishment, mockery, parturition, the law of the father, and the maternal word—all of which are connected to Stephen's first confrontation with authority (that of his parents, but also God the father, Mother Church, and Mother Ireland).

In terms of chronology, Joyce's self-quotation in the *Portrait* epiphanies provides the mechanism that sets his structures of repetition and variation ticking, though in practice, the repetitive movements of the novel are inseparable from its epiphanic workings. A good example is the second epiphany in *Portrait*, a moment as carefully prepared for as the endings of *Dubliners*. Confined to the infirmary after having been shouldered into the square ditch, Stephen thinks, "How pale the light was at the window!" (25), recalling a series of phrases like the "cold sunlight outside the window" (21–22) that echoes back to the pale chilly air and the gray light at the beginning of the section (4). These repetitions serve as temporal and physical markers, correlated with Stephen's febrile condition as he drifts in and out of fitful sleep (he wakes to see a "pale sunlight," feeling "weak" and "rough," while "his face and body were very hot" [18]). A few lines later, "The sunlight was queer and cold," and it is the "queer" word "suck" that reminds Stephen of the water cocks in the lavatory at the Wicklow hotel, making him "feel cold and then hot" ("That was a very queer thing" [8]). Thus, the strange power of a word Stephen considers onomatopoeic comes to dominate the section (cf. Attridge 2001, 59–77) as hot and cold become repeated motifs in which the cold of the playing fields and the cold slime of the latrine, the cold dark sea, and cold smell of the chapel are contrasted with the fire at home, or in the peasants' cottages, and the warmth of his bed (a theme first heard in the overture: "When you wet the bed first it is warm then it gets cold" [3]).

At the end of the section, Joyce recalls both these motifs through the associations of pale, cold light and warm firelight, metamorphosing into waves that introduce the epiphany:

> How pale the light was at the window! But that was nice. The fire rose and fell on the wall. It was like waves. Someone had put coal on and he heard voices. They were talking. It was the noise of the waves. Or the waves were talking among themselves as they rose and fell.

As the waves are personified, Stephen sees them taking shape:

> He saw the sea of waves, long dark waves rising and falling, dark under the moonless night. A tiny light twinkled at the pierhead where the ship was entering: and he saw a multitude of people gathered by the waters' edge to see the ship that was entering their harbour. A tall man stood on the deck, looking out towards the flat dark land: and by the light at the pierhead he saw his face, the sorrowful face of Brother Michael.
> He saw him lift his hand towards the people and heard him say in a loud voice of sorrow over the waters:
> —He is dead. We saw him lying upon the catafalque. A wail of sorrow went up from the people.
> —Parnell! Parnell! He is dead!
> They fell upon their knees, moaning in sorrow.
> And he saw Dante in a maroon velvet dress and with a green velvet mantle hanging from her shoulders walking proudly and silently past the people who knelt by the waters' edge. (25)

This passage offers a wavelike repetition of the original epiphany:

> A moonless night under which the waves gleam feebly. The ship is entering a harbour where there are some lights. The sea is uneasy, charged with dull anger like the eyes of an animal which is about to spring, the prey of its own pitiless hunger. The land is flat and thinly wooded. Many people are gathered on the shore to see what ship it is that is entering their harbour.

Unlike the first epiphany, which is similar to its sources, the differences here are pronounced, yet several features suit the epiphany to this point in the narrative. The first is its dreamlike quality, combining a series of simple, anaphoric sentences ("The ship," "The sea," "The land") with subtler patterns of repetition and variation, ranging from the aural echoes of alliteration, assonance, and rhyme ("which . . . waves gleam feebly," "night/lights," etc.) to imagistic transformations (gleaming waves—lights in the harbor—glowering eyes). This lyrical-symbolic mode is particularly effective because it provides a culminating moment for the section, drawing together Stephen's earlier imaginings and linking them to the imagery of cold and heat, darkness and light, sickness and convalescence. Illness and recovery indicate another function: when the scene is reused in *Portrait*, it goes beyond feverish fantasy to symbolize death and resurrection. Brother Michael returns to announce the death of Parnell, but the phrase he uses ("We saw him lying upon the catafalque") recalls Stephen's earlier daydream, when he imagined dying like Little and having a requiem mass, with "yellow candles on the altar and round the catafalque" (*P* 22). In his revery, Stephen imagines being "buried in the little graveyard of the community" (*P* 22), and as Hans Walter Gabler has pointed out, Stephen's return to health is carefully synchronized with the return of Parnell's body to Ireland, so as Stephen returns from his imaginary death, he is symbolically linked to the spirit of Parnell.[4]

This link is strengthened each time the scene is recalled. Its first repetition occurs in the Christmas dinner scene when Stephen "remember[s] the evening in the infirmary in Clongowes, the dark waters, the light at the pierhead and the moan of sorrow from the people when they had heard" (35). Given Casey's remark that "the priests' pawns broke Parnell's heart and hounded him into his grave" a page earlier, it is natural that Stephen recalls his vision here, especially after his father's outburst: "Sons of bitches! . . . When he was down they turned on him to betray him and rend him like rats in a sewer" (33). Recalling that Stephen fell sick after being shouldered into an open sewer where "a fellow had once seen a big rat jump" (11),[5] there is a subtle link between Stephen and Parnell, and just as Parnell's career was torn apart by powerful religious and political tensions, Stephen finds himself caught between the same violent tensions at his first family Christmas.

This memory is clearly formative because in chapter 2, when Stephen's "monstrous" sexual fantasies throw him "beyond the limits of reality," so that he can "scarcely recognise . . . his own thoughts" and even the most basic placeholders of existence (origin, identity, location) are chiastically reversed and emptied of meaning ("Victoria [Hotel] and Stephen and Simon. Simon and Stephen and Victoria."), he recalls four names clearly: "Dante, Parnell, Clane, Clongowes" (98). As "the memory of his childhood suddenly [grows] dim," he involuntarily remembers the moment when he

> watched the firelight leaping and dancing on the wall of a little bedroom in the infirmary and dreamed of being dead, of mass being said for him by the rector in a black and gold cope, of being buried then in the little graveyard of the community off the main avenue of limes. But he had not died then. Parnell had died. (98)

Again, Stephen is linked with Parnell, his return to vitality at the moment Parnell dies associating Stephen with the uncrowned king of Ireland. There is as much irony here as in "Ivy Day," where Hynes's poem summons Parnell to "Rise, like the Phoenix from the flames" (*D* 132), but the connection remains important until the end of the novel, when Stephen goes forth "to forge in the smithy of [his] soul the uncreated conscience of [his] race" (277). Many readings of this line are possible, but all gain potency from the associations with Parnell. Read straight, as the triumphant cry of a godlike artist, one can hardly overlook the nationalist rhetoric that inspires Dedalus's literary aspirations, especially in the light of the rapid political events that unfolded in the years following *Portrait*'s publication; read ironically, there is perhaps a pun on "forge," linking Dedalus's hubris to Piggot's forged confession of the Phoenix Park murders, whose disclosure provided Parnell with a brief moment of triumph before his fall.

In the first two chapters, Parnell is a dominant presence, but by the end of the novel, "[t]he Ireland of Tone and of Parnell seem[s] to have receded in space" (199), Stephen has roundly rejected Davin's nationalism (220), and the infirmary scene is forgotten. It last occurs during the retreat, when Stephen recalls the cemetery "where he had dreamed of being buried; the firelight on the wall of the infirmary" and "the sorrowful face of Brother Michael" (116). "His soul, as these memories came back to him, became again a child's soul," as though to contrast Stephen's childish innocence with his state of sexual experience at the start of chapter 3. This change may explain why the scene is not repeated further, but it also indicates how Stephen's character is constructed around a series of striking memories. Memories like the firelight in the infirmary, when Stephen imagined his death and dreamed of Parnell, hold the place for his own lost identity as a boy ("How strange to think of him passing out of existence in such a way, not by death but . . . by being lost and forgotten" [99]). Facing symbolic death, these memories provide the record of Stephen's being, which helps explain both the structure of *Portrait* and why readers find it so vivid: constructed around a series of unforgettable scenes, each of which contains a cluster of eidetic images, the novel constantly returns to its key moments, like variations on a theme. This structure ensures that incidents like the infirmary epiphany are never forgotten for long—or rather, the half-forgotten is forever being recalled, weaving complex images that soon escape the woof and warp of binary logic. This is partly a problem of overdetermination, as Joyce's matrices constantly overlap, not only within the text but also through intertexutal echoes. But it is not only a problem of complexity: even a fully glossed paleographic text would be inadequate to account for the kind of meaning *Portrait* generates, because the gap is a necessary condition for the echo. Even the most finely woven cloth is a tissue of holes, and as Joyce discovered in the epiphanies, it is these very gaps that produce new images and new meaning.

* * *

I have shown three effects of repetition and variation in the infirmary scene: first, the passage draws together the major themes of section two; second, it aligns Stephen with Parnell, overlaying his portrait with the history of Irish nationalism; third, by reflecting on memory and textual memory, the echoes from "The Ship" to Stephen's self-image in Cork suggest that the structure of Joyce's epiphanies is akin to the epiphanic structure of *A Portrait of the Artist as a Young Man*. This is particularly clear in the diary section that concludes the novel, where Joyce uses three epiphanies (#29, #27, #30) in four pages. Although the *Workshop* numbers are conjectural, there are clear stylistic and thematic links between the last epiphanies in *Portrait* and the missing epiphany in the sequence, "The Ship" (#28). In fact, the source for all four is Stanislaus Joyce's "Selections in Prose from Various Authors," where they appear in reverse order: #30, #27, #29, #28. This is probably no more than chance, but given the importance of chiastic structures in *Portrait*, the parallel may be significant;[6] in any case, the similarities are close enough that the infirmary epiphany proleptically echoes the ending, which may explain why Joyce uses "The Ship" so early in the novel.

In chapter 2, I showed how "The Spell of Arms and Voices" is linked to Stephen's Janus-faced self-portraiture, imagining himself as both Daedalus and Icarus, and in the next section I will demonstrate the role of the *Portrait* epiphanies in forging Stephen's identity, but for the present my purpose is to uncover the structural matrix they establish. "The Spell" brings together a series of echoes from earlier epiphanies, the most important of which is "The Ship." The "tall ships that stand against the moon" in the former are reminiscent of the ship entering the harbor in the latter, though there it is "[a] moonless night." In "The Spell," the ships carry a "tale of distant nations," just as "The Ship" carries the news of Parnell's death in *Portrait*. These tidings are conveyed by the raised hand and voice of Brother Michael, before his cry is taken up by the people (*P* 25); likewise, epiphany #30 casts a "spell of arms and voices" in which "the black arms of tall ships" are "held out to say: We are alone,—come. And the voices say with them, We are your people." In *Portrait*, the epiphany ends with the figure of Dante "walking proudly and silently past the people who knelt by the waters' edge," just as "The Spell" ends with the narrator's kinsmen "making ready to go"; and both texts echo epiphany #27, which concludes with the sound of distant hoofs hurrying "to what journey's end—what heart—bearing what tidings?"

These "hoofs that shine amid the heavy night like diamonds" begin another chain, recalling the "lank brown horses" in "The Last Tram" who "shake their bells to the clear night, in admonition" (*P* 72). In *Portrait*, this epiphany is reused after a series of three vignettes, each beginning "He was sitting" (*P* 70–71),[7] which serve to introduce Emma, providing the occasion for Stephen's first poem. Hence, Stephen's fledgling artistry is directly inspired by a moment based on "The Last Tram," and this moment is recalled when Stephen composes his villanelle. The second vignette is based on epiphany #5 ("Is That Mary Ellen?"), one of three scenes in which Stephen "chronicle[s] with patience what he [sees]" (70), "reshaping the world about him into a vision of squalor and insincerity" (69), recalling Joyce's dramatic epiphanies.[8] In *Portrait*, the firelight and distant voices of the epiphany are expanded to echo "The Ship"; at the same time, "the sound of voices at the fire" leads Stephen to imagine "winding galleries and jagged caverns" (71), foreshadowing "Images of Fabulous Kings" with its "long curving gallery" and "pillars of dark vapours" (*P* 272).

Again, silence and repetition create the conditions for the image, a process Benjamin connects to dreams (204–5). "Images of Fabulous Kings" is explicitly introduced as a dream in *Portrait*, and the passages based on "Hoofs" and "The Spell" probably record dreams as well, just as "The Ship" is feverish and dreamlike. All four share close thematic and imagistic echoes, but beyond these similarities, it is the lyrical language of "Fabulous Kings" that links it to the other dream epiphanies.[9]

In this regard, it may be significant that, aside from minor changes in punctuation, the only difference between "The Spell" epiphany and the text in *Portrait* is the word "people," which becomes "kinsmen" in the diary, bringing additional associations of "relationship, affinity, genus, race" and "generation" into play (Skeat). Similarly, only one word is changed from "Images of Fabulous Kings," where "ascend" replaces "arise." There are a few more alterations to "Hoofs," but these can mostly be explained by context: "summer" is omitted, since the entry is dated April 10; "Dublin" is cut, as the setting is clear; "town" is changed to "city." In contrast to the radical revision of "The Ship," Joyce inserts his epiphanies virtually unchanged, because the diary provides a perfect narrative structure for a series of fragmentary texts, with little need for introduction or explication. Nevertheless, Joyce ensures continuity by making many of the diary entries resemble epiphanies, recording "the vulgarity of speech or of gesture" or "a memorable phase of the mind" (*SH* 216): in addition to four dream epiphanies, there are lyrical passages of reflection, such as Stephen's thoughts on time and beauty (273), the old man from the West (274), and Platonic love (275), while Stephen also notes "little errors and gestures—mere straws in the wind" (*MBK* 126) by which people betray themselves (270, 275).

This stylistic resemblance between diary and epiphanies is strongly reinforced by their structural similarities. Like the epiphanies, Stephen's diary is discontinuous, with a gap of four days after the April 10 epiphany, and ten days after the last epiphany; even when multiple entries are recorded on the same day, there is always a break between them. Then again, Joyce creates continuity by returning to earlier concerns and repeating phrases within the diary. In the first entry, Stephen records a "long talk with Cranly" about his "revolt" and "love for one's mother," apparently referring to the discussion they have just concluded (270; 259–69), and he pursues the same theme on March 24, March 30, and the penultimate entry, April 26. Similarly, when Stephen recalls the word "tundish" on April 13, this is only the most obvious of many verbal echoes from earlier scenes, including a raucous reappropriation of phrases from the climax to chapter 4: "Wild spring. Scudding clouds. O life! Dark stream of bogwater . . . Eyes of girls . . . Houp-la!" (273). Repetition is also frequent within the diary, from the "exhausted loins" and freedom of the first three entries, to the play on "mud" and "crocodiles" (272–73), to the final repetition, "Old father, old artificer."[10]

Thus, Stephen's diary, like Joyce's epiphanies, comprises a series of linked but discontinuous moments, both radiant in themselves and reflecting on each other. As mentioned, the novel is composed of a series of striking vignettes separated by narrative breaks—the same basic structure that governs the diary and the epiphanies is replicated in each of its chapters. Any outline of part 1 would surely include the apologize, square ditch, infirmary, Christmas dinner, pandybatting, and rectorate scenes, but it would also have to indicate gaps between sections (e.g., the jump to Christmas between 1.2 and 1.3 and the return to Clongowes), as well as those within each section. The problem with a linear summary is that Joyce's scenes are discontinuous yet interwoven, bridging narrative ellipses with repetition. Exacerbating the difficulty, Joyce provides few deictic indications for temporal and spatial shifts, leaving readers to rely on other clues for orientation, like the imagery of fire, holly, and ivy at the beginning of section three, which provides a link back to Stephen's thoughts of Christmas (18, 25–26). Here, plot is subordinate to patterned imagery, indicating that the novel is not fixed and sequential but reciprocal and self-varying, "an endless reverberation" (*P* 177) of echoes.

The structure of each part is even more evident in the novel as a whole: with little explicit indication, shifts between chapters, like the jumps from Clongowes to Blackrock to Dublin (spanning some eight or ten years), emphasize the elliptical narrative, organized around epiphanic scenes. As mentioned, many of these are based directly on epiphanies, such as the apologize scene, the infirmary, the encounter with the prostitute, and Stephen's vision of "the hell reserved for his sins" (*P* 148–49); others, like the moment Stephen meets Emma and writes his first poem, his composition of the villanelle, and the diary, are structured around several epiphanies, and significantly these are the key moments in which we see Stephen's growth as an artist. It is not surprising, therefore, that other climactic moments not based on any known epiphany, like the fetus scene or the birdgirl on the strand, are frequently dubbed epiphanies.[11] These set pieces stand out for their lyrical qualities and their evident symbolic function, but just as often, the passages based on epiphanies in *Portrait* are unremarkable—only a reader familiar with the "Mary Ellen" or "Last Tram" epiphanies is likely to notice any difference between their occurrence in the novel and the paragraphs surrounding them. Critics have tended to focus on the first kind, but the second group gives a much fuller picture of the extent to which both the structure and style of *A Portrait* are based on the epiphanies, not only in the climaxes to each chapter but also in the quiet lulls that follow. Indeed, these unobtrusive, largely unnoticed epiphanies point to a shortcoming in previous studies of the *Portrait* epiphanies, where critics typically read back from climactic moments in the novel (the bird-girl, etc.) to the epiphanies, and not the other way around. Their approach is legitimate in view of the relative importance of each text in Joyce's oeuvre, but by putting the focus on *Portrait*, they obscure the crucial role of the epiphanies in structuring the novel.

Portrait's Stylistic Fusion

The epiphanies provide nodal points for *Portrait*'s major articulations, as well as the twin strands of repetition and variation that run like a double helix through every twist and turn of the novel. It follows that any passage will exhibit the structural and stylistic principles of the epiphanies, but just as there is a genesis from the epiphanies to *Portrait*, so too there is clear stylistic development within Joyce's *Künstlerroman*, reflecting Stephen's maturing consciousness through growing linguistic complexity.

The epiphanies shape this stylistic development, with Stephen's artistic growth reaching its fullest expression in his final journal entries, many of which are modeled on epiphanies. Likewise, Stephen's first poem is inspired by two epiphanies (#3, #5; *P* 72–74); the "instant of inspiration" (235) that occasions the villanelle comes immediately after "The Girls, The Boys" (234–35); in the midst of its composition, he recalls a scene based on "She Dances with Them in the Round" (238) that furnishes "the radiant image of the eucharist" to complete the poem;[12] and immediately upon doing so, he returns to "The Last Tram" to reflect on his artistic development (241).[13] Thus, Stephen's art in *Portrait* grows out of Joyce's art in the epiphanies, and Stephen's growth as an artist leads him to precisely the point when he is able to write the Joycean epiphany.[14]

In the last section, I showed how little Joyce revised the diary epiphanies, but there is one significant change: in *Portrait*, he adds an entire paragraph after epiphany #29:

> *25 March, morning.* A troubled night of dreams. Want to get them off my chest.
>
> A long curving gallery. From the floor ascend pillars of dark vapours. It is peopled by the images of fabulous kings, set in stone. Their hands are folded upon their knees in token of weariness and their eyes are darkened for the errors of men go up before them for ever as dark vapours.
>
> Strange figures advance as from a cave. They are not as tall as men. One does not seem to stand quite apart from another. Their faces are phosphorescent, with darker streaks. They peer at me and their eyes seem to ask me something. They do not speak. (272)

The "[s]trange figures" may represent a new dream or a continuation of the epiphany; in either case, the rhetorical mode of the second paragraph is indistinguishable from the first. It may be based on a lost epiphany, just as the Mabel Hunter and Harold's Cross sections that begin "He was sitting" (*P* 70–72) may be drawn from more than thirty epiphanies that seem not to have survived, but it is equally likely that Joyce composed the scenes for *Portrait*; either way, the dream is framed as *Stephen's* epiphany, highlighting how closely the style of the diary, and *Portrait* as a whole, is modeled on Joyce's ur-texts.

Nevertheless, there is a clear evolution in the way epiphanies are reused in *Portrait*. At the beginning of the novel, there is little if any irony in the "Apologise" epiphany or the infirmary scene, but by the end of the diary, Stephen distances himself from his April 10 epiphany: "Read what I wrote last night. Vague words for a vague emotion" (274). As Bowen argues, this seems to prepare the ground for Stephen's ironic view of the epiphanies in "Proteus" (Bowen 1979; *U* 3.141–44), but it is also possible to read the comment positively ("Would [Emma] like it? I think so. Then I should have to like it also" [274]). In chapter 4, Stephen contemplates "an inner world of individual emotions mirrored perfectly in a lucid supple periodic prose" (181), suggesting that if the emotion is as vague as a dream, its representation demands an equally dreamlike style, which is precisely what the dream epiphanies create. All Stephen's reveries, whether waking or sleeping, have this quality, and the diary has many such passages, but by the end of the novel, their rhythm has changed, becoming increasingly staccato.

One would expect the lyrical-symbolic mode of the dream epiphanies to create an unbroken flow of associations, but Stephen's diary combines this with frequent ellipsis, which punctuates the rhythm. This combination plays a key role in shaping Dedalus's stream-of-consciousness style in *Ulysses*, but it is important to recognize that this is not a fundamentally new voice; on the contrary, it unfolds from Joyce's underlying structure of silence and repetition. For instance, the entry for March 21, night, reads:

> Free. Soulfree and fancyfree. Let the dead bury the dead. Ay. And let the dead marry the dead. (270)

Despite rapid-fire sentences, Joyce's prose remains supple and periodic. This syncopated rhythm is created by runs of repetition and variation (the first playing on "carefree," the second on the Gospels[15]), so that the pauses between sentences are more graphic than aural, indicating Stephen's train of thought. Likewise, the previous entry, dated the same morning, combines short, staccato sentences with recondite reflection, inviting readers to join Stephen's elliptical thoughts into a coherent stream of consciousness. Interestingly, both passages allude to epiphanies in Luke and Matthew, propagating further associations.[16]

This conjunction of silence and repetition suggests the diary is analogous to the epiphanies, but *Portrait* goes much further in fusing the poles: whereas the dramatic epiphanies foreground resonant hiatuses, and the dream epiphanies are characterized by lyrical symbolism, by the end of *Portrait*, Joyce combines them in equal measure.

This tendency is already apparent in the overture, with its "quick-cut glimpses" (Kenner 1991, 12) of childhood: in a page and a half, Joyce presents the tale of baby tuckoo, "the wild rose" song, wet beds, "the sailor's hornpipe," Uncle Charles and Dante, Dante's brushes for Michael Davitt and Parnell, the Vances, and the injunction to "Apologise." Each paragraph provides a snapshot, like a discontinuous sequence of early memories; even the sentence structure is paratactic. Yet repetition bestows order and continuity on the sequence, like the final pages of *Portrait*. As with the diary, Joyce combines lyrical-symbolism with ironic realism: two songs on the first page foreground repetition ("Tralala lala / Tralala tralaladdy"), accruing symbolic associations through variation ("O, the wild rose blossoms / . . . O, the geen wothe botheth"[17]), while the overture concludes with the first epiphany, a dramatic sketch constructed around the resonant hiatus of why Stephen is being punished and the silence of who says, "Pull out his eyes" (4). Thus, for all their apparent differences, the structure of the opening mirrors the diary at the end; Stephen's language and reflections become more complex, but the underlying pattern remains.

The generative structure of *A Portrait* becomes apparent when the dialogue and narrative of *Dubliners* are compared to those of *Portrait*: whereas in *Dubliners* the two are relatively distinct, and can be characterized, respectively, by Joyce's modes of ironic realism and lyrical symbolism (chapter 3), *Portrait* brings them together. That is, the dialogue in *Portrait* is frequently elevated to lyrical or impassioned rhetoric, while even its most lyrical passages are undercut by irony. Regarding the former, epiphany #1 provides a perfect example, as young Stephen transforms spoken threats into poetry ("Pull out his eyes / Apologise . . ."). In *Portrait*, these lines are no longer even dialogue, but a pure form of lyrical symbolism. Mutatis mutandis, the power of the Christmas dinner scene is created not only by the realism and irony of its dialogue (though it has that in spades) but also by its impassioned rhetoric, which thrills, terrifies, and enflames Stephen (38–39), making the visceral power of language a highly charged motif.[18] Another example is provided by Stephen's thirteen-page disquisition on aesthetics, which culminates in a narrative epiphany no more, and no less, lyrical than Dedalus's monologue (*P* 221–33; "The Girls, The Boys"). The same point holds true for the dialogue in chapter 5: for all their irony and realism, the long conversations with Davin, the dean of studies, Lynch and Cranly are replete with lyrical symbolism, and this mode applies as much to Stephen's interlocutors as to himself. For instance, Davin's tale, recounted in a lilting Hiberno-English brogue, "[calls] up before Stephen's mind a strange vision" (196) whose lyrical associations ("The last words of Davin's story *sang* in his memory") of "a batlike soul waking to the consciousness of itself" (198) are repeated verbatim as Stephen forges an image to complete his villanelle (239–40). Lyrical-symbolic effects such as these are found in every chapter, such as Uncle Charles's refined diction, which colors the surrounding narrative by association (62; see Kenner 1975, 15–38); the jouissance occasioned in young Stephen by Dumas's line, "Madam, I never eat Muscatel grapes" (65); the strange power of the *Confiteor*, which awakens a "sudden memory" in Stephen, carrying him "as if by magic" to "another scene" (82); Father Arnall's hell sermons (126–45);[19] the voices of Stephen's brothers and sisters modulating from the boro-boro language of children into an angelic choir (177); and the boyish whoops of joy that echo in Stephen's ears as he goes to encounter the bird-girl on the beach (182–83).

Hence, the dialogue in *Portrait* retains the ironic realism of *Dubliners* and the dramatic epiphanies but adds the lyricism and symbolic significance associated with dream epiphanies; conversely, the narrative mode of *Portrait* is always undercut by irony. This is typically the result of a gap between Stephen's romantic imaginings and the apparent reality of the situation he describes; yet this deconstruction of lyricism through tonal ambiguity enhances its power. Perhaps the best example is the famous ending to chapter 4, where a girl gazing out to sea—possibly a cocklepicker—undergoes a lyrical-symbolic metamorphosis in Stephen's imagination: "She seemed like one whom magic had changed into the likeness of a strange and beautiful seabird" (185). One has only to compare similar passages in Synge and D'Annunzio to see the delicacy and intensity of Joyce's lyricism,[20] but his emphasis on "her long slender bare legs" and full thighs, "bared almost to the hips," revealing "the white fringes of her drawers" (185), counteracts the symbolism of Stephen's extended avian simile. Stephen's natural desire casts doubt on the purity of the angelic "image" he creates—"a wild angel . . . , the angel of mortal youth and beauty, an envoy from the fair courts of life"—leaving "the holy silence of his ecstasy" ringing with rapturous longing, and these carnal motivations are written into his credo: "To live, to err, to fall, to triumph, *to recreate life out of life!*" (186, my emphasis). Joyce's line resonates on many levels, picking up on all the major themes of chapters 3 and 4, but it is significant that at the moment Stephen affirms his self-sufficiency as an artist-creator, the text underscores his Daedalian ambitions with the basic instincts of reproduction.

These sexual drives can be read ironically, as John McGowan does when he interprets the scene "in terms of Stephen's troubled relation to women; his separation from the girl, with whom he exchanges 'no word' makes his substitution of the warm embrace of mother earth take on a comic note" (439; see *P* 187). This is perceptive, and McGowan is right that "Stephen's sexual confusions" ask us to interpret "his aesthetic theories in relation to his frustrated romantic longings" (439; see *P* 187). Joyce seems to mock Stephen's artistic pretensions as flowery aestheticism by reflecting on the lurid description of sunset: "A world, a glimmer, or a flower?" (187). But this doesn't negate the dreamlike beauty of the sunset passage; rather, it opens another perspective, allowing us to enjoy Joyce's lyricism all the more by disarming critical resistance. Likewise, the satirical potential of sexual undercurrents does not undermine the epiphanic quality of the bird-girl passage; in fact, by yoking Stephen's creative impulses to reproductive instincts, Joyce offers the possibility of physical incarnation to art and imagination, making the bodily and the spiritual one, which actually reinforces the "heroic" reading of *A Portrait of the Artist as a Young Man*.

This paradoxical function of irony and realism to heighten Joyce's lyrical symbolism is seen in the climax to each chapter. At the end of chapter 2, for instance, Stephen's encounter with the prostitute expands on the poetic language of epiphany #31, whose "dark presence" moves "subtle and murmurous as a flood" through the passage (*P* 106), adding the religious symbolism of gas lamps "burning as if before an altar" and prostitutes arrayed "as for some rite" to the "maze of narrow and dirty streets" in Dedalus's Nighttown; at the same time, this lyrical symbolism is interpenetrated by the ironic realism of the encounter, powerfully manifest in a series of puns and double entendres ("Good night, Willie dear" [cf.106–8]). As with the ellipses in *Dubliners*, these euphemisms may be explained by the pressures of censorship, which allows Joyce to tease the reader with the ambiguity of what takes place. Hovering between (French) kiss and intercourse (in both senses), this ambiguity allows Joyce to make the physical movement of "her softly parting lips" a fluid exchange of tongues, speech, fantasy, and sex: here, ironic realism creates a teeming, indeterminate orifice that presses upon Stephen's "brain as upon his lips," and presumably his penis, "as though they were the vehicle of a vague speech," disseminating meaning through the confluence of language, fantasy, and sexuality.

The uncertainty about what happens at the end of part 2 creates a euphemistic silence that stems from the repetition of "Upon Me from the Darkness," and this conjunction is replicated in the many phrases that recall Stephen's "mortal sin" at the beginning of chapter 3. "From the evil seed of lust all other deadly sins [spring] forth" (113), we read, but the chapter begins with Stephen's gluttony and ends with his eager anticipation of white pudding, sausages, eggs, and tea "the morning after the communion" (158), adding a homely, ironic-realist twist to his reflections on the simplicity and beauty of life as he receives the host.[21] Again, the effect is not so much to negate the significance of Stephen's communion as to return the symbolism of transubstantiation to the substance of survival.

Almost all the meals in *Portrait* are overlaid with eucharistic imagery, like the sad, parentless supper of tea and sugared bread supplemented by the children's singing in chapter 4 (176–77) and the breakfast of watery tea and crusts of fried bread at the start of chapter 5 (188), where the "dark pool" of dripping recalls the "turfcoloured water of the bath in Clongowes" (188) as well as the last figures islanded in "distant pools" at the end of chapter 4 (187). Thus, the movement of climactic, even epiphanic, chapter endings followed by down-to-earth, ironic-realist openings described by Kenner, Booth, and Riquelme is reductive,[22] for the two modes are continuously in operation: the lyrical symbolism of the endings is enhanced by levels of realism and irony, just as the apparently realistic scenes that commence each new chapter are overlaid with lyrical and symbolic associations, like the Eucharistic breakfast and baptismal bath at the beginning of chapter 5.

This conjunction of stylistic modes governing the climax of each chapter, and the novel as a whole, also applies in each of its parts. As I argued in chapter 3, the purest and simplest form of Joyce's ironic realism is silence, while the quintessence of his lyrical-symbolism is repetition. It follows that the synthesis of these modes involves the union of silence and repetition. Since the two modes originate in the epiphanies, it is not surprising to find them in the *Portrait* epiphanies, but whereas straightforward repetition of the early texts would imply a stylistic movement from the first dramatic epiphany to the lyrical epiphanies in the diary, as Gabler suggests (*JJA* 7.xxvii), the novel brings the poles together. This interweaving of silence and repetition is explicit in the diary, where "silence is cloven by alarm as by an arrow" ("Hoofs"; *P* 274). Sundering and adhering to the silence, the "arrow" is a sign of repetition—primarily of the "hoofs upon the road," which are first heard "through the silence," then on the bridge, then again under the windows, and finally far away, "hoofs that shine amid the heavy night as gems." I have already shown how this phrase echoes "The Last Tram," which is itself recycled twice in *Portrait* (72, 241), and how the diary entry as a whole is linked to epiphanies #28, #29, #30 and the passages based on them. The arrow-like repetitions of the hoofs that cleave (to) the silence ripple outward, with the ambiguity of the verb "to cleave" indicating how repetition oscillates between bifurcation and doubling, giving form to silence by opening a space for (self-) reflection while simultaneously bridging the difference.

The impulse generated by this oscillation shapes the wavelike surface of Joyce's text, an endlessly repeated succession of ever-varying crests separated by troughs of silence, and the same pattern is evident in the genesis of *Portrait*'s epiphanies. As noted, the major difference between epiphany #1 and *Portrait* is the loss of speech headings and stage directions, which leave the repeated verses either unspoken or unattributed. Elsewhere, speech is reduced to pure materiality, the repetition of meaningless sound. For instance, Joyce's revision of epiphany #6 makes the satirical "Half-Men, Half-Goats" move repetitively "in slow circles, circling closer and closer to enclose, to enclose, soft language issuing from their lips." Their malleable utterance is as unintelligible as the fecal matter that surrounds them, so that in Joyce's "Epiphany of Hell" (Cornell 2.A.16), speech is figured as logorrhoea, or verbal diarrhoea, an endlessly repeated, reified, and unintelligible production. Semantic reduction, accompanied by the reification of sound, can also be seen in the transformation of "Upon Me from the Darkness," whose cry "for an iniquitous abandonment" (*PSW* 191; *P* 106) becomes almost "inarticulate" as Stephen "moan[s] to himself like some baffled prowling beast," feeling the murmurs of a dark presence break from him in "a cry which was but the echo of an obscene scrawl which he had read on the oozing wall of a urinal" (106).

In these epiphanies, speech is rendered as inarticulate or unintelligible sound: a silence of signification reduces spoken language to empty repetition. These physical properties furnish one half of Stephen's epiphanic theory of language incarnate; the other comes from its signifying function, represented as silence that speaks. In the last quotation, an "obscene scrawl" on "the oozing wall of a urinal" (note the sound patterns) is echoed in a cry ("Fuck"?): silent letters speak through repetition. This indicates that, as well as representing the materiality of language "silently emptied of instantaneous sense" (*P* 193), the *Portrait* epiphanies figure speech and writing as repetition in silence.[23] For instance in epiphany #24, Joyce describes a young woman (perhaps Hannah Sheehy) whose "eyes have revealed her—secret, vigilant, an enclosed garden" (*PSW* 184). This window to her soul echoes the Song of Songs, evoking a response in the speaker: *Inter ubera mea commorabitur* (Songs 1.13). In *Portrait*, the epiphany is reused to describe the "inaudible voice" Stephen hears caressing his soul as he reads Alphonsus Liguori, echoing back phrases from the canticles, until Stephen hears his "soul answer with the same inaudible voice, surrendering herself: *Inter ubera mea commorabitur*" (*P* 164). Here, the young woman's revealing eyes set off a train of association that makes the silence speak. Likewise, in "Images of Fabulous Kings," the eyes of statues are "darkened" with opaque significance, but in the paragraph Stephen adds, "strange figures . . . peer at [him] and their eyes seem to ask [him] something," though "they do not speak" (*P* 272).

In the bodily production of inarticulate language and silent reflections of the gaze, these epiphanies define two patterns: the repetition of silence and the silence of repetition. Ultimately, these interwoven patterns form a single braid, but it is easier to see this by separating the strands. Silence in repetition first. The "Images" epiphany (#29, quoted above; *P* 272) provides a ready example: the "weariness" of the "fabulous kings" who gaze with "darkened eyes" on the errors of men echoes Stephen's villanelle ("Are you not *weary* . . ." 236, 243), Jonson's lyric, "I was not *wearier* where I lay" (190), Newman reading Virgil (177), and a whole sorry tale of weariness going back to Stephen's reflections on the green earth and maroon clouds in his geography textbook, weighed down as they are by politics and the name of God (13). It is impossible to bear all these reverberations in mind, because ancillary associations with Jonson, Newman, Virgil, Parnell, Davitt, and so on create a potentially infinite regress. One moment in the chain is particularly striking, however, because it expresses this very condition. As Stephen listens to his siblings singing in the gathering dusk, he hears "with pain of spirit . . . the overtone of weariness behind their frail fresh innocent voices": "He heard the choir of voices in the kitchen echoed and multiplied through an endless reverberation of the choirs of endless generations of children: and heard in all the echoes an echo also of the recurring note of weariness and pain" (177). This "recurring note of weariness and pain" might recall "the hole we all have" (*WD* 29), but its overtones reverberate endlessly precisely because its associations are imaginary. Stephen listens to his siblings' voices, no doubt with echoes and harmonics, but the overtones he hears are not confined to sound: in his imagination, a metonymic chain of choirs sings the same note to infinity, creating a genuinely resonant hiatus. The musical analogy adds a certain complexity, since overtones can be sung by different voices, but in literature, at least, the "subtle or elusive implication[s] or association[s]" of *figurative* overtones (*OED*) lie wholly within the text. Indeed, the multilevel implications of overtones bring attention to the tonal properties of language. Describing voice and color, tone is discerned in music, speech, and writing, yet it has no overt marker: whatever overtones or undertones we may detect, the text remains the same. In this sense, the tone of writing is silent, an invisible mark of difference in repetition (note, for instance, the difference between identical lexical items in the sentence quoted above, like the subtle shift from literal voices to figurative echoes in the repetition of "heard"). The irony so many readers detect in *Portrait* illustrates this perfectly: opening a gap between what is said and how it is understood, meaning multiplies. Yet irony is only one aspect of the tonal ambiguity that characterizes all of Joyce's work, from *Dubliners* to *Finnegans Wake*; like the ironic-realism of the dramatic epiphanies, it universalizes the potential for semantic ambiguity, opening an invisible gap or silent mark of difference that makes every word resonate.

As well as the silence within repetition, there is also repetition in silence. "[C]hiasmic symmetry pervades" *A Portrait*, from the "quick-cut glimpses" of the overture reflected in the final diary fragments, or the counterpart visions of prostitute and bird-girl that end chapters 2 and 4, to countless examples of chiasmus in the text (Kenner 1991, 11–13). As Kenner points out, at the structural center of the novel, between the second and third of four sermons that form the innermost section of the central chapter, "The preacher took a chainless watch from a pocket within his soutane and, having considered its dial for a moment in silence, placed it silently before him on the table" (*P* 126). At the center of the novel, then, is a moment of silence, a pause, a hush, like the tain of the mirror, which reflects everything but itself. That is to say, the mirrored repetitions that form *Portrait*'s chiastic structure are centered on a moment of silent reflection. Indeed, Kenner's analogy between self-portraiture, like Rembrandt's "A Portrait of the Artist as a Young Man" (of which there are several) and Joyce's autobiographical novel, implies that silence is to the text as the mirror is to the painting:

Background	Painter	Mirror	Painter's image	Background's image
	Dublin	Joyce	Stephen	"Dublin"

Kenner argues that books provide silent mirrors of the world: "When the busy sounding world has passed through the novel's kind of mirror into a book, its sounds lie hushed in the mimicry of silent type" (13). Traditional notions of mimesis might justify Kenner's conclusion, but Joyce's work challenges mimetic theories of art by foregrounding the materiality of language. Insisting on graphemes as textual objects, Joyce suggests that the "kind of mirror . . . silent type" provides is not fundamentally representational but self-referential. In this model, textual silence is analogous to the thin layer of tinfoil that makes reflection possible, though it cannot reflect itself; likewise, the materiality of language is a condition for representation, although it cannot signify itself. It follows that, in addition to the material form of the signifier, there must be a gap for representation to take place; this space is the silence of signification. Just as there is never a total absence of sound, or a material void, textual silence cannot be represented directly: all representation necessarily contains a space of silence, but silence can be summoned into being only through representation. Again, the poles are uroboric: representation (the relation of similitude-in-difference) depends upon silence, and silence depends upon material representation. If this seems abstract, consider the diagram above. When Kenner invites the reader to inscribe silence in the blank space of its absence, a genuine hiatus carries the trace of its own signifier, offering a paradigm of the linguistic epiphany.

Kenner's reading is paradigmatic because *Portrait*'s chiastic structure hinges on silence: a central silence enfolds all others, even as it opens the space for mirrored repetition. Borrowing Derrida's term, silence in *Portrait* is "*la brisure*," the hinge that joins and divides; "designating difference and articulation," it is the "origin of all repetition," instantiating "*the différance* which opens appearance and signification*"* (1976, 65). Likewise, Joyce's silence both cleaves and is cloven by repetition, because the silent pause at the center of *Portrait*'s chiastic structure is mirrored by silence within each repetition, pointing to a silence that lies before inscription and beyond the text.

As this suggests, the same structure is replicated throughout the novel, so that Kenner's central silence is one of many. Kenneth Burke situates the "point of *farthest internality*" (324) just after the retreat, as Stephen prays silently on the threshold to his room:

> He waited still at the threshold as at the entrance to some dark cave. Faces were there; eyes: they waited and watched.
> —We knew perfectly well of course that though it was bound to come to the light he would find considerable difficulty in endeavouring to try to induce himself to try to endeavour to ascertain the spiritual plenipotentiary and so we knew of course perfectly well—

> Murmuring faces waited and watched; murmurous voices filled the dark shell of the cave. (147)

Burke's choice of center is cryptic, but the one clue he provides—"circular" (147)—may refer to the chiastic structure of the passage: "dark cave. Faces . . . waited and watched . . . perfectly well . . . try to induce himself . . . induce himself to try . . . perfectly well . . . faces waited and watched . . . dark . . . cave." This mirrored repetition replicates in miniature the structure of the book, and here too it encloses a moment of silence. In the central paragraph, the words quoted are thought, not spoken; echoing in Stephen's mind, they recall a motif: "The echoes of certain expressions used in Clongowes sounded in remote caves of his mind. // His ears were listening to these distant echoes amid the silence" (170; cf. 71, 193, 272 and epiphanies #5, 29).

Burke's "point of *farthest internality*," deep in the cavern of Stephen's self, offers an alternative center to Kenner's, but others are equally plausible. Indeed, the epiphany that begins on the following page is more deeply embedded than the scene Burke singles out, where Stephen's room is presented as a cave (147): when Stephen crawls into bed and wraps himself in his blankets, trying to shut out the memory of his sins and close "the senses of his soul" (148), he has gone much deeper into himself than when he stands on the threshold of the room. It is at precisely this moment that Stephen has his personal vision of hell, based on Joyce's "hell" epiphany ("Half-Men, Half-Goats"), which, as the central epiphany in *Portrait*, provides another structural center to the novel. I have shown how Joyce adapts the epiphany to reflect on silence and repetition, but Stephen's vision also reflects the "vision of hell" Father Arnall describes a few pages earlier:

> —A holy saint (one of our own fathers I believe it was) was once vouchsafed a vision of hell. It seemed to him that he stood in the midst of a great hall, dark and silent save for the ticking of a great clock. The ticking went on unceasingly; and it seemed to this saint that the sound of the ticking was the ceaseless repetition of the words—ever, never; ever, never. (143)

Following Burke's logic of internality, this point could be taken as central, and here again, we find the same repetitive mechanism ticking ceaselessly in the silence.

The word silence appears almost a hundred times, including its adjectival and adverbial forms; virtually every scene in *Portrait* is accompanied by silence, from the silent air over the playing fields in the opening to the cloven silence of the dream epiphanies in Stephen's diary. In between, there are awkward silences at the Christmas dinner table, a "dead silence" before the pandybatting, and silence in the rectorate; when Stephen meets Emma, his manner is silent and watchful (70–72, cf. epiphanies #5 and #3); his vision of the word "foetus" arises in the silence of the anatomy theater, just as "Stephen's inarticulate cries" break the silence of the prostitute's chamber at the end of chapter 2. In part 3, Stephen takes pleasure in "penetrating into obscure silences" (113), and there are plenty of them in the loaded silences before and after the retreat, as well as between the sermons, where Stephen suffers silently in his need for confession (136). Afterward, his soul is "clear and silent" (158), but he knows that he will "fall silently" back into temptation, for he already feels "the silent lapse of his soul" (175). The bird-girl scene is suffused in an atmosphere of "holy silence" (186), as is the composition of the villanelle, and after writing out his poem, Stephen feels an "oceanic silence" (245) filling his heart. This moment recalls "the enchantment of the heart" Stephen describes in "the luminous silent stasis of esthetic pleasure," which summons up "a thoughtenchanted silence" (231), and silence is of course the first of Stephen's "arms," simultaneously a means of attack, defense, and expression (268–69).

Like the inaudible backdrop to *Dubliners*, there is an everpresent air of silence in *A Portrait*, and this silence, the silence *of* language, is unchanging, yet the silences *in* each narrative have a different quality.[24] In the last chapter, I identified silence as the essence of Joyce's ironic realism, creating resonant hiatuses in the text, and this, I believe, is their primary function in *Dubliners*, whereas the "oceanic" silences in *Portrait* are both lyrical and symbolic. The silence of language is necessarily present in narrated silences, so the difference is not fundamental, but the implicit mechanism of *Dubliners* becomes increasingly explicit. Portraying the "thoughtenchanted" silences of *Portrait* in a lyrical-symbolic vein, Joyce implies that silence gives rise to repetition, while each repeated image runs back into the same silent sea. Just as repetition enfolds silence, even when there is no marked difference (e.g., through tonal ambiguity), this fusion of the poles means that the named silences in *Portrait* explicitly embody their propensity to proliferate.

Language Incarnate: The Epiphany of the Word

If the structural and stylistic principles of the epiphanies are conjoined throughout the novel, then *Portrait*'s language is itself epiphanic. In this section, I take up this argument, showing that for Joyce, the real site of epiphany is the word, as language becomes a manifestation of spirit. To flesh out this notion of linguistic embodiment, I adopt Jean-Jacques Lecercle's concept of the remainder.

As Derek Attridge explains, for Lecercle, "[a]ny language [. . .] operates in accordance with four propositions":

1. Language is a material product of the body.
2. Language is an abstract system, independent of the body.
3. The speaker speaks the language, saying freely what he or she means.
4. The language speaks, and meaning belongs to the community before it belongs to the speaker. (Attridge 2001, 65)

The "commonsensical" view of language relies on propositions 2 and 3 (Lecercle 1995, 107); but when 1 and 4 "transgress their allotted frontiers . . . we become aware of the remainder" (66). Examples include glossolalia ("Derevaun Seraun! Derevaun Seraun!" [*D* 33]), liturgical language (e.g., the act of contrition in *Portrait*, which is prescribed by the community, not the individual: *P* 146), and words that carry a bodily or sexual charge ("rump," "suck," "kiss," "smugging"). Attridge focuses on the third group to show how "a word can resonate physically and often erotically" (77). In passing, he mentions the role of nineteenth-century philology in emphasizing the "historical and material specificity" of words (70), implying that words can be "made strange" (73) either by *divesting* them of meaning or by *investing* them with a complex history of morphological and semantic change, which explains why the remainder "may just as easily be manifested in an excess of meaning as in a lack of it" (66).

As I showed in chapter 2, Joyce's lyrical and dramatic epiphanies manifest precisely this excess and lack of meaning, although the relationship between them is uroboric. Likewise, semantic proliferation and indeterminacy are defining characteristics of the epiphanies in *Portrait*, determining the structure and style of the novel. More fundamentally, these qualities are present in the materiality of language, with all its supra-individual networks of signification. As such, these dual aspects of the "remainder" are not fractional leftovers but ubiquitous properties of language. In *Portrait*, they are presented in quasi-divine terms, as the epiphany of the word.

This is evident in two ways. First, Stephen dwells on the materiality of language, a bodily production with a physical life of its own. This body is, of course, composed of sound waves and graphic inscriptions, which *Portrait* figures as repetition in silence, but Stephen's immaculate conception of the word made flesh, with its recurrent imagery of watery words precipitating from ethereal clouds (235–42), provides a powerful image of language formation as a spiritual incarnation. Second, Stephen gradually realizes that the language he speaks is not his own: English belongs to others, like the dean of studies, before him (205), while speaking through them both, like a "tundish" funneling meaning (203–5, 274). The "unrest of spirit" Stephen feels is not simply a matter of colonial history; language always casts a "shadow" (205) because any word undergoes phonological, graphological, and semantic change. Since the history of these changes lies behind each utterance, the physical form of language provides a conduit for thought. Representing the symbolic manifestation of an intelligence greater than any individual, Lecercle's fourth proposition provides a succinct account of this aspect of Joyce's linguistic epiphany, continuously affirming the human spirit as each word modifies a history of repetition and variation.

* * *

Attridge demonstrates the visceral power of words like "suck" and "kiss," emphasizing the erotic charge of the "remainder," but the physical production of language is stressed from Stephen's first utterance ("O, the geen wothe botheth": Riquelme 2007, 1.12), while the nascent sexuality encoded in words like "smugging" is linked to Stephen's artistic growth, allowing him to reproduce his creative fantasy through incarnated language. In *The Incarnation of Language*, Michael O'Sullivan gives a good example of linguistic embodiment:

> A soft liquid joy like the noise of many waters flowed over his memory and he felt in his heart the soft peace of silent spaces of fading tenuous sky above the waters, of oceanic silence, of swallows flying through the sea-dusk over the flowing waters.
>
> A soft liquid joy flowed through the words where the soft long vowels hurtled noiselessly and fell away, lapping and flowing back

and ever shaking the white bells of their waves in mute chime and mute peal, and soft low swooning cry; and he felt that the augury he had sought in the wheeling darting birds and in the pale space of sky above him had come forth from his heart like a bird from a turret, quietly and swiftly. (245)

O'Sullivan notes how "[t]he words of the description become part of the description itself; the vowels hurtle and lap, taking on the physical and material state of the waves that have caused his epiphany" (87). Perceptive as this is, the scene is not based on any extant epiphany (although stylistically it resembles the lyrical prose poems), and O'Sullivan implies that Stephen is by the sea, while it is primarily the nomadic swallows that exalt him as he stands on the steps of the National Library in central Dublin. In this context, the hurtling, falling vowels imitate the flight of the birds and their "soft low swooning cry" (*P* 245), suggesting that Joyce's language embodies the paths of the birds traced at the start of the scene,[25] re-creating their cries through lyrical runs of softly modulated alliteration and assonance. Significantly, it is only when the free indirect discourse embodies their movement and gives voice to their cries that Stephen feels "the augury he had sought in the wheeling darting birds . . . come forth from his heart like a bird from a turret" (245).

Nevertheless, marine imagery is as present as avian imagery in the text, so O'Sullivan's impression is not ungrounded. Indeed, it can probably be explained by the fact that the "soft liquid joy" flowing over Stephen's memory and the "soft peace" he feels "in his heart," along with the bird motif and the "silent spaces of fading tenuous sky above the waters," recall the end of chapter 4, where Stephen's "outburst of profane joy" at the birdlike woman slowly subsides into "the peace and silence of the evening" above the shallow water (186–87). In this way, Stephen's experience on Sandymount Strand seems to hover over the scene, explaining why the passage "imbibes the form of the villanelle Stephen has just mouthed to himself" (O'Sullivan 87). Although the immediate context points back to Yeats's lines from *The Countess Cathleen*, the "soft liquid joy" of these "soft long vowels" flowing over Stephen's memory recalls the end of the previous section (5.2), where language is figured as liquid and mysterious, a bodily production that takes fluid form, even spilling into the text with the reproduction of the completed villanelle.[26] There is a kind of jouissance in its repetition: Stephen feels "a glow of desire" kindle his soul and fire his body as he imagines Emma, "the temptress of his villanelle," becoming "conscious of his desire"; her dark, languorous eyes return him to a state of rapture in which "[h]er nakedness yielded to him," causing "the liquid letters of speech, symbols of the element of mystery, [to flow] forth over his brain," just as the poem flows forth over the text.[27]

Onanistic implications throughout the section provide a comical subtext to the villanelle as a kind of linguistic ejaculation, the bodily production of Stephen's jouissance.[28] There is surely irony in these autoerotic undercurrents, but the underlying conception of language is central to the novel. Joyce's use of "soul" and "spiritual life" for the realm of fantasy recalls the climaxes to chapters 2 and 4, illustrating how language, sexuality, and fantasy are interwoven in *Portrait*; there is an implicit analogy between the imaginative ardor of sexual fantasy that issues in orgasmic ejaculation and the ecstasy of the spirit that issues in language. This analogy can be traced back from Emma's "nakedness yield[ing]" to Stephen's fantasy (242)—causing the poetic emission of the villanelle—to his earlier projection that "she would unveil her soul's shy nakedness" to an ordinary cleric, "rather than to him, a priest of the eternal imagination, transmuting the daily bread of experience into the radiant body of everliving life" (240). Here, the artist is portrayed as epiphanist, manifesting the sacred through the profane, and in a sense, Stephen's poem is itself an imaginative transmutation of everyday desire into a "eucharistic hymn," whose "ardent ways" combine passionate emotion, religious fervor, and flaming desire. Giving physical embodiment through "liquid letters" to immaterial fantasy, Stephen envisions poetry (< ποεῖν, to create) as incarnation: "In the virgin womb of the imagination the word was made flesh."

It has been suggested that Stephen's "dewy wet" soul is a euphemism for nocturnal emissions as he wakes from a wet dream, providing a humorous, down-to-earth interpretation of "the word . . . made flesh." The possibility is certainly implied, contributing to the satirical reading of Stephen, but at the same time it makes Stephen's doctrine of the logos comically real: language is literally incarnated through the physical embodiment of fantasy, the dewy distillation of thought. Effectively, Joyce suggests that an immaculate conception takes place each time thought arises in the imagination. As a literary product, Stephen's images naturally take shape in sounds and letters, a shape no less tangible, or potentially fertile, than his bodily emissions. This emphasizes the bodily incarnation of language, a literal interpretation of John 1.1–14, and this vision of the linguistic epiphany is strongly reinforced by descriptions of Stephen giving form to the villanelle through a cloudlike condensation of spirit.

The section opens with a series of decadent, almost Pateresque periods about Stephen's morning inspiration, leaving "His soul . . . all dewy wet" (235). "An enchantment of the heart!" Stephen thinks, recalling his dream, and also the phrase used by Luigi Galvani, which Stephen likens to "a spiritual state" produced by "the luminous silent stasis of esthetic pleasure" in his theory (235, 231). Recalling Shelley's description of the mind as a fading coal at the moment of poetic inspiration (235, 231), Stephen's aesthetic theory hovers behind the "instant of inspiration":

> The instant of inspiration seemed now to be reflected from all sides at once from a multitude of cloudy circumstance of what had happened or of what might have happened. The instant flashed forth like a point of light and now from cloud on cloud of vague circumstance confused form was veiling softly its afterglow. (235–36)

Again, the potential irony of Stephen's Romanticism in no way invalidates his epiphanic vision; rather, by undercutting univocal claims to truth, Joyce's *second degré* discourse multiplies significance, exactly as described: Stephen's "instant of inspiration" flashes forth like lightning and is reflected back on all sides from a "multitude of cloudy circumstance." These vague, oneiric clouds are both the source and reflection of Stephen's luminous inspiration; their light fills his spirit with "the purest water, sweet as dew" (235), and at the end of the section, the image of his muse, Emma,

> enfolded him like a shining cloud, enfolded him like water with a liquid life; and like a cloud of vapour or like waters circumfluent in space the liquid letters of speech, symbols of the element of mystery, flowed forth over his brain. (242)

Joyce's recurrent use of cloud imagery here, in which poetic inspiration is represented as a shining cloud of vapor that precipitates liquid letters, draws on Exodus, where God appears as "a pillar of cloud" by day and "a pillar of fire" by night to lead the Israelites to the promised land (13.21–22).[29] This Old Testament *shekinah* becomes increasingly important in *Ulysses* and *Finnegans Wake*, where cycles of water and light become dominant linguistic tropes. As this development indicates, Joyce reifies the heavenly apparitions offered by biblical clouds, which ultimately congeal into language. In *Finnegans Wake*, Issy, in the guise of "Nuvoletta" ("little cloud" [*FW* 157.8]), condenses into tears and urine, only to return, like Marvell's dew, to her heavenly source, and there is a similar cycle in *Portrait*, whose watery words return to their nebulous origins.

This cycling and recycling of language is most apparent in chapter 4, when Stephen draws "forth a phrase from his treasure":

>—A day of dappled seaborne clouds.
>
>The phrase and the day and the scene harmonised in a chord. Words. Was it their colours? He allowed them to glow and fade, hue after hue: sunrise gold, the russet and green of apple orchards, azure of waves, the grey-fringed fleece of clouds. No, it was not their colours: it was the poise and balance of the period itself. Did he then love the rhythmic rise and fall of words better than their associations of legend and colour? Or was it that, being as weak of sight as he was shy of mind, he drew less pleasure from the reflection of the glowing sensible world through the prism of a language manycoloured and richly storied than from the contemplation of an inner world of individual emotions mirrored perfectly in a lucid supple periodic prose? (180–81)

Here Stephen reflects on both the material and supra-individual properties of the remainder. The phrase is presented as a product of the body: in the treasure-house of memory Stephen stores precious words, prizing their shape and sound, and he draws them out by speaking them aloud. Phrase, day and scene (contextual and intertextual), harmonize "in a chord," which brings both the spatial dimension of geometric chords and the aural field of music into *ac*cord. This musicality is present in "the poise and balance of the period itself," a perfect line of iambic tetrameter (*a dáy of dáppled séaborne clóuds*) whose regular rhythm and alliterative opening are offset by the harmonious modulation of short and long vowels. It is significant that this "rhythmic rise and fall of words" is found in an apparently banal line of prose (the phrase comes from Hugh Miller's *Testimony of the Rocks*, a book on sacred geology), emphasizing that aural qualities are not the exclusive province of poetry.

For Stephen, every phrase has its rhythm, even when apparently devoid of sense: the "wayward rhythms" of lines like "The ivy whines upon the wall, / And whines and twines upon the wall . . . band and disband" as Stephen's "consciousness of language . . . ebb[s]" and "trickl[es] . . . into the very words" (193). Stephen dismisses the verse as "drivel," a waste bodily fluid "trickling" from his brain, but tellingly, this poetic "remainder" arises when Stephen finds himself "glancing from one casual word to another... in stolid wonder that they had been so silently emptied of instantaneous sense until every mean shop legend bound his mind like the words of a spell... as he walked on in a lane among heaps of dead language" (193). Echoing the Cork scene where Stephen "could scarcely interpret the letters of the signboards of the shops" (98), literary legends are reduced to pure materiality, "heaps of dead language," yet, paradoxically, they bind Stephen's mind like a spell (193).

Likewise, the associations of "legend and colour" mesmerize Stephen in "A day of dappled seaborne cloud," because the processes of reading (*legere*) and writing activate the legends, or stories of words through association. These associations emphasize verbal vitality, rather than Stephen's dead letters, illuminated by his choice of colors:[30] "sunrise gold" connects to the dawning of "a day"; "seaborne" suggests "azure" waves; the provenance of "greyfringed fleece of clouds" is self-evident. These correspondences imply that "dappled" is "the russet and green of apple orchards," and it is here that the "associations of legend" go with color, for etymologists compare "dappled" with Old French *pomelé*, and Old English "æppled," as in "æpplede *gold*" (*OED*). Skeat, quoting Wedgwood, regards the resemblance as accidental (perhaps because he focuses on apple-*grey*), but in the *OED*'s first citation, Mandeville describes the giraffe as "a faire beste, wele dappled" while the Cotton manuscript has "a best pomelee or spotted." Whether Joyce knew this source,[31] read it in the *OED* (first entry 1894), or discovered the connection elsewhere, "the russet and green of apple orchards" that color "dappled" reanimate the word with the associations of an obsolete legend.

As well as explaining the colors, the phrase explains what Stephen means by the associations of "legend": reading back through a written record to rediscover the story of a word. Seeking his own identity in the name of his forbear, Stephen Dedalus is as enthusiastic about etymology as the character he is derived from. In *Stephen Hero*, Daedalus, whose name is closer to the Greek, reads "Skeat's *Etymological Dictionary* by the hour" (32): "It was not only in Skeat that [Daedalus] found words for his treasure-house, he found them also at haphazard in the shops, on advertisements, in the mouths of the plodding public. He kept repeating them to himself till they lost all instantaneous meaning for him and became wonderful vocables" (*SH* 36). Again, Stephen's alexia is linked to both loss of meaning and heightened signification. Reduced to pure sound, phonemes become "wonderful vocables," an estrangement of sense that manifests the strange form of language. At the same time, Stephen finds "the plodding public" "strangely ignorant of the value of . . . words," while he is "hypnotised by the most commonplace conversation" because he *resists* semantic "reduction" and therefore hears "wonderful vocables" in the constituents of speech (*SH* 32, 36). This is a prime example of Lecercle's fourth proposition, where "[t]he language speaks, and meaning belongs to the community before it belongs to the speaker" (Attridge 2001, 65), which means that the words in Stephen's "treasure-house" embody both aspects of the remainder: materiality and the language of the community. Indeed, the doubly "wonderful vocables" are two manifestations of Joyce's linguistic epiphany, and both are present in Stephen's treasured phrase, "[a] day of dappled seaborne clouds"—although demonstration will require a diversion into Victorian philology.

Philology was one of the most dominant intellectual disciplines of the late nineteenth century, influencing new fields like linguistics, anthropology, and psychology. Stephen's own approach can be characterized as sacred philology: "Phrases came to him asking to have themselves explained. He said to himself: I must wait for the Eucharist to come to me: and then he set about translating the phrase into common sense. He spent days and nights hammering noisily as he built a house of silence for himself wherein he might await his Eucharist" (*SH* 36). Following two references to Skeat, here Stephen extends etymology into quasi-mystical reverence. Paradoxes abound: personified phrases seek their own interpretation; Stephen awaits communion with consecrated language but attempts to translate it back into "common sense"; he hammers noisily to build a house of silence. There is no way to resolve these contradictions, but it is interesting to note the conjunction of repetition and silence in Stephen's Eucharistic image of language, which gives a personal twist to one of the mainstays of Victorian philology: the idea that language embodies eternal truth and that etymology provides the means to discover it.

In the preface to his *Etymological Dictionary* (1882), Skeat concludes: "The speech of man is, in fact, influenced by physical laws, or in other words, by the working of a divine power. It is therefore possible to pursue the study of language in a spirit of reverence similar to that in which we study what are called the works of nature; and by aid of that spirit we may gladly perceive a new meaning in the sublime line of our poet Coleridge, that 'Earth, with her thousand voices, praises God'" (xii). Skeat's views can be explained by his turn to philology from theology, but he is not alone in his sentiments. Richard Chenevix Trench, perhaps the most popular and influential philologist of the nineteenth century, whose papers "On Some Deficiencies in our English Dictionaries" (1857) provided the impetus for the New (later Oxford) English Dictionary, held similar views.[32] In the first lecture of *The Study of Words* (1851), Trench urges his audience to "behold the great spiritual realities which underlie our common speech," for God has "pressed such a seal of truth upon language, that men are continually uttering deeper things than they know." As dean of Westminster, and later archbishop of Dublin (1864–1884), Trench believed that "God gave man language, just as He gave him reason, and just because He gave him reason; for what is man's *word* but his reason, coming forth that it may behold itself? They are indeed so essentially one and the same that the Greek language has one word for them both"—*logos*.[33]

Nevertheless, Trench stopped short of believing that all speech was divine. In *Proverbs and Their Lessons*, a book Joyce owned (Gillespie 1986, 240–41), Trench offers an extended commentary on the Latin proverb, *vox populi vox Dei*: "If it were affirmed in this that every outcry of the multitude . . . ought to be accepted as God's voice speaking through them, no proposition more foolish or more profane could well be imagined. But the voice of the people here is some thing very different from this. The proverb rests on the assumption that the foundations of man's being are laid in the truth; from which it will follow, that no conviction which is really a conviction of the universal humanity, but reposes on a true ground" (130). The difficulty for Trench is to discover "that true voice of humanity, which . . . we have a right to assume an echo of the voice of God," so as to be sure "that we have not taken some momentary cry, wrung out by interest, by passion, or by pain, for *the voice of God*" (131). Interestingly, this is exactly what Stephen does in "Nestor," when he hears the hockey players celebrate a goal and tells Mr. Deasy, "That is God . . . A shout in the street" (*U* 2.378–86), suggesting that Joyce extended Trench's view of the divine origins of language and the sacred truth of proverbs to every utterance.

It is significant that Joyce kept *Proverbs and Their Lessons* in his Trieste library while writing *Portrait*, for there are important similarities between Stephen's epiphanic vision of language and Trench's. Although Trench died when Joyce was four, in September 1904 Joyce shared the Martello Tower with Trench's grandson, Samuel (later Dermot) Chenevix Trench, who became the principal model for Haines in *Ulysses*. Joyce may have rejected Trench's Unionist politics and religion, but the connection to Dermot, the book he owned, and Richard's fame means there is every likelihood Joyce would have known of Trench's other work, especially his most popular book, *The Study of Words*. The first sentence of Trench's introductory lecture acknowledges the commonplace that in "worthy books are preserved and hoarded the *treasures* of wisdom and knowledge which the world has accumulated" (my emphasis). "[N]ot in books only," Trench continues, "but often also in words contemplated singly, whether they relate to highest spiritual things, or our common words of the shop and the market . . . , there are boundless stores of moral and historic truth, and no less of passion and imagination," from which "lessons of infinite worth may be derived" (1; cf *CW* 28, 29). Whereas *Proverbs and Their Lessons* expounds the moral teaching contained in the "treasure of our native proverbs," especially those drawn from "the rich treasure-house of the Eternal Wisdom," in *The Study of Words*, Trench regards all of language and literature as a source of treasured wisdom, much as Stephen Dedalus does in *Portrait*.

Indeed, the metaphor Trench uses to describe the buried treasure of language is revealing with regard to Stephen's reflections on language. Borrowing the phrase from Emerson, Trench characterizes language as "fossil poetry": "Just as in some fossil, curious and beautiful shapes of vegetable or animal life . . . are permanently bound up with the stone, . . . so in words are beautiful thoughts and images, the imagination and the feeling of past ages . . . preserved and made safe for ever. . . . Many a single word also is itself a concentrated poem, having stores of poetical thought and imagery laid up in it" (18–19). This concept of words as concentrated poems containing stores of ancient wisdom lies behind Trench's advocacy of etymology, first citations, and chronological accounts of semantic change for the *New English Dictionary*; it also sheds light on Stephen's conception of language in *Portrait*. The phrase Stephen recites, "a day of dappled seaborne clouds," is adapted from Hugh Miller's *Testimony of the Rocks*, whose subtitle, *Geology in Its Bearings on the Two Theologies, Natural and Revealed*, indicates Miller's purpose: by digging into the fossil record (the natural theology of the book of nature), Miller attempts to uphold the literal truth of the Bible. Attempting to explain how the earth could have been created in six days and have existed for little more than six thousand years, Miller interprets "the six days of creation as vastly extended periods" corresponding to geological ages. This endeavor to reconcile "the Geologic and Mosaic Records" leads Miller to essay "a *possible* poem," whose argument sketches out an epic vision of creation. On the first day, after the war in heaven, Lucifer and the fallen angels are expelled to "our present earth, existing as a half-extinguished hell" (275; cf. Gen. 1.1–5). Countless centuries roll by; land forms; volcanic activity subsides; plant life takes root; animals appear; the sixth day dawns, and we await the arrival of man (275; cf. Gen. 1:6–24). In wonder, Lucifer watches "scene [succeed] scene, and creation [follow] creation," "and when calling up in memory what once had been, the features of earth seemed scarce more fixed to his view than the features of the sky in a day of dappled, breeze-borne clouds" (277–78). Thus, the phrase Stephen recalls links earth and sky in a vivid image of protean transformation as the world takes shape. Each day and scene in Miller's account lasts eons, adding intertextual overtones to Stephen's reflection that "the phrase and the day and the scene harmonised in a chord." Like Miller, Stephen treasures "the rhythmic rise and fall of words," writing a "lucid supple periodic prose" that aspires to poetry.[34] Framed by invocations to Milton and Coleridge, Miller's account of creation is a vision of "poems that might be" (279); at its center, the "day of dappled, breeze-borne clouds" anchors Miller's epic vision in a precise, natural image. Representing creation in flux, the phrase synthesizes everything from the primeval creation of the earth upon the void to the "sublime revelation" when "man enters upon the scene" as "God, made manifest in the flesh" (278–79).

Joyce's choice of phrase for Stephen's treasure is surely not accidental. As a novel about the formative years of an artist, culminating in his first literary creations, and his final intention "to forge in the smithy of [his] soul the uncreated conscience of [his] race," there are various senses in which *A Portrait of the Artist as a Young Man* can be read as a creation myth. With his mythical links to Daedalus and Icarus, Stephen's mazes and imaginative flights are rooted in "the fabulous artificer" (183),[35] but the first epiphany also links him to Prometheus (*P* 4) and the creation of man. Stephen seeks his destiny in the mythological origins of his name while trying to forge a personal identity through the various roles he assumes—sinner, saint, artist manqué—each of which is presented as a spiritual rebirth. Yet he arrives at his poetic vocation only by growing into language, developing his craft to the point at which he can create his own self-portrait in the diary. And as Miller's phrase reveals, *Portrait*'s creation myths go beyond Stephen, touching on the creation of the wor(l)d.

In Miller's "poem," the whole history of creation passes before Lucifer's eyes in the moment before the birth of man; for Stephen, all of language is present like distant nebulae behind each epiphany of the word. Whereas Miller literally digs into the book of nature to unearth ancient fossils that will reveal the truth of scripture, for Stephen, language is a kind of "fossil poetry" whose etymological roots offer the promise of true meaning. For Miller, there are two sources of revelation: natural theology and the Bible; for Stephen, nature has to be read and interpreted ("Signatures of all things I am here to read" [*U* 3.2]), while not just sacred scripture but all of language becomes "a sudden spiritual manifestation." No matter how ordinary or banal the thought behind it, spoken language is literally in-spired (*inspirāre:* to blow or breathe into), and spirit is always incarnate in the word, whether through the physical embodiment of language or the diachronic networks of signification that stretch beyond any individual; both aspects pertain to the remainder, and both are present in Stephen's reflections on "[a] day of dappled seaborne clouds."

* * *

The material body of the word and its collective histories are present whenever Stephen reflects on language, because Joyce creates an image of language in the process of becoming, manifesting a "continuous affirmation of the human spirit" through each verbal production. From the beginning of the novel, the visceral impact of words is amplified by Stephen's nascent sense of their polysemy, from the two meanings of "belt" (5) to the "queer word," "suck" (8), and his extended preoccupation with "smugging" (42–45), whose meaning belongs to a community beyond the speaker. Smugging can mean to caress or fondle (*OED*), possibly even to copulate, as in Bob Doran "fornicating with shawls" (slang for prostitutes) "and hugging and smugging" them in "Cyclops" (*U* 12.803–7), but it is more common as a dialect term for juvenile petty theft (Hotten's *Slang Dictionary*). Both meanings are in play in *Portrait*, where the word carries an obscure sexual charge related to the boys' activity in the latrines (42–43), as well as being connected to the putative theft of altar wine or a monstrance from the sacristy (47). The latter is significant because the word can also mean stealing, copying surreptitiously, hushing up or arresting (*OED*): the boys have been arrested; their misdemeanor has been hushed up; having broken his glasses, Stephen copies his spelling crib surreptitiously (46); and Joyce has smuggled all these suggestions into a word whose powerful affect belies its uncertain origins.[36] In the midst of these reflections, Stephen returns, via Tusker Boyle, to Eileen's "long thin cool white hands . . . like ivory; only soft," providing a bodily explanation for "*Tower of Ivory*," just as her golden hair explains "*House of Gold*" (43; cf. 35), but it takes him many years to connect the materiality of the word "ivory" to a living tradition that makes the word shine "brighter than any ivory sawn from the mottled tusks of elephants. *Ivory, ivoire, avorio, ebur.*" Stephen's etymology, via French and Italian to Latin, is not a return to a "dead language" (193) but a recognition that language is "a complex coherent organism . . . that can maintain its identity as it grows and evolves in time; that can remember, that can anticipate, that can mutate" (Kenner 1979, 96). As Kenner says, "Latin is not a dead language; everyone in Paris speaks it, everyone in Rome, everyone in Madrid. The poetic of our time grows from this discovery" (Kenner 1979, 96), and in *A Portrait of the Artist as a Young Man* we see Stephen making it.

Linking the bodily production of language to its diachronic development, Joyce's linguistic epiphany is in the process of becoming. Miller's "day of dappled breeze-borne clouds" provides an image of the creation of the world, and Joyce's variations on the same phrase suggest that language is constantly in flux. Still thinking of the line, Stephen looks back along the bay to Dublin, which appears "[l]ike a scene on some vague arras [< a town in Artois, ca. 1400], old as . . . the thingmote," a large Scandinavean mound that stood in the center of Dublin until 1685. Gazing through language to the distant past, Stephen forms "an image of the seventh city of christendom" (perhaps recalling the seven churches, seals, and trumpets of Revelation), and then turns to "the slowdrifting clouds, dappled and seaborne. They were voyaging across the deserts of the sky, a host of nomads on the march, voyaging high over Ireland, westward bound. The Europe they had come from lay out there beyond the Irish Sea, Europe of strange tongues and valleyed and woodbegirt and citadelled and of entrenched and marshalled races" (181). Precursors of the migrating swallows in chapter 5, which are themselves figures of thought and language, these nomadic clouds convey waves of political and linguistic invasion: European vagrants slip into the strange tongues they speak, embodied in the contrast between Latinate terms ("valleyed," "citadelled," "entrenched") and those with Germanic roots ("woodbegirt," "marshaled"). Although the meaning and etymology of these words are distinct, the conjunctions and genitives seem to fold them together, as though Europe had one history and one language. This may explain why Stephen hears "a confused music within him as of memories and names which he was almost conscious of" as he tries to uncover the origins of these words, and why, although they keep receding from consciousness, "from each receding trail of nebulous music there fell always one longdrawn calling note, piercing like a star the dusk of silence" (181–82).

In this image, language is a kind of cloud-music whose trails blaze across the sky like shooting stars and whose long-drawn-out notes pierce the silence. Combining repetition and silence with trails of cloud and light (cf. Exodus 13.21–22), language is presented as a heavenly apparition. Stephen's "one longdrawn calling note" implies belief in unitary truth, but Joyce immediately undercuts this notion of transcendence with the cries of Stephen's schoolmates "calling" to him: "—Hello Stephanos! /— Here comes The Dedalus!" (182). Their calls put a different light on the "one londgdrawn calling note" Stephen hears, and by playing on his name ("Bous Stephanoumenos! Bous Stephaneforos!"), they put the notion of identity into flux.

This is crucial, because Stephen Dedalus seeks his identity in the meaning of his name. From the start of the novel, he is trying to answer Nasty Roche's question, "What kind of a name is that?" (5). Inscribing his jotter: "Stephen Dedalus / Class of Elements / Clongowes . . . / Ireland . . . / The Universe (12)," he tries to affix his name and place. Although he soon realizes that "there were different names for God in all the different languages," Stephen still thinks "God's real name was God" (13). Likewise, even when the boys call him in Latin ("Stephanos Dedalos!"), and mock him in Greek ("Stephaneforos"), Stephen believes in his destiny: "Now, as never before, his strange name seemed to him a prophecy" (183). His soul "soaring sunward," he vows to "create proudly out of the freedom and power of his soul, as the great artificer whose name he bore, a living thing, new and soaring and beautiful" (184). Yet the boys' banter, accompanied by unaffected whoops of joy (183–84), brings Stephen's artistic aspirations back down to earth, offering an epiphany in the here and now, rather than the mythical past or its predestined future. This is important, because even at his most triumphant moments of affirmation, Stephen is plagued with doubts ("What did it mean? . . . Where was his boyhood now? . . . where was he?" [183, 185]). These questions speak to Stephen's uncertainty, and his loss of connection to the past, suggesting that there is no stable identity to repose on, bringing us back to the "queer name, Dedalus," which, like Athy's queer name, poses a riddle.

This riddle raises two key points. First, the changing identity of the character named Stephen Dedalus provides *Portrait*'s most extended example of linguistic mutation, replacing fixed meaning ("one . . . note") with endless self-variation. As I have shown, this structure of repetition and variation is replicated throughout the text, creating an image of language in the process of becoming. For instance, in its final repetition, the "day of dappled seaborne clouds" merges with Stephen's vision on the strand, mirroring cloud and sea in chiastic silence: "the clouds were drifting above him silently and silently the seatangle was drifting below him." (185). This vision affects Stephen powerfully: "a new wild life was singing in his veins" (185), allowing the "wild angel" who calls his "soul . . . to recreate life out of life" to be traced back to the treasured phrase that inspired Stephen's vision of language and his vocation to "create . . . a living thing" (184). Yet Joyce's variations on Miller's line, which gradually mutates almost beyond recognition, mean that the image of linguistic creation it embodies is not one of original and permanent being but perpetual becoming.

Second, as Stephen seeks to forge himself, his language, and his race, he is constantly confronted by lack of identity, linguistic uncertainty, and the gap to the other. On a journey back to his ancestral homelands, when Stephen seeks his father's (and his own) initials in the anatomy theater, he is struck by the strange word "*Foetus*," whose engraved "legend" sends Stephen "beyond the limits of reality" (98). Maud Ellmann points out that the fetus is connected to Stephen's "strandentwining cable of all flesh" (*U* 3.37) at the navel, a scarified knot of the umbilicus (1982, 96–97). But this "scar" is also an aperture; like the hole in epiphany #19, it can open again, a powerful reminder of "the hole we all have here," which is also a remainder, the hole *in* language. And with this in mind, it is striking that the one word Stephen looks up, the word "tundish" whose origin he seeks, shares a structural similarity with the umbilicus. As the fetus is nourished through the umbilical cord, Stephen's tundish is a funnel or conduit to fill the lamp of the intellect. But since the lamp he refers to is, initially at least, the aesthetic illumination provided by "one or two ideas of Aristotle and Aquinas" (202), its light is the inspiration of language.[37] When the dean of studies tries to bring this lamp back down to Epictetus's homely objects of iron and earth, Stephen recalls the philosopher's remark that "the soul is very like a bucketful of water," and soon the words become fused with "the smell of molten tallow" as the dean of studies lights the fire. "[T]he jingle of the words, bucket and lamp and lamp and bucket," indicates the presence of the remainder in the chiastic repetition of empty words, although Stephen too is trying to ignite the fire of his intellect in answer to the dean's questions about his aesthetic theory. But this remainder, which at first seems devoid of meaning, becomes supersaturated with significance when the dean returns to the metaphorical lamp, advising Stephen to choose his authorities (i.e., his reading) with care: "You must choose the pure oil and you must be careful when you pour it in not to overflow it, not to pour in more than the funnel can hold" (203). Thus, language is figured as a liquid fuel that fills the bucket of the soul or lamp of the intellect—an image that is reminiscent of the "drops of water falling softly . . . into the brimming bowl" at Clongowes and the "liquid letters of speech" distilled from the "shining cloud" of Stephen's poetic inspiration (61, 242). In each case, language is presented as an epiphany through the incarnation of spirit in the word, but there is always a hole, a silent unknowable, whether in the virgin womb of the imagination, the immaculate conception of the word, the silence of the air, or the obscurity of the word "tundish."

Both Stephen and the dean dwell on the word, uttering it six times in twenty lines, with the dean vowing twice to look it up. At the end of the novel, Stephen records in his diary, "That tundish has been on my mind for a long time. I looked it up and find it English and good old blunt English too. Damn the dean of studies and his funnel! What did he come here for to teach us his own language or to learn it from us"[38] (274). This "little word" that turns the "rapier point of his sensitiveness" against the dean clearly has historical and political import. After eight centuries of English oppression, Stephen is right to feel sensitive, because the history of words *is* the history of their use, but at the same time, this linguistic history goes further than the colonial imposition of English on the Irish. It is not only to Stephen that the English language is "so familiar, so foreign"; however different the words "home, Christ, ale, master" on the dean's lips and Stephen's (a question of pronunciation, or the bodily production of the word, as much as Anglo-Irish history), "Christ" comes from the Greek, "master" is Latinate, "home" is Teutonic, and "ale" is as close to Gaelic as Anglo-Saxon. Nor is it by any means clear that "tundish" is "good old blunt English"; Skeat traces "tun" back to low Latin *tunna* (also found in

Irish), and "dish" is Latinate (from *discus*). Hence, the word is not simply a Shakespearian relic (cf. *Measure for Measure* 3.2.72) preserved by the Irish and forgotten by its colonial masters; its origins are uncertain, and no amount of etymological digging in the fossil records of language will unearth it. There is no single source or meaning; the word is founded on the void, and for all its symbolic significance as the conduit of light, spirit, thought, and power, Joyce suggests that it is in this silence, if anywhere, that the epiphany of language shows forth.

6

Permutations of Epiphany in *Ulysses*

Table 2 provides an overview of the epiphanies in *Ulysses*. All told, fourteen epiphanies are reused in *Ulysses*, the same number as *Stephen Hero* and two more than *Portrait*, debunking Scholes's assertion that "the epiphany seems never to have been in [Joyce's] recorded thoughts except in *Stephen Hero*" (1964, 72). In this section I outline the role of these epiphanies in *Ulysses*, showing that even as the epiphanies fade into the background, a ghostly trace of their imprint remains, like a watermark on the page.

The first epiphany in *Ulysses*, "She Comes at Night" (quoted on page 15, above), records a dream in which Joyce was visited by the specter of his mother (*MBK* 229–30). In the introduction, I showed how the dream-mother's knowledge of the "inmost heart" is alluded to but never revealed, creating a textual lacuna. The possibilities suggested are as "susceptible of change" as the figure in the epiphany, thereby exerting an "imaginative influence" over the reader as well as the text, and it is this symbiotic relationship between resonant hiatuses and semantic proliferation that characterizes Joyce's epiphanies. Reduced to their simplest form, the qualities that emerge from the dramatic and lyrical epiphanies are silence and repetition; and paradoxical though it seems, the two are interconnected.

This original structure is evident in the use Joyce makes of epiphany 34 in *Ulysses*. The epiphany is echoed four times in the opening twenty pages, resurfaces in Stephen's thoughts several times during the day (e.g., 9.439–40), and is explicitly recalled at the end of "Circe," a moment often considered the climax of the book. Stanislaus Joyce's account of the oneiric origins of the epiphany around the time of their mother's death (*MBK* 229–30) sheds light on the first appearance of the epiphany in "Telemachus": "Silently, in a dream she had come to him after her death" (1.112–13). But the passage in *Ulysses* fuses the epiphany with another dream, recorded under "Mother" in Joyce's Trieste notebook: "She came to me silently in a

Table 2. Epiphanies in *Ulysses*

Chapter	Major Use	Echoes and Allusions[a]
"Telemachus"		34. "She Comes at Night" (1.112–13, 270–79)
"Nestor"		34. "She Comes at Night" (2.139–50) 29. "Images of Fabulous Kings" (2.155–72)[b] 32. "The Race" (2.307–12)
"Proteus"		5. "Is That Mary-Ellen?" (3.70–75) 33. "They Pass in Twos and Threes" (3.205–15) 16. "An Arctic Beast" (3.300–309) 28. "The Ship" (3.503–5) 30. "The Spell of Arms and Voices" (3.503–5)
"Hades"	21. "Two Mourners" (6.517–20)	
"Aeolus"		33. "They Pass in Twos and Threes" (7.720–24)
"Scylla and Charybdis"		18. "The Stars on Joyce's Nose" (9.939–44)
"Wandering Rocks"		15. "The Lame Beggar" (10.239–56)
"Nausicaa"	38. "Is Mabie Your Sweetheart?" (13.64–74)	39. "The Lesson That She Reads" (13.107–27)
"Circe"	34. "She Comes at Night" (15. 4194–204)	32. "The Race" (15.3962–83) 35. "Fred Leslie's My Brother" (15.4795–97)
"Ithaca"		5. "Is That Mary-Ellen?" (17.139–41) 18. "The Stars on Joyce's Nose" (17.1256–58)
"Penelope"		15. "The Lame Beggar" (18.346–47)[c]

Notes: a. Numbers refer to those given in *WD* and *PSW*; the titles are taken from Beja (in Bowen and Carens, 712–13). Some of my examples are drawn from the previous source and McFadzean (229).

b. Beja and McFadzean detect thematic echoes here, though there are few repeated phrases. The same applies to epiphany #16 in "Proteus," #18 in "Scylla and Charybdis," and #39 in "Nausicaa."

c. Although there are no direct echoes of the epiphanies in "Penelope," "when I threw the penny to that lame sailor for England home and beauty" (18.346–7) recalls the coin flung to the one-legged sailor in "Wandering Rocks" (10.228–53), a passage that echoes epiphany #15, indicating how the epiphanies become woven into Joyce's text. I include this as a representative example; if indirect echoes were admitted throughout, the table would be extensive.

dream after her death: and her wasted body within its loose brown habit gave out a faint odour of wax and rosewood and her breath a faint odour of wetted ashes."[1] Comparing this passage with the scenes in "Telemachus" (1.112–15, 1.270–73) shows how similar the lines are, although the variations are equally revealing: in the first echo her breath becomes "mute, reproachful" (1.105), and in the second it is "bent over him with mute secret words" (1.272), suggesting a link to the silent, secret knowledge of the heart possessed by the ghostly mother in the epiphany. This connection is strengthened by Stephen's memories of "[h]er glazing eyes, staring out of death. . . . Her hoarse loud breath rattling in horror. . . . Her eyes on me to strike me down," the prayer, "*Liliata rutilantium*," and "Ghoul! Chewer of corpses!" in the following lines (1.274–79), all of which are recalled in quick succession when May Dedalus's ghost returns in "Circe" (15.4157–240). As with Stephen's earlier memories, the Nighttown apparition draws on the Trieste notebook (e.g., "*her breath of wetted ashes*" [15.4182]), as well as Mulligan's recriminations from the Martello tower episode, but the text is now centered on Joyce's epiphany: "Who had pity for you when you were sad among the strangers? . . . Years and years I loved you, O, my son, my firstborn, when you lay in my womb" (15.4197, 4203–4). Thus the two dreams, from the Trieste notebook and the epiphany, become fused in *Ulysses*, allowing the "silent word" uttered by the ghoul (15.4161) to suggest at once the "mute secret words" she breathes in "Telemachus" (1.272), the "inmost heart" of epiphany 34, and the "word known to all men" (15.4192–93), which may or may not be "Love" (9.429–30).[2]

The epiphany seems to be travestied in "Circe" ("Get Dilly to make you that boiled rice every night after your brain work" 15.4195, 4202–3), but at the same time, these realist details strengthen the mother's pleas for Stephen's repentance, while the ironic reappropriation of earlier lines (e.g., "Our great sweet mother!" [4180]) places the reader in the same position vis-à-vis the text as Stephen before the ghost, which only he can see. As with the closet scene in *Hamlet*, there is a gulf between what Stephen sees and everyone else does; readers are made aware of this gap (e.g., at 4208, when Florry says "Look! He's white"), providing a privileged perspective to judge the apparition (i.e., as the return of Stephen's repressed guilt) and his reaction to it. Likewise, differences between the scene in "Circe" and the textual details it repeats (notably those based on the epiphany) invite readers to analyze Stephen through the transformation from interior monologue to interior dialogue. Far from negating the significance of the epiphany, irony opens a gap in the text that allows meaning to proliferate. The effect is comic but not insincere; as Joyce told Budgen, "There's only one kind of critic I . . . resent. . . . The kind that affects to believe that I am writing with my tongue in my cheek" (108).

Ironic realism, derived from the dramatic epiphanies, plays a crucial role in "Circe," but the lyrical symbolism of epiphany 34 is also manifest in May Dedalus's reproach to Stephen: "You sang that song to me. *Love's bitter mystery*" (15.4189–90). This is the song Stephen hears Buck Mulligan sing in "Telemachus": "And no more turn aside and brood, / Upon love's bitter mystery; / For Fergus rules the brazen cars" (1.239–40). The following lines of Yeats's "Who Goes with Fergus?" are woven into Stephen's thoughts of "Woodshadows" and the "White breast of the dim sea" (1.242–45),³ providing another thread in the tapestry of repetition and variation that weaves Joyce's text, for not only is the image of the sea spun from Yeats's ("Wavewhite wedded words shimmering on the dim tide" 1.246–47), but a few lines later Stephen thinks of "Fergus' song: I sang it alone in the house, holding down the long dark chords. Her door was open: she wanted to hear my music. Silent with awe and pity I went to her bedside. She was crying in her wretched bed. For those words, Stephen: love's bitter mystery" (1.249–53). According to Richard Ellmann, in August 1903, as his mother lay on her deathbed, Joyce sang Yeats's lyric to her, accompanying himself on the piano, just as he had a year before to his dying brother George (*JJ* 141, 98), which explains why the ghost-mother in "Circe" accuses Stephen of killing her by singing "that song" (15.4189).

If Ellmann can be trusted, Joyce seems to have consciously patterned this repetition-in-death through Yeats's song, and, as I showed in chapter 2, he does the same thing in the epiphanies, four of which concern Georgie's death and three of which are related to the loss of his mother. In this context, it is tempting to think that the decaying chords Stephen desists from in *Stephen Hero* (168) are the same "long dark chords" he remembers "holding down" at the end of "Fergus' song" in "Telemachus," before going silently to his mother's bedside, just as the protagonist in *Stephen Hero* is bent over the keyboard "in silence" (*SH* 168; cf. epiphany #19) when his mother questions him about the "matter coming away from the hole in Isabel's . . . stomach." As I have shown, this navel is both a void—"The hole we all have /. . . . . here" (*PSW* 179)—and the "strandentwining cable of all flesh" (*U* 3.37); linguistically, it is both a hiatus (the referential hole in every signifier) and the opening in language through which all signs link up in the play of signification.

Earlier, I argued that these limits of language—referential indeterminacy and semantic proliferation—first come to the fore in Joyce's death epiphanies, and it is notable that the second major epiphany in *Ulysses* occurs in "Hades":

> Two mourners push on through the crowd. The
> girl, one hand catching the woman's skirt,
> runs in advance. The girl's face is the face
> of a fish, discoloured and oblique-eyed; the
> woman's face is small and square, the face
> of a bargainer. The girl, her mouth distorted,
> looks up at the woman to see if it is time
> to cry; the woman, settling a flat bonnet,
> hurries on towards the mortuary chapel.

Said by Stanislaus to have been written two or three months after May Joyce's funeral (*MBK* 235), Joyce reused this epiphany, with the minimum changes necessary to fit the past tense narrative, for Isabel in *Stephen Hero* (172), whose death is based on Georgie Joyce's. The "[t]wo mourners" at the beginning of the scene are hurrying to the "mortuary chapel," whose origins (*mortuus*) indicate the mortal nature shared by "all the living and the dead" (*D* 225).[4] Joyce emphasizes this continuity when he reuses the same epiphany for an unnamed child in "Hades": "Mourners came out through the gates: woman and a girl. Leanjawed harpy, hard woman at a bargain, her bonnet awry. Girl's face stained with dirt and tears, holding the woman's arm, looking up at her for a sign to cry. Fish's face, bloodless and livid" (6.517–20). David Hayman suggests that "'Leanjawed harpy' carries out some of the underworld themes of 'Hades,' besides being sharper and quicker than the first version" (Hart and Hayman 106). This stylistic change is equally evident in "Fish's face," which compresses a sentence of twelve words into a single phrase, drawing each syllable into focus.[5] Here, Joyce's cuts allow the piscan features to be attributed to either the girl or the woman, while the change of adjectives shifts attention from vehicle (the "discoloured" fish, with side-facing eyes) to tenor (where the tear-stained girl might seem pale or "bloodless," the rapacious bargainer "livid"). As in the original epiphanies, interpretations multiply, but this change is paradigmatic, cutting to the heart of the chapter. Revised from "discoloured," "bloodless and livid" suggests deathly pallor, embodying the shades of "Hades," but "livid" originally referred to a bluish, leaden color (Skeat) and can be applied to purple, red, black, or white, especially in relation to bruises (*OED*). In each case, discoloration is due to circulation: temporary breaks cause blood to drain from the face (white, "bloodless"); excess blood makes one "livid" with rage; ruptured capillaries trap blood beneath the skin, forming varicolored contusions. Again, indeterminacy allows associations to proliferate, and the ambiguity of "livid" brings out a vital connection to circulation, showing how a central rift sets the chain of signification in motion.

Circulation is the governing trope for this motion in *Ulysses*: blood circulates through the body, citizens circulate through the city, money circulates on the waters of civic finance, news is circulated by the organs of the press, words and letters circulate through the book.[6] The theme can be traced back to the digestive and generative cycles of "Calypso," or even earlier, to the textual and intertextual recycling that begins in the Telemachiad, but "Hades" breaks the cycle, introducing an underworld variation. Naturally enough, this break is occasioned by death, as Bloom pauses to wonder would Paddy Dignam's cut corpse bleed? "He would and he wouldn't," Bloom supposes: "The circulation stops," but "some might ooze out of an artery" (6.432–34). "[B]loodless and livid," the mourners embody this ambivalent condition in the land of the living, and this in turn leads to Bloom's thoughts on broken hearts "pumping thousands of gallons of blood every day. One fine day it gets bunged up: and there you are" (673–75): "The circulation stops." In a similar vein, "Aeolus" begins "IN THE HEART OF THE HIBERNIAN METROPOLIS" where trams circulate citizens along Dublin's arteries, "vermilion mailcars" put letters into circulation, and "A GREAT DAILY ORGAN" pumps (mis)information into the collective bloodstream (7.1–2, 16, 84; see M. Ellmann 2008, 55); but by the end of the chapter, the tramcars stand motionless in their tracks, "becalmed in short circuit" (7.1043–47), just as the end of Deasy's letter has been torn away (7.521), and Bloom's call to Monks, the dayfather, about Keyes's ad produces a break in the text, marked by the line of botched type ".)eatondph 1/8 ado dorador douradora" (16.1257–58). Notwithstanding the importance of circulatory systems in the symbolic economy of *Ulysses*, these breaks become increasingly dominant because they thematize the break in the text itself.

These breaks draw attention to the circulating system, allowing the material quality of each paralyzed element to be examined in isolation, like the eight lines of tramcars and trolleys individually enumerated at the end of "Aeolus" (7.1043–47); at the same time, they reveal the conditions necessary to set the circuit in motion. Hence, an analogy can be drawn between breaks in circulation and the silence and repetition of the epiphanies: both lead to an acute awareness of the materiality of language, coupled with heightened self-reflexivity as Joyce's text doubles back on itself. Together, this heightened materiality of the text and the self-reflexive awareness it manifests of its own textuality create the conditions for the linguistic epiphany.

The Epiphany of Language

Between these epiphanies of death, there is a telling echo in "Nestor." As the boys play hockey outside, Stephen is called into Mr. Deasy's study. While Deasy types out the end of his letter on foot-and-mouth disease, Stephen notices framed images of famous nineteenth-century racehorses, which remind him of an incident at the racetrack with Cranly, "hunting his winners among the mudsplashed brakes, amid the bawls of bookies on their pitches and reek of the canteen, over the motley slush. Fair Rebel! Fair Rebel! Even money the favourite: ten to one the field. Dicers and thimbleriggers we hurried by after the hoofs, the vying caps and jackets and past the meatfaced woman, a butcher's dame, nuzzling thirstily her clove of orange" (2.307–12). Although the general atmosphere of "The Race" has been retained along with similar phrases ("bawls of bookies . . . motley slush. . . . Nuzzling thirstily her clove of orange"), the passage has been substantially rewritten to fit its new context. The most significant transformation is that in *Ulysses* the scene is truncated: whereas the original epiphany ends with a marked contrast between "[h]uman creatures . . . swarming in the enclosure" and the romantic image of "[a] beautiful brown horse . . . flash[ing] far away in the sunlight" (*PSW* 192), Stephen's reverie is interrupted by the shouts and whistle of a goal outside, sending his thoughts back to his own boyhood among "battling bodies in . . . the joust of life." Recalling "that knockkneed mother's darling," Stephen sees himself in Cyril Sargent, tying this scene back to the history lesson ("Time shocked rebounds") and "She Comes at Night" (2.139–50). But as well as bringing back the past, the boys' shouts on the playing field echo forward to the moment Stephen counters Deasy's Hegelian view of history moving toward "one great goal, the manifestation of God" with his own view of God manifest in the hockey players' spontaneous shouts of celebration ("Hooray! Ay! Whrrwhee!)," which Stephen, feigning indifference, or perhaps uncertainty ("shrugging his shoulders"), generalizes to any vocal utterance: "A shout in the street." This deferral of the manifestation underscores both its arbitrariness and universality, suggesting that for Dedalus any moment is the occasion for epiphany, but equally the boys' shouts (2.313, 378) are echoed by the "shout in the street" (386), a vocal manifestation.

Joyce returns to this scene near the end of "Circe." With faint echoes of *Hamlet* 1.4, Stephen challenges his father to a battle of the spirits (15.3940–1), at which point a sleepy Simon Dedalus swoops down to castigate his son for "stabl[ing]" with Mulligan and Haines. In the hallucinatory hunt that follows, Stephen's fox, "having buried his grandmother," is pursued by a motley crowd that "bawls of dicers, crown and anchor players, thimbleriggers, broadsmen," while "hoarse bookies in high hats clamour deafeningly: . . . Card of the races. Racing card!" (3960–63). Soon after "A dark horse, riderless, bolts like a phantom past the winningpost," followed by a field drawn from the day's Gold Cup ("Sceptre, Zinfandel . . .") and the "Skeleton horses" from Deasy's wall ("Shotover, Repulse, . . . Ceylon"), with Garrett Deasy himself brandishing a hockeystick as he rides "Cock of the North" (3974–82). Like the shouts outside the window in "Nestor," Stephen's reverie, which condenses and displaces "The Race," is broken only by the sound of discordant singing beneath the window: "Hark! Our friend noise in the street" (3998), recalling Dedalus's vocal manifestation of God as a "shout in the street" (2.386).

Behind the complex web of repetition in this passage, a pattern emerges from the epiphanies. Echoes of "The Race" close the scene, while the airborne battle it begins with, pitting Stephen's "vulture talons" against his father's "buzzard wings," and his cries against his father's (e.g., "An eagle gules volant" [3948–49]), can be traced back to "Apologise" and "Upon Me from the Darkness." Moreover, the riddle of the fox (15.3952–53, 2.101–50) is connected to "She Comes at Night," which recurs soon after (15.4157ff), so that the first epiphanies in *Ulysses* are repeated in reverse order at the end of the "Odyssey" (episodes 4–15). Returning to themes raised at the beginning of the novel (mourning, love, religion, filial bonds), this chiastic structure provides a sense of closure at the end of "Circe," and following this mirroring, Stephen is finally able to free himself from the specters of authority.

Four moments, all connected to "She Comes at Night" and "The Race," can be identified in this break with authority: at the end of "Telemachus," with the prayer for his dead mother still ringing in his ears, Stephen rejects Mulligan's hold over him, vowing to return neither to the tower nor to his home (1.740); preferring a shout in the street to mammon or universal history, Stephen rejects Deasy's gods in favor of a shouted epiphany; the same faith, bolstered by recourse to Joyce's ur-texts, defends him against the internalized voice of the father, which threatens to break his spirit and his art; so when Stephen smashes the chandelier (15.4243–34), dispelling the ghostly apparition of his mother, his cry of "*Nothung!*" (needful, 4242) can be read as an attempt to exorcise the guilt he feels over her death, and for having left the Church, as well as a broader rejection of institutional authority. Morris Beja argues that this break from filial bonds creates the necessary space for Stephen to recognize Bloom "as his father," and following "the thematic unification achieved by this epiphany" all that remains is for Bloom to "recognise his role" (1971, 106–11). For Beja, "he does so in the most effective moment of vision in all of Joyce" (111), the apparition of eleven-year-old Rudy as Bloom stands guard over Stephen at the end of "Circe."

There *is* a sense of wonder here, but it is more ambiguous than Beja suggests. The "climactic epiphany" (Beja, 1971, 111) is not based on any of Joyce's extant epiphanies, and the connection between Bloom and Stephen is never overtly stated. Far from recognizing his father, when Bloom rouses the unconscious Stephen, the latter responds "Who? Black panther. Vampire," and the song he returns to reveals the grip of the dead: "Who . . . drive . . . Fergus now" (4932–43). Punctuated by ellipses, Stephen's last lines take him back to the loss of his mother, showing the repetitive drive of the death epiphanies. As Beja intimates, Bloom's vision of Rudy reading "from right to left inaudibly" is a distorted reflection of the poem Stephen "murmurs." When Bloom "calls inaudibly" to Rudy, he sees his son in Stephen, but the vision is filled with irony. Holding Stephen's hat and ashplant, Bloom sees Rudy wearing "a little bronze helmet" and "a slim ivory cane with a violet bowknot" (4936–67), and in the final line of the episode, Bloom sees a white lambkin peeping out of Rudy's waistcoat, having just undone the buttons of Stephen's waistcoat. These ironies are accentuated by Bloom standing guard "in the attitude of a secret master" and Rudy's apparition as "a fairy boy . . . , a changeling, . . . dressed in an Eton suit with glass shoes" (4957–58), adding humor to the scene while multiplying its significance through hybrid imagery (Masonic, Greek, Hebraic).

Bloom himself is "wonderstruck" by the vision, and after the climax of Stephen shattering the chandelier, and the abrupt fall to earth following his altercation with Carr, there is something wondrous about this resonant silence. Appearing almost artless, the moment is akin to Stevens's "The Snow Man," revealing "[n]othing that is not there and the nothing that is." The fact that it occurs in the wake of Stephen's "[n]*on serviam!*" (15.4228), as he lies semiconscious on the ground, suggests that only by breaking with traditional notions of epiphany as intense, climactic moments of revelation was Joyce able to extend his epiphanic aesthetic to the rest of his texts. For it is notable that from this point on, few epiphanies are explicitly reused in *Ulysses*; instead, in the final three episodes that constitute the *nostos*, or return, the epiphanic quality of language comes to the fore.

A good example of this generalization of epiphany is the echo of "Is That Mary Ellen?" in "Ithaca." Ellmann considers it a "major use," even though Joyce reduces a fourteen-line epiphany to a single listed item in *Ulysses*. Without contextual knowledge, the reader is more likely to associate this scene with "The Dead," but biographical evidence enables us to recognize the fire kindled by Stephen's "godmother Miss Kate Morkan in the house of her dying sister Miss Julia Morkan at 15 Usher's Island" (17.139–41) as the fire described in the "Mary Ellen" epiphany (*PSW* 274n; *JJ* 84, 286).[7] Several critics have noted the similarity between the fire in the epiphany and the fire Bloom kindles in "Ithaca" (17.126–33), as well as the series of "similar apparitions" Stephen thinks of—"others elsewhere in other times who . . . had kindled fires for him" (17.134–35), including Brother Michael in the infirmary at Clongowes (cf. *P* 21, 25), his father, his mother, and the dean of studies in *Portrait* (*P* 199ff; *U* 17.134–47). Of course, the dean's "art in lighting a fire" (*P* 200) is closely associated with Stephen's aesthetics and the theory of language he struggles to articulate in *Portrait*, so the recollection of this moment, along with the infirmary scene that culminates in "The Ship" and the fireplace on Usher's Island, points again to the relationship between Joyce's epiphanies and his aesthetics. Moreover, the obvious connection to "The Dead" indicates the role Joyce's epiphanies play in bringing back "others elsewhere in other times," including one's former self, for subjectivity, like language, is founded on a lacuna.

This structure of the self-replicating lacuna is reiterated in all of Joyce's epiphanies, and even as the epiphanies fade from the text, a ghostly trace of their imprint remains, like a watermark on the page. The following epiphany offers a good example:

> [Dublin: at the corner of
> Connaught St, Phibsborough]
>
> The Little Male Child —*(at the garden gate)*. . Na. .o.
> The First Young Lady —*(half kneeling, takes his hand)* —Well, is Mabie your sweetheart?
> The Little Male Child —Na . . . o.
> The Second Young Lady —*(bending over him, looks up)* —*Who* is your sweetheart?

In "Nausicaa" this becomes:

> —Tell us who is your sweetheart, spoke Edy Boardman. Is Cissy your sweetheart?
> —Nao, tearful Tommy said.
> —Is Edy Boardman your sweetheart? Cissy queried.
> —Nao, Tommy said.
> —I know, Edy Boardman said none too amiably with an arch glance from her shortsighted eyes. I know who is Tommy's sweetheart. Gerty is Tommy's sweetheart.
> —Nao, Tommy said on the verge of tears. (13.66–74)

None of the eight "Anatomies of 'Nausicaa'" in Benstock's *Critical Essays* (1989) mentions this epiphany: it has become practically invisible. Perhaps this is because the scene merits no more attention than Scholes paid in calling it "a showing forth of banality and vulgarity," an "insipid episode" easily translated to "Nausicaa" (*WD* 48). Yet the episode appears far from insipid when read as a comment on the role of desire in language acquisition. Tellingly, the first dialogue in the chapter shows Cissy Caffrey instructing baby Boardman to

> Say out big, big. I want a drink of water.
> And baby prattled after her:
> —A jink a jink a jawbo. (13.26–8)

A little later, Cissy tells baby to "Say papa," mimicking her own speech in infantile form: "Say pa pa pa pa pa pa pa" before being interrupted by the baby's attempt to do so: "Haja ja ja haja" (13.392). Joyce's phonetic representation of baby talk is humourously childish but also pleasurable, eliciting a kind of jouissance, because he evokes both aspects of "the remainder": language as a material product of the body, and the fact that meaning belongs to the community before it belongs to the individual.

Both these qualities manifest Joyce's linguistic epiphany, and in this context, the toddler's repeated syllables are as interesting for their form as their referential content. In the epiphany, the boy's reluctance to reply to the young ladies' questions is emphasized by ellipsis (". .Na. .o," "Na . . . o"). When the second young lady "looks up" (at the first?), one might think they collude in mocking him, which would explain his reticence, a reading strengthened by Edy's "arch glance" in "Nausicaa." Yet substitutions of the "sweetheart" suggest the endless deferral of desire, from which it follows that desire must be denied to be perpetuated, providing an alternative explanation for Tommy's paralyzed discourse, as he hypnotically repeats a single negative diphthong. However, "Cissy's quick motherwit" guesses that Tommy's tears are not related to the questions at all; the boy's symbolic negations are charged by a real need to urinate. Banal as it might appear, this is as good an example of *lalangue*, that meaningless, infantile babble by means of which Lacan claimed Joyce was able to graft the Symbolic order onto the Real, as may be found anywhere in Joyce.[8] The fact that it occurs in one of the most unremarkable epiphanies in *Ulysses* indicates that this endlessly circling rupture is a fundamental property of (Joyce's) language, everpresent in the simple repetition and variation of phonemes ("Habaa baaaahabaaa baaaa" 13.398) and the circulation of letters that constitutes writing (recall Wisdom HELY'S sandwich boardmen, with "apostrophe S" trailing behind). Indeed, the great cycle of life and death Bloom imagines in "Lestrygonians" always commences with the same repeated vagitus: "maaaaaa" (8.483), extending the first vowel indefinitely from its voiced bilabial origins into the newborn's first word, calling back the (m)other.

Mind the Gap

If the epiphanies in *Ulysses* become invisible, refined out of existence, one might wonder why Joyce chose to reuse them. Reasons of economy have been suggested, with some validity, but when this is reckoned solely as a saving in labor, the account is incomplete; there is also wastage involved in reduplicating texts, as Nora was quick to note.[9] In fact, both James and Stanislaus Joyce recycled paper, and many of Joyce's earliest fragments are preserved on the versos of other texts, such as Stanislaus's diary. This physical recycling provides a useful analogy with the way Joyce's epiphanies are reused in his later texts, including *Ulysses*, where they increasingly seem to remain within or behind or beyond the text, like God—or the artist—in *A Portrait*. However fleeting (e.g., "Mary Ellen") or unremarkable ("Is Mabie Your Sweetheart"), the epiphanies Joyce recycles create intertextual links, and since their phrasing is typically repeated (e.g., "She Comes," "The Race"), they also create *intra*textual patterns of repetition and variation.[10] Like *Portrait*, these variations weave the complex *entrelace* of the text as innumerable scenes and passages are interwoven through multiple threads of repetition, while different strands of the same motif allow associations to propagate. The end of "Proteus" provides a ready example as Stephen, with echoes of Hamlet leaving Ophelia, turns his head over his shoulder, "rere regardant" (*U* 3.503; cf. *Hamlet* 2.1.108–12) and sees "[m]oving through the air high spars of a threemaster, her sails brailed up on the crosstrees, homing, upstream, silently moving, a silent ship" (3.503–5). In the silent arrival of the ship, echoes of "The Ship" and "The Spell" may be heard, with all the resonance they accrue in *Portrait*,[11] but even if these epiphanies are not recalled, the structure of repetition and variation is evident: Joyce himself drew attention to the importance of the word "crosstrees," repeated in "Scylla and Charybdis" (9.496),[12] and DB Murphy, the memorable sailor who arrives on "the threemaster *Rosevean*" (16.450), recalls not only the ship and the themes of wandering and return (e.g., at 16.421) but also introduces a mini-cycle of epiphanic repetition since his first appearance in the "Wandering Rocks" episode clearly echoes epiphany 15 (10.239–53). This scene is itself echoed when he sings "*For England, home and beauty*" in "Eumaeus" (16.420) and again in "Penelope" as Molly remembers throwing a penny "to that lame sailor for England home and beauty" (18.346–7). Here, then, is another small but significant example of the lyrical-symbolic method Joyce devised in the narrative epiphanies, demonstrating how the Joycean text is composed of a tissue of repetition and variation, both intratextual and intertextual; in both cases, resonant gaps between similar but nonidentical passages allow imagery to proliferate (Benjamin 201–16; Miller 9).

However, there is a significant shift in emphasis between the epiphanic structure of *Portrait* and that of *Ulysses*. In *Portrait*, the nonidentical similarity between two textual elements (repeated and repeating) defines a gap between them, whereas in *Ulysses*, Joyce homes in on the gap itself, allowing textual limits to be defined from within. This can be understood as the difference between a traditional concept of repetition as the doubling of some preexistent whole (however inexact the copy) and the notion of "originary doubling" (Gasché 227). Gasché argues that subjectivity entails relating to oneself, which is only possible through a space of self-difference, so that doubled and double come into being simultaneously through self-reflection: an "originary duplication" (225–39).[13] Gasché's "General Theory of Doubling" extends to language, both in the act of writing or reading and within the signifying system (*différance*). Admittedly, it is hard to reconcile this abstract notion of repetition that originates in an act of spacing, or opening, with the linear text on the page, but as soon as one tries to theorize the creative act of writing, it seems clear that all texts arise from silence, from an imaginative space that precedes them, and that the writer typically assesses the words composed according to the accuracy with which they are perceived to represent some hitherto unarticulated thought.[14] This should not be taken to imply that writing represents preverbal thought; rather, I am suggesting that thought and language come into being together from a space of silence. And it is this space of silence, this originary act of linguistic creation, that Joyce reopens in the Ulyssean epiphanies.

To give a concrete example, consider "The Stars on Joyce's Nose" (quoted on pages 58–59, above). I analyzed this epiphany, and its relationship to the César Abín caricature, in chapter 2, but there is one moment I wish to return to: the curious gap between Sheehy's question and Joyce's response. Joyce's complete non sequitur, foreclosing the conversation, could be taken as a snub by Sheehy (who himself seems to be poking fun at Joyce), but instead this gap becomes the point of departure for a new turn in the dialogue. If one reads the text aloud, it becomes clear that the break does not function as a pause between utterances; rather, Joyce's studied response issues from silence, initiating a new turn. Joyce deliberately evades Sheehy's question; the force of his turn, in both its ordinary and linguistic sense, depends upon difference—a difference that also defers the question. This *différance*, arising from a silence in the text, is marked by the epiphanic phenomenon par excellence: the appearance of the stars. Twice "the stars" follow an ellipsis: in a momentary silence the "phenomenon" appears. Thus, far from ending the conversation, Joyce's unexpected observation opens a new cycle of repetitive dialogue orbiting around ellipses: phenomenon ... phenomenon ... star ... star ... phenomenon. The entire cycle issues from a silence in the epiphany, providing an early illustration of one of Joyce's major developments in *Ulysses*, where attention shifts from the gaps defined between iterations to the silence before speech. Before returning to these original silences, however, we need to consider how they are manifest in *Ulysses*, particularly through the celestial imagery that transforms the biblical epiphany of the star into a linguistic phenomenon.

"the heaventree of stars"

Ulysses is replete with celestial apparitions and epiphanic imagery, creating its own epiphany of the stars. For instance, when Stephen ascribes the significance of William Shakespeare's name to the fact that a new star appeared "as the signature of his initial" in the W-shaped constellation of Cassiopeia at the time of his birth,[15] Thomas Lyster, "the quaker librarian" (9.928–42) asks:

> Was it a celestial phenomenon?
> —A star by night, Stephen said. A pillar of the cloud by day. (942–44)

This "celestial phenomenon" may carry a trace of the "star ... phenomenon" in the epiphany, but the obvious allusion is to Exodus 13:21, where God appears to Moses and the Israelites "by day in a pillar of a cloud, to lead them the way; and by night in a pillar of fire, to give them light." This Old Testament *shekinah* is important in *Portrait*, and the same verse is cited repeatedly in *Ulysses* (e.g., 7.865–6, 15.1407, 17.1999), while clusters of related cloud and star imagery recur throughout, showing the significance of Old Testament epiphanies, as well as the apparition of the star in Matthew and Luke.

The most famous examples occur in "Ithaca," when Stephen and Bloom emerge silently into the penumbra of the garden to see "the heaventree of stars hung with humid nightblue fruit" (17.1039), and Bloom demonstrates various constellations, including Orion with its nebulous belt, and "new stars such as Nova," which appeared in February 1901 (17.1040–51). Indeed, among the "various features of the constellations" considered are "the condensation of spiral nebulae into suns" (1108)[16] and

> the appearance of a star (1st magnitude) of exceeding brilliancy . . . about the period of the birth of William Shakespeare over delta in the recumbent neversetting constellation of Cassiopeia and of a star (2nd magnitude) of similar origin but of lesser brilliancy which had appeared in and disappeared from the constellation of the Corona Septentrionalis about the period of the birth of Leopold Bloom and of other stars of (presumably) similar origin which had (effectively or presumably) appeared in and disappeared from the constellation of Andromeda about the period of the birth of Stephen Dedalus, and in and from the constellation of Auriga some years after the birth and death of Rudolph Bloom, junior, and in and from other constellations some years before or after the birth or death of other persons. (17.1118–32)

Here, with clear echoes of "Scylla and Charibdis," Bloom and/or Stephen extend the original epiphany of Christ to Shakespeare, themselves, Rudy, and anyone else; but quite apart from the questions of tone raised by this heretical appropriation of epiphany, which simultaneously bestows Christ-like significance on each human being and destroys the unique status of the Son of God, the imprecision of "some years before or after the birth or death" indicates a characteristically Joycean gesture, making epiphany both everpresent and arbitrary. This gesture is evident in Stephen's epiphany of God as "a shout in the street" (substituted, with a shrug, for shouts on the playing field [2.386]) and again in his conception of the world as God's book ("Signatures of all things I am here to read, seaspawn and seawrack, the nearing tide, that rusty boot" [3.2–3]).

How sincerely Stephen is supposed to believe in the vision of world and language he espouses is open to interpretation, but Joyce's text certainly undercuts the Romantic ideal of epiphany as something absolute, universal, and immanent—the Wordsworthian moment ever ready to appear. The chief difference is that Joyce foregrounds a void of meaning that has no place in the Romantic epiphany, and this hole undercuts the significance of Joyce's epiphanies even as epiphanic significance is extended to all phenomena. The hiatus I identified in "The Stars on Joyce's Nose" provides one example, but the linguistic world of *Ulysses* is riddled throughout by the same "incertitude of the void," as the word "phenomena" makes plain. In "Cyclops," for example, when Bloom tries to explain the "natural phenomenon" of "a morbid upwards and outwards philoprogenitive erection *in articulo mortis per diminutionem capitis*" (i.e., the hanged man's "poker," 12.464–65, 477–78), he is mocked for "his jawbreakers about phenomenon and science and this phenomenon and the other phenomenon" (466–67), a motif that is continued in the "hubbub of Phenomenon" answering Bloom's explanation of thunder in "Oxen" (14.424–28, 436) and the onanistic suggestions of the natural phenomena he recalls in "Circe" (15.2795–96, 3354–55). These manifest ironies undercut any claim to empirical certitude, drawing all phenomena down to the same level, just as every word is riddled with uncertainty. Yet the word "phenomenon" is derived from *phainein*, the same root as "epiphany," while in the plural it has a long-standing association with astronomy, suggesting that, notwithstanding their incertitude, all phenomena have universal significance.[17] These meanings are in play in the epiphany quoted above, as they are in "Ithaca," both in the list of "attendant phenomena" following the starbirth passage (17.1132–6, above) and in Bloom's expectation of an everyday epiphany:

> What prospect of what phenomena inclined him to remain?
> The disparition of three final stars, the diffusion of daybreak, the apparition of a new solar disk. (17.1256–59)

In this "diurnal phenomenon" (1262), epiphany has again been generalized, becoming both universal and arbitrary, for Joyce reminds us that epiphany takes place daily (in fact, at every moment, somewhere in the world), each time our closest star appears.

Œmissions

Stephen and Bloom have a shared interest in the stars, but they view the heavens quite differently. For Stephen, as we have seen, the apparition of

Tycho's star is a symbol of Shakespeare's literary stardom, whereas Bloom seeks to explain celestial phenomena scientifically. Stephen tends to symbolize the world through art, transforming experience into language, whereas Bloom seeks to reify symbols, making sense of language through empirical data. Thus, for Stephen, the significance of stars is figurative, whereas for Bloom they are literal, and Stephen seeks meaning in signifiers, whereas Bloom looks to the signified. The linguistic parallax between them is expressed most clearly in the difference between Stephen's fascination with proper nouns and Bloom's with phenomena.

Stephen's theory of *Hamlet* rests on the coincidence of a few proper nouns. The "celestial phenomenon" (9.942–43) that Stephen interprets symbolically is offered as empirical evidence of the revelatory significance of appellations. Having discussed Hamlet/Hamnet, Richard and Edmund, Stephen turns to the identity of the father/son/ghost/brother/maker ("He has hidden his own name, a fair name, William, in the plays. . . . He has revealed it in the sonnets where there is Will in overplus" [9.921–24]), and asks "What's in a name? That is what we ask ourselves in childhood when we write the name that we are told is ours" (9.927–28). As he "read[s] the skies" (939), finding "the signature of [W. Shakespeare's] initial among the stars" (931), this thought takes Stephen back to his own name, initials, and astrological "configuration," as well as the nicknames he had as a child ("Bous Stephanoumenos"), recalling his musings on the same theme in *Portrait*. "Your own name is strange enough," Eglington remarks, echoing Mulligan on the opening page ("your absurd name, an ancient Greek!" [1.34]), which brings back the mythical associations of Daedalus that Stephen dwells on in *Portrait* ("Fabulous artificer. The hawklike man . . . Lapwing. Icarus"), implying that the Stephen of *Ulysses* believes as fervently as his literary forbear that the meaning of a name will reveal the identity of its bearer.

If Stephen seeks the light of logos to illuminate experience, Bloom seeks to reify the signifier by determining its empirical referent. In "Nausicaa," for example, as dusk falls on Dollymount Strand, Bloom gazes up at the darkening sky: "A star I see. Venus? Can't tell yet. Two. When three it's night" (13.1076–77). Whereas Stephen's star is abstract, a symbol of William Shakespeare, Bloom gazes at real stars that serve to define the precise moment night arrives. This moment is clearly mirrored by Bloom's thoughts of daybreak in "Ithaca," announced by "the disparition of three final stars" (17.1257, qtd. above); in both cases, he may be thinking of the Talmud,[18] but the result is the same: beginning with phenomena, in the Kantian sense, Bloom seeks to attach a precise sensory experience to the words "night" and "day," as though all nouns could be made concrete. He applies the same strategy to foreign words, seeking familiarity in the material (e.g., "*Corpus*: body. Corpse" [5.350]), to dead metaphors such as Kernan's "inmost heart," which Bloom returns to its visceral organ (6.670–76), and to clichés like "stream of life" ("Because life is a stream" [8.95]) used in reference to the river Liffey, whose name means "life," and only by extension to the figurative flow of Dublin (8.88–95).

Both Stephen and Bloom seek a determinate relationship between signifiers and signifieds that will reveal the true meaning of the sign. In doing so, they seek a linguistic epiphany that corresponds to the Romantic revelation of the immanent. Yet Joyce's language continuously manifests the impossibility of achieving this revelation due to the arbitrary nature of the sign, while, paradoxically, the gap between signifiers and signifieds becomes the site of epiphany. This double gesture explains why the epiphanies in *Ulysses* seem arbitrary, meaningless, or ironic, and also funny, since Joyce's unexpected gaps of meaning possess endless potential to signify anew.

But signifiers can also be defined in relation to other signifiers, emphasizing formal and semantic relationships. These may be authorized by folk etymology or reference works, but regardless of status they are never fixed; they exist in a state of play, showing how signification is generated. In *Ulysses*, this playful approach characterizes Molly, who breaks unfamiliar words into their constituent letters and sounds, spinning new meanings from the threads she untwines, like Penelope weaving and unweaving her web—think of "met him pike hoses," for example. Faced with an unfamiliar word, Bloom tries the same approach: "Parallax. I never exactly understood . . . Par it's Greek: parallel, parallax" (8.110–12), and although his derivation rests on surer ground, he recognizes the similarity to Molly ("Met him pike hoses she called it till I told her about the transmigration" [8.112–13]).[19] As I showed in the last chapter, in *Portrait* Stephen is also fascinated by the sound and etymology of words (e.g., *kiss, suck, ivory, tundish*). In *Ulysses*, he rarely breaks words down; instead, they are given for us to decode. "[P]ostprandial, do you know that word?" [3.222] offers an easy example, but try "*Autontimorumenos*" or "*Stephanoumenos*" (9.939;

cf. *P* 182). These words come from the same passage on names in "Scylla and Charibdis," where Stephen plays on the materiality of his own name: "Stephen, Stephen, cut the bread even. S. D: *sua donna*." (9.940), showing how this kind of word play, common to children, leads to more complex nicknames like *"Bous Stephaneforos"* (*P* 182; *U* 9.939). This verbal invention becomes central to Stephen's "theolologicophilolological" portmanteaux (9.762), and however much we may suspect him (or his creator) of taking the piss here (the word is followed by *"Mingo, minxi, mictum, mingere"* [9.762], conjugations of the Latin verb *micturire, to urinate*), Joyce too discovers the common root of theology, logic, and philology in *logos*.

Stephen's, Bloom's, and Molly's shared interest in the materiality of language, along with the pleasure they derive from playing with sound, letters, and signification, is fundamental to the aesthetics of *Ulysses*, because as Joyce draws attention to the materiality of language, he shows phonological, graphological, and semantic change *in play*. Paronomasia, or wordplay, demonstrates linguistic change in real time, showing how verbal invention depends on difference—that is, difference *from* a recognizable unit of signification—and how this variation leads to formal change and/or new meaning. This procedure is so fundamental to Joyce's verbal invention that practically any line could be cited, but as a paradigm case, consider Molly's substitution of "omissions" for *e*missions when she recalls the doctor "asking me had I frequent omissions where do those old fellows get all the words they have omissions" (18.1170). The context is ambiguous, passing from bowel movements to menstruation (1163–70), and since Molly is seated on the chamberpot where the flow of her thoughts accompanies (1) the beginning of her menstrual cycle (1105–10), (2) her urination (1142–44), (3) recollections of "that white thing coming from me" (1152–53), and (4) her subsequent visit to Dr. Collins, a gynaecologist (1153–74), her "omissions" include a range of bodily secretions, including the secret of Boylan's emissions ("anyhow he didn't make me pregnant" [1123]) that she has omitted to tell Bloom. This extension from Molly's and Milly's emissions to Boylan's and Bloom's is authorized in the next section when she refers to Bloom's ejaculation as "his omission," compressing "a period of 10 years, 5 months and 18 days during which carnal intercourse had been incomplete, without ejaculation of semen within the natural female organ" (17.2282–84) into the change of a single letter. Besides their narrative significance, the bodily functions and desires expressed by this substitution provide a paradigm for the linguistic epiphanies in *Ulysses*, where a textual hole, an omission, in the body of the text emits, or disseminates, an unlimited stream of linguistic associations. In a word, œmissions.

"Remember your epiphanies . . . ?"

How do œmissions relate to epiphanies and their permutations in *Ulysses*? The answer is in Joyce's aesthetics, which, though not confined to the epiphanies, can be traced back to them, as Stephen does in "Proteus": "Remember your epiphanies written on green oval leaves, deeply deep, copies to be sent if you died to all the great libraries of the world, including Alexandria? Someone was to read them there after a few thousand years, a mahamanvantara. Pico della Mirandola like. Ay, very like a whale. When one reads these strange pages of one long gone one feels that one is at one with one who once" (3.141–46). The irony of this passage is frequently noted, but it is worth recalling that the first part is based on Joyce's comment to Stanislaus (*JJ* 113) and that as a young man Joyce modeled his character and his writing on Pater.[20] Clearly Joyce outgrew the florid style and aestheticism of *The Renaissance*, but his continuing use of the epiphanies, right through to the *Wake*'s ricorso, shows that he never outgrew their aesthetics. Indeed, the irony of *Ulysses* is a consequence of his epiphanic language—far from negating the significance of his early work, this passage contains, in nebulous state, a development of their aesthetics.[21]

The clue is Stephen's allusion to Hamlet mocking Polonius:

> Hamlet. Do you see yonder cloud that's almost in shape of a camel?
> Polonius. By th' mass, and 'tis like a camel indeed.
> Hamlet. Methinks it is like a weasel.
> Polonius. It is back'd like a weasel.
> Hamlet. Or like a whale.
> Polonius. Very like a whale. (*Hamlet*, 2.2)

Echoing Polonius echoing Hamlet, Stephen's "very like a whale" (3.144) can be read in a number of ways, positioning himself as mocker, mocked, or both; but the image of the protean cloud, and the protean language it precipitates, is central to the episode and the novel. Like their Danish ancestors, Stephen and Bloom view the same cloud from different perspectives, one of the clearest examples of parallax in the book. Stephen sees it artistically: just as he thinks of *Hamlet* in the "epiphanies" passage, he first sees the cloud colored by Yeats's "Who Goes with Fergus": "A cloud began to cover the sun slowly, wholly, shadowing the bay in deeper green" (1.248). By contrast, Bloom's first impressions, which occur at almost the same moment,[22] are more literal than literary: "A cloud began to cover the sun slowly, wholly. Grey. Far" (4.218). Thirteen hours later, when Bloom counts the stars and sees "nightclouds" metamorphose, unlike Stephen's literary symbolism, their transformations are brought back down to physical phenomena: "A star I see. [. . .] Two. When three it's night. Were those nightclouds there all the time? Looks like a phantom ship. No. Wait. Trees are they? An optical illusion. Mirage" (13.1076–79). Following Stephen's allusion to *Hamlet* in the "epiphanies" passage, it seems reasonable to assume that these lines echo the same scene, thereby implying a connection between Stephen's reflections in "Proteus" and Bloom's in "Nausicaa." As well as the star and cloud clusters discussed above, Bloom's "phantom ship" recalls the oneiric vessels in "The Ship" and "The Spell," whose imagery is echoed in the "silently moving" ship at the end of "Proteus." Indeed, the word "phantom," derived from *phainein*, is cognate with "epiphany," "phenomenon," and "fantasy"; like the phantom mother in "She Comes at Night," the fantastical phenomenon of Bloom's nightcloud is "susceptible of change."

Taken alone, these threads constitute a minor motif, but numerous parallels between the episodes bring out the pattern: Stephen and Bloom walk along the same strand, seeing the same objects—hoops, bottles, rocks, and so on—that lead them to closely related reflections; both fantasize about women on the beach (Stephen's midwives, Bloom's Gerty) before relieving themselves through the same bodily organ; and each episode climaxes with an act of writing that reflects the perpetual flux of language.

As one might expect, Bloom's text is more straightforward. Picking up a stick from the beach (to mirror Stephen's ashplant), Bloom writes a message in the sand:

I.
. . .
AM. A.
No room. Let it go.
Mr Bloom effaced the letters with his slow boot. (13.1258–66)

Bloom's unfinished message to Gerty suggests many endings, ranging from the confessional to the revelatory (e.g., Fritz Senn proposes "' . . . a cuckold,' ' . . . a naughty boy,' ' . . . alone,'" "an incomplete half of the Christ of Revelation (who is A *and* O, beginning and end)," and "a faint adumbration of a Jehovean I AM THAT I AM" [in Hart and Hayman, 294–95]). These biblical allusions suggest the epiphanic nature of the text, but it is an everchanging manifestation, in which *any* noun could follow the indefinite article: the gap in Bloom's text is both meaningless and limitless. Drawn from the resonant hiatuses of the dramatic epiphanies, Bloom's composition goes beyond them, and beyond the ephemeral nature of traditional revelations, to show the transience of the epiphany itself, effaced by Bloom even before the tide has a chance to wash it away.

The connections between Bloom's physical inscription, erased by his boot, and Stephen's protean poetry are manifold: "Signatures of all things I am here to read," Stephen thinks, for "these heavy sands are language tide and wind have silted here" (3.2, 288–89), foreshadowing Bloom's legend, while Bloom sees "rocks with lines and scars and letters" (13.1261) in the midst of writing his message in the sand, recalling the poem Stephen composed upon a rock. Similarly, the "bottle with story of a treasure in it" that Bloom sees (or imagines) recalls the "porterbottle" Stephen sees after remembering his epiphanies (13.1249–50; 3.152). Bloom's bottle probably wasn't "thrown from a wreck" (13.1250), just as Stephen's is unlikely to be a relic of the "lost Armada" (3.149); Stephen's is an empty "sentinel" of the "isle of dreadful thirst" (153–54), and Bloom's is an example of countless unknown objects encountered among "[a]ll those holes and pebbles on the beach" (1248–49). These echoes ensure that when the bottle becomes the imaginary repository of "a piece of paper" Bloom finds on the strand ("Letter? No. . . . Page of an old copybook" [1247–48]), the torn page recalls the poem Stephen writes on the torn end of Deasy's letter in "Proteus."

It requires careful reading to realize that Stephen is writing a poem in "Proteus," and it is only in the "???" section of "Aeolus" (some seventy pages later), when Myles Crawford asks who tore Deasy's letter, that we finally hear it:

On swift sail flaming
From storm and south

> *He comes, pale vampire,*
> *Mouth to my mouth.* (7.522–25)

These lines are recognizably Dedalian when we recall the words he scribbled on the blank end of Deasy's letter earlier in the day:

> He comes, pale vampire, through storm his eyes, his bat sails bloodying the sea, mouth to her mouth's kiss.
> Here. Put a pin in that chap, will you? My tablets. Mouth to her kiss.
> No. Must be two of em. Glue em well. Mouth to her mouth's kiss.
> (3.387–400)

Stephen's poetry is risible, but by emphasizing the physical properties of the fragment, and then reflecting back on it, Joyce creates a self-reflexive text. Its buccal image stems from the epiphanies, since Stephen's imagery is drawn from memories of Parisian prostitutes "shattering with gold teeth *chaussons* of pastry, their mouths yellowed with the *pus* of *flan Breton*" (3.214–15), itself based on epiphany #33's description of prostitutes eating pastries in Paris.[23] With some irony, Stephen searches for an ending in birth and death ("mouth to her moomb. Oomb, allwombing tomb"), but he winds up thinking "Why not endless till the farthest star? Darkly they are there behind this light, darkness shining in the brightness, delta of Cassiopeia, worlds" (408–10).

These lines take on greater significance in the light of Stephen's theory of names and literary stardom, but like the move from the unique star that heralds Shakespeare's birth in "Scylla and Charibdis" to the universally meaningless celestial events that accompany human life and death in "Ithaca," there is a move from the "word known to all men" that Stephen ponders in "Proteus" to the chameleonic language of "Rhymes and Reasons," where multicolored words exchange letters like garments:

> Mouth, south. Is the mouth south someway? Or the south a mouth? Must be some. South, pout, out, shout, drouth. Rhymes: two men dressed the same, looking the same, two by two.
>
> > . . . . *la tua pace*
> > . . . . . *che parlar ti piace*
> > *Mentre che il vento, come fa, si tace.*
>
> He saw them three by three, approaching girls, in green, in rose, in russet, entwining, *per l'aer perso*, in mauve, in purple, *quella pacifica*

oriafiamma, gold of oriflamme, *di rimirar fè più ardenti*. But I old men, penitent, leadenfooted, underdarkneath the night: mouth south: tomb womb. (7.714–24)

The Dantean rhymes (peace, pleases, falls silent) are significant, as is the context (*Inferno* 5), but Stephen seems to associate the interlocking rhymes of Dante's terza rima with the two old men, dignified and grave, in Dante's heavenly pageant (*Purgatorio* 29.134–35), while the verses come in threes, like the wings of the cherubim ("three and three") or the trio of brightly colored virtues (29.110, 121–29). Dressed in red, green, and white, they represent faith, hope, and charity, but the procession emerges from a "burst of incandescence," led by seven golden candlesticks emitting a spectrum of light (29.16, 43–78). This heavenly pageant, interpreted self-reflexively, connects the passage with "the prism of a language multicoloured and many-storied" in *Portrait*, explaining why Stephen's personified verses change color. In *Portrait*, Stephen imagined "A day of dappled seaborne clouds" glowing with "sunrise gold, the russet and green of apple orchards, azure of waves, the grey-fringed fleece of clouds" (*P* 180); here too, Stephen's feminine rhymes wear gold, russet, and green. But whereas Stephen's synesthetic vision of language in *Portrait* was founded on the idea of a singular meaning animating each word through all its changing forms—an identity that could be traced back to its etymological root—the metamorphoses of Stephen's rhymes in "Aeolus" point to a fundamentally protean view of language, in which the strandentwining cables of philology (the art of "Proteus") are not only hollow "navelcord[s]" but also link back to an original void ("no navel" [3.42]). Yet this notion of language as "Creation from nothing" (3.35) is anything but empty; like the carefully camouflaged heading, "Rhymes and Reasons," Joyce gives a positively plural spin (both/and) to the negative he plays off, *neither* rhyme *nor* reason.

Stephen's protean vision of language constantly coming into being, where chameleonic words change their appearance as easily as their significance, gradually becomes generalized to Joyce's text, permitting Stephen's reflections on poetry to become a self-reflexive poetics. In the cabman's shelter of "Eumaeus," Stephen stares at "nothing in particular" (Wallace Stevens would be proud), vaguely listening to a "synopsis of things in general," and hears "all kinds of words changing colour like those crabs about Ringsend in the morning burrowing quickly into all colours of different sorts of the same sand" (16.1141–45). Here again, Stephen's chromatic hearing pictures the physical form of language changing, and although we never see those crabs in "Proteus," Stephen's colored words burrowing into the shore recall his earlier reflection: "These heavy sands are language tide and wind have silted here" (3.288). With linguistic crustaceans burrowing down into the sand and rock sediment writ by the elements, Stephen's geological (geo, Earth + logos) transformations recall the "fossil poetry" of Trench and Miller, except that Stephen's "words changing colour" show that this process is not only diachronic, the long, slow process of language change, but also chameleonic, changing shades of meaning before our eyes.

Metaphorically decrepit, the tired "old" narrative of "Eumaeus" (Gilbert schema) is particularly rich in examples (see Senn 1995, 156–75). For instance, when Bloom misunderstands Stephen's scholastic use of the word "simple" to describe the incorruptible soul, Bloom feels "bound to enter a demurrer": "Simple? I shouldn't think that is the proper word. Of course . . . you do knock across a simple soul once in a blue moon" (16.756–65). Throughout "Eumaeus," Joyce comically, but conclusively, explodes the possibility of irreducible, incorruptible meaning, as even simple words like "simple" become anything but. In the following lines, Bloom provides a colorful figure for this anything but simple, anything but empty language of the shelter: "a horse of quite another colour" (16.770–71). Senn points out how the chapter, "in analogy to its phrasal horses, varies its colour," as does *Ulysses* (1995, 156–58). In this passage, for instance, the incongruity of Bloom's cliché makes the horse-image a kind of hologram,[24] since Joyce's modification defamiliarizes a relatively uncommon idiom, allowing it to latch onto more familiar Ulyssean metaphors. For example, Bloom is twice figured as a "dark horse" in "Cyclops" (12.1557–58), and the same phrase appears in "Eumaeus" when the 20–1 winner, "Throwaway recalls . . . Capt. Marshall's dark horse Sir Hugo" (16.1242–43). This recollection picks up on the "dark horse" who "bolts like a phantom past the winningpost" in "Circe," followed by a field including Deasy's spectral racehorses from "Nestor" and the runners from the day's Gold Cup. As well as coloring Bloom's clichéd horse with various equine shades, these echoes weave the passages based on "The Race" back into the account Bloom reads (16.1276–89), in which he, the "dark horse," is metaphorically associated with the winning outsider, Throwaway.

Picking up on mutations of the horse and the epiphany, Joyce's incorporation of real and fictional articles from the *Evening Telegraph* creates a high degree of self-reflexivity. In "Cyclops," Bloom is "on his high horse" (12.1798), and in "Eumaeus," he is "Nettled not a little by" his misnomer, "L. Boom," and "the line of bitched type": ".)eatondph 1/(ador dorador douradora," "not forgetting the usual crop of nonsensical howlers of misprints" in the notice of Paddy Dignam's funeral (16.1248–61). However, he is "tickled to death simultaneously by C. P. M'Coy and Stephen Dedalus B. A. who were conspicuous, needless to say, by their total absence (to say nothing of M'Intosh)," Joyce's cloaked representative. When Bloom points out the unreliability of print, seeing the day's events change before their eyes, he receives an extraordinary reply: "Is that first epistle to the Hebrews, [Stephen] asked as soon as his bottom jaw would let him, in? Text: open thy mouth and put thy foot in it" (1268–69). Picking up on Deasy's subject, foot-and-mouth disease, as well as Stephen's poem, "mouth to thy mouth" (Stephen has reason to think he may have put his foot in it by tearing Deasy's letter—see 7.521), the sentence also refers to the syntax of Stephen's question, delaying the preposition until he can open his mouth.

Here, by echoing the bodily production of speech in self-reflexive text, Joyce articulates a new aesthetic of errancy as the source of linguistic creativity.[25] This focus on creative uncertainty can be traced back to the resonant hiatuses of the epiphanies, but *Ulysses* goes much further than Joyce's earlier works in showing how the materiality of language begins to change the moment it is produced, like the baby talk of "Nausicaa," or the "[i]nked characters fast fading on the frayed breaking paper" of the freshly printed *Freeman's Journal* (6.160). In *Portrait*, Stephen prefers the word "phase" to epiphany, and *Ulysses* carries his aesthetic one step further, showing language in a state of flux, for even as meaning is produced, it is riddled with uncertainty. Instead of "dagger definition[s]" ("horseness is the whatness of allhorse" [9.84]), Joyce gives us linguistic horseplay, making the revelations in *Ulysses* increasingly comic, and this shift in the overall tenor can be measured by the change of organic metaphor: in *Portrait* Stephen earnestly seeks a new terminology to describe the processes of artistic conception, gestation, and reproduction but pointedly fails to find it, whereas "Oxen" uncovers a new word, the "postcreation,"[26] replacing the metaphor of reproduction with a new aesthetics of mutation.

172 · Panepiphanal World: James Joyce's Epiphanies

Mutation and Irony in "Oxen of the Sun"

Portrait's epiphany of language is an image of creation, *Ulysses*'s a self-image in mutation. The most explicit example in "Oxen" is its catalog of real and imaginary human deformities, including "aprosopia due to a congestion, the agnathia of certain chinless Chinamen," and "multiseminal, twikindled and monstrous births conceived during the catamenic period or of consanguineous parents—in a word all the cases of human nativity which Aristotle has classified in his masterpiece with chromolithographic illustrations" (14.968–77). In fact, *Aristotle's Masterpiece* mentions neither aprosopia (the absence or imperfect development of the face) nor agnathia (complete or partial absence of one or both jaws), but the reference to this pseudo-medical treatise on midwifery (not, it goes without saying, by Aristotle) is interesting because it is one of the works Bloom leafs through at the bookstall in "Wandering Rocks": "Mr Bloom turned over idly pages of *The Awful Disclosures of Maria Monk*, then of Aristotle's *Masterpiece*. Crooked botched print. Plates: infants cuddled in a ball in bloodred wombs like livers of slaughtered cows. Lots of them like that at this moment all over the world. All butting with their skulls to get out of it. Child born every minute somewhere. Mrs Purefoy" (10.585–90). A 1900 edition contains six plates that fit Bloom's description (e.g., figure 3), while earlier editions offer more explicit illustrations (e.g., figure 4), suggesting that Bloom's interest in the image is more likely to be prurient than anatomical, just as his interest in *The Awful Disclosures of Maria Monk* is probably salacious rather than puritanical. With its scandalous allegations of sexual liaisons between the nuns of the Hotel Dieu convent in Montreal and the monks of a neighboring monastery, whose offspring were baptized before being strangled and buried in the convent's basement, Monk's *Disclosures* (1836) belongs to the same anti-Catholic genre as Rebecca Reed's *Six Months in a Convent* (1835) and Edith O'Gorman's *The Escaped Nun* (1871). The latter, it will be recalled, is the novel Dick Sheehy asks Joyce if he has read in "The Stars on Joyce's Nose," prompting Joyce's turn to the celestial apparition. In "Wandering Rocks," the same non sequitur is made in reverse, from Bloom "pointing out all the stars and the comets in the heavens" (apparently oblivious to his wife's earthly infidelities) to Maria Monk's *Awful Disclosures*, marked even more clearly by a break in the text (see 10.567–86). This line of three asterisks (Joyce's characteristic section break) comes between sections 9 and 10 of the episode—that is, at the

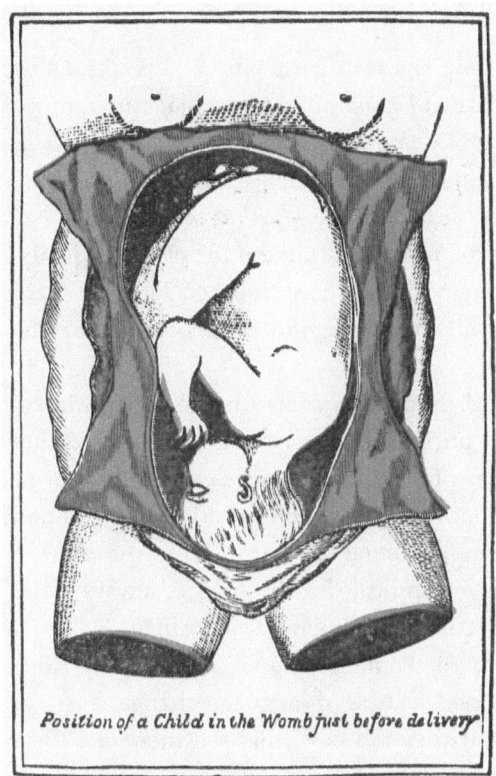

Figure 3. "Position of a Child in the Womb." *Aristotle's Masterpiece* (London: Published for the booksellers, 1900), plate 4.

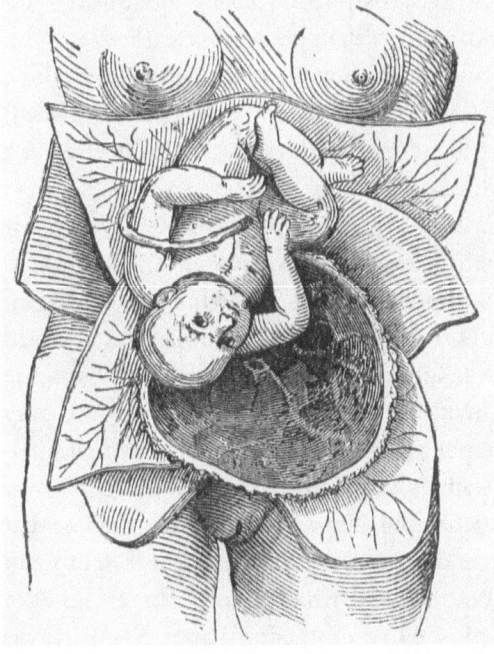

Figure 4. "Form of a Child in the Womb." *Aristotle's Masterpiece* (New York: Published for the trade, 1846), 16.

center of the episode (comprising eighteen parts plus a coda), and since "Wandering Rocks," which Marilyn French calls "a series of epiphanies of Dublin" (1976, 117), is often considered as the central episode in *Ulysses*, these stars centered on a white line can be regarded as the structural center of the novel. As with *A Portrait*, one could locate other centerpoints, such as the break between episodes 9 and 10 (treating the 18 episodes equally), a moment comparable to epiphany 18 and the stars at 10.584, for it marks a significant break in the text while remaining indissolubly linked to what has gone before.

This linguistic structure, and the aesthetic that develops from it, can be termed "mutation." On this principle, the very idea of pure repetition, of perfect reproduction, is sterile, for evolution, whether linguistic or organic, takes place through variation, introduced genetically by random mutation and linguistically through actual language use. In the realm of *parole*, at least, language is *never* identical, for the context always varies, leading to semantic, phonological, and orthographical change.

These mutations arise from the same gaps and silences that riddle Joyce's epiphanies. A fundamental feature of language change, they can be traced across his oeuvre, but they are particularly evident in "Oxen of the Sun." In a letter to Frank Budgen, Joyce describes the chapter as "a nineparted episode without divisions introduced by a Sallustian-Tacitean prelude (the unfertilised ovum), then by way of earliest English alliterative and monosyllabic and Anglo-Saxon" to Mandeville, Malory, the Elizabethan chronicle style, Milton, "and so on through Defoe-Swift and Steele-Addison-Sterne and Landor-Pater-Newman until it ends in a frightful jumble of Pidgin English, nigger English, Cockney, Irish, Bowery slang and broken doggerel" (*LI* 139–40). Joyce links this literary and linguistic progression with "the natural stages of development in the embryo and the periods of faunal evolution in general," showing how ontogenesis recapitulates philogenesis, both in an individual human fetus named Mortimer Purefoy and a single chapter in the history of English literature titled "Oxen of the Sun." Estimations of Joyce's stylistic imitations vary from virtuoso ventriloquism to poor pastiche, but regardless of their quality, studies of Joyce's sources, such as Saintsbury's *History of English Prose Rhythm* and Peacock's *English Prose from Mandeville to Ruskin*, concur that the *differences* between Joyce's rendition of, say, Anglo-Saxon English and the original are at least as great as the similarities. Indeed, Robert Janusko and James Atherton show that Joyce had no qualms about distorting his sources or introducing anachronisms into his history of English literature (Atherton, in Hart and Hayman; Janusko 1983, 58–60); in all probability, he did so deliberately, suggesting that he viewed the differences between model and imitation, or one period and another, as more fertile sources of literature than faithful reproduction. In a letter to Harriet Shaw Weaver, Joyce gives this principle the first and last word when he states that the nine-parted embryonic development of "Oxen" begins and ends with "a headpiece and tailpiece of opposite chaos" (*LIII* 16). In view of the governing metaphor of genesis, this chaos seems to represent something like the primeval chaos of creation, a chaos that itself stems from the void, so the entire episode (representing in miniature the history of English literature and the development of the English language) is flanked by two passages whose "opposite chaos" represents, in literary form, the incertitude of the void. Again, what we see here is not a gap being opened between repetitions but an originary gap from which linguistic representation emerges.

Yet perhaps the most striking feature of these sections at the beginning and end of "Oxen" is their opacity. Difficulty generates a chaos of meaning, and in opposite ways: the opening chiefly through its Latinate vocabulary and convoluted syntax; the ending by virtue of unfamiliar idiomatic phrases and the lack of deictic references with which to ascribe them to speakers. With painstaking labor, both passages can be restored to order (see Turner 1997; Mamigonian and Turner 2002), but this probably misses the point, since the immediate effect is to enforce an intense awareness of the materiality of language and the way in which graphic and aural similarities encourage the reader to produce meaning in or from uncertainty. By occluding (but never effacing) the referential function of language, Joyce forces readers to participate in producing whatever significance they find in "Oxen" directly from the material and significatory constituents of its language. This is a similar experience to that provided by the *Wake*, although there Joyce estranges the process even further by breaking those constituents down to phonemes and graphemes; he does so, I would suggest, to show that these hermeneutic processes are always at work, no matter how transparent a text may appear.

A typically jocoserious example occurs in "Oxen" as Bloom stares at a bottle of Bass ale, letting the voices of Stephen, Mulligan, Lenehan, Crothers et al. "blend and fuse in clouded silence" (14.1078). The voices Bloom hears return to the "infinite," all-encompassing space of silence (1079), a "clouded silence" in which his "soul is wafted over regions of cycles of generations that have lived," recalling both the end of "The Dead" and the "endless reverberation of the choirs of endless generations" Stephen hears in *Portrait*. These "cycles of generations" heard in the blended silence of unattended voices can also be read as the vast histories of language change that resonate behind each word, those endless echoes and repetitions that fill the clouded silence of our utterances. Although the entire passage is comically colored by Bloom's thoughts and De Quincey's prose, leading some critics to conclude that Bloom's "trance" is sheer nonsense, a parody of sententiousness, which lures readers into "looking for sense where possibly there is none" (Beckett 2006, 314), the serious substrata should not be dismissed. The twilight and dusk, scattering its perennial dew of stars, seems to parody the Celtic revival (along with Dedalus's poetry in *A Portrait*), but at the same time, star and cloud imagery, drawn from Exodus and a long tradition of biblical epiphanies, form leitmotifs in both *Portrait* and *Ulysses*, where they always occur in an epiphanic setting. In this case, the echoes of *Giacomo Joyce* ("a mare leading her fillyfoal" [*U* 14.1083])[27] point to the fragmentary, lyrical-symbolic quality of Bloom's reveries. Twice described as "phantoms," these figures must refer to Molly and Milly, but they also bring back other phantoms: Bloom's jumbled recollections of "Agendath" and "Netaim" (1086–87) echo back to "Calypso"; the "ghosts" of biblical and zodiacal "beasts," stalked by Parallax personified, are all phrases that haunt the text; and so it continues. Clearly Bloom is being satirized, all the more flagrantly when the red triangle of the Bass label transforms ("wonder of metempsychosis"!) into "the everlasting bride, harbinger of the daystar," mother Mary, thence to Martha, and finally to "Millicent, the young, the dear, the radiant . . . coifed with a veil of what do you call it gossamer" (14.1099–1104; cf. 13.1020); but at the same time, the passage contains epiphanic hints about the nature of writing, particularly in the "clouded silence" of the opening and the "mysterious writing" in the sky that concludes the passage (1078, 1107). The adverb "writhing," and the fact that "after a myriad metamorphoses of symbol, it blazes" back into the "ruby and triangled sign" on a bottle of ale leaves no doubt that this is ironic (1107–9), but that doesn't invalidate it. On the contrary, its full significance can *only* be conveyed through irony: far from being a single, determinate, or transcendental vision of the logos, the "myriad metamorphoses" of each symbol are central to Joyce's epiphanic vision of language, which means that the linguistic embodiment of this theory *must* contain the self-distanciating gap that irony provides.

At the structural level, divergence emerges as a key aesthetic principle, governing not only the difference between each part of "Oxen," its intertexts, and the preceding styles but also the remarkable diversity of Joyce's Odyssey, where each episode seems to embark on a break from its predecessors, just as the epiphanies form a set of discrete units whose gaps belie a dense network of interlacing repetition. When it comes to the function of irony, whether the stylistic imitations in "Oxen" are regarded as parodies, pastiches, or travesties is irrelevant; what matters is that there is a recognizable gap between each one and the text it is supposed to imitate. This gap creates tonal uncertainty by opening a distance between the surface meaning of the text (insofar as that can be ascertained) and what it is thought to imply. In its most general sense, irony always depends on this gap, and its recognition causes readers to double back and question the significance of the text just read. This potential for irony, or more generally, tonal ambiguity, to reveal the epiphany in *any* utterance explains why it is so central to Joyce's texts: through the internally echoing tonal resonance we call irony, Joyce writes self-reflexive readings into his texts, bringing heightened awareness to the materiality of language, its signification, and the gap between them, until the strange form(s) of language come to seem both devoid of significance and supersaturated with it.

* * *

In chapter 2, I postulated two limits of language: indeterminacy and semantic proliferation, whose central mechanisms are silence and repetition. To recapitulate, the dramatic epiphanies foreground silence through resonant hiatuses, while the lyrical epiphanies depend principally on repetition, but both modes go hand in hand, as *Dubliners* and *Portrait* make apparent. These stylistic poles remain evident in the first half of *Ulysses*, but as I have attempted to show, there is a significant break in Joyce's later treatment of epiphany. Whereas the previous works employed structures of repetition and variation to foreground epiphanic silences, in *Ulysses* Joyce homes in on the gap itself, showing how the text unfolds from an originary silence. The "Stars" epiphany provides a good example, both in itself and in the way that this text, though absent from *Ulysses*, seems to hover behind its epiphanic leitmotifs of star and cloud, as well as Stephen's and Bloom's reflections on language and names, their respective compositions in "Proteus" and "Nausicaa," and the three-starred break between the central sections of "Wandering Rocks." The structure of that episode is itself metonymic of the structure of the novel, which can in turn be compared to the structure of Joyce's original epiphanies (taken as a collection), while each of the fourteen epiphanies Joyce reuses in *Ulysses* replicates this structure in miniature, through features such as pauses and breaks in conversation or the mysterious lacunae left ringing by Joyce's prose-poetic mode.

The same could be said of the epiphanies reused in *Portrait*, but I have tried to indicate the evolution of Joyce's Ulyssean epiphanies in three ways. First, I showed how the central gap they stem from is thematized through Joyce's breaks in circulation—the stopping of the bloodflow in death, the short-circuiting of the tram system, breaks in communication caused by interruption, and so on. These breaks are analogous to the silence between repetitions in the epiphanies, but by singling out the *rupture*, Joyce deconstructs the circulating system of language, bringing a heightened, self-reflexive awareness of both the materiality of language and its limitless capacity to signify.

Second, I highlighted *divergence* as a stylistic and structural principle in *Ulysses*, governing the relationship of part to part, both within an individual episode (such as "Oxen") and between episodes; again, this divergence is a natural consequence of the gap between repetitions and can thus be traced back to the epiphanies, but it emerges as a new aesthetic of mutation in "Oxen," where Joyce celebrates diversion—even random, "artless" change—over perfect repetition (which is in any case shown to be impossible), because these gaps are the source of linguistic originality and vitality.

Finally, I have attempted to describe the actual process of coming-into-being that I call the linguistic epiphany. To reiterate, this process depends upon a gap becoming visible. In Joyce's epiphanies, as in *Dubliners* and *A Portrait*, the gap is typically produced in one of the following ways: a) through the difference between similar, but not identical, repetitions; b) by producing narrative hiatuses through ellipses, silences, pauses, euphemisms, and associated figures. In *Ulysses*, Joyce employs both these means, but increasingly, he also offers the reader c) a humorous or ironic recognition of a gap between what we expect to encounter and what we in fact read, and d) moments of self-reflexivity in which we reflect back on the text from a new perspective. Both these strategies differ from technique a) in that they do not depend upon a difference from some earlier textual instance and from b) in that the gap is not posited as something missing that we are invited to speculate upon but as something actually present in the text. The result of this is that Joyce invites the reader to reflect upon a gap that is *already present in language*—a gap that shares the same fundamental indeterminacy and semantic proliferation as the resonant hiatuses of the epiphanies. This gap can, in a sense, be called silence, but it is the silence *of* language, the silence that puts the endless cycle of repetition and variation that constitutes the signifying chain into play; by rupturing that chain, even if only for a moment, Joyce brings our attention back to the self-reflexive silence language stems from.

As a final illustration, consider the word "wimbles" from the end of "Aeolus": "DIMINISHED DIGITS PROVE TOO TITILLATING / FOR FRISKY FRUMPS. ANNE WIMBLES, FLO / WANGLES—YET CAN YOU BLAME THEM?" (7.1069–71). According to Stuart Gilbert, "wimbles" is an example of *hapax legomenon*, a word used only once. If this were true and the word carried no history, one would expect it to be unguessable, but in fact the physical sound and shape of the word are suggestive, and since it is paired with "Wangles" as a verb, the narrative of the "Frisky Frumps" already lies behind any attempt to decode its meaning. Moreover, the word does have a history, and it would seem unlikely that Joyce did not know it from other sources,[28] but even if he didn't, and even supposing the word had been used only once (like *moly* in Homer, famously), that still does not preclude or delimit its meaning, because as soon as we read the word, we immediately bring a range of interpretive strategies to bear (syntactic position, grammatical relations, etymology, aural and graphic similarities, contextual factors, and so on). As soon as a word is read, we attempt to decode it in relation to the signifying networks of the language(s) we know, so even a word like "wimble," which seems to rupture the signifying chain, is never a complete blank; instead, it *wimbles*, "boring *into*" language, and the holes it opens are the very openings through which it threads the interwoven strands of signification, "wimbling" the haybonds of language (*OED*). By deconstructing language in this way, Joyce suggests that no rupture in language is complete; even the most meaningless string of sounds or letters has the potential to generate signification, and the revelation of this vast, ancient, complex, fecund, *wimbling* system constitutes the linguistic epiphany.

Critics have long been at odds over the stylistic thread that connects *Ulysses* and *Finnegans Wake*. "Sirens," "Oxen," "Circe," "Eumaeus," and "Penelope" have all been proposed as prototypes for *Wakean* language,[29] yet throughout *Ulysses* Joyce brings attention to the teeming, cornucopian void of signification that forms the nucleus of his *Work in Progress*. This focus on incertitude and infinitude is first evident in the epiphanies, and their constant reworkings in *Portrait* and *Ulysses* attest to Joyce's intense preoccupation with these qualities of language; by homing in on the epiphanic gap between repetitions, the epiphanies in *Ulysses* begin a self-reflexive deconstruction of language that leads to *Finnegans Wake*.

7

The Panepiphanal World of *Finnegans Wake*

Introducing the work that brought "epiphany" to Joyce's readers, Theodore Spencer claims that "all of human history" is "epiphanised" in the *Wake* (*SH* 23), while Irene Hendry's seminal essay, "Joyce's Epiphanies," states that "Joyce's work is a tissue of epiphanies . . . from the briefest revelation in his lyrics to the epiphany that occupies one gigantic, enduring 'moment' in *Finnegans Wake*" (461). Since the 1970s, these claims have come under fire, even by authorities on the modernist epiphany, such as Morris Beja, who objects to the "common and persistent" tendency to refer to "an entire short story or even novel as 'an' epiphany—that *Finnegans Wake*, say, is regarded as a sudden spiritual manifestation." Beja points out that "no one who has actually read the book will easily say that it is in itself sudden . . . and the word *sudden* is the first one in Stephen's definition of epiphany" (1984, 719). However, Joyce's aesthetics are not necessarily the same as Stephen's, particularly by the time we get to *Finnegans Wake*, and even Daedalus's account of epiphany has three phases, including analysis, which demands spatial and temporal extension; while Spencer and Hendry's claims need qualification, they cannot be dismissed so easily. In this chapter, I reexamine the long-neglected link between Joyce's first literary compositions and his last, showing how both works offer an epiphany of language.

In *The Aesthetics of Chaosmos*, Umberto Eco argues that, in dialectical tension with chaos, Joyce replicates the medieval order of being, whereby everything is connected to everything else: "*Finnegans Wake* is that great epiphany of the cosmic structure resolved into language" (1989, 77). A similar view is echoed in Lucia Boldrini's study of Joyce and Dante: "In the language of the *Wake*, every word, theme, motif, and the book as a whole can be the occasion of an epiphany, the revelation of the essential nature of what is known, what pertains to everyday reality, to history, to myth" (138). Eco's and Boldrini's interpretations shift the site of the *Wakean* epiphany toward language, but they emphasize what it signifies ("the cosmic structure," knowledge, "everyday reality"), rather than signifiers themselves, and are thus not fundamentally different from Spencer's view that the *Wake* "epiphanise[s] . . . all of human history."

By contrast, for Giorgio Melchiori, the *Wakean* epiphany is shown forth through a "process of translation": "The language of *Finnegans Wake* is a constant epiphanisation of the current, familiar, obvious everyday language, by a process of translation that intensifies to the utmost its semantic values, so that the banal becomes memorable, the common word becomes a wonderful vocable. *Finnegans Wake* is a single, gigantic epiphany, the epiphany of the human language" (4). Many readers will object to the notion that "*Finnegans Wake* is a single, gigantic epiphany," but whatever justification there may be for Melchiori's "epiphany of . . . language" clearly depends on the nature of its "translation." Melchiori defines this broadly as "breaking up a linguistic pattern and recreating a new one" (5). He implies that every language act is translational, suggesting that the radical linguistic transformations of the *Wake* reveal something fundamental about "familiar, . . . everyday language," opening up the startling prospect that *Finnegans Wake* is not an eccentricity but "the central text in the Western literary tradition" (Attridge 1988, 233).

If it can be shown that *Finnegans Wake* reveals something essential about literary language—and indeed, language per se—then there is a rational basis for the proposition that *Finnegans Wake* offers an epiphany, or showing forth, of language. That is precisely what I intend to demonstrate by tracing the surprising similarities between the extraordinary language of the *Wake* and the ordinariness, or "vulgarity," of Joyce's epiphanies. Although several critics have applied the term "epiphany" to the *Wake*, no one, to my knowledge, has analyzed the way Joyce's ur-texts shape its language. In this chapter, I explore the connection between the two texts, beginning with the manuscript epiphanies recycled in *Finnegans Wake*, followed by the numerous passages that draw explicitly or implicitly on the traditional language of epiphany, before turning to *Wakean* language. In doing so, I use the word "epiphany" to cover a lot of ground, from Joyce's ur-texts, read against their classical and biblical contexts, to what I call the linguistic epiphany; but I do so of necessity, for in *Stephen Hero* and the letters, Joyce uses the term with the same latitude, covering both

Daedalus's theory and his own praxis, where epiphanies are manifestations of language.

Epiphanies in *Finnegans Wake*

Litz notes one epiphany in *Finnegans Wake* (*PSW* 273), with Beja adding two "notable similarities" (1984, 712–13). Four more can be identified, bringing the total to seven (see appendix). In some cases, these echoes are reduced to a single word, indicating that the epiphanies occupy a relatively minor place in *Finnegans Wake*, yet the fact that Joyce reused at least seven, decades after they were written, demonstrates his continued interest. Despite their fleeting presence, the gradual development, or unfolding, of the linguistic epiphany that I have traced in previous chapters continues in Joyce's last work, manifesting the central qualities of Joyce's epiphanies (silence, repetition, materiality, self-reflexivity) in the epiphanic language of the *Wake*.

As with *Ulysses*, the most striking epiphany in *Finnegans Wake* is "She Comes at Night," recording a dream in which Joyce was visited by the specter of his mother (*MBK* 126). Joyce echoes the epiphany in Shem's response (as Mercius) to Shaun (Justius) at the end of 1.7:

> Pariah, cannibal Cain, I who oathily forswore the womb that bore you and the paps I sometimes sucked, you who ever since have been one black mass of jigs and jimjams, haunted by a convulsionary sense of not having been or being all that I might have been of you meant to becoming, . . . it is to you, firstborn and firstfruit of woe, to me, branded sheep, pick of the wasterpaperbaskel, . . . dweller in the downandoutermost where voice only of the dead may come, because ye left from me, because ye laughed on me, because, O me lonly son, ye are forgetting me!, that our turfbrown mummy is acoming (*FW* 193.33–194.22)

The speech heading and stage direction ("Mercius (of hisself)" [193.31]) suggests that Shem is referring to both himself and Justius (*his* self) as "Pariah, cannibal Cain" (193.32), in the same way that Justius speaks "(to himother)," beginning "Brawn is my name and broad is my nature," before addressing Shem directly: "Macadamson [son of Adam's son, or perhaps his two sons, Cain and Abel], you know me and I know you" (187.24–36).

Of course, the theme of fraternal rivalry and affinity, embodied in Shem and Shaun, runs right through the *Wake*, providing one of the clearest examples of Giordano Bruno's principle of the *coincidentia oppositorum*. But by the end of the passage, Shem's voice begins to flow into ALP's: "our turfbrown mother is acoming, alpilla, beltilla, ciltilla, deltilla, running with her tidings, all the news of the great big world" (194.22–24), which suggests that the next chapter, "Anna Livia Plurabelle," is in some ways a continuation or response to the epiphanic end of 1.7. This makes good sense in relation to the original epiphany, which describes the apparition of a ghostly mother in the third person ("She comes . . . She comes . . . She knows . . ."), before turning to the first person when she speaks: "I am susceptible of change . . . Who has pity for you when you are sad among the strangers? Years and years I loved you when you lay in my womb." Whereas these words are ostensibly spoken by the mother in the epiphany, here they are spoken by the Shem/Mercius figure who merges with both Justius/Shaun and ALP. Yet the references to "firstborn" and "O me lonly son" in the *Wake* echo "Circe" more closely than epiphany #34 (cf. "Years and years I loved you, O, my son, my firstborn, when you lay in my womb" [*U* 15.4203–4]), which suggests that, as well as the references to Stanislaus (Shaun), and the memory of George Joyce, the brother-double figure is partly based on May Joyce's firstborn, John Augustine Joyce, who died on December 1, 1880, little over a year before James Augustine was born. This might explain why Mercius "forswore the womb that bore you and the paps I sometimes sucked," and why he is "haunted by a convulsionary sense of not having been or being all that I might have been of you meant to be becoming." It may be stretching the interpretation to suggest that May Joyce's lost firstborn is born again as James Joyce, but ultimately it doesn't matter whether the passage is addressed to Joyce's dead brother or not, for the specter of John Augustine Joyce is only one apparition of a general principle in *Finnegans Wake* whereby original and reproduction are indistinguishable and identity is tied to alterity. In "She Comes," the dream-narrator is projected into the voice of his mother, while *Finnegans Wake* embodies these principles in Shem and Shaun: opposites who can exchange roles (e.g., 2.2) and are at times inseparable. Whether identical (as in *The Comedy of Errors*, which Joyce plays on), or dizygotic (i.e., two-yoked, as in Castor and Pollux), the twins are both split and doubled, reflecting on both themselves and each other, like Issy's refracted image, which provides a figure for the language of the *Wake*.

As I have shown, there is a powerfully self-reflexive quality to this epiphany, which is preserved in *Finnegans Wake*. Indeed, 1.7 is the most self-reflexive chapter in the book. From the first line, "Shem is as short for Shemus as Jem is joky for Jacob" (169.1), the autobiographical aspect of Joyce's self-portrait, split between Shem and Shaun, is apparent; in the epiphanic passage at the end of the chapter, "jimjams," as well as being slang for delirium tremens, clearly points to James Joyce, and there are dozens of references of this kind. Much of the chapter consists of an amusing parody of Joyce's life, including his early poverty, self-imposed exile, notorious drinking (not forgetting his penchant for Fendant du Valais, or "Fanny Urinia" [171.29]), and his eye problems. Joyce refers to virtually all of his own works in the chapter, including "chambermade music" (*Chamber Music*, 184.04), "eggshells" (*Exiles*, 184.04), and "a certain holy office" (190.14), as well as Shem stippling "endlessly inartistic portraits of himself" (*Portrait*, 182.19), "making believe to read his usylessly unreadable Blue Book of Eccles, *édition de ténèbres*" (*Ulysses*, 179.27–28), and his cunningly disguised list of titles from every story in *Dubliners* (185.13–186.15). In this context, it is telling that the chapter ends by going back to the origins of Joyce's work, the epiphanies, and that this epiphany is the only text to be substantially incorporated into Joyce's *Wakean* autobiography.[1]

I will return to the materiality of 1.7, epitomized by Shem writing "over every square inch of the only foolscap available, his own body," with ink concocted from his bodily excretions (185.14.37), as well as the self-reflexivity of the text (that is, reflections in and on the language of *Finnegans Wake*, as opposed to autobiographical or biographical allusions). Before turning to these qualities, however, it will be useful to consider how the other epiphanies are reused.

In addition to "She Comes at Night," Morris Beja identifies two "similarit[ies] worth noting" (#6 and #16 at *FW* pages 352–53 and 15–16, respectively [1984, 713]), although it would be nice to know exactly where he sees the similarity. The closest connection to "An Arctic Beast" I can find is on page 17, between the "[c]ountlessness of livestories . . . netherfallen by this plage, flick as flowflakes" (*FW* 17.26–28) and the "white mist . . . falling in snowflakes" from the start of the epiphany, but the "flowflakes" could also echo the end of "The Dead."[2] As for "Half-Men, Half-Goats," there is a reference to "the mangoat" at 353.2, which, following the "sulphuring" hell and "the pungatories of sin praktice" (352.37–353.1) recalls Joyce's "hell" epiphany, particularly as it is reused after the sermons in

Portrait; however, the same passage includes a "shittery pet," a werewolf ("lou garou"), a "sabre tooth" tiger, a bear ("Ussur Ursussen": Lat. *ursus:* bear) and "a bull in a meadows" (*FW* 353.29–353.13), so the satyrs of epiphany #6 are only one manifestation of these "confused forms."

Besides these, there are several epiphanies in *Finnegans Wake* that have not been noted. The first is on page 10, where, as Margot Norris points out, "the big wide harse" of Wellington's horse (10.21) may be derived from Bennett, the "whitearsed bugger" in "Circe" (*U* 15.4796–97; Norris 1976, 133); what she doesn't note is that the colorful phrase from Nighttown is a direct recycling of Eva musing on her brother Fred Leslie in epiphany #35: "O, 'e's a whoite-arsed bugger" (*WD* 45). Similarly, in the Games chapter, Glugg's second guess (*FW* 233.21–26) recalls not only "Nausicaa," as McHugh notes, but also the "Sweetheart" epiphany (cf. *U* 13.66–74; *WD* 48); in each case, catechistic dialogue connects infantile language and erotic secrets (sweethearts in the epiphany and *Ulysses*; the color of Issy's underwear in *FW* 2.1), suggesting that language manifests desire, a characteristically Joycean epiphany. These are little more than passing references, a particular word or phrase Joyce echoes from his earlier work, but they are unmistakable. There may be others (e.g., an echo of "Apologise, / Pull out his eyes" from epiphany #1 in "apullajibed" [*FW* 317.31], the oracular hole of epiphany #19 at 323.5–6, or a rhythmical chime of "She Comes" at 548.10–12), but they are little more than echoes, of the same order as the similarities Beja notes to epiphanies #6 and 16. With the exception of "She Comes at Night," it is clear that the epiphanies Joyce reuses in *Finnegans Wake* are not nearly as central to its structure, themes, or style as those in *Stephen Hero*, *Portrait*, or *Ulysses*. Nevertheless, the fact that Joyce used seven epiphanies in the *Wake*, up to thirty-five years after they were written, shows their continued importance to him, and a final example shows wherein their importance lies.

Clive Hart identifies three levels of dreaming in *Finnegans Wake*, followed by a mystical awakening in Book 4. These correspond to the three Viconian ages (Divine, Heroic, Civic), followed by a *ricorso*, and they also map onto the "microcosmic syllable," AUM:

The four constituent parts of the word represent the four state[s] of consciousness:

A	The Waking State
U	Sleep, disturbed by Dreams

M	Deep Sleep
SILENCE,	. . . a higher plane of consciousness—a state in which the 'adept'
or ECHO	can apprehend the Real Self and the true nature of Being. (97)

Whatever one thinks of Hart's dream-cycles, the philosophy of the Upanishads, or Theosophical mysticism, there is no doubt that Joyce was interested in the "holy syllable," as shown by the benevolent mockery of Russell in "Circe" ("Aum! Baum! Pyjaum!" [*U* 15.2275]) and the extensive notes on "Om" in Joyce's copy of Heinrich Zimmer's *Maya der indische Mythos* (Connolly 1957, 42–47). But Hart goes further, suggesting that "Joyce was aware of these categories of consciousness very early in his career," citing "a sentence from *A Portrait* which names the last three and implies the first: 'Faintly, under the heavy night, through the silence of the city which has turned from dreams to dreamless sleep as a weary lover whom no caresses move, the sound of hoofs upon the road'" (97). In fact, this sentence (and the entire April 10 diary entry in *Portrait*) is taken, almost word for word, from "Hoofs upon the Dublin Road," whose next sentence describes how "the silence is cloven by alarm as by an arrow," while at the end of the epiphany, the hoofs echo distantly (*PSW* 37). What interests me here is the silence being sundered and reunited (cloven, in both senses) by echoes, like the fourth stage of Aum, where "the last overtone of the syllable dies away into *laya* (dissolution), the boundary between a faint hollow echo and true silence" (Hart 96). Whether "true silence" exists is debatable, but Hart points out that in the Hamsa Upanishad "the *laya* is paradoxically described as having a sound like a peal of thunder" (96), which provides an explanation for "the shocking silence" of the *Wake* (393.25). In any case, Hart convincingly demonstrates that when "Justius concludes his denunciation of Shem with the yawning religious formula: '*Insomnia, somnia somniorum. Awmawm*' (193.29), . . . Shaun is intoning the holy syllable" (Hart 103). Indeed, the first three words "seem to represent respectively the Waking State, Sleep (with Dreams), and Deep Sleep," while "'*Awmawm*' may also include the word *maunam*, meaning 'silence'" (Hart 103). This echoing silence can be traced back to the cloven silence of the epiphany; "Awmawm" is Justius's last word, emphasizing its physical sound and gesture through a kind of ritual incantation whose long-drawn final syllables are intoned while pointing "the deathbone" and stilling "the quick" (193.29);[3] and this speech act is immediately followed by Mercius's reply, based on "She Comes at Night," so that in these lines we see the key characteristics of *Finnegans Wake*'s epiphanic language: silence, repetition, materiality, and self-reflexivity. I will analyze each of these aspects after considering the importance of such passages in the *Wake*.

Epiphanic Passages in *Finnegans Wake*

Readers drawn into the *Wake* tend to become ensnared in a mesmerizing web where "every pun and portmanteau word . . . is related to every other via a proliferating and multidimensional network of connections" (Clark 1990, 746).[4] One consequence of this work-wide web is that specific qualities of its language, such as materiality, self-reflexivity, silence, and repetition, cannot easily be isolated from the whole (which is in any case dynamic), but in an attempt to order the "chaosmos of Alle" (*FW* 118.21), I will divide the epiphanic passages of the *Wake* into those where (a) the word "epiphany" is present, or the traditional language of epiphany is invoked, and (b) notebook passages, sometimes called "epiphanoids" (Hayman 1990, 27), which have been compared to the epiphanies. Since my primary interest is the language of epiphany, I will focus on (a), but first I want to briefly consider the case for (b).

Perhaps the most general and widespread example of Joyce's epiphanic method in *Finnegans Wake* is his continued practice of incorporating real-life revelations, especially through "the vulgarity of speech or of gesture" (*SH* 216). In 1.7, we hear how "All the time [Shem] kept on treasuring with condign satisfaction each and every crumb of trektalk, covetous of his neighbour's word" (172.30–31). Eugene Jolas recalls Joyce telling him, "Really it is not I who am writing this crazy book. It is you, and you, and you, and that man over there, and that girl at the next table" (400), a remark that brings to mind Gogarty's account of Joyce "slipp[ing] politely from the snug . . . to make his secret record" of conversation. Gogarty's objection "to be[ing] an unwilling contributor to one of [Joyce's] 'Epiphanies'" was not ungrounded, for Joyce wrote about him in "Is that for Gogarty," and perhaps Gogarty's snide remark, "Which of us had endowed [Joyce] with an 'Epiphany' and sent him to the lavatory to take it down?" (293–95, qtd. in *WD* 7), was not so wide of the mark, for in "Shem the Penman" we hear how Shem, "with help of the simulchronic flush in his pann" (simultaneous (and chronic) flash in the pan/flash in the brain/flush in the toilet) "scrabbled and scratched and scriobbled and skrevened nameless shamelessness about everybody ever he met" (182.11–14).

There is good evidence that Joyce continued this practice in *Finnegans Wake*, recording hundreds of similar jottings for his *Work in Progress*. David Hayman calls these moments "epiphanoids," defined as "a brief notebook entry that records something overheard, intercepted, perceived . . . that reveals an internal (personal) dynamic of such force as to solicit its preservation in language" (1999, 27). According to Hayman, there are at least five hundred epiphanoids, some of which "are very close to the early epiphanies" (e.g., Buffalo VI.A.271, qtd. in Hayman 29), although he underlines that they are not "sudden spiritual manifestation[s]"; rather, they reveal the "quasi-realistic underpinnings" of the *Wake*, as Joyce made use of everything that came his way in "the creative manipulation of lived experience" (41). Hayman's attempt to distinguish entries based on Joyce's own experience from literary quotations or factual records is problematic, since many of the passages Hayman calls "epiphanoids" were in fact copied from newspapers and other texts rather than spontaneous conversation.[5] Yet Hayman regarded "lines taken from newspapers and other printed texts as functioning for Joyce precisely as would personal observations" (27), so the distinction is not critical. Whether "fragments of colloquy" or quotations, and whether a page long or a single word, each of these notes records material for composition. One might see a difference between Joyce recycling epiphanies almost verbatim in his first novels and jotting down single lexical items for his later works, but the difference is quantitative, not qualitative: in *Finnegans Wake*, for instance, epiphanies are reduced to a single word (e.g., "apullajibed" [317.30]). Indeed, this spectrum suggests that the broad range of manuscript materials Joyce drew on, from the epiphanies to the *Finnegans Wake* notebooks, can all be regarded as "relics of the workings of the mind," "memorable phases" and phrases from Joyce's *Umwelt*, or "extended mind" (Van Hulle 225–27). As Van Hulle points out, the change from epiphanies to notes is gradual, not sudden, suggesting an underlying continuity, so that one can still make a case for epiphanoids. However, there are practical difficulties with this approach, because the "extended mind" of *Finnegans Wake* occupies thousands of pages of notes and drafts (*JJA* 28–63). Rather than working from manuscripts to text, therefore, I will begin with the published version, concentrating on passages that employ either the word "epiphany" or its traditional language.

The most important of these passages is the Berkeley and St. Patrick vignette in Book 4, based on the legendary contest of doctrine between saint and druid. Drafted from July to August 1923, it is one of the earliest sections Joyce composed for *Work in Progress* and a key stage in the evolution of Wakean language. The first version begins with the archdruid explaining "the illusion of the colourful world, its furniture, animal, vegetable and mineral, appearing to fallen men under but one reflection of the several iridal gradations of solar light, that one which it had been unable to absorb while for the seer beholding reality, the thing as in itself it is, all objects showed themselves in their true colours, resplendent with the sextuple glory of the light actually contained within them."[6] As Pierre Vitoux has shown, although the archdruid is called Berkeley in the second and fourth drafts, his theory is based on Newton's *Opticks*, where Newton concludes, much as the druid does here, that color is not an innate property of objects but rather that "bodies become coloured by reflecting or transmitting this or that sort of rays more copiously than the rest; it is to be conceived that they stifle in themselves the rays which they do not reflect or transmit" (4.116, qtd. in Vitoux, 171). This explains "the illusion of the colourful world," whose "furniture" (Berkeley referred to the totality of material objects as the "furniture of the earth" [McHugh]) appears as "one reflection of the several iridal gradations of solar light," while "for the seer beholding reality, the thing as in itself it is," objects reveal the "true colours" of the wavelengths they absorb (which are naturally invisible). "To eyes so unsealed King Leary's fiery locks" appear "the colour of sorrel green, His Majesty's saffron kilt of the hue of brewed spinach, the royal golden breasttorc of the tint of curly cabbage," since orange and green are opposites, but the patriotic blinkers of the druid make a farce of his own theory as he sees everything through green-tinted glasses, including the "azure eyes" and "violet" features of King Leary.

In the fourth draft (August 1923), Joyce keeps the gist of Berkeley's theory while adding considerable complexity:

> Tunc. Bymeby, bullocky vampas tappany bobs topside joss pidgin fella Balkelly, archdruid of islish chinchinjoss in the his heptachromatic sevenhued septicoloured roranyellgreenlindigan[7] mantle finish he show along the his mister guest Patholic with alb belongahim the whose throat hum with of sametime all the his cassock groaner fellas of greysfriaryfamily he fast all time what time all him monkafellas

with Same Patholic, quoniam, speeching, yeh not speeching noh man liberty is, he drink up words, scilicet, tomorrow will recover will not, all too many much illusiones through photoprismic velamina of hueful panepiphanal world spectacularum of Lord Joss, the of which zoantholitic furniture, from mineral through vegetal to animal, not appear to full up together fallen man than under but one photoreflection of the several iridals gradationes of solar light, that one which that part of it (furnit of heupanepi world) had shown itself (part of fur of huepanwor) unable to absorbere, whereas for numpa one puraduxed seer in seventh degree of wisdom of Entis-Onton he savvy inside true inwardness of reality, the Ding hvad in idself id est, all objects (of panepiwor) allside showed themselves in trues coloribus resplendent with sextuple gloria of light actually retained, untisintus, inside them (obs of epiwo). (611.4–24)

The first version, written in relatively straightforward English, clearly mocks the druid, and it could be argued that the fourth draft simply dresses up the same illogical theory in borrowed raiments, but equally, Joyce's transformation of the passage, and his multilingual additions, bring out one of the central problems in the *Wake* through the complex relationship between language, light, and color. As we have seen, Joyce drew on Dante for images of the word as an infinitely varied spectrum, "reflect[ing]" and refracting "the glowing sensible world through the prism of a language multicoloured and richly storied" (*P* 180–81; *U* 7.713–24). Lucie Léon recalls Joyce asking her for detailed information about shades and ranges of colors, saying that he intended to use them in the *Wake* (15). He did so in many ways, from Issy's underwear to the rainbow girls, but the most striking chromatic image of all is Berkeley's "hueful panepiphanal world," a phrase that reaches back to the original meaning of epiphany as literal illumination, later generalized to an apparition, manifestation, or showing forth. This suggests that the all-manifest world as it appears to us through visible light is an illusion, veil ("velamina" in Latin [611.10]), or spectral play ("spectacularum" 611.11: spectrum, spectacle, from *spectaculum*, play), whereas for the leading paradoxical seer, "the true inwardness of reality, the Ding hvad in idself id est" is shown through the "light actually retained" in "all objects." Joyce's transformation leaves no doubt that this is Kant's Ding an sich, the noumenal thing in itself (as well as the Freudian unconscious, and perhaps the whatness [in Danish, *hvad* means what] or quidditas of Stephen's epiphany, when the object appears as "that thing which it is" [*SH* 218]),[8] and it is obvious that the "light actually *retained*" (611.23–4; my emphasis) in the object can no more be perceived than Kant's noumenon. Thus, the paradox of the "hueful panepiphanal world" is that, while the words suggest an all-visible, all-manifest apparition, Balkelly's polychromatic world is a phenomenal illusion, forever hiding its "true colours." This condition is summed up succinctly in the fourth of Joyce's parenthetical insertions, "(obs of epiwo)," which, reducing the earlier abbreviations ("furnit of heupanepi world," etc.), condenses numerous possible meanings: the *objects* of the epiphanal world (cf. "objects (of panepiwor)" 611.22), *observation* of these visible objects (whether real or illusory), and the *opposite* or *obverse* of the phenomenal world—that is, a hole in appearance.

It is not just the resonance of Joyce's "panepiphanal world" that makes this passage so important; as Joyce told Budgen shortly after *Finnegans Wake* was published, "Much more is intended in the colloquy between Berkeley the archdruid and his pidgin speech and Patrick the archpriest and his Nippon English. It is also the defence and indictment of the book itself, B's theory of colours and Patrick's practical solution of the problem" (*LI* 406). Out of context (Budgen's letter is lost), Joyce's reply raises more questions than it answers: what charge is being brought against *Finnegans Wake*, and what might justify it? Is Berkeley's theory offered as the defense to Patrick's indictment, and if not, how are the druid-priest pair related to the juridical terms? Yet perhaps it is fitting that there are no answers, leaving the significance of the colloquy to the book a question of equivocation. Seen in this light, Berkeley's theory of colors is analogous to Joyce's Wakean language: polychromatic, shimmering, and playful but also elusive and perhaps illusory, veiling words in a "heptachromatic mantle," so that any interpretation we may wish to impose is as subjective as the green-tinted glasses with which Berkeley views his panepiphanal world. Indeed, the wor(l)d of *Finnegans Wake* is panepiphanal in just this sense, for any hermeneutic lens will present the text in a new light; and no matter how clear one's vision, there is always a blind spot on the retina. Once again, the ambiguity is typical of Joyce's epiphanies, whose endless capacity for signification is founded upon referential uncertainty, so that if the book is charged with obscurity, as it so often was, then it is Joyce's illumination of this very obscurity—like the unseen spectrum of light in all that is visible or manifest—that constitutes its epiphanic defense.

Whereas Berkeley, clad in a pure white "heptochromatic mantle," splits white light (unity) into an infinitely varied spectrum (diversity), before challenging "guest Patholic" to see "that with pure hueglut intensely saturated," everything is "tinged uniformly" green, Patrick's "practical solution" is syncretic, cleverly unifying Berkeley's nationalism and his worship of light, along with a dash of Judaism, into the Christian doctrine of the Trinity. Unimpressed by Berkeley's color theory, "the petty padre" addresses his adversary condescendingly as "Bigseer," rejecting his prismatic theory as that of a "pore shiroskuro [Japanese *shiro*: white; *kuro*: black; *chiaroscuro*] blackinwhitepaddynger." In place of the druid's abstractions, Patrick points "aposterioprismically" to a crock of gold at the end of "Irismans ruinbow" and has no hesitation in whipping out a "handcaughtscheaf of synthetic shammyrag" (or fake chamois handkerchief in the shape of a shamrock) with which to illustrate the verdant trefoil Trinity (three in one demonstrated in the year "four three two," when St. Patrick returned to Ireland[9]), before bowing down thrice before the "Balenoarch" (evil fire flash whale-arched rainbow [*arcobaleno*]). Praying to the Father, the Son, and the Holy Ghost in the rainbow ("the firethere the sun in his halo cast": 612.30), Patrick echoes the divine light of Dante's *Paradiso* (33.115), which is at once unity and Trinity, encompassing all things (33.43–145), and there is added significance in the echoes of Genesis, where God seals his covenant of peace ("Gudstruce!" [God's truth+ truce]: 613.12) with Noah through the epiphany of the rainbow (bringing back into play Shem and Shaun as versions of Shem, Ham, and Japheth), but the immediate significance of the passage is that Patrick opportunistically turns Berkeley's theory of light and color, including the green glow he casts over King Leary, into a totemic "sound sense sympol" (*symbol*, literally meaning thrown together, as well as *simple*, both in its philosophical sense and its common or garden definition, as a single-stemmed, three-leafed blade of clover found "in a weedwayedwold" [612.30]).

In a letter to Olga Howe dated May 23, 1930, Paul Léon, who rarely commented on Joyce's work, outlined a theory of *Work in Progress*, based on "ipsissima verba," or the word itself:

> When St. Patrick went to baptise Ireland he found some difficulty to explain the sense of the Holy Trinity when suddenly his eyes fell on the ground where he saw a most commonplace little flower, trodden by the people, dirtied by the animals which had a three-leaf forming

a single one. He took it and showed it to the people who shouted: Credimus, Credimus!

Now does not every word we use represent a Trinity: it has a sense, a sound, a power to evoke pictures. One does not feel it as rule unless "something goes wrong" i.e. either the sense is stupid, or the picture obsolete, or the sound false. (qtd. in Noël, 45)

There is no evidence that Léon's theory originated with Joyce, but Léon, who was an accomplished linguist, as well as professor of philosophy and sociology, studied "Joyce's process of creation" for many years, looking up "words in various languages" for his friend, and was therefore particularly well placed to judge Joyce's "mental process and the metamorphosis of language he indulges in" (8). Now Léon's theory is perhaps too facile and could be made more concrete by replacing the "power to evoke pictures" with the graphic form of words (yoking imagery to sense), in which case the trinity comprises the material shape and sound of words with their potential for signification (where the last leaf is self-reflexively cloven). But allowing for such adjustments, it is generally the case, as Léon points out, that ordinarily one does not notice the sound, shape, or signifying function of words unless "something goes wrong," which is exactly what happens in *Finnegans Wake*, indicating that its strange contortions are common or garden sympols.

Berkeley's spectrum of light and Patrick's trefoil shamrock are both epiphanic doctrines of the manifold: the rainbow combines the Old Testament theophanies of light and cloud, which become central Wakean tropes, while New Testament epiphanies, from the coming of Jesus to the *logos* of Saint John, are revelations of the Trinity. This theological bridge, particularly through the arc of the covenant, brings their doctrines into accord, just as Patrick's ability to reunify Berkeley's green-tinted spectrum completes the Viconian cycle of unity-discord-diversity-unification outlined by Muta in the preceding dialogue (which poses the question Berkeley and Patrick debate): "So that when we shall have acquired unification we shall pass on to diversity and when we shall have passed on to diversity we shall have acquired the instinct to combat and when we shall have acquired the instinct of combat we shall pass back to the spirit of appeasement?" (610.23–27). However, the final word is given to neither of the antagonists; first the Kantian terms of appearance and reality are rejected—"Yet is no body present here which was not there before," and then the real epiphany occurs in a literal illumination, as the sun streams "benedictively" through the oriel windows "when saint and sage have had their say" (613.13–16). The importance of this moment can scarcely be overstated, because for Joyce, like John, light is the visible manifestation of the logos.

Written soon after the Roderick O'Connor and St. Kevin episodes, the Berkeley-Patrick dialogue was one of the first sections Joyce wrote for *Work in Progress*,[10] and it has special significance because "it was the first piece to be written in *Wakean* language" (Hulle, in Crispi and Slote 2007, 442–43). In fact, the development of Wakese can clearly be traced between the first draft (quoted above), written in English, and the second draft, which begins: "Topside joss pidgin fella Berkeley, archdruid of the Irish josspidgin, in his heptachromatic sevenhued roranyellgreeblindigan mantle." Here we see the introduction of Chinese pidgin (*topside* = superior; *joss* = God) and slang (fella),[11] linguistic borrowings ("heptachromatic," from the Greek *heptachromatikos*), and portmanteau words, such as the six-colored adjective (missing violet). Indeed, Laurent Milesi argues that with Berkeley's Chinese pidgin and St. Patrick's "Nippon English," "la gamme des parlers anglais *s'oriente* vers un champ nouveau en *s'orientalisant*; on peut à juste titre considerer cet épisode comme la première étape de la voie royale qui conduira l'écrivain vers sa langue universelle" (1985, 166).[12] The tendency toward universality, exemplified by the meeting of Occident and Orient, is one aspect of the *Wake*'s polyglossia,[13] but the incomprehension caused by diverse tongues is equally important.

Indeed, it has been suggested that Berkeley's idiom, and perhaps even the language of the *Wake*, is an attempt to re-create the "Dark Tongue" of Ireland. Adaline Glasheen (1963) notes that Joyce made extensive use of R. A. Macalister's *The Secret Language of Ireland*. Although Macalister's book was not published until 1937, there can be no doubt about Joyce's debt, because he took extensive notes in VI.B.46 (Crispi and Slote 2007, 240), and as Clive Hart has confirmed, "all the Shelta, Ogham, Bog Latin, and Bearlagair Na Saer" Glasheen quotes "was added to the text at the galley stage or was included in passages composed after 1937" (1963, 3). One of the most interesting correspondences is to "A darktongues, kunning" (223.28)—"a gloss to the *Senchus Mor* tells how two *file* (poets) . . . spoke 'in a dark tongue' so that the chieftains standing by were unable to understand them"—a legend that was turned into "The Colloquy of the Two Sages" who "confound each other with obscure allusive kennings"

(Glasheen 1963, 2). This is clearly reminiscent of the colloquy between the archdruid and the archpriest, a comparison George Cinclair Gibson takes up in "The Recovery of the Dark Tongue." At times, Gibson's perspective seems distorted by nationalist sympathies,[14] but he makes a fascinating comparison between *Bélra na filed*, or the "Dark Tongue," an artificially constructed, ritualistic language of the theological poets of ancient Ireland, and Joyce's language in the *Wake*. Indeed, the similarities are striking: *Bélra na filed* is "nearly incomprehensible in its polyglot logorrhea," a baffling construction "riddled with puns, neologisms, and a plethora of polysemes and portmanteaus; language literally loaded with thousands of words misspelled and malformed, bent, folded, twisted, mutilated or torn into pieces" (220–21). He goes on to note the threefold darkness of the *Filidh's* tongue: *duibhe*—obscurity; *dorchatu*, its mysterious, enigmatic, or even magical quality; and *dluithe*, its arcane techniques of "semiotic and linguistic compression" (227). On this basis, it is hard to deny the resemblance to Joyce's "writing of the night" (*JJ* 559). There is also an intriguing connection to the Archdruid Berkeley sketch, the first piece written in Wakese, although Gibson goes too far when he concludes that "[t]he *Wake* . . . is the re-creation of the Rites of Tara, and the Dark Tongue is *the* language of the Rites" (235).

These similarities point to the obscure, enigmatic, and ritualistic qualities of epiphany in the *Wake*, which are given the same importance as traditional revelation in Joyce's epiphanic allusions. "[O]n the night of the Apophanypes" (626.4–5) combines both the revelatory and doomsday aspects of Apocalypse with the Feast of the Epiphany (the context alludes to a severe storm that struck Dublin on January 6, 1839 [McHugh]). Similarly, "the Verily Roverend Father Epiphanes" (341.27) may refer to St. Epiphanes of Besançon, Antiochus Epiphanes, the "abomination of desolation" (Daniel 11.31), or a racehorse of that name. From the context (radio or television coverage of "*the worldrenownced Caerholme Event . . . given by* The Irish Race and World" [341.19–20]), the latter is most likely, but as with the night of the "Apophanypes," the figure of "Father Epiphanes" is triangulated between salvation, destruction, and fact, all of which are placed on one plane.

This humorous conflation of the sacred and the profane in the literal typifies the *Wake's* epiphanies, exemplified by their curious connection to the story of Buckley shooting the Russian General.[15] The anecdote, told by John Joyce, was one of Joyce's favorites, and he regarded it as typical of Irish humour (*JJ* 411; Glasheen 42). The story concerns an Irish volunteer named Buckley who comes upon a Russian General; first impressed by his medals and decorations, then dismayed by the undignified sight of the Russian defecating, Buckley cannot bring himself to shoot until the General wipes his backside with a sod of turf. Beckett's verdict, "another insult to Ireland" (*JJ* 398 n.), brings out the comedy and political significance, but it is nonetheless difficult to see why Joyce gave this story such prominence, or why he associated it with epiphany. Yet the "Father Epiphanes" passage continues "Backlegs shirked the racing kenneldar," and a few lines later there is "a shote of excramation! Bumchub! Emancipator, the Creman hunter (Major Hermyn C. Entwhistle)" (341.29–30, 342.19–20). Here, the shout of exclamation includes shite (one of John Joyce's favorite words) and excrement, while "Bumchub!" seems to be Buckley, the Emancipator and Crimean Hunter, but this is odd because it associates ECH with Buckley, whereas usually HCE is the General, as in the parenthesis that follows, in which case perhaps Emancipator, a racehorse sired in 1927 (McHugh), is the General's steed, and "Bumchub!" refers to his exposed posterior. "[D]eretane denudation with intent to excitation," or mooning (557.23), is one of the charges brought against HCE, and several versions of the incident in the park seem to involve indecent exposure (both frontal and rear), as in 3.4, where HCE exposes both his genitals and his backside to his children, provoking outrage and wonder. In any case, there is a clear connection between the Russian General, Earwicker, and the fall, which is linked to epiphany in HCE's defense ("I . . . fell clocksure off my ballast" [*FW* 550.37–551.1]),[16] while the curious "tail" of Willingdone being shot "on the back of his big wide harse" (*FW* 10.19–21; cf. epiphany #35) culminates in the Russian General dropping his pants:

—How culious an epiphany!
—*Hodie casus esobhrakton?* (508.11–12)

Hodie is Latin for today, *casus* means fall, and in modern Greek, *esôbrakôn tôn* means "their underpants." Today their underpants fall: how curious, and *cul*ious (*cul*: ass) an epiphany! Yet, by making a humorous revelation out of the ridiculous and scatological, Joyce suggests that *anything* can become the subject of epiphany, exposing the anal aesthetic of indecency itself through the return of the repressed, in all its forms, which allows the full range of human experience not only to be redeemed but placed on one level, where everything, from the sublime to the ridiculous, is made literal—which is to say, epiphanized—at least on the level of the text.

Joyce's use of the traditional language of epiphany to create this leveling of the sacred and the profane is surprisingly frequent in *Finnegans Wake*, so I will limit my discussion to a few examples from the New Testament that can be traced back to the Greek root *phaino*. The word first occurs in Matthew 1:20: "Behold, the angel of the Lord appeared [*ephanē*] unto [Joseph] in a dream," announcing Mary's immaculate conception, and is repeated in Joseph's second dream-epiphany, which the King James Version translates using the same formula: "an angel of the Lord appeared [*phainetai*]" (Matt. 2:13). The phrase is also used for the annunciation and the nativity in Luke (cf. Luke 1:11, 2:9 [KJV]), and Joyce echoes it repeatedly in *Finnegans Wake*. For instance, in Book 1, chapter 3, which is largely taken up with reports of Earwicker's crime in the park, an assailant who has allegedly tried to rob HCE claims that at the time of the incident he was on an almighty pub crawl, from "the House of Blazes" to "the Holy Lamb, . . . till the engine of the laws declosed unto Murray" (combining May Joyce's maiden name, Murray, with her given name, Mary) "the gatestone pier," which he mistook for a "cattlepillar" (policeman). Irreverence also shrouds HCE's plea in 3.3, where he calls on "the oragel of the lauds" (552.25), or angel of the Lord, to protest his innocence by trumpeting his healthy sex life ("tellforth's glory" [552.26]), to which the four bray in derision ("Hoke! / Hoke! / Hoke! / Hoke!" [31–34]). Recalling the conclusion of the "MaMaLuJo" chapter ("Mattheehew, Markeehew, Lukeehew, Johnheehewheehew! / Haw!" [399.32–33]), the third watch of Shaun ends with the four evangelists braying like asses: "Matahah! Marahah! Luahah! Joahanahanahana!" (554.10), and the following chapter opens with a "pallyollog*ass*," a "cuddy" (slang for donkey), a "donk," and an "onage" (onager = wild ass [555.11–20]). These obscure references may recall Jesus riding into Jerusalem on a donkey, as blatant an example of the sacred in the mundane as his birth in a manger, but as the pun implies, the ass in *Finnegans Wake* offers a culious kind of epiphany.

There are several other echoes of "the angel of the Lord" in *Finnegans Wake*, including three in Book 4. As well as the Gospels, the first—"It is not even yet the engine of the load with haled morries full of crates" (*FW* 604.9–11)—recalls the Angelus, which begins "The angel of the Lord declared unto Mary, . . . Hail, Mary, full of grace" (*Enchiridion of Indulgences*,

June 29, 1968). Traditionally recited at 6 a.m., noon, and 6 p.m., its immediate significance is to indicate the time (not yet 06:00), but it also extends the epiphanic allusions from the synoptic gospels to John, particularly in the third versicle, which passes from the Annunciation to the Incarnation: "And the Word was made flesh, And dwelt among us—Hail Mary, full of grace." Joyce echoes John 1:14 ("And the Word was made flesh, and dwelt among us . . . full of grace and truth") repeatedly in *Finnegans Wake* (138.08ff.), just as he echoes the opening of John's gospel: "In the beginning was the Word, and the Word was with God, and the Word was God" (cf. *FW* 17.22, etc.). As Atherton has shown, the first five references also allude to Genesis 1:1, while the last four refer "in the first place" to the Evangelist (1974, 177),[17] but the opening of John is in many ways a rewriting of Genesis chapter 1, and Joyce's allusions combine both scriptures: "In the buginning is the woid" (word/void 378.29; cf. Gen. 1:2). Thus, God's act of creation in Genesis, beginning with heaven, earth, and light, is traced back to the Word in John, which becomes God, life, light, and Christ (John 1:1–14). Through a series of complex references to "the angel of the lord" and the Angelus (cf. 63.27–28), Joyce brings together the principal epiphanies of Matthew and Luke (the Annunciation and Incarnation), with the original, universal epiphanies of Genesis and John, allowing all four to shine through his own language, which is by turns brilliant and obscure, like Berkeley's theory of color, or John's epiphany of light: "And the light shineth [*phainei*] in darknesse, and the darknesse comprehended it not" (1:5).

Epiphany originally meant a literal illumination, and it is interesting to note that the same word is used for the revelation of Jesus Christ to John of Patmos, as it is again near the end of Revelation, where God enlightens the holy city without need of sun or moon (Rev. 1:16, 21:23). It is worth recalling that Joyce copied the entire book of Revelation at a formative stage of his career, most likely while composing his epiphanies, for in some ways *Finnegans Wake* can be considered as Joyce's Revelation, although his "night of the Apophanypes" is as much a revelation of darkness as of light. Alternatively, as David Spurr has shown, *Finnegans Wake* can be considered as "Joyce's Countergospel," although Joyce's purpose is not only to bear witness to the light of logos, like John (1.6–9), but also the incertitude of the "woid."[18]

Joyce attached great importance to being born on Candlemas (February 2), commemorated on the fourth Sunday of the Epiphany season, when

Jesus is presented in the temple as a "light" and "revelation" (Luke 2:32), but it is of course the first Sunday that Catholics celebrate as the Feast of the Epiphany (January 6). In Luke, Jesus's revelation is announced to the shepherds by the "angel of the lord," whereas in Matthew it is the star that guides the wise men. Intermixing the Lucan and Matthean accounts, images of the Epiphany are recurrent in the *Wake:* for instance, after the unexpected appearance of an angel, a star brings "three kings of three suits and a crowner" flocking to baby Yawn (474.17–20). As I have shown, the "angel of the lord" passages also draw on epiphanies in Luke and Matthew, but as well as echoing the Gospels, Joyce's celestine imagery points to real heavenly bodies and Old Testament *shekinahs*.

In Book 4, "the engine of the load" refers to "the angel of the lord," the first recital of the Angelus, and to daybreak, or more precisely, sunrise, as an astrological apparition ("Calling all downs to dayne": 593.2). The moment is akin to Bloom and Stephen's stargazing in "Ithaca," with Bloom's recollection of sunrise, except that here celestial motion is mapped onto terrestrial transportation: the "Sideral Reulthway" is a star-sent Railway (sidereal + Irish *réal*, star), or "vialact coloured milk train" (*Via Lactia* = the Milky Way), "with its endless gallaxion of rotatorattlers," including the "waggonwobblers" of the Plough. Literal interpretation is possible, since stars do in fact wobble due to the gravitational effect of orbiting planets, but the allusions to fruit and husbandry suggest that the wobbling stars of the Plough, ready to fall to earth, include an echo of Revelation: "And the stars of heaven fell unto the earth, even as a fig tree casteth her untimely figs, when she is shaken of a mighty wind" (Rev. 6:13). This verse, which Joyce alludes to in *Portrait* (121, cf. 260), provides added resonance to "the eversower of the seeds of light" at the start of Book 4, particularly in answer to the preceding line: "A hand from the cloud emerges, holding a chart expanded,"[19] which seems to undo the Apocalyptic image of heaven departing "as a scroll when it is rolled together" [Rev. 6:14]).

The words "cloud," "star," and "fire" occur hundreds of times in *Finnegans Wake*, often appearing together. As with the nebulae and constellations of *Portrait* and *Ulysses*,[20] this conjunction reflects Joyce's literal interpretation of God leading Moses and the Israelites to freedom, going "before them by day in a pillar of a cloud, to lead them the way; and by night in a pillar of fire, to give them light" (Ex. 13:21).[21] As mentioned earlier, the motifs in the *Wake* are inextricably intertwined, so that it is inevitably reductive to disentangle them, but that danger becomes unavoidable as soon as one ventures an interpretation. With this caveat in mind, I want to suggest that Joyce associates the imagery of fire, stars, and *light* with HCE (and, to a lesser extent, the male children, Shem and Shaun), while the cloud-rain-river-water cycle is associated with ALP and Issy. Both clusters provide an image of the book: Berkeley's "hueful panepiphanal world" of infinitely varied appearances, where the true color of the noumenal object is always invisible, reflects the nature of Joyce's "collideorscape"; while in the preceding dialogue, Muta describes Joyce's "kingly work in progress" (625.13–14) as "wolk [cloud] in process." This image is reminiscent of Stephen's "instant of inspiration . . . reflected from all sides at once from a multitude of cloudy circumstances," except that in *Finnegans Wake* the emphasis is not on the immaculate conception of the word as a unique epiphany but rather on the linguistic *process*, a course of becoming. As such, it represents both the illumination and the obscurity of the *Wake*, the "[c]umulonubulocirrhonimbant heaven" (*FW* 599.25) and "the fog of the cloud in which we toil" (599.30).

"[W]olk in process" also sheds lambent light on the cryptic hint Joyce gave Budgen, immediately following his comments about the Berkeley-Patrick colloquy being "the defence and indictment" of the book: "Hence the phrase in the preceding Mutt and Jeff banter 'Dies is Dormimus master' = Deus est Dominus noster plus the day is Lord over sleep, i.e. when it days" (*LI* 406). Here is the "banter" Joyce refers to:

> Muta: Quodestnunc fumusiste volhvuns ex Domoyno?
> Juva: It is Old Head of Kettle puffing off the top of the mornin.
> Muta: He odda be thorly well ashamed of himself for smoking before the high host.
> Juva: Dies is Dorminus master and commandant illy tonobrass.
> Muta: Diminussed aster! An I could peecieve amonkst the gatherings who ever they wolk in process?
> Juva: Khubadah! It is the Chrystanthemlander with his porters of bonzos, pompommy plonkyplonk, the ghariwallahs, moveyovering the cabrattlefield of slaine. (609.24–34)

Muta (change) begins by asking in Latin, "what now is that smoke rolling out of the Lord?" The answer, of course, is St. Patrick's paschal fire, lit by the "Chrystanthemlander" on the hill of Slane, in contravention of King Leary's decree that all fires should be extinguished until the druids had kindled their sacred blaze. Legend has it the druids warned the king that if the fire were not extinguished at once it would blaze forever, but there is more to this "smoke . . . of the Lord" than the fiery fervor of Ireland's conversion to Christianity. *Deus est Dominus noster* (God is our Lord) probably refers to the Athanasian creed: "*Est ergo fides recta ut credamus et confiteamur, quia Dominus noster Jesus Christus, Dei Filius, Deus et homo est*" (the true faith is: we believe and profess that our Lord Jesus Christ, the Son of God, is both God and man).[22] In use since the sixth century, this creed offers the first explicit statement of faith in the Trinity, alluded to here because the prayer attributed to St. Patrick, supposedly composed in preparation for his victory over paganism, begins and ends with an avowal of "the Trinity in the Unity."

This faith in the trinity as a divine manifold accounts for "Patrick's practical solution of the problem" in the rainbow spectrum of light and the trefoil shamrock, but it is less clear what this has to do with day and night. One answer is simply that Book 4 represents the coming of day, the everyday epiphany of sunrise, when our nearest star, bringer of light and life, appears. But the "wolk in process" is also the cloud of smoke made by Patrick and his band of monks, while "Diminussed aster!" (Greek *aster* = star) picks up on "Dorminus master": the mastery of day (Latin: *deis*) over our sleep (*dormimus*) is expressed through the transition from the diminishing star of the druids to a rising cloud of Christian smoke.[23] Since the pagans are fireless while Patrick has ignited a paschal blaze, I think it likely that Joyce is playing again on God's apparition by day as a pillar of cloud and by night as a pillar of fire in the Pentateuch, underscoring how Joyce's "wolk in process" provides a nebulous image of epiphany.

If the primary element of HCE, embedded in the landscape of Dublin and environs, is earth, then ALP, as the river Liffey, is water, but in *Finnegans Wake*, the earth is connected to heaven, fire, and light, while the water cycle passes through air, congealing into cloud. In a sense, this creates two images of epiphany, masculine and feminine, which are both associated with day; but it goes without saying that Joyce's dichotomies are never so simple, and by the end of the book, they begin to converge. The cloud is initially associated with Issy as Nuvoletta (e.g., *FW* 157–59), but by the end of the book, when ALP addresses her daughter, she too seems to be projected into the cloud, so that it becomes not only Issy's mother, but ALP's, and by extension, everybody's (597.26–34): "I was sweet when I came down out of me mother. My great blue bedroom, the air so quiet, scarce a cloud. In peace and silence. I could have stayed up there for always only. It's something fails us. First we feel. Then we fall. And let her rain now if she likes" (626.8–12). As Anna Livia approaches the sea, her tidal waters become salty, no longer the "sweet" rainwater of her origins. With the wind whipping up waves, she feels "near to faint away. Into the deeps . . . Where you meet I." Here, "the old man in the sea" (HCE) meets "the old woman in the sky" (ALP, as riverine cloud: 599.35–36), but as the waters merge, ALP is "getting mixed," and HCE is "changing, sonhusband, and . . . turning" into "a daughterwife," so that the "mere [+ *mer, mère, mare*] size" of her "cold mad feary father," the ocean, makes it both mother and father, masculine and feminine, like *la mer* and *il mare*. This merging of masculine and feminine is already implicit in the figure of ALP as the convergence of manifold streams and rivers (e.g., in 1.8), representing "the river of lives, . . . The untirities of livesliving being the one substance of a streamsbecoming" (597.7–8).[24] But in the final lines, this figure of unity in diversity represented by the confluence of cloud, river, and sea becomes a counterpoint to Berkeley and Patrick's rainbow of light (recalled through the sunrise that occurs simultaneously with the meeting of the waters), and both images are united in the traditional imagery of epiphany: like the angel of the lord appearing to Mary, ALP (as cloud and river) imagines HCE (as sun and sea) "bearing down on me now under whitespread wings like he'd come from Arkangels," and then, remembering a cherished moment in their courtship, she invokes Moses in the reeds and the vision of the burning bush: "We pass through grass behush the bush to. Whish!"

The burning bush is another recurrent image of epiphany in the *Wake*, from "avoice from afire" bellowing "mishe mishe" (i.e., Moses: *FW* 3.9), to the "burning bush" atop HCE's "hierarchitectititptitoploftical" tower (see *FW* 4.18–5.4), to Joyce's irreverent admonition of Kendall Bushe (author of *Cease Your Funning*): "cease your fumings, kindalled bushies! . . . For here the holy languge. Soons to come" (256.11–15). Again, this provides an image of revelation in nature, which itself becomes emblematic of the book; through a series of motifs, including thunder, trees, stones, rivers, clouds, fire, and light, Joyce seems to suggest that language, like other natural objects, is a continuous revelation. Of course, there is a traditional association between Holy Scripture and nature as the book of God, but Joyce extends this to all of language (taking John's Gospel in the most literal sense possible), including silence. Indeed, the sense of epiphany at the end of *Finnegans Wake* is achieved not so much by its rich imagery and lyricism but by the return to silence in the *ricorso*, behushing the burning bush ("Whish!") as the text trails into white space, letting "the last half versicle repurchas[e] his pawned word" (596.31–32).

The Epiphany of Language

So much has been written on the language of *Finnegans Wake* that it is impossible to provide an adequate survey, but to situate my argument, it may help to outline three trends in the literature: early criticism, written during the composition of *Work in Progress*; critical and theoretical approaches in the decades following publication; and recent scholarship on its genesis. Although excellent work has been done in each area, rarely are the results brought together; doing so helps to bring out similarities between the epiphanies and *Finnegans Wake*. Both works combine dreamlike lyricism and enigmatic dialogue; by turns ironic, irreverent, playful, and funereal, Joyce's early works prepare the ground for his jocoserious "*funferal*" (*FW* 433.8, 120.10); characterized by riddles, ambiguity, incertitude, and polyvalence, both texts evade conventional interpretation; disjunctive and interconnected, aleatory and universal, they are open to endless recombination. Any of these links could be singled out, but the many fine analyses that have already been written suggest that they form a chain connected by four linchpins: silence, repetition, materiality, and self-reflexivity. Reviewing the relevant literature, I will show how these qualities run through the language of the *Wake*.

As Sylvia Beach recorded, the first group of Joyceans consisted of "writers, friends and collaborators of Joyce" who "had the advantage of hearing the hints that he would let fall" as they composed their hortations and defenses of *Work in Progress*. Many of these appeared alongside episodes of Joyce's novel as it appeared in the *Transatlantic Review* and *transition*. *Work in Progress* was the centerpiece of Eugene Jolas's review, and many of the essays he published formed the backbone of *Our Exagmination Round His Factification for Incamination of Work in Progress* (1929). In the first of these essays, "Dante . . . Bruno. Vico. . Joyce," Beckett introduces three key linguistic principles. First, his famous pronouncement, "form *is* content, content *is* form," indicates the principle of *imitative form:* "When the sense is sleep, the words go to sleep . . . When the sense is dancing, the words dance" (14). These examples demonstrate Beckett's dictum that "[h]is writing is not *about something; it is that something itself"* (14), indicating a second aspect, the *materiality* of Joyce's text. Beckett underlines this by describing words that "elbow their way on to the page, and glow and blaze and fade and disappear" (16); the same vision of living, physically embodied print is echoed in many of the following essays, such as Victor Llona's description of words that "skip and prance, shout, lisp, sing or speak their lines" (95), Robert McAlmon's "Irish Word Ballet" (105–16), or G.V.L. Slingsby's impression of Joyce "making words serve as music" (190). For Beckett, these personified words "are alive" (Beckett 16), participating in "endless verbal germination, maturation, putrefaction, the cyclic dynamism of the intermediate," a Viconian cycle orbiting around Jolas's fundamental insight that Joyce's revolutionary language "is in *a constant state of becoming*" (82; my emphasis).

These principles are common knowledge, as are the texts they come from, but it is worth rehearsing some of the Exagminers' seminal insights into the language of *Finnegans Wake*, because key claims have been forgotten or overlooked.[25] The thunderous epiphany is a case in point: according to Beckett, the linguistic life cycles described above are derived from Book 2 of *La Scienza Nuova*, titled "Poetic Wisdom," where Vico "evolve[s] a theory of the origins of poetry and language" from thunder, which inspired fear of the gods, man's first word, religious awe, respect for authority, sexual shame, and the beginnings of society, as primitive man retreated to caves for shelter (*OE* 5). The three-part cyclical history that unfolds from these beginnings, with its recurrent theological, heroic, and civic ages, followed by a short *ricorso* (developed by Joyce into a major structural principle), is, as numerous commentators have shown, pertinent to the structure of *Finnegans Wake*, as well as to its central preoccupations: history, myth, family, religion, and language. Yet it seems to have been forgotten that in the first readings of Joyce and Vico, thunder is a divine apparition, the primordial epiphany.

It could be argued that Vico is subtler than Beckett and Gilbert suggest, but as Beach points out, Joyce's aides and acolytes benefited from his hints, which should not be overlooked. Vico's interest in philology is well known, but the epiphanic origins of his language deserve more attention. According to Stuart Gilbert, Vico sought to rediscover the universal antidiluvian language through etymology, thereby achieving "a synthesis of history and of language, a task which . . . is being realised by James Joyce in his latest work" (54). Beckett's derivation of *legere* (to read, originally to gather) from *Lex* (law, crop of acorns [11]) provides a good example, and

Gilbert, whose glosses were probably prompted by Joyce (much like his book on *Ulysses*), shows how Joyce developed these etymological principles into the "*divertissement philologique*" that is *Finnegans Wake* (*OE* 95):

> For Vico, the etymology of 'Jupiter' is *jus* + *pater:* the sky is not merely the allfather but also the source of law and justice, of the family tie and social consciousness. But not only did the voice of the thunder inspire the brutish giants with ideas of shame and justice; the strong emotion of their fear loosened their tongues and they ejaculated the first monosyllable of the language, the name of father, that word which in all tongues has the same root. It is significant that *Work in Progress* opens with a crash of thunder. (*OE* 53)

Gilbert could not be clearer about the role of thunder, yet critics have shied away from the epiphanic nature of the thunderwords. For instance, Eric McLuhan passes over their Viconian origins, arguing that *Finnegans Wake* is a Menippean satire. I find his reading unpersuasive, but the sixty-page glossary he devotes to explicating 1,001 letters in the thunderwords offers a preeminent illustration of Stuart Gilbert's early recognition that "as a mine of suggestion and allusion [*Work in Progress*] is practically inexhaustible" (67). This offers a more promising interpretation of the thunderwords representing the fall of (or into) language, beginning with a stuttering approximation to the fall of the tower of Babel ("bababadal . . .").

Laurent Milesi argues that the Babelian parable lies at the origin of the *Wake*'s polyglossia (1985, 153), and, perhaps, its impulse toward a new universal language, but Joyce's thunderwords are as Viconian as they are biblical, and both myths rest on an epiphany: the descent of God to Shinar in Genesis (11.1–9) or the "*forma poetica dello spirito*" (qtd. in *OE* 10). Ostensibly, Croce's phrase means that the spirit has a poetic form, but it can also be read as the poetic form created (< poesis) by the spirit;[26] both readings offer valid interpretations of Vico's conclusion to *The New Science*. Returning to the first thunderclaps after the universal flood, which cause the giants to "subject themselves to a higher power which they *imagined* as Jove" ("s'assoggettissero ad una *Forza Superiore, ch'immaginarono Giove*": 3.143), Vico emphasizes that the states so formed were "sotto il *governo* d'un *ottimo Massimo*, ch'essi stessi si *finsero*, e si *credettero*, al balenar di que' *fulmini*; tra' quali rifulse loro questo *vero lume di Dio*, ch'egli *governi gli uomini*" (3.143–44). Bergin and Fisch render this "under the *government of a Greatest and Best* whom they themselves *created for their faith* out of the flash of the *thunderbolts*, in which this *true light of God* shone forth for them: that *He governs mankind*," but more than "*created*," "si *finsero*, e si *credettero*" suggest that the giants *made up* and *convinced* themselves of the "*ottimo Massimo*," while "*rifulse*," from rifulgere, to "glow, radiate, or shine brightly," makes it clearer that the "true light of God" they imagine comes from the fulminations of thunder and lightning. This subtle ambiguity helps to explain Beckett's comment that for Vico language is neither materialistic nor transcendental, neither "polite and conventional symbolism" nor "a gift from the Gods" (*OE* 10); it is, rather, an *immanent* capacity that unfolds from the "first dumb form" of language as gesture, to "Homer's 'language of the Gods'" (*OE* 10), to the complex expression of *Finnegans Wake*, like the primitive poets making fables of immortal gods from flashes of lightning and rumbles of thunder, revealing the divinity within their vision of nature.

This is a good description of the manner in which we are encouraged to approach the language of *Finnegans Wake*, at least in *Our Exagmination*, where the first extended passage offered for analysis "alludes to the dawn of pre-history when Vico's thunderclap came to rescue man" (59, quoting *FW* 289.5–10). As support, Gilbert (again, most likely at Joyce's prompting), points to "flash and crash" days, "live wire," "Benjamin Franklin, inventor of the lightning conductor," and "Funkling" (from the German Funke, a spark); he also notes that Benjamin means "son of the right hand" (cf. Gen. 35:18), an allusion to Lucifer that is continued with a "clear, if colloquial, allusion to the angel's panic flight before the fires of God," "the doom of Prometheus," "Lucifer's exile in the void," "Empyre" (suggesting "Empyrean," the highest heaven), "and the archangel's fall from grace."

It is interesting that Gilbert should choose this passage as a representative sample of Joyce's work, but the general import, as Gilbert explains, is that "This passage illustrates the manner in which a *motif* foliates outwards through the surrounding text, beginning from a single word—here the 'flash' in 'flash and crash' has 'electrified' the words which follow. . . . All through *Work in Progress* similar foliations may be traced, outspreading, overlapping, enmeshed together; at last deciduous, as new and stronger *motifs* thrust upwards into the light" (*OE* 60). Gilbert's arboreal metaphor suggests both the repetition of motifs and the difference between variations, the essential mechanisms of Joyce's epiphanies. His image of electrified motifs thrusting "upward into the light" suggests the epiphanic force of Joyce's language, and just as Beckett's etymological tree of reading (*legere*) is traced back to a lexical acorn, *Lex*, Gilbert's seminal example provides a holotype for reading the epiphanic language of the *Wake*.

Perhaps the clearest example is the portmanteau: when Gilbert differentiates Joyce's complexity from Carroll's portmanteaux and Lear's nonsense rhymes, the critical exfoliations of his approach can be traced through a series of subsequent comparisons between "Dodgefather Dodgson" (VI.B.33.184h; cf. *FW* 482.1), and "ghem of all jokes" (193.9), the best of which are to be found in *Dublin's Joyce* and *The Books at the Wake* (124–36). Atherton, in particular, identifies an impressive list of verbal tricks they have in common, from the change of a single letter (cf. Joyce's "hesitency" and Carroll's "Litterature"), word ladders (or "Doublets," as Carroll calls them), spelling reversals and palindromes, and, of course, portmanteaux. Later critics have developed these studies into an extensive list of techniques that characterize Wakean language: Michael Begnal notes polysemy, puns, permutations, reversals, disguised names, proverbs and quotations, anagrams, words broken up by unorthodox spacing, acronyms, and "myriad numbers of little puzzles" (637). Nevertheless, his account is conservative in comparison to those of critics like Margot Norris and Derek Attridge, which develop sophisticated deconstructivist accounts of Joyce's language based on general principles of iterative difference that can be traced back to the twin poles of silence and repetition in the epiphanies.[27]

One of the first studies of Joyce's language, published just a few months after *Finnegans Wake*, perceptively notes that Joyce's "polysemantic verbal patterns" run the risk "of charging the language with so many counterpointed meanings that in the end it signifies nothing," requiring the reader "to fill in lacunae, supply links, embroider upon associations, rearrange the cunningly separated elements of a single pattern" (Schlauch 483–90). As with Gilbert, this emphasis on counterpointed verbal patterns of repetition and variation, and their inherent lacunae, set the template for the second wave of criticism in the decades following Joyce's death, much of which is predominantly concerned with one or other of these aspects. For instance, the first words of Campbell and Robinson's *Skeleton Key to* Finnegans Wake dub the book a "[r]unning riddle and fluid answer" (3), while Tindall's *Reader's Guide* (1959) proclaims that "[i]n the great design of repetition with variation that the *Wake* shares with life, . . . motifs, more than devices or connective threads, become the fabric itself" (12). These works have largely been superseded by McHugh's *Annotations* (1980–2015), but Adaline Glasheen's three censuses of *Finnegans Wake*

(1957–1977), Atherton's *Books at the Wake* (1959), Hart's *Structure and Motif* (1962), McHugh's *Sigla of* Finnegans Wake (1976), and more recently Raphael Slepon's FWEET website (2005–present) remain indispensable guides to Joyce's last work, all of them essentially concerned with its repetitive structures of character, intertextuality, motif, sigla, word, and allusion. Conversely, some of the strongest single-thesis monographs on the *Wake*, such as Patrick McCarthy's *Riddles of* Finnegans Wake (1980), John Bishop's *Joyce's Book of the Dark* (1986), and Norris's *Decentered Universe of* Finnegans Wake (1976), concern the riddles, gaps, silences, obscurity, and uncertainty of the *Wake*.

Norris's book also heralds what can broadly be termed a post-structuralist turn in Joyce studies, where the interrelationship between silence and repetition is brought to the fore. One of the earliest and best of these studies is Jennifer Levine's "Originality and Repetition in *Finnegans Wake*" (1979), which argues that "throughout the *Wake*, every word makes a repetition, carries a past along with it, and as such invites the whole question of origins and originality," even as "the reader is constantly aware of missing connections . . . , the space between words and their points of origin" (112). Describing the same effect in less fundamental terms, Colin McCabe characterizes Wakese as "a language which constantly creates new words by fusing and shortening old ones or by borrowing from the many European languages that Joyce knew," resulting in a "deformation of language" so that "every word carries more than one meaning and each sentence opens out onto an infinity of interpretations" (1982, 29–30). Joyce did not, in fact, restrict himself to European languages, and "deformation" carries the wrong connotation (what Joyce reveals is the normal state of language), but the basic connection between linguistic difference and semantic proliferation is perceptive, and Rabaté extends the point to narrative in his well-known essay "Silence in *Dubliners*": "The endlessness of the other narratives relies on such a victorious silence [as 'The Sisters'], and this is the real link between the stories in *Dubliners* and those of *Finnegans Wake*" (1982, 51). More recently, David Spurr's "Fatal Signatures" (2002) shows how forgery, understood as "a gesture of displacement and usurpation whose conditions of possibility are those of absence," undermines the authority and authenticity of the paternal logos, leading to *Finnegans Wake*'s "language of excess," a textual embodiment of feminine jouissance characterized by "overflow, abundant superfluity, and inexhaustible possibility" (104, 112). Similarly, in "Joyce's Countergospel," Spurr suggests that the "nothingness at the heart" of *Finnegans Wake* "makes possible the language of Joyce's book" (2015, 30–31), just as for Derrida, absolute nihility "makes possible, opens, splits, or renders infinite the other" (1996, 29, qtd. in Spurr 2015, 31). Finn Fordham sums up this basic condition of *Wakean* language in his 2013 introduction: "What prevents 'nouns' from being true in *Finnegans Wake* is both the potential multiplicity and nullity of their referentiality" (in Brown 2008, 76).

Lest it be thought these insights are purely theoretical, the same fundamental conception of Joyce's language underlies the work of Fritz Senn, whose close reading of *Finnegans Wake* is second to none. For instance, when Giorgio Melchiori claims that "*Finnegans Wake* is a constant epiphanisation of . . . everyday language, by a process of translation that intensifies to the utmost its semantic values" (4), his "process of translation" rests on Senn's term "dislocution." The choice is apt, for Senn's coinage functions as an umbrella for "all manner of metamorphoses, switches, transfers, displacements," modifications, and reversals whereby an author uses novel linguistic forms or misquotations "to exploit original semantic energy for deflected intrinsic ends" (Senn 1984, 207).[28] Senn writes that "*Finnegans Wake* is dislocutory throughout in all possible senses. . . . Its language is everything implied in the Latin prefix *dis-*" (209). Ultimately, *dis-*, "apart," is derived from Greek δύο, "two" (Skeat), and according to the *OED*, its primary meaning is "two-ways, in twain," so the root implies both bifurcation and doubling, the essential properties of Joyce's epiphanic language.

Senn's work on the *Wake* emphasizes these dislocutions through deviations (including negations and reversals) of expected sense and forms of repetition (e.g., quotations, allusions, intertextuality, translations). A case in point is his "Reading Exercise in *Finnegans Wake*," where the "practical demonstration" of how Joyce's "[s]emantic potential is released" in two sentences "of medium to light opacity" from Jaun's Sermon (432.35–433.2) remains, to my mind, unsurpassed as a piece of *Wake* exegesis. Following five pages of close reading, Senn asks "Do *I* make this . . . up?"; recalling the imagery of Stuart Gilbert, he concedes that "[s]ome of the foregoing exfoliation is one particular reader's imaginative weaving of the textual threads." But that is because the writer, as poet, or "maker," is joined by the reader, as "maker-up," and (following the analogy of "our jocosus inkerman" in the passage under discussion), "making things up seems to be part . . . of our mission": "*Finnegans Wake* seems to send us abroad into far away fields (linguistic, historical, here hagiographical) . . . to engage us in our own spiritual exercises" (1984, 90–95). Such rhetorical flights are rare in Senn's explications, but an underlying credo can usually be inferred—in the same essay, for example, he discusses how "hindsight, rather 'culious an epiphany' [508.11], affects the linguistic structure" of *Finnegans Wake*—and out of print he readily admits his substantial agreement with Melchiori, for his dissatisfaction with the term "epiphany" as it is usually employed, or Joyce's epiphanies in themselves, is simply that he regards each of Joyce's words as an epiphany.

Despite the paucity of criticism examining the relationship between the epiphanies and *Finnegans Wake*, the epiphanic qualities of silence, repetition, materiality, and self-reflexivity are central to the studies discussed, providing a missing link between their diverse perspectives. In the remainder of this chapter, I will examine each of these aspects in turn, considering silence and repetition in light of recent trends in genetic criticism, before relating these principles to the physical and reflexive properties of language in order to develop a unified theory of the epiphany.

Silence

From the first chapter of *Finnegans Wake*, "silence speaks the scene" (13.3). There are a number of references to silence in the notebooks: "Sylvia Silence, the girl detective" (VI.B.10.22h), first appears in the rumours chapter, 1.3, before returning in 2.3 and 3.3 (*FW* 61.1–11, 337.17, 523.2–4); "the sublime art of sonorous silence" Joyce cribbed from Wagner's love letters lies behind the *Wake*'s "science of sonorous silence" (VI.B.3.77a; *FW* 230.22–23); and in VI.B.5.92b Joyce notes a fascinating contradiction: "noise or silence drove ᛖ mad" (cf. *FW* 98.3).[29] McHugh goes further, suggesting that the parenthetical break "(Silent.)" (14.6) in the first chapter is linked to HCE's demise, as are the line breaks inscribed "(Silents)" and "SILENCE" at 334.31 and 501.6, which he reads as *ricorsi*, or gaps between ages. This silence in death makes sense, for elsewhere HCE is associated with the amplified, stuttering voice of the paternal logos. In 2.1, the fulminating, balbutient babble of "Loud," "Clearer of the Air from on high," is "moguphonoised" (megaphonically amplifying his mogiphonia, or difficulty in producing vocal sounds) by that strange phenomenon, or "phonemanon," speech (cf. Gk *phonema*: discourse [258.20–22; cf. 257.28–259.9]), in opposition to the maternal principle of silence enacted by "Mummum"

(259.10). The association between mothering, acting (or mumming), and silence (to keep mum) recurs frequently (e.g., "Mum's mutyness" [53.3] or "Mum's for's . . . Silance" [228.15–17]), with a cluster of examples centered around "the abnihilisation of the etym" (353.22): Taff's "momstchance ministring" (mumchance means both a hazardous venture and acting or keeping silence) produces "words of silent power" (pointing at the beertap) that elicit "another guidness," or Guinness, from the barman; near the end of the chapter, the connection between "Mommery" as mummery, or dumbshow, and language as "Silence in thought!" emerges more clearly through allusions to Jesperson and a return to Joyce's creationism: "In the buginning is the woid [word, void], in the muddle is the sounddance and thereinofter you're in the unbewised again" (378.30–34). In German, *unbeweisen* means "unproven," while the adjective *unbewusst* means "unconscious"; add the proximity between mum (or "mim") and "Whisht" (Hiberno-English for "silence" [e.g. 366.35–337.1]) and the fact that every occurrence of the "whisht" motif, right through to the "Whish!" in the final lines (628.13), carries the double sense of silence and *wish*, the standard English translation of Freud's *Wunsch* (*désir* in Lacan), and I think we can begin to see how silence in *Finnegans Wake* is not only a pause between speech, or the *ricorso* between epochs, but also the polarized tension of repressed desire from which language and subjectivity spring.[30]

Repetition

"[U]pon the silence of the dead, from pharoph the nextfirst down to ramescheckles the last bust thing. The Vico road goes round and round to meet where terms begin" (452.20–22). Thus does Issy remake Vico in her own image (and that of Vico Road, Dublin), transforming "cyclewheeling history" (186.2), in which the *ricorso* plays a minor role, into "vicous cicles" (134.16) of repetition and variation that "repose, upon the silence." These patterns are familiar enough that I will limit my remarks to a single example, the "seim anew."

Near the end of 1.8, the washerwomen gossiping on the banks of the river describe HCE's bigamy and the seven dams on the Liffey in the language of Revelation ("seven dams to wive him. And every dam had her seven crutches. And every crutch had its seven hues . . ." [215.15–17; cf. Rev. chs 2–16]). The seven hues are also the colors of the rainbow, paling to pastel as dusk falls ("pinky lemony creamy birnies and their turkiss indienne mauves" [20–21]). "But at milkidmass"—Michaelmas, or the Day of St. Michael and All Angels, which principally celebrates the banishment of Lucifer (light)—his spouse was ALP, so "all that was was fair" (21–22). As night falls, with the last light gleaming on the river, the scene becomes elven: "Tys Elvenland! Teems of times and happy returns. The seim anew. Ordovico or viricordo. Anna was, Livia is, Plurabelle's to be" (22–24). The run of rivers (Ty, Elv, Elfenland, Teme, Tees, Seim . . .), a constant theme in the chapter, suggests the diversification and unification of the water cycle, just as at the end of the book, the Liffey delta branches out into Dublin Bay only to be absorbed back into the ocean. In the same way, one diurnal cycle nears an end here with the fall of night, while another begins with daybreak at the end of book 4. Both these cycles of water and light thematize the "seim anew," embodied in HCE and ALP, the masculine and the feminine. The play on "same anew" clearly points to a fundamental principle of difference-in-repetition, but it is noteworthy that Joyce's variation of the "seim anew. Ordovico or viricordo" takes the *physical* form of a river flowing toward the Ordovician rocks north of Dublin, while his Viconian cycle seems as *reflexive* and reversible as the grammar of *vi ricordo* (I remember you, or remind you of something), which is not the case for Vico's ages.

There are numerous variations on this theme: "the same roturns" (18.5), "remews [remains, renews, re-moults] the same" (134.17), "the same renew" (226.17). In the first chapter, the Prankquean tells Jarl van Hoother "there was a brannewail [brand new fire wail] that same sabbaoth night of falling angles [plus angels]" (21.17–18), suggesting a somewhat epiphanic association between "starshootings" (22.12) and the renewal of the same, while the riverine motif of 1.8 is clearly echoed in 2.2: "For as Anna was at the beginning lives yet and will return after great deap sleap rerising . . . as shower as there's a wet enclouded . . . We drames our dreams tell Bappy returns. And Sein annews" (277.22–28). Here again, fire and cloud imagery are prominent in the theme of resurrection as renewal, with HCE and ALP becoming merged in "Bappy" (Pappy), whose return is both awaited and foretold, as being (German: *Sein*) and dreams (*sen* in Czech and Polish) are renewed in the tidal Seine ("Sein annews"). The combination of long, Germanic vowel and soft, Latinate consonant permit the remaking of the *sign*, while the final recurrence of this theme near the end of the book, "Time after time. The sehm asnuh" (620.15–16) might suggest the seme made new (cf. "semetomyplace" 114.18, "seems to same" 527.1).[31] This may be stretching things, but "sehm" is an anagram of Shem ("asnuh" = Shaun), spelled Sem in French, a root Joyce plays on when Shaun mentions the "increasing lack of interest in his semantics [including Shem's antics]" (173.32–33). Semantics comes from Greek σῆμα, sema, but it is worth comparing the German word *Sema*, meaning both "sign" and "same," particularly given the cluster of Teutonic words like *sehen*, to "see," and *nu*, "now." This cluster is continued in the next line, "To bredder as doffered as nors in soun," where bredder suggests both riverbanks (from Norwegian *bredder*) and brothers (German *Brüder*), while "doffer," "nors," and "soun" are Dutch for pigeon, surly, and kiss/peace, respectively. Hence, the phrase suggests the brothers are as different as north and south, or the banks of a river, but in both cases, opposites are defined by the same point of reference, a difference that is doffered, or dovetailed, implying that the two are brought together like noise and sound, or surliness in peace, conjoining synonyms (the same anew) with Bruno's *coincidentia oppositorum*.

Genetics Aside

As I have indicated, from the *Skeleton Key* to FWEET, a considerable portion of *Wake* criticism is concerned, in one way or another, with silence and repetition. Similarly, much of the best recent work in genetic criticism is devoted to detailed analysis of the changes Joyce made in each successive draft of a given section, which is to say studying the text as a series of iterations, a complex palimpsest consisting of multiple layers of repetition and variation. I have attempted to do this for the epiphanies, showing how they are reiterated in Joyce's later texts, but there is more detailed scholarship on the genesis of the *Wake* that extends the point further. For instance, after analyzing thirteen successive stages of composition over a fourteen-year period of a single "Sentence in Progress" (449.27–450.2), David Hayman's seminal essay concludes that *Wakean* sentences "resemble nothing more than views of a cross section of some organism seen under varying lighting conditions" (Hayman 1958, 152). Perhaps recalling the organic metaphors of *Our Exagmination*,[32] or Campbell and Robinson's claim that Joyce "re-enact[s] the 'genesis and mutation of language'" in *Finnegans Wake* (14), Hayman's characterization of evolving, mutating language is equally congruent with Kenner's account of modernists like Pound, Eliot, and Joyce making "the slow discovery of *language*, a complex coherent organism . . . that can maintain its identity as it grows and evolves in time; that can remember, that can anticipate, that can mutate" (1972, 96). Even among a generation of critics who habitually avoid such far-reaching claims, Hayman's approach remains widely influential: Finn Fordham's "The Writing of Growth and the Growths of Writing" (2007–2008) is a case in point.[33]

As well as developing the methodology of genetic criticism, Hayman can be credited with unlocking one of its most important discoveries: the "nodality" of the *Wake*, organized around a cluster of key scenes that recur in frequent variations. Hayman's "epiphanoids" provide a paradigm case, and while it is not clear exactly how these "epiphanoids" are to be differentiated from other notebook entries, this apparent weakness in fact strengthens Hayman's case for the epiphanic genesis of the *Wake*. Indeed, the recycling of the epiphanies themselves offers perhaps the single clearest example of the underlying structure of repetition and variation that genetic critics trace.

Materiality

Besides holograph notebooks and drafts (*JJA* 28–43), a vast body of proofs and typescripts await genetic inquiry (*JJA* 44–63). As well as revealing further stages of Joyce's iterative composition, these texts, typed letter by letter, mark by mark, from Joyce's almost indecipherable handwriting (or even more laboriously, set by the printer's hand), bring home the manufactured nature of the text (see Kenner 1992). Again, the materiality of *Finnegans Wake* is a well-worn subject, from *Our Exagmination*'s formal emphasis on sound and shape over referential content, to the fascination of tonguetwisting thunderwords and other linguistic bizarreries, to the difficulty of reproducing Joyce's "Doodles family" in print (*FW* 299.F4). It is also well known that Joyce thematizes the physical properties of language in the *Wake*. Earlier, I showed how he uses the language of nature (trees, stones, light, water, clouds, thunder) to reflect upon the nature of language, and when Shem concocts ink from his own faeces and urine to write upon his body, he graphically illustrates two of its fundamental truths: that language is a material product of the body (see Attridge 2001, 65) and that it has a body of its own. This material body of the text is more than a theme in *Finnegans Wake*: it *is Finnegans Wake*, a recognition underscored each time the letter returns.

While our fascination with Shem's bodily emissions may seem anal,

Joyce's scatology serves a serious, and perhaps revelatory, purpose: Clive Hart ends his book on *Structure and Motif in "Finnegans Wake"* with Joyce's "aim of distilling universal beauty from scatology" (208); Father Boyle links the "alshemi[cal]" transaccidentations of I.7 (185.35–186.4) to the Eucharist; and Vincent Cheng argues that *Finnegans Wake*'s "goddinpotty" (59.12) completes a bodily cycle, expressing "the word made flesh made shit made text" (in Bollettieri Bosinelli et al. 1992, 95). These interpretations emphasize Joyce's conflation of sacred and low, God and excrement, in the literal word, underscoring the universal nature of the linguistic epiphany, indifferently present in every utterance.

The Letter

Scratched from the "midden" of history "(dump for short)" by "that original hen," Belinda Doran (110.22–111.5), there are a number of similarities between the "letter from litter" (615.1), stained with tea (111.20), pee ("pee ess": 111.18), or worse, and Shem's bodily effusions, as Vincent Cheng (94–95) and Clive Hart (200–208) have shown. For Hart, there are two types of "motif-agglomeration" in the *Wake*: a simple catalog or list of "juxtaposed motifs," on the one hand, and "the technique of amassing motifs into a matrix or complex," on the other. The preeminent example of the latter is the letter (179–80).

While this distinction is helpful in thinking about the difference between lists like the names of HCE or the titles of the mamafesta, and motifs like the Quinet quotation (14.35–15.11, 281.4–13, 615.2–4) or the chicken and egg (81.22, 220.21, 615.10–616.21), both are the result of the same basic technique. Nevertheless, Hart is right that "the Letter must rank first among the many 'expanding symbols' in *Finnegans Wake*," for it "recurs in literally hundreds of places in more or less fragmentary form, making its presence felt in the most widely divergent contexts" and touching "every theme in *Finnegans Wake*, so that it quickly comes to stand for the book itself" (200). By tracing its genesis, Laurent Milesi argues that "[t]he displacements and echoic dissemination to which the 'Letter' complex was subjected generated the first major example of leitmotivistic composition" in the *Wake* (1990, 96). Milesi argues for a "dual parentage" of the first variants of the letter in the narrative from the *Exiles (I)* and "Circe" sections of *Scribbledehobble* (c.1922–23: VI.A.271, 754),[34] before showing how the composition of these passages was preceded by the

"Revered" letter (615.12–619.19), which was elaborated in December 1923 but put aside until 1938, when Joyce thoroughly revised it for insertion near the end of the *Wake*. According to Milesi, "this crucial step led to the discovery of the basic architecture of the book," although his causal arrow should probably be reversed, for it is not so much the displacement and dissemination of the letter complex that generated Joyce's method of "leitmotivistic composition" as the opposite. Indeed, the holotropic fractal that patterns *Finnegans Wake* extends from the cyclical structure of the book as a whole to every "blotch and void" of "penstroke, paperspace" left after the "abnihilisation of the etym."

Patrick McCarthy raises six objections to the notion that the letter represents the book: (1) no two versions are identical; (2) each version is so ambiguous that defense turns into accusation; (3) attention constantly shifts from its contents to its form; (4) it is difficult to separate the letter from its commentaries; (5) the letter has been damaged in the course of its burial and resurrection; (6) its authorship is doubtful. Yet each of these objections points to the nature of Joyce's epiphanic text: (1) its structure of repetition and variation; (2) Joyce's uncertainty principle; (3, 5) the materiality of the text; (4) the role of "anticollaborators" (*FW* 118.25); and (6) the linked questions of origins, authenticity, and authorship. The latter are particularly revealing. Although 3.1 suggests the letter, delivered by Shaun, was dictated by ALP to Shem in defense of HCE (420.17–19), and the last epistle would appear to corroborate ALP as author, defending her husband, the earliest notebook evidence attributes the missive to Issy, with Maggy as sender (Milesi 1990). Since Maggy is both Issy's split personality and her mirror image (420.7, 457.24–61.32), Issy emerges as writer and recipient of the "letter selfpenned to one's other" (489.33–34), even if "a multiplicity of personalities," including the entire Earwicker household, lies behind the slippery *bordereau* (107.22–23). Here again, Joyce makes possibilities proliferate from uncertainty, creating an original figure of the writer-reader split and doubled in a symmetrical siglum ╌╂╌ whose implications extend beyond authorship of the letter(s) in *Finnegans Wake* to the "problematic origin of language" (Milesi 1990, 79).

The difficulties McCarthy raises reflect readers' experiences of the *Wake*, a point he later concedes: "The letter is free—that is, irreducible to a consistent level of meaning, or even to a definitive text. In this, as in other respects, it is a model of the mysterious, compelling, kaleidoscopic work of which it is a microcosm" (732). McCarthy makes the same point in his

1984 introduction: "To a large extent, the subject of the letter is the letter, just as the subject of *Finnegans Wake* is *Finnegans Wake*" (577), for "the letter is, ultimately, all documents, and its subject matter is human life on all its levels" (in Bowen and Carens 1984, 576). This echoes Atherton's comprehensive summary: "The letter stands as a symbol for all attempts at written communication including all other letters, all the world's literature, *The Book of Kells*, all manuscripts, the sacred books of the world, and also *Finnegans Wake*" (62–63; cf. McHugh 1976, 30). The hyperbole of "human life on all its levels" and "the sacred books of the world" may rile, but the textual claim is justified, for the letter is not only a representation of *Finnegans Wake* but also a reflection of (and on) textuality.

There are, naturally, two mirrored aspects to this self-reflection: the first is the heightened attention Joyce brings to the materiality of language—its sound and shape—by emphasizing the physical form of the letter. Obviously, this is not limited to the "everydaylooking stamped addressed envelope," its teastained, fork-punctured, "written on with dried ink scrap of paper," or the "blots and blurs and bars and balls and hoops and wriggles" of its individual handwriting (118.29–33); rather, it is a reflection on the character of letters as graphemes, or the nature of writing itself (Rasula), which opens onto the second aspect, reflexivity.

Self-Reflection

There is an intimate connection between materiality and self-reflexivity, because "within the inbuilt critical dimension of Joyce's texts representation 'itself' . . . is exposed, beyond its canonisable techniques and resources, to a reflexion on representability and representativity" (Milesi 2003, 9). Milesi signals how the materiality of Joyce's language constitutes nothing other than the thin sheet of tinfoil behind the glass: "The mirror traditionally held up to nature has revealed the tain that enables its (self-)reflexions" (9). This observation clearly recalls Rodolphe Gasché's *The Tain of the Mirror*,[35] specifically his "General Theory of Doubling," which argues that Derrida's philosophy of reflection emerges from the notion of "originary doubling," whereby repeated and repetition come into being simultaneously (225–39). This central *brisure* is already inscribed in "the *alteration* of the originary *iteration*" that constitutes "repetition, reproduction, representation" (Derrida 1976, 209), but the theory of originary doubling is most fully developed in "Plato's Pharmacy," where the privilege accorded to living speech over dead writing is not simply overturned but also deconstructed, as both speech and writing are shown to originate in a self-othering act of repetition (1981, 63–171).[36] Split and doubled at the source, the traces of this cloven language underwrite Derrida's cryptic comment that "the whole of *La Pharmacie de Platon* was only 'a reading of *Finnegans Wake*'" (in Attridge and Ferrer 1984, 150), because a reproductive chain reaction of dividing and doubling is exactly what Derrida describes as the "paradigm" of Joyce's "fission": "[Joyce] tries to make outcrop, with the greatest possible synchrony, at great speed, the greatest power of the meanings buried in each syllabic fragment, subjecting each atom of writing to fission in order to overload the unconscious with the whole memory of man: mythologies, religion, philosophies, sciences, psychoanalysis, literatures" (149). "Joyce's ghost is always coming on board," because "everything we can say after [*Finnegans Wake*] looks in advance like a minute self-commentary with which this work accompanies itself," Derrida writes (1987, 149); in this case, his remarks on fission and the *pharmakon* look like a commentary on the first page, where Dublin is doubled in Georgia (motto: "Doubling all the time!")—or in Joyce's words, "doublin their mumper all the time" [3.8–9]). Doubling all the time is precisely what we get in *Finnegans Wake*, although much of it occurs almost indistinguishably within the original apparition, as in 1.4, where "[t]he boarder incident prerepeated itself" (81.33). In this incident, "man may not say" (nor woman neither) whether the antagonists represent Napolean engaging Wellington, Buckley reconnoitering the Russian General, the Cad attacking his "Adversary" (81.18–20), Shem and Shaun, warring brothers, or any son fighting his father, because ultimately they stand for every pair in *Finnegans Wake*, showing how in Joyce's "leitmotivistic composition," repetition is always prerepeated.

These self-echoing pairs can be conceived as identical twins, split and doubled from a single egg, or as a figure of union-in-opposition, like the fusion of Shem-Shaun, but the most powerful example of Joyce's fission is the doubling of Issy. Of the myriad examples, I will concentrate on 3.3, where Issy, appearing as a witness in HCE's trial, gazes in the mirror and addresses her own reflection: "Listenest, meme mearest" (527.3). The play on *même* (same) and the doubling of me-me is repeated more than once: "Listen, meme sweety" (527.21), "It's meemly us two, meme" (527.24), opening the cleft in which Issy and her image are doubled and redoubled ("joyfold," no less [527.22]). The origins of this cleft have been traced back to 1927, when Joyce split Issy into Isolde la Belle and her rival, Isolde Blanchemains (Tristan's wife); hence the split siglum for question 10 in the Quiz chapter,[37] and the difficult relationship between "me . . . his belle" and "your extensions to my personality" in that section (144.12–145.2). But this split is not simply between Issy and her reflection, as Henkes and Bindervoet state (§10), because in 3.3 we find allusions to both "Blanchemain[s]" and Bédier's "Fairhair[ed]" La Belle ("my arms are whiter": 527.20–21) before the mirror, while the two Maggies, "Sester Maggy" and "Madge, my linkingclass girl" (458.10, 459.4), appear *in* the mirror, like the earlier reflection of "two Madges on the makewater" (420.7).[38] In fact, both schisms are more complex than this. First, Issy's narcissistic self-gaze, figured as the girlish (self-)love of *mon beau* for *ma belle*, conjures up a Carrollesque production (Isa Bowman played Alice in a famous stage adaptation) that becomes iridescent: "How me adores eatsother simply (Mon ishebeau! Ma reinebelle!) [double rainbows are inverted]." Like the twenty-eight dancing girls (days of February, lunar month, menstrual cycle, 4 × 7), the rainbow is consistently associated with Issy throughout *Finnegans Wake*, showing how an original split generates unlimited variation, like light refracted into seven bands of an infinite spectrum.

As shown, in the Patrick-Berkeley vignette, the manifold nature of light reflects the "panepiphanal" language of the *Wake*, here traced back to the originary doubling of Issy's self-reflection, but the split in the image also becomes epiphanic through the prism of Maggy and Mary. Addressing her fading image ("meme nearest . . . I'm fading") as "esster" (Swift's two Esthers, dubbed Vanessa and Stella), Issy promises to "be clue" to "who knows you, pray Magda, Marthe with Luz and Joan" (528.10–15). Joyce's grammar is ambiguous: on one reading, Maggy splits into a transgender MaMaLuJo; on another, she is known by them. In either case, she becomes associated with Mary (Mary *Magda*lene or the sisters Mary and Martha of Bethany [see Luke 10:38–42, John 11:20–27]). Moreover, since the mirror has already been associated with the litany of the Blessed Virgin, remembered from *Portrait* ("Mirror do justice, taper of ivory, heart of the conavent, hoops of gold!" [527.22–23][39]), Issy's reflection, Maggy, is also Mary, mother of God. Once conjured, this mirror image epiphanizes the magical trick of doubling: "Think of a maiden, Presentacion. Double her, Annupciacion. Take your first thoughts away from her, Immacolacion. Knock and it shall appall unto you. Who shone yet shimmers will be e'er scheining" (528.19–22). On one level, the maiden is Issy (or any number of her personalities), doubled in the mirror, but the language is that of a stage-trick, employing Marian symbolism, while its interpretation is neo-Kantian. Derived from the Protoevangelium of James, in the Liturgy the Presentation of the Blessed Virgin Mary (November 21) celebrates Mary's precocious devotion to God "under the inspiration of the Holy Spirit who filled her with grace at her Immaculate Conception." Hence, "take your first thoughts away from her" is partly addressed to Joseph (or any doubtful husband), but the mystery of paternity can also be read as a comment on authorship: if "in the virgin womb of the imagination the word was made flesh" (*P* 236), then "where do thots come from?" (*FW* 597.25). "Immacolacion" clearly refers to the immaculate conception, but it seems to contain a pure or immanent collation (bringing together) or colation (straining, as in riddling or sieving) as well; "Knock" refers to the apparition of the Virgin at Knock, County Mayo, in 1879, as well as "Knock and it shall be opened unto you" (Matt. 7:7, Luke 11:9). But a knock can also cant (German *kanten*), so that from the appalling aperture of the initials I. K. ("Immacolacion. Knock)," Immanuel Kant seems to appear. If this canting apparition upsets the lifeboat of mariolatry, the entry is at least licensed by "e'er scheining": Mary who shone once and shimmers still will always shine, because the "thing in such" (528.15) or the Ding an sich (i.e., the noumenon) will always keep appearing (Kant's term for the phenomenon is *Erscheinung*, meaning "apparition"). What makes this example so powerful is that the very opposition between the thing-in-itself and its appearance is in the process of being deconstructed as it is played out by Issy gazing in the mirror. Here Issy *is* the noumenon, yet she can see herself only as a reflection, whereupon she is inevitably split; yet the phenomenon in the mirror also possesses physical properties that appear in different lights ("fading," "fay," it "appal[s]"), like a Ding an sich. Thus, the Kantian split occurs on both sides (ambi-) of the doubling: Issy has "an ambidual act herself in apparition with herself" (528.25).

The implications of this "ambidual act" are profound. By representing Issy's self-reflection *in* the *Wake*, Joyce reflects upon the self-reflexivity *of* the *Wake*, or indeed, reflexivity in general. Already doubled on both sides of the reflection (ambidual), Issy provides the perfect illustration of Derrida's notion of originary doubling, whereby repetition does not repeat some preexisting whole but comes into being together with the thing as it is presented. Another way to understand this is that, contrary to Gasché, there is no tain *of* the mirror; the tain *is* the mirror, all metal and no glass. Put differently, the signifying function of language, its referentiality, is inseparable from its materiality; the two are inscribed as one, and each is double: shape and sound always signify, and signification is always embodied. Indeed, this is precisely what self-reflexive language reveals: by drawing heightened attention to itself, it makes manifest the strange, often opaque form of graphemes and phonemes, their irreducible materiality, while simultaneously asking us to reflect on the phenomenological associations they evoke.

The Linguistic Epiphany

Recalling that the primary senses of "epiphany" are manifestation and appearance, this mirror held up to (or rather, in) self-reflexivity reveals the epiphanic nature of language. Joyce helps us see that language is always both: the physical manifestation of a bodily production, and the endless appearances it generates through reflection. Again, there are connections between the material manifestation of language, on the one hand, and its appearance as "repetition, reproduction, representation" (Derrida 1976, 209), on the other, just as there are between silence and repetition, or materiality and reflexivity. These connections can be traced all the way back to the epiphanies that prefigure the language of the *Wake*, manifesting the self-reflexive nature of language.

Any passage from either text could serve as an example, for language is inherently self-reflexive, but *Finnegans Wake* is exceptional in the extent to which it manifests this recognition, making metatextuality its dominant mode as "the book of Doublends Jined" doubles back on itself (*FW* 20.15–16). Early on, readers are invited to bend down for a closer look at its strange textual objects, stooping or submitting to the text even as it voices resistance: "(Stoop) if you are abcedminded, to this claybook, what curios of signs (please stoop), in this allaphbed!" (18.18–19). When the curious sign of a Greek alphabet consecrated to Allah is as familiar as the Old English word abecede, "Can you rede"—a variant of read, meaning "rule," "direct," "guide," "deliberate," "resolve," "advise," and much else besides—"its world?" Both writing and reading have been defamiliarized, yet the tale of the *Wake* "is the same told of all" (18.19–20). We "may have our irremovable doubts as to the whole sense" of its "variously inflected, differently pronounced, otherwise spelled, changeably meaning vocable scriptsigns" (117.35–118.28), especially when referred back to a mutating palimpsest of drafts, typescripts, and proofs "very like a whale's egg farced with pemmican . . . , calling unnecessary attention to errors, omissions, repetitions and misalignments" (120.9–16),[40] but at least if "You is feeling like you was lost in the bush," without "the poultriest notions what the farest he all means" (112.3–6), there's "Mr. Himmyshimmy" to fall back on, "unconsciously explaining, . . . with a meticulosity bordering on the insane, the various meanings of all the different foreign parts of speech he misused" (173.27–36).

These examples illustrate how Joyce's self-reflexive text is composed with conscious, and explicit, awareness of its own textuality and how metatextual recognition invites readers to reflect on their own reading. The heightened attention Joyce brings to this process of making meaning shows how language offers a continuous epiphany as the manifestation of thought. It might be objected that these remarks apply, if at all, to *Finnegans Wake*, not language as a whole, but here again the letter is instructive. Given that it stands for *Finnegans Wake*, the letter is inherently self-reflexive, but if it is also true that it stands for all documents, then it reveals the epiphanic, self-reflexive nature of textuality. This synecdochal relation to literature (understood in the broadest sense) is often implied in the *Wake* (e.g., "every letter is a hard but yours sure is the hardest crux ever" [623.33–34]), as is the corollary reading it demands: "Leave the letter that never begins to go find the latter that ever comes to end" (337.11–13). Appearing between "a beautiful thought" called or "cull[ed]" "sub silence" (337.16–17) and the "semeliminal salmon" of knowledge caught on the ladders of the Liffey (337.9–10), "end" (13) is both noun and verb: the "latter" (ladder, last, literature) always comes to fruition. As Derek Attridge has shown, the portmanteaux in *Finnegans Wake* "help make the book conceivable as a central, rather than a peripheral, literary text" because they shatter "any illusion that the systems of difference in language are fixed and sharply drawn, reminding us that signifiers are perpetually dissolving into one another" (1988, 204); "semeliminal" (a seminal, subliminal, liminal sign) epitomizes this *Wakean* conception of language as an interrelated system of differences.[41] I have tried to isolate two related movements of this structure, silence and repetition, tracing their interplay from the epiphanies to *Finnegans Wake*, but the location of meaning in the slippage between mutually defined differences has a venerable history from Saussure to Derrida, illustrating why, for many readers, the *Wake* "may offer itself as the central text in the Western literary tradition" (Attridge 1988, 233). Although it "can no more be *intrinsically* central" to the canon "than it can be intrinsically on the edge" (237), by presenting readers with "an extreme version of what we do with all literary texts" (Attridge 1990, 21), the *Wake* reveals the twin principles not only of literature but of language, which is why Derrida could write with no real contradiction that "Plato's Pharmacy" is an indirect commentary on *Finnegans Wake*, a network of difference in repetition, or *différance*, that "repeats and mobilises and babelises the (asymptotic) totality of the equivocal." In the particular is contained the universal.

8

Conclusion

Three interwoven strands connect the epiphanies to the *Wake*, as the structural, stylistic, and linguistic patterns sketched out in Joyce's "earliest important literary compositions" (*PSW* 157) are elaborated in his subsequent texts. Indeed, William York Tindall regards Joyce's entire oeuvre as "one great work" (1959, 11); to the extent that he and Litz are right, the epiphanies lie at its origin, both temporally and as an originary stage of development.[1] But it is also true that each of Joyce's works is quite different; while the epiphanies play a key part in every subsequent work, their role is constantly evolving.

Fourteen epiphanies are reused in *Stephen Hero* and twelve in *A Portrait of the Artist as a Young Man*, forming "the principal building blocks" (*WD* 6) of those novels. *Ulysses* also recycles fourteen epiphanies, with seven allusions in *Finnegans Wake*, but in the later works they no longer form fulcrums of the plot. By contrast, *Dubliners*, composed concurrently with *Stephen Hero*, contains none of the epiphanies Joyce reserved for his autobiographical novel. Yet this very absence marks an important stage in the development of Joyce's epiphanic method, because his short stories work out the structural, stylistic, and linguistic principles of the later fiction.

As an ensemble of discrete but interconnected texts, *Dubliners* is analogous in structure to the epiphanies, constructing a model of narrative unity that bears comparison to *Portrait*, *Ulysses*, and the *Wake*. Stylistically, the two types of epiphany, dramatic and lyrical, represent "the twin poles of Joyce's art" (*PSW* 158); *Dubliners* illustrates how Joyce applies the ironic realism of the dramatic epiphanies to dialogue and the lyrical symbolism of his prose-poetic epiphanies to narrative. These techniques remain important in *Portrait*, albeit the structure becomes more unified and the poles become fused. Joyce's stylistic modes can also be detected in the "initial style" (*L I*, 129) of *Ulysses*, although Joyce's odyssey soon moves on to more complex innovations, such as the parodies and pastiches of "Cyclops" and "Oxen." Yet these ironies, like those in *Dubliners* and *Portrait*, are not fundamentally different from the irony of the dramatic epiphanies, whose complexity depends upon a recognizable but unassimilable gap between what is said and what it is thought to signify. Ultimately, this pervasive tonal ambiguity, like Joyce's rich semantic ambiguity, is a corollary of his epiphanic principles: the silence of the dramatic epiphanies and the repetition of the lyrical epiphanies combine to create resonant hiatuses and symbols of indeterminate but inexhaustible significance.

This linguistic nucleus is first evident in the "fragment of colloquy" that precipitates Daedalus's definition; it remains charged throughout the epiphanies; and it sets off a chain reaction that leads to *Finnegans Wake*. As Joyce fuses his epiphanic styles in *Portrait*, the fundamental charge of each pole, silence and repetition, form a single circuit, but whereas *Portrait* channels this semantic energy to forge myths of literary creation, *Ulysses* breaks the flow of its own textual current, creating a new aesthetic of mutation. This difference can be explained by the relative functions of silence and repetition within each work: complex patterns of repetition and variation in *Portrait* define gaps between repeated and repeating elements, and these gaps, or silences, between similar but nonidentical phrases allow associations to propagate, like Benjamin's Proustian image (201–16); by contrast, *Ulysses* homes in on the gap itself, which becomes the site of productive variation, showing how creativity and originality issue from linguistic difference, just as evolution depends upon mutation.

This original silence has a mystical ring, but as repetition necessarily includes silence, if only in the intervening text or the act of signification, so too silence must be manifest as presence through textual representation. True silence would exist only in a void; textual silence must be signified, and language is embodied. Yet, by definition, language is also reflexive, requiring a gap between that which is represented and that which represents. Thus, the elaborate patterns of repetition and variation that weave all of Joyce's work, from the epiphanies to *Finnegans Wake*, constantly evoke silence. This silence, powerfully thematized in *Dubliners*, is repeatedly and explicitly invoked in the later works, and as silence comes to the fore, not only through named silences but also through the self-differing silence of the text, Joyce draws heightened attention to the materiality and reflexivity of language. Indeed, the ever-sharper focus Joyce brings to the physicality of language is inherently self-reflexive, emphasizing strange-sounding polysyllables in "The Sisters" (*D* 1), the visceral charge of Old English monosyllables like "kiss" and "suck" in *Portrait* (5, 11–12), the infantile babble of *lalangue* in "Nausicaa" (*U* 13.28, etc.), fermenting phonemes in *Finnegans Wake* (e.g., 3.12–13), and countless examples of the "remainder" (Attridge 2001, 65). Another way of saying this is that self-reflexivity turns a lens on textuality, bringing both the materiality of the text and the process of representation into focus, and it does so *inside* the mirror of language. Hence, as silence, repetition, materiality, and self-reflexivity become increasingly central to Joyce's work, they reveal an ever-clearer epiphany—or showing forth—of language: *Dubliners* taps the currents of the epiphanies; *Portrait* harnesses them for literary creation; *Ulysses* explores their endless potential for linguistic innovation; and the *Wake* offers an epiphany of language perpetually at the point of becoming.

In chapter 2, I showed how Joyce extends the domain of epiphany beyond traditional manifestations of the transcendent, or Romantic revelations of the immanent, to language. In the same way, by tracing the similarities between Stephen Daedalus's aesthetics of epiphany and Kant's aesthetic of the sublime, I argued that Joyce's epiphanies locate the site of the sublime in language rather than in nature or the mind. Joyce's underlying principles of silence and repetition can be related equally well to the Lacanian concept of desire, endlessly seeking to fill the void that provokes it by fixating on one object after another, and the Derridean notion of iteration as repetition with a difference.[2] In one sense, Joyce's focus on silence and repetition simply lays bare the underlying movement of *différance*, play, and supplementarity in what Gasché calls the "infrastructural chain" (185–224), but this deconstruction of language reveals that silence and repetition are fully implicated in one another and ultimately inextricable. Moreover, Joyce's epiphanies offer concrete instantiations of these principles, bringing to light the fundamental connection between the silence of signification and the materiality of the sign, a recognition that reinstantiates the signifier through self-reflection. Thus, the epiphanies reveal a single nucleus of silence and repetition whose twin charges are equivalent both to each other *and* to materiality and self-reflexivity, a linguistic manifold composed of four fundamental properties that *always* appear in the sign.

Robert Langbaum has claimed that "the epiphanic mode," derived from Wordsworth, "is to a large extent the Romantic and modern mode—a dominant modern convention" (336), yet Joyce's foregrounding of silence, repetition, materiality, and self-reflexivity defines modernism's "epiphanic mode" more precisely, disclosing key linguistic features that illuminate the work of his contemporaries. According to Suzette Henke, Virginia Woolf regarded Joyce as her "artistic 'double'" (1986, 41); beyond the formal similarities in their stream of consciousness styles, or the comparable aesthetics of Joyce's epiphanies and Woolf's moments of being, the doubling of linguistic preoccupations in Woolf and Joyce is uncanny. "[T]here is a zone of silence in the middle of every art. The artists themselves live in it," Woolf writes in "Walter Sickert" (2011, 39), including herself in the same compass, for, as Patricia Laurence has shown, Woolf's work is steeped in silence. Yet this central zone is marked out by repetition: Hillis Miller's *Fiction and Repetition* includes a brilliant analysis of the structural and thematic importance of repetition in *Mrs. Dalloway* (176–202), a point that can be extended to the repetitive language in each of Woolf's major novels. Moreover, Woolf's silence and repetition, like Joyce's, are conjoined in the materiality of self-reflexive words. For example, in the echoing silence of Woolf's "play-poem" (1980, 139), *The Waves*, Bernard thinks or says, "Drop upon drop [. . .] silence falls. It forms on the roof of the mind and falls into pools beneath. For ever alone, alone, alone,—hear silence fall and sweep its rings to the farthest edges. [. . .] let silence fall, drop by drop" (172). These pools of silence are associated with thought, speech, and writing, including the first impulse that gave rise to the novel,[3] for silence pervades *The Waves*, like the inaudible murmuring of the sea heard "all through" *To the Lighthouse* (1980, 34). And since Bernard, the writer and storyteller who relates the novel in its final part, is also associated with the strange figure of "[t]he lady" writing inside *The Waves*'s fictional house (185, 191, 206, etc.), there is a powerfully self-referential aspect to Woolf's silence, akin to the metatextual moment when Woolf holds a mirror up to the audience in *Between the Acts* (219).

In *The Unnamable*, Beckett employs a similar trope to express the liquid silence of language: "The words are there, somewhere, without the least sound, [. . .] words falling, you don't know where, you don't know whence, drops of silence through the silence" (2009, 376; cf. 403–7, etc.).[4] These named silences *in* the text are examples of "First-degree silence" (30), but by equating falling words with drops of silence, Beckett also summons a "Second-degree silence" *of* the text that pervades language (Loevlie 2003, 30). As with Woolf, this silence is framed by repetition: Steven Connor's post-structuralist study, *Samuel Beckett, Repetition, Theory and Text*, draws on Derrida and Deleuze to demonstrate the centrality of repetition in Beckett's work, from his early fiction to his late drama. Indeed, the late plays, or "dramaticules"—which are perhaps the closest literary relations to Joyce's epiphanies—provide the most direct representation of Beckett's central nexus. *Act Without Words I* and *II* stage silence and repetition through mime, while Beckett's *Film* and the television plays, *Quad* and *Nacht und Träume*, put silence on screen. While none of these works contains dialogue, the single "sssh!" in *Film* (2006, 325), the sound of footsteps in *Quad*, and the last bars of Schubert's song in Beckett's eponymous play point to the impossibility of "true" silence, which must always be signified. This is especially evident in the theater, where, no matter how minimal the staging, the audience is always aware of their own presence in the performance space, a central recognition in Beckett's drama as physical aspects of performance are isolated and emphasized. By deconstructing the theatrical experience, both on stage and for the viewer (e.g., through the self-reflexive representation of [self-]perception in *Film*), Beckett stresses both the materiality of his medium and its metatheatrical quality (think of *Play*, for example). Beckett's most concise play, *Breath*, is paradigmatic, presenting the audience with a spotlit mouth above a litter-strewn stage, the amplified sound of a newborn's first cry, and a single elongated breath that rises from, falls back into, and is punctuated by silence, inviting the audience to reflect on the innumerable inspirations and exhalations that pass from the first breath to the last. Only thirty seconds long, *Breath* offers a Joycean epiphany translated from the page to the stage.

Beckett and Joyce were on close terms in Paris, where Beckett assisted his countryman with *Work in Progress*, a literary apprenticeship that may explain why silence, repetition, materiality, and self-reflexivity are so central to his work. The relevance of these qualities to the trilogy and the major plays needs no demonstration, but even the radio plays contain a surprising number of pauses, whose isolation of sound helps to clarify that all dialogue is constructed around repetitive patterns of talk punctuated by silence. These silences mark both the difference and the connection between turns, drawing heightened, self-reflexive attention to the words themselves. This conjunction, familiar from Joyce, is a key aspect of Beckett's work, illustrated by *Come and Go*, which opens and closes (like every play, but here explicitly directed) in silence. After one line of dialogue, Ru calls for it again, both shrouding recollections of the past and opening the silences that surround each character's exit, leaving the pair onstage to whisper about them. Each character's return is greeted by one of the remaining figures "put[ting] her finger to her lips" (354–55), thrice hushing a secret in a gesture that recalls the "Hush! Caution! Echoland!" of the *Wake* (13.5). When all three join hands in a ritualized handclasp, the "rings" Flo feels, circled by "*silence*" above and below (355), suggest both the physical connection between them and the resonance of the silence they maintain, an echo that ripples out into the audience and is self-reflexively embodied on the page.

While Beckett's drama suggests that silence and repetition are constitutive features of dialogue, Jonathan Culler's *Theory of the Lyric* makes the same principles fundamental to poetry, whose complex patterns of rhythm and repetition physically affect readers and listeners, producing a miniature version of the sublime (132–85). Of course, if silence, repetition, materiality, and self-reflexivity are general properties of language, they will naturally be found in all literature, but modernist writers like Joyce, Woolf, Beckett, Stein, and Eliot make these features the central and explicit subject of their work.[5] Just as Joyce's literary experimentation reveals the nature of his medium, and Beckett's experimental drama creates a sense of epiphany in the theater, so too Eliot's poetry offers an epiphany of language. Moreover, this epiphany reveals the same fundamental properties as Joyce's, exemplified, for instance, by the original epigraph for *The Waste Land*, where repetition circles the void:

> Did [Kurtz] live his life again in every detail of desire, temptation, and surrender during that supreme moment of complete knowledge? He cried in a whisper at some image, at some vision,—he cried out twice, a cry that was no more than a breath—
> "The horror! The horror!" (Conrad 2010, 117; Eliot 1971, 3)

On Pound's recommendation, Eliot changed the epigraph, but the published version still alludes to Conrad, with *Heart of Darkness* shadowing the speaker as he looks "into the heart of light, the silence" (2015, 1.41). Hence, Eliot's transformation conjoins two visions of modernism: the horror of the void witnessed in Conrad and Lowry, and the Quakeresque plenitude of silence cherished by Dorothy Richardson.[6] These contrasting aspects, associated with emptiness, absence, death, and sterility, on the one hand, and a redemptive vision of beauty and resurrection, on the other, bring out many of *The Waste Land*'s central themes, encapsulated in the near-silent "whisper music" of the woman who "fiddle[s]" the "strings" of her hair and the inaudible echoes of baby-faced bats whistling "in the violet light" (5.378–81).

Eliot is not alone in this regard: the silences of Joyce, Woolf, Beckett, and Stevens also oscillate between emptiness and fullness, but Eliot is instructive because silence and repetition are central to both his secular and his religious poetry. *The Waste Land* embodies silence in its imagery (e.g., the jungle "humped in silence"), so that when silence breaks into thunder, it is not so much rent by sound as emanated through it, creating an epiphany of language that repeats the same Indo-European root differently for every hearer, like the long-drawn final syllables (peace, tranquility, quiet) trailing into space.

Eliot's thunder of the Upanishads is comparable to the Viconian thunderwords in the *Wake*, creating an epiphany of language as physically embodied silence that differs from itself in every repetition. *Burnt Norton* creates a similar vision of silent light "[a]t the still point of the turning world," a silence that "Words, after speech, reach / Into" (4.9–10, 5.3–4). In Eliot's later poetry, "The Word" is increasingly associated with the Logos of Saint John (*Burnt Norton*, 5.19; cf. "Choruses from 'The Rock,'" III, VII, etc.), so that his own "intolerable wrestle / With words and meanings" that "[rise] and slowly [fade] into silence," varying and "repeating" their "raid[s] on the inarticulate," is presented as the search for "a further union, a deeper communion" with the Word of Jesus Christ (*East Coker*, 2.20–21, 3.33–46, 5.8). Like "the sudden illumination" of *The Dry Salvages*, we get the experience in Eliot's poetry but perhaps miss the meaning (2.44–45)—unless the "lucid stillness" (*Burnt Norton*, 3.4) is "half-heard" between "waves" of repetition (*Little Gidding*, 5.37–38), calling us back to the words we started from.

It has often been stated that, with the exception of Hopkins's theophanies and Eliot's later poetry, the modern literary epiphany, epitomized by Joyce, is a secular form, but the similarities between Joyce's linguistic epiphany and Eliot's are much greater than their differences. In *The Book of God*, Colin Jager debunks a widely held perception that the world we inhabit has become increasingly secular since the Industrial Revolution; if anything, the available evidence points in the opposite direction, although the trend is far from uniform, with diverse regions developing differently at various times (26–28). In the same way, while there may be a general drift away from organized religion in modernist literature, the commonplace idea that this entails post-Enlightenment loss of faith is misinformed, for secularization is best understood as a process of institutional differentiation (Jager, 28–29). What stands out from this brief survey of modernist writers is the diversity of their literary visions, from Joyce's faith in language to Woolf's intersubjectivity, Conrad's dark abyss to Richardson's lucid silence, Beckett's negative theology to Eliot's conversion, and the many others I have omitted, such as Pound's *logopoeia* and Stein's echolalian exactitude. At the same time, what all these writers have in common is a reverence for their medium, exploring new structures of silence, repetition, materiality, and self-reflexivity to reveal the epiphany of language.

APPENDIX

EPIPHANIES IN JOYCE'S WORK

Epiphany[a]	WD no.	Source	Stephen Hero	Portrait	Ulysses	Finnegans Wake
"Apologise"	1	Buffalo I.A-1		4		317.31
"A Story of Alsace"	2	Cornell 17.47–48				
"The Last Tram"	3	Cornell 17.44	67–68	72		
"Forty Thousand Pounds"	4	Buffalo I.A-5				
"Is That Mary-Ellen?"	5	Cornell 17.56		70–71	3.70–75, 17.135–41	
"Half-Men, Half-Goats"	6	Cornell 17.57–58		148–49		352.37–353.1
"Holy Queen, Mother of Mercy"	7	Cornell 17.46–47				
"The Big Dog"	8	Cornell 17.42	38			
"There's Nothing Like Marriage"	9	Buffalo I.A-12	251			
"The Priest That Writes Poetry"	10	Buffalo I.A-13				
"Ibsen's Age"	11	Buffalo I.A-14	46			

Note: a. The titles are taken from Beja (in Bowen and Carens, 712–13). See this source, as well as *PSW* 273 and McFadzean 40–41, for similar, but less extensive tables.

Epiphany[a]	WD no.	Source	Stephen Hero	Portrait	Ulysses	Finnegans Wake
"Your Favorite Poet"	12	Buffalo I.A-16	43			
"It's a Terrible Life"	13	Buffalo I.A-19				
"Order, Order!"	14	Buffalo I.A-21	45			
"The Lame Beggar"	15	Buffalo I.A-22	244–45		10.239–56	
"An Arctic Beast"	16	Buffalo I.A-26	33–34		3.300–309	17.26–28
"The Day of the Rabblement"	17	Buffalo I.A-28				
"The Stars on Joyce's Nose"	18	Buffalo I.A-30			9.939–44, 17.1256–58	
"The Hole in Georgie's Stomach"	19	Buffalo I.A-42	162–63			323.5–6
"Poor Little Fellow!"	20	Cornell 17.45–46	165			
"Two Mourners"	21	Buffalo I.A-44	167, 244		6.517–20	
"I Was Sorry"	22	Buffalo I.A-45	169			
"His Dancing"	23	Cornell 17.50–51				
"Her Arm on My Knees"	24	Cornell 17.41		164		
"The Girls, the Boys"	25	Cornell 17.61–62	183–84	234–35		
"She Dances with Them in the Round"	26	Cornell 17.45		238		

Appendix: Epiphanies in Joyce's Work · 235

Epiphany[a]	WD no.	Source	Stephen Hero	Portrait	Ulysses	Finnegans Wake
"Hoofs upon the Dublin Road"	27	Cornell 17.42–43		274		
"The Ship"	28	Cornell 17.57		25	3.503–5	
"Images of Fabulous Kings"	29	Cornell 17.57		272	2.155–72	
"The Spell of Arms and Voices"	30	Cornell 17.40–41	237	275	3.503–5	
"Upon Me from the Darkness"	31	Cornell 17.53		106		
"The Race"	32	Buffalo I.A-52			2.307–12, 15.3962–83	
"They Pass in Twos and Threes"	33	Cornell 17.51–52			3.205–15, 7.720–24	
"She Comes at Night"	34	Buffalo I.A-56			1.102–3; 1.270–79; 2.140–43; 15.4194–204	193.33–194.22
"Fred Leslie's My Brother"	35	Buffalo I.A-57			15.4795–97	10.21
"The Two Sisters"	36	Buffalo I.A-59				
"I Lie Along the Deck"	37	Buffalo I.A-65				
"Is Mabie Your Sweetheart?"	38	Buffalo I.A-70			13.64–74	233.21–26
"The Lesson That She Reads"	39	Buffalo I.A-71			13.107–27	
"Is That for Gogarty?"	40	Cornell 18				

Note: a. The titles are taken from Beja (in Bowen and Carens, 712–13). See this source, as well as *PSW* 273 and McFadzean 40–41, for similar, but less extensive tables.

NOTES

Chapter 1. Introduction

1. Examples include Irene Hendry, "Joyce's *Epiphanies*," *Sewanee Review* 54 (1946): 449–67; Joseph Prescott, "James Joyce's Epiphanies," *Modern Language Notes* 64, no. 5 (1949): 346; William York Tindall, *A Reader's Guide to* Finnegans Wake (London: Thames and Hudson, 1959); Florence L. Walzl, "The Liturgy of the Epiphany Season and the Epiphanies of Joyce," *PMLA* 80, no. 4 (1965): 436–50.

2. See Robert Scholes, "Joyce and the Epiphany: The Key to the Labyrinth?" *Sewanee Review* 72 (1964): 65–77; Robert Scholes and Florence L. Walzl, "The Epiphanies of Joyce," *PMLA* 82, no. 1 (1967): 152–54.

3. Twenty-two holograph epiphanies at Buffalo were published by O. A. Silverman in 1956. The first complete edition appeared in *The Workshop of Daedalus*, edited by Robert Scholes and Richard M. Kain (1965). They are also included in *Poems and Shorter Writings* (*PSW*), ed. Richard Ellmann, A. Walton Litz, and John Whittier-Ferguson (1991), which is now the standard edition.

A note on the title: both Silverman and *PSW* italicize *Epiphanies*, giving them the status of a major work. This brings out their importance, but it also implies that the forty surviving pieces form a single work, which is questionable, because we don't know how many there were originally or the order(s) they were arranged in; Joyce chose to reuse individual epiphanies rather than to publish them as a collection. Scholes and Kain capitalize "Epiphanies," which has the advantage of distinguishing Joyce's ur-texts from other passages one might wish to call epiphanies, but this distinction becomes problematic when Joyce recycles his early works in the later (does a fleeting reference such as "apullajibed" [*FW* 317.30] constitute an Epiphany?). I preserve the ambiguity by avoiding italics, quotation marks, and capitalization.

4. Dates from 1899 to 1904 have been proposed (*JJ* 87; *WD* 5; *PSW* 157); I assess the evidence in MacDuff, "The Yale Epiphanies: A New Typescript," *Genetic Joyce Studies* 17 (Spring 2017): 1–15, 1–4.

5. See MacDuff, "The Yale Epiphanies," 1–15. http://www.geneticjoycestudies.org/articles/GJS17/GJS17_Macduff.

6. Joyce told Adolph Hoffmeister, "My work is a whole and cannot be divided by book titles," suggesting that there was "a straight line of development" from *Dubliners* onward, but one could also point to Joyce's poetry, criticism, fiction, and drama as points of origin (qtd. in Morris Beja, *James Joyce: A Literary Life* [Basingstoke: Macmillan, 1992], 31).

7. As Richard Ellmann notes, Joyce borrows the phrase from Flaubert: "*La beau . . . est la splendour du vrai, comme disait Platon*" (qtd. in *CW* 141). Reused in his aesthetics, *Stephen Hero*, and *Portrait*, this splendor of truth is associated with Dedalus's third phase of beauty, *claritas*, which he translates as radiance and equates with quidditas (whatness) at the moment of epiphany (*SH* 216–18; *P* 230–31).

8. The decorative title and large, neat script indicate a juvenile hand.

9. This copy, printed by G. Eyre and A. Strahan for the British and Foreign Bible Society (London, 1825), is now in the Harry Ransom Center at the University of Texas.

10. The Greek word *zōon* is often translated as "beast" or "animal" but also means "living thing." Here Joyce's change is closer to the Douay version ("living creature"), but sometimes he retains "beast," as in the Authorized Version (e.g., 13.3). This is more common in the later chapters, suggesting a distinction between the positive images of "living beings" in chapters 4–6 and the apocalyptic "beasts" of earth, sea, and armageddon (chapters 13–17).

11. See *transition* 16–17: 13, 18: 7, 176–210, 19–20: 141–220, 22: 125–26.

12. The twenty-two manuscript epiphanies included in the Joyce exhibition of 1949–50 (now at Buffalo) may have been restored to the collection after Joyce's death, but there is no record of this among the papers of Maria Jolas, who acted as Joyce's literary executor, preparing the sale after sorting a trunk Joyce left with her in Saint-Gérand-le-Puy and the papers Alex Ponizowski and Paul Léon rescued from his flat in Paris in 1940. Similarly, the typescript of nineteen epiphanies in the Jolas papers at Yale might be posthumous, and Joyce could have been quoting from memory when he reused his epiphanies in *Ulysses* and *Finnegans Wake*, but it is more probable that he kept a copy with him.

13. The source for this epiphany is a holograph manuscript in the University of Buffalo (I.A-42). The title is taken from Morris Beja, "Epiphany and the Epiphanies," in Bowen and Carens, 712–13. It was numbered 19 by Robert Scholes and Richard M. Kain in *The Workshop of Daedalus*; the same numbers are used in *Poems and Shorter Writings*. The *Workshop* sequence is not entirely satisfactory, however, and there are occasional transcription errors in *WD* and *PSW*, so the epiphanies quoted in this book are transcribed from the manuscripts in

Buffalo, Cornell, and Yale. See the appendix for a full list of titles, sources, and *WD* numbers.

14. See Morris Beja, "The Incertitude of the Void: Epiphany and Indeterminacy," *Joyce, the Artist Manqué, and Indeterminacy: A Lecture and an Essay* (Gerards Cross: Colin Smyth, 1989); and Beja in Wawrzycka and Zanotti, 115–22 on ellipsis in the epiphanies.

15. Stanislaus emphasizes Georgie's stoicism in the face of death, "only saying to his terrified mother:—I am very young to die" (*MBK* 134), but at the corresponding moment in *Stephen Hero*, Isabel's body is wracked by involuntary sobbing ("her bosom began to heave loudly beneath the bedclothes" [169]).

16. According to Lacan, "The relation of the subject to the Other is entirely produced in a process of gap [*béance*]" (Seminar 11, 206). This gap is the lack that gives rise to desire and is thus constitutive of the Symbolic order. Indeed, the connection to speech is already present in Lacan's term, *béance*, which means both a large hole and the opening of the larynx.

17. Hugh Kenner, for one, guessed that "death" was the "word known to all men" long before the corrected edition; Kenner, *Ulysses* (London: Allen and Unwin, 1982), 129. See also Jean Kimball, "Love and Death in Ulysses: 'Word Known to All Men,'" *James Joyce Quarterly* 24, no. 2 (1987): 143–60.

18. In *Silence: Lectures and Writings* (Middletown, Conn.: Wesleyan University Press, 1961), Cage describes entering an anechoic chamber, or room without echoes, and hearing "two sounds, one high and one low. . . . [T]he high one was my nervous system in operation, the low one my blood in circulation" (8). The story is retold as an epiphany in *Indeterminacy* (#6: 5.02–5.58). These two versions, and the titles of the works they appear in, indicate that the poles of Cage's art are silence and indeterminacy, whereas Joyce's are silence and repetition.

Chapter 2. From Genesis to Joyce: A Brief History of Epiphany

1. Examples from classical literature include the *Iliad* 2.324 and the *Odyssey* 3.173. *Phainos* appears thirty-one times in the New Testament, of which thirteen are in Matthew. *Epiphaneia*, from which the English word is derived, occurs six times (2 Thess. 2:8; 1 Tim. 6:14; 2 Tim. 1:10; 2 Tim. 4:1; 2 Tim. 4:8; Tit. 2:13).

2. See Augustine, *Sermons for Christmas and Epiphany* (New York: Newman, 1978), 154–82, and the breviary for January 13 and February 2.

3. Joyce's correspondence and the definition in *Stephen Hero* (216) suggest that he thought of epiphanies as a literary genre. Ellmann argues that Joyce turned to prose as a reaction against his contemporaries: Joyce admired Yeats but felt unable to rival him, just as the shadow of Ibsen (and later Synge) loomed large in his imagination (*JJ* 87), which explains why he abandoned his early poetry (*Moods* and *Shine and Dark*) and why it took him so long to write another play after *A*

Brilliant Career (1900) and *Dream Stuff* (ca. 1901). The form he devised in their place, the epiphany, can be understood as Joyce's first attempt to unite poetry and drama in prose, combining "the quintessence of Ibsenism" (Shaw's phrase) with Yeats's "Symbolism of Poetry."

4. See Morris Beja, *Epiphany in the Modern Novel* (Seattle: University of Washington Press, 1971); Robert Langbaum, "The Epiphanic Mode in Wordsworth and Modern Literature," *New Literary History* 14, no. 2 (1983): 335–58; Ashton Nichols, *The Poetics of Epiphany: Nineteenth-Century Origins of the Modern Literary Moment* (Tuscaloosa: University of Alabama Press, 1987); Wim Tigges, *Moments of Moment: Aspects of the Literary Epiphany* (Amsterdam: Rodopi, 1999); Birgit Neuhold, *Measuring the Sadness: Conrad, Joyce, Woolf and European Epiphany* (Frankfurt am Main: Peter Lang, 2009).

5. See Felix Jacoby, *Die Fragmente Der Griechischen Historiker* (Berlin: E. J. Brill, 1968), 334, 81; and Verity J. Platt, *Facing the Gods: Epiphany and Representation in Graeco-Roman Art, Literature and Religion* (Cambridge: Cambridge University Press, 2011).

6. The word most commonly used for divine manifestations in the Old Testament is *mareh* (הָאַרְמ: sight, appearance, vision), which appears 104 times in a variety of contexts, including Moses ascending Mount Sinai to receive the tables of the law (Ex. 24.17): "And the sight [הָאַרְמוּ: *appearance*] of the glory of the Lord was like devouring fire on the top of the mountain in the eyes of the children of Israel" (*KJV*). Joyce recreates this moment in "Aeolus" (*U* 7.862–69), providing an epiphanic account of the origins of writing.

7. In *Le sacré et le profane* (Paris: Gallimard, 1992), Mircea Eliade describes the creation of the world as the archetypal Judeo-Christian "*hiérophanie*" or sacred manifestation, which all subsequent epiphanies re-create by making manifest the presence of spirit in the world (25–32).

8. See in particular Richard Chenevix Trench's *The Star of the Wise Men* (Philadelphia: H. Hooker, 1850). In addition to his theological works, Trench was a prominent philologist, providing the founding impulse for the *OED*. Archbishop of Dublin from 1864 to 1884, Trench was known to Joyce, who shared the Martello tower with Richard's grandson, Samuel Chenevix Trench, the model for Haines in *Ulysses*. Joyce owned Trench's *Proverbs and Their Lessons: Being the Substance of Lectures Delivered to Young Men's Societies* (London: Macmillan, 1869), a work best described (like Skeat's *Etymological Dictionary*) as sacred philology.

9. Isaiah 7:14; Micah 5:1; Hosea 11:1; Jeremiah 31:15; Isaiah 4:3, ordering the narrative into five scenes: Joseph's first dream; Herod and the magi; Joseph's second dream; Herod and the children; Joseph's third dream (Brown 51).

10. In Luke, the star appears to shepherds who are led to a manger. Both accounts emphasize the humble nature of the epiphany, which seems to have

appealed to Joyce, who singled out Yeats's homely, enigmatic tale, "The Adoration of the Magi," for lavish praise in his early essay "The Day of the Rabblement" (*CW* 71).

11. While Beja's argument is persuasive, its force depends on the meaning of "secular." In its original sense, "[o]f or pertaining to the world" (*OED*), the modern epiphany is largely "secular"; however, in its connotations of the "non-sacred" or the "profane," the word is misleading: modern literary epiphanies typically reconceive the spiritual through subjective experiences of time, memory, consciousness, or language.

12. Joyce provides a cryptic reference to this scene ("to Legge before" [127.8]) in the first question of *Finnegans Wake* 1.6, which Henkes and Bindervoet interpret as a key to the work.

13. See http://www.augustinus.it/latino/contro_parmeniano/ 3.4.24.

14. See http://catalogue.nli.ie/pdflookup.php?pdfid=vtls000194606_02 (17–19).

15. One might object that Dedalus's reading of *Hamlet* centers on an epiphanic theory of the name, but this is not so much Shakespeare's revelation as Stephen's application of an Old Testament shekinah to Shakespeare. Stephen's vision of the celestial name appearing as "[a] star by night, . . . [a] pillar of cloud by day" (*U* 9.944, adapting Ex. 13.21–22) can be traced back to *Portrait* and through to *Finnegans Wake*, providing an increasingly prominent emblem of the linguistic epiphany, but its origins are obviously in the Bible, not the Bard.

16. "Si jamais quelque chose a ressemblé à une inspiration subite, c'est le movement qui se fit en moi à cette lecture; tout à coup je me sens ma tête prise par un etourdissement semblable a l'ivresse. Une violente palpitation m'oppresse, souleve ma poitrine; ne puvant plus respirer en merchant, je me laisse tomber sous un des arbres de l'avenuë, et j'y passé une demie heure dans une telle agitation qu'en me relevant j'apperçus tout le devant de ma veste mouillé de mes larmes sans avoir senti qu'en repandois" (Second letter to M. de Malesherbes, January 12, 1762, qtd. in Neuhold, *Measuring the Sadness*, 43).

17. For instance, de Man claims that for Wordsworth, imagination marks "a possibility for consciousness to exist entirely by and for itself" (16), but it is almost impossible to conceive of the imagination functioning "independently of all relationship with the outside world" (16). We should be especially wary of divorcing imagination from sensory experience, because Wordsworth's "language of the sense" is a kind of proto-phenomenology, hinting at both the materiality of language and a reflexive awareness of its signifying systems. Paul de Man, *The Rhetoric of Romanticism* (New York: Columbia University Press, 1984).

18. Compare Revelation 1:8–18, 21:6 and *Paradise Lost* 5.153–65. Max Wildi, in "Wordsworth and the Simplon Pass," *English Studies* 40 (1959): 224–32, points out

that descriptions of Alpine sublimity were a standard topos in eighteenth-century travel writing.

19. In *The Book of God: Secularization and Design in the Romantic Era* (Philadelphia: Pennsylvania University Press, 2007), Colin Jager suggests that in the second half of *The Prelude*, Wordsworth shifts the domain of design from the book of nature to the poem (186–87).

20. Blake, for one, was not convinced: "You shall not bring me down to believe such fitting & fitted I know better & Please your Lordship": http://www.blakearchive.org/exist/blake/archive/erdman.xq?id=b12.12.

21. See the introduction and MacDuff, "Death and the Limits of Epiphany: Wordsworth's 'Spots of Time' and Joyce's Epiphanies of Death," *James Joyce Quarterly* 53, nos. 1–2: 61–74.

22. "To burn always with this hard, gemlike flame, to maintain this ecstasy, is success in life" (Pater, *The Renaissance*, 1873, 210).

23. These passages are quoted in Beja, *Epiphany in the Modern Novel*, 17–19, 52–54, 112.

24. See, for example, Thomas B. Stroup, "Bottom's Name and His Epiphany." *Shakespeare Quarterly* 29, no. 1 (1978): 79–82; Martin Bidney, *Patterns of Epiphany: From Wordsworth to Tolstoy, Pater, and Barrett Browning* (Carbondale: Southern Illinois University Press, 1997); Gerald Gillespie, *Proust, Mann, Joyce in the Modernist Context*, 2nd ed. (Washington, D.C.: Catholic University of America Press, 2010); D. K. Danow, "Epiphany in 'Doctor Zhivago,'" *Modern Language Review* 76, no. 4 (1981): 889–903; Sharon Kim, *Literary Epiphany in the Novel, 1850–1950: Constellations of the Soul* (New York: Palgrave Macmillan, 2012); and Paul Maltby, *The Visionary Moment: A Postmodern Critique* (New York: State University of New York Press, 2002).

25. Other critics who have argued for the continuing importance of epiphany in Joyce include Marilyn French, S. L. Goldberg, Robert M. Scotto, Jay Losey, Zack Bowen, and Vivian Heller.

Chapter 3. "Remember your epiphanies . . . deeply deep"

1. Robert M. Adams has a "low estimate of the epiphanies" in *James Joyce: Common Sense and Beyond* (New York: Random House, 1966), ix; Vicky Mahaffey regards them as naive and humourless (in Attridge, *The Cambridge Companion to James Joyce* [Cambridge: Cambridge University Press 1990], 185–87); Robert Scholes considers them "supercilious" in "Joyce and the Epiphany: The Key to the Labyrinth?" *Sewanee Review* 72 (1964): 65–77, 73.

2. One exception—and one of the most original and insightful essays on the epiphanies—is Catherine Millot's Lacanian reading, "Épiphanies," in *Joyce Avec Lacan*, ed. Jacques Aubert (Paris: Navarin, 1987), 87–95.

3. Ellmann and Scholes suggest 1900 to 1903 (*JJ* 87; *WD* 5); Litz proposes 1901/02 to 1904 (*PSW* 157).

4. Stanislaus also copied three of the epiphanies out twice, in the same order (Cornell 4609 Bd Ms 3), and there is a typescript of nineteen epiphanies in the Eugene and Maria Jolas papers at Yale (Gen Ms 108.15.63: see http://www.geneticjoycestudies.org/articles/GJS17/GJS17_Macduff).

5. As well as the obvious connection between the snatches of dialogue and lyrical vignettes each records, there is a structural similarity between Joyce's epiphanies and Baudelaire's *Petits Poèmes en Prose* (Paris: Larousse, 2009): "On ne pourrait pas dire, sans injustice, qu'il n'a ni queue ni tête, puisque tout, au contraire, y est à la fois tête et queue, alternativement et réciproquement" (1).

6. For example, Hayman 1998, 647; Vivian Heller, *Joyce, Decadence, and Emancipation* (Urbana: University of Illinois Press, 1995), 15.

7. As John Paul Riquelme points out, chapters 19–25 in Theodore Spencer's edition of *Stephen Hero* should read 18–24. I use the corrected numbers.

8. My transcription. Cf. *JJA* 7:45.

9. Rutland Square, now renamed Parnell Square, encloses the Rotunda hospital and gardens in north central Dublin. In 1903, the most likely date for this epiphany, Gogarty was a medical student at the Rotunda.

10. The standard account is given by Maria Jolas: "Someone had called him 'a blue-nosed comedian,' so he insisted that a star be put on the end of his nose to illuminate it" (*JJ* 658).

11. The black derby hat was to symbolize his mourning for his father and his "chronic dejection"; his superstitious belief that he was cursed with uncommonly bad luck is represented by the cobwebs and the number 13; the patches on his knees signify poverty; and the roll of paper in his pocket bears the song, "Let me like a soldier fall," from William Vincent Wallace's opera, *Maritana* (1845), referred to by Mr. Browne in "The Dead" (*D* 200; *JJ* 658).

12. John Joyce is said to have disdained his in-laws, regarding Lillie Murray as common.

13. For a range of interpretations of Stephen's aesthetics, see Irene Hendry, "Joyce's *Epiphanies*," *Sewanee Review* 54 (1946): 449–67; William T. Noon, *Joyce and Aquinas* (New Haven: Yale University Press, 1957); Florence L. Walzl, "The Liturgy of the Epiphany Season and the Epiphanies of Joyce," *PMLA* 80, no. 4 (1965): 436–50; Morris Beja, *Epiphany in the Modern Novel* (Seattle: University of Washington Press, 1971); Ashton Nichols, *The Poetics of Epiphany: Nineteenth-Century Origins of the Modern Literary Moment* (Tuscaloosa: University of Alabama Press, 1987); Robert Langbaum, "The Epiphanic Mode in Wordsworth and Modern Literature," *New Literary History* 14, no. 2 (1983): 335–58; Birgit Neuhold, *Measuring the Sadness: Conrad, Joyce, Woolf and European Epiphany* (Frankfurt am

Main: Peter Lang, 2009); Wim Tigges, *Moments of Moment: Aspects of the Literary Epiphany* (Amsterdam: Rodopi, 1999); Paul Maltby, *The Visionary Moment: A Postmodern Critique* (New York: State University of New York Press, 2002); Sharon Kim, *Literary Epiphany in the Novel, 1850–1950: Constellations of the Soul* (New York: Palgrave Macmillan, 2012); Richard Kearney, "Epiphanies in Joyce," in Fogarty and O'Rourke, 239–59; and Jūratė Levina, "The Aesthetics of Phenomena: Joyce's Epiphanies," *Joyce Studies Annual* (2017): 185–219. However, none of these critics attend to the linguistic implications of Stephen's interpretations.

14. See Lorraine Weir, "The Choreography of Gesture: Marcel Jousse and *Finnegans Wake*," *James Joyce Quarterly* 14, no. 3 (1977): 313–25; and Stephen Heath, "Ambiviolences: Notes for Reading Joyce," in *Post-Structuralist Joyce: Essays from the French*, ed. Attridge and Ferrer, 31–68 (Cambridge: Cambridge University Press, 1984).

15. For example, William T. Noon, *Joyce and Aquinas* (New Haven: Yale University Press, 1957), 67–68; Zaniello, "The Epiphany and the Object-Image Distinction," *JJQ* 4 (1967): 286–88; Morris Beja, *Epiphany in the Modern Novel* (Seattle: University of Washington Press, 1971), 77–81; Hugh Kenner, *Dublin's Joyce* (New York: Columbia University Press, 1987), 138.

16. See http://catalogue.nli.ie/Record/vtls000194606 (17–19).

17. Kant criticized Baumgarten on etymological grounds, arguing that aesthetics is not the "science of the beautiful" but the science of sensory perception (1998, A21).

Chapter 4. Silence and Repetition in *Dubliners*

1. For example, *JJ* 169; Florence L. Walzl, "The Liturgy of the Epiphany Season and the Epiphanies of Joyce," *PMLA* 80, no. 4 (1965): 436–50, 432; Warren Beck, *Joyce's Dubliners: Substance, Vision, and Art* (Durham, N.C.: Duke University Press, 1969), 21–25; James Joyce, *Dubliners*, Viking Critical Edition, ed. Robert Scholes and A. Walton Litz (New York: Viking, 1969), 253–56.

2. By his own admission, Steppe had not actually read the letter, placing faith in John O'Hanlon's opinion, even though Stuart Gilbert, Richard Ellmann, and Eugene Roche (curator of the Curran collection) concur that Joyce wrote "epicleti" (*LI* 55; *JJ* 169; personal communication). After studying a facsimile of the letter alongside a selection of Joyce's terminal s's and i's, I believe "epiclets" is most likely, but it is impossible to be certain.

3. See, for example, Terence Brown's Penguin edition (*D* xxxiii–xxxvi), and *Dubliners: An Illustrated Edition with Annotations*, ed. John Wyse Jackson and Bernard McGinley (New York: St. Martin's Griffin, 1995).

4. For example, in a brilliant reading of "Clay," Attridge challenges the critical assumption that the "soft wet substance" Maria feels is the clay of the title, thereby

bringing referentiality into question; see Derek Attridge and Daniel Ferrer, eds., *Post-Structuralist Joyce: Essays from the French* (Cambridge: Cambridge University Press, 1984), 35–51.

5. For a discussion of this letter in relation to epiphany in *Dubliners*, see Morris Beja, "One Good Look at Themselves: Epiphany in *Dubliners*," in *Work in Progress: Joyce Centenary Essays*, ed. Richard F. Peterson, Alan M. Cohn, and Edmund L. Epstein, 3–14 (Carbondale: Southern Illinois University Press 1983).

6. Compare, for instance, "[t]hrough one of the broken panes I heard the rain impinge upon the earth, the fine incessant needles of water playing in the sodden beds" (*D* 23) with "The Girls, The Boys": "The quick light shower is over but tarries, a cluster of diamonds, among the shrubs of the quadrangle where an exhalation arises from the black earth." Or compare the first sentence of "Two Gallants" with the first sentence in "Hoofs upon the Dublin Road."

7. Kenner argues that Frank is less than frank about his motives in whisking Eveline away to Buenos Aires (slang for a life of prostitution, apparently). But the real irony is not in Frank's name, his motivation, or the possibility of sailing from Dublin to Argentina (see Phillip F. Herring, *Joyce's Uncertainty Principle* [Princeton, N.J.: Princeton University Press, 1987], 5–7); it is structural, in the gap between Eveline's and Frank's points of view.

8. Joyce is known to have read his brother's diaries, which include Stanislaus's record of a visit to the Rotunda theater, where he met a "handsome, dark-haired" woman (*MBK* 160), who, according to Stanislaus, provided the inspiration for Mrs. Sinico. Stanislaus notes that Duffy shares many of his own characteristics, such as "intolerance of drunkenness, hostility to socialism, and the habit of noting short sentences on a sheaf of loose pages pinned together" with a brass pin, like Mr. Duffy (*MBK* 160). These notes, which James Joyce referred to as *Bile Beans* (*JJ* 138; *D* 103), include Duffy's epigrammatic sentences in "A Painful Case": "Every bond is a bond to sorrow" and "Love between man and man is impossible" (*D* 160). But these sentences are themselves close paraphrases of Nietzsche (Marvin Magalaner, "Joyce, Nietzsche, and Hauptmann in James Joyce's 'A Painful Case,'" *PMLA* 68, no. 1 (1953): 95–102), and Magalaner points out that Joyce had translated Hauptmann's *Michael Kramer*, the same play Duffy is translating in "A Painful Case" (Magalaner 95; *D* 103; *JJ* 91), implying that Joyce's irony is directed toward himself as much as Stanislaus.

9. Nannie is not entirely deaf, as the aunt could have shouted at her, and she is not mute either, as she mutters her prayers in front of the coffin, but within the space of the story, she communicates entirely through gesture (6). As such, she figures as the silent sister to Eliza's repetitive discourse.

10. Recall the boy's feeble smile in the dream, "as if to absolve the simoniac of his sin" (3). Given that the only exchange in the story that could conventionally

be described as simony is the High Toast the boy brings when he receives religious instruction, and that Eliza has just hinted at some hidden connection between the snuff and the priest's decline, there is a certain logic in the boy's unconscious wish to absolve his part in the death.

11. Cf. Burton Waisbren and Florence Walzl, "Paresis and the Priest: Jame's Joyce's Symbolic Use of Syphilis in 'The Sisters,'" *Annals of Internal Medicine* (1974): 758–62; Zack Bowen and James F. Carens, eds., "Joyce and the Epiphany Concept: A New Approach," *Journal of Modern Literature* 9, no. 1 (1981): 103–14, 106–7.

12. The critical events in all but two of the stories take place at or after nightfall, and the imagery of light and darkness is pervasive throughout. Candles play a significant role in "The Boarding House," "Ivy Day," and "The Dead"; they also have a special significance for Tom Kernan in "Grace." Eveline Hill and Tommy Chandler are both found staring out of windows while the image of the lighted window reappears in "Araby" and "The Dead."

13. Euclid defines the gnomon as a parallelogram with a similar parallelogram missing from one of its corners: BCDEFG in figure 2 (*Elements* II, Def. 2). The earliest recorded use of "gnomon" in the *OED* refers to a sundial, metaphorically extended to the nose, and then other "instruments serving as 'indicators.'" Derived from the Greek γνώμων (indicator), the word can refer to a carpenter's square, which may explain why gnomon also means "[a] rule, canon of belief or action" (4). Citing Leonard Albert, Norris, in *Suspicious Readings of Joyce's Dubliners* (Philadelphia: University of Pennsylvania Press, 2003), asserts that gnomon's Greek root "means 'model, criterion, standard,'" which allows her to claim that the first story is "the gnomon of the book": "with its gaps and silences . . . , 'The Sisters' serves as a synecdoche for a collection of fictions without wholeness" (18). But in "Gnomon Inverted," in Bollettieri et al., eds., *The Languages of Joyce* (Philadelphia: John Benjamins, 1992), Fritz Senn points out that the gnomon is not only "The Figure with Something Missing, The Gap to Be Filled" but also an accretive symbol. Euclid's definition "makes it appear incomplete. But it might have been defined just as well as an addition: if you take one parallelogram and join a smaller one to its corner (with parallel sides) you get the same result: a construction of *both and*" (249–50). Senn's geometry is slightly askew (think of a square, for example), but the general point holds. This structure of the infinitely repeatable figure defined by both its lack and its surplus combines the poles of silence and repetition that unify *Dubliners*.

Chapter 5. "A day of dappled seaborne clouds": *A Portrait of the Artist*'s Epiphany

1. The earliest surviving pages begin with "The Spell of Arms and Voices"; many of its most powerful scenes are based on epiphanies (e.g., Isabel's death is

dramatized through four epiphanies in seven pages), and the manuscript breaks off soon after Stephen's aesthetics of epiphany. Ilaria Natali analyzes Joyce's rewriting of the epiphanies in *Stephen Hero*; see Ilaria Natali, "A Portrait of James Joyce's Epiphanies as a Source Text": http://www.humanicus.org/global/issues/humanicus-6-2011/humanicus-6-2011-3.pdf.

2. See Morris Beja, *Epiphany in the Modern Novel* (Seattle: University of Washington Press, 1971) and "Epiphany and the Epiphanies," in Bowen and Carens, 707–25; Zack Bowen, "Epiphanies, Stephen's Diary, and the Narrative Perspective of *A Portrait of the Artist as a Young Man*," *James Joyce Quarterly* 16 (1979): 485–88, and "Joyce and the Epiphany Concept: A New Approach," *Journal of Modern Literature* 9, no. 1 (1981): 103–14; Robert Adams Day, "Dante, Ibsen, Joyce, Epiphanies, and the Art of Memory," *James Joyce Quarterly* 25, no. 3 (1988): 357–62; Kate Harrison, "The *Portrait* Epiphany," *James Joyce Quarterly* 8 (1971): 142–50; David Hayman, The Purpose and Permanence of the Joycean Epiphany," *James Joyce Quarterly* 35 (1998): 633–56; Vivian Heller, *Joyce, Decadence, and Emancipation* (Urbana: University of Illinois Press, 1995); Vicki Mahaffey, "Joyce's Shorter Works," in Attridge 1990, 185–211; John McGowan, "From Pater to Wilde to Joyce: Modernist Epiphany and the Soulful Self," *Texas Studies in Literature and Language* 32, no. 3 (1990): 417–45; Robert M. Scotto, "'Visions' and 'Epiphanies': Fictional Technique in Pater's *Marius* and Joyce's *Portrait*," *James Joyce Quarterly* 11 (1973): 41–49.

3. The threat of blindness also foreshadows Stephen's broken glasses, itself strangely prophetic of Joyce's eye troubles.

4. Gabler argues that Stephen is taken to the infirmary on October 10, 1891, in which case, the "moonless night" in the epiphany occurs on October 10–11 (Gabler says daybreak). Parnell died on October 6, but his body was returned to Ireland in the early hours of October 11, when he was buried in Glasnevin cemetery. See Gabler, "The Genesis of *A Portrait of the Artist as a Young Man*," in Brady and Carens, 1998, 106–7.

5. Stephen remembers the rats in the infirmary: "That was the way a rat felt, slimy and damp and cold" (20).

6. There is another intriguing chiasmus in the genesis of *A Portrait*: the surviving pages of *Stephen Hero* begin in the middle of epiphany #30, while *Portrait* ends a few lines after the same epiphany.

7. Two of these passages are based on epiphanies, suggesting that "The beautiful Mabel Hunter" scene may have been too, though no such manuscript epiphany survives (see Beja, *Epiphany in the Modern Novel*, 90).

8. Cf. Daedalus's conviction that "it was for the man of letters to record" the "vulgarity of speech or of gesture" with "extreme care" (*SH* 216).

9. For example: stone/folded/token, errors/men/them/ever; "from the floor,"

"set in stone"; "A lóng cúrving gállery"; "dark vapours . . . darkened . . . dark vapours."

10. Many of the motifs for Cranly come from the Trieste notebook (ca. 1907–1909), where, under the heading for John Francis Byrne, Joyce recorded details such as "He is exhausted," "He hears confession without giving absolution: a guilty priest," and "he dislodged an old figtree from a rotten tooth" (*WD* 93–94), all reused in *Portrait*, chapter 5.

11. For example, Beja, *Epiphany in the Modern Novel*; Kenneth Burke, "Fact, Inference, and Proof in the Analysis of Literary Symbolism," in *A Portrait of the Artist as a Young Man: Authoritative Text, Backgrounds and Contexts, Criticism*, ed. John Paul Riquelme, 311–28 (New York: Norton, 2007); David Hayman, "The Purpose and Permanence of the Joycean Epiphany," *James Joyce Quarterly* 35 (1998): 633–56; Vivian Heller, *Joyce, Decadence, and Emancipation* (Urbana: University of Illinois Press, 1995).

12. Altering the dialogue of "She Dances" (#26), Stephen imagines himself as a "monk," while Emma fears he is "a heretic," leading Stephen to replace "[h]is own image" with "the image of the young priest in whose company he had seen her last" (*P* 238). Dedalus bemoans the fact that "she would unveil her soul's shy nakedness" to "a priested peasant, . . . rather than to him, a priest of eternal imagination, transmuting the daily bread of experience into the radiant body of everliving life" (239–40). This chain links the epiphany to "the radiant image of the eucharist" that shapes the final tercets.

13. Echoing "The Last Tram," Joyce brings out the power of the initial scene (cf. 240, 74). Immediately after writing his first poem, Stephen goes "into his mother's bedroom and gaze[s] for a long time at his face in the mirror" (74). This mirror stage, a formative moment for the artist, is implicitly connected to the description of Simon Dedalus contemplating his earthly perfections "in the pierglass above the mantelpiece" (26) and Stephen's reflections on God "the Father contemplating from all eternity as in a mirror His Divine Perfections" (161). See Thomas C. Singer, "Riddles, Silence, and Wonder: Joyce and Wittgenstein Encountering the Limits of Language," *ELH* 57, no. 2 (1990): 459–84. These subtle reflections indicate the various senses in which *Portrait* is a book about creation.

14. Two stanzas in *Stephen Hero* indicate what Stephen's poem to Emma may have been like ("The dawn awakes with tremulous alarms" *SH* 42). According to Stanislaus Joyce, Stephen's villanelle was written during the *Shine and Dark* period (ca. 1900–1901), when Joyce was about eighteen (*MBK* 100–101; *JJ* 86). The epiphanies were composed ca. 1901–1904.

15. Cf. Luke 9:60: "Jesus said unto him, Let the dead bury their dead: but go thou and preach the kingdom of God"; Matt. 8:22: "But Jesus said unto him, Follow me; and let the dead bury their dead."

16. "[E]xhausted loins" repeats Stephen's thoughts about Cranly the previous evening, linking his elderly parents to Elizabeth and Zacchary, who were "very old" when the angel Gabriel "appeared" (*phainein*) to announce the birth of John the Baptist (*P* 270; Luke 1:7–25). There are clear parallels between the epiphany in Luke, and the first Matthean epiphany, when "an angel of the Lord appeared [*phainein*]" to announce the immaculate conception; in both gospels, chapter 2 narrates the apparition of the star leading to the nativity. In this context, John is "the precursor" to Christ (but also "saint John" the Evangelist: *P* 270); following the analogy, Cranly becomes the precursor to Stephen. There is surely a degree of irony here, but at the same time, Stephen asks himself, "Why was it that when he thought of Cranly he could never raise before his mind the entire image of his body but only the image of the head and face? Even now against the grey curtain of the morning he saw it before him like the phantom of a dream, the face of a severed head or a deathmask" (*P* 192).

17. Replacing a "wild rose" with a "geen wothe" (Joyce, 2007, ed. Riquelme, 1.12) questions the relationship between language and nature ("you could not have a green rose. But perhaps somewhere in the world you could": *P* 9). In Stephen's version, language "blossoms" through repetition ("botheth").

18. When Stephen notices his father's face "glowing with anger," he feels "the glow rise to his own cheek as the spoken words [thrill] him" (38), and when Casey sobs over the death of Parnell, Stephen is "terrorstricken" to discover tears in his father's eyes (39). Likewise, at the end of the chapter, as the rector studies Dedalus in silence, Stephen feels "the blood rising to his face and the tears about to rise to his eyes" (58).

19. Joyce's art of lyrical symbolism is evident if one compares Giovanni Pinamonti's *Hell Opened to Christians*, the scriptural citations, and Ignatius Loyola's *Spiritual Exercises* (especially "A Meditation on Hell"). On the sources, see James R. Thrane, "Joyce's Sermon on Hell: Its Source and Its Backgrounds," *Modern Philology* 57, no. 3 (1960): 172–98; Elizabeth F. Boyd, "James Joyce's Hell-Fire Sermons," *Modern Language Notes* 75, no. 7 (1960): 561–71; James Doherty, "Joyce and 'Hell Opened to Christians': The Edition He Used for His 'Hell Sermons,'" *Modern Philology* 61, no. 2 (1963): 110–19.

20. For example, in *The Aran Islands*, Synge records that among the islanders gathering seaweed, there was "a party of young girls" who "looked strangely wild and seal-like." As the tide recedes, they are islanded with birds in a tempestuous sunset that leaves Synge "trembling and flushed with exultation" (qtd. in *A Portrait of the Artist as a Young Man: Authoritative Text, Backgrounds and Contexts, Criticism*, ed. John Paul Riquelme, 311–28 [New York: Norton, 2007], 272).

21. There is perhaps an echo here of "A Story of Alsace," where the speaker eagerly anticipates "tea and bread and butter, and white pudding" (*PSW* 162).

22. "[E]ach chapter closes with a synthesis of triumph which in turn feeds the sausage-machine set up in the next chapter" (Hugh Kenner, "The *Portrait* in Perspective," *Kenyon Review* 10, no. 3 [1948]: 361–81, 379). "Each of the first four sections ends a period of Stephen's life with what Joyce, in an earlier draft, calls an epiphany: a peculiar revelation of the inner reality of an experience, accompanied with great elation, as in a mystical religious experience. Each is followed by the opening of a new chapter on a very prosaic, even depressed level" (Wayne Booth, "The Problem of Distance in *A Portrait of the Artist*," in Wollaeger 2003, 62). "At the end of each of *A Portrait*'s five parts, Joyce uses elevated language to suggest that Stephen achieves a momentary insight and intensity through a transforming experience. . . . At the start of each succeeding part, Joyce counters and ironises the intensity of the preceding conclusion by switching immediately and unexpectedly to a realistic style" (Riquelme in Derek Attridge, ed., *The Cambridge Companion to James Joyce* [Cambridge: Cambridge University Press, 1990], 117).

23. In part 1, the repetitive sounds of balls and birds in the silent air image speech as a sequence of repeated and varying soundwaves. In part 5, Joyce's aerial and ornithological imagery represents writing as the trace of repetitive movements across the "silent spaces" of the sky (245).

24. Elisabeth Marie Loevlie, in *Literary Silences in Pascal, Rousseau, and Beckett* (Oxford: Oxford University Press, 2003), distinguishes between "First-degree silence," designating "a silence that is described in the narrative" and "Second-degree silence, . . . a dynamic that arises from the text" (30).

25. "[F]lying high and low but ever round and round in straight and curving lines . . . from left to right" (243), the birds trace script-like figures across the temple of the sky, and Stephen tries to read their portent.

26. For an intriguing psychoanalytical interpretation of Joyce's "Watery Words," see Randolph Splitter, "Watery Words: Language, Sexuality, and Motherhood in Joyce's Fiction," *ELH* 49, no. 1 (1982): 190–213. On the villanelle, see Charles Rossman, "Stephen Dedalus' Villanelle," *James Joyce Quarterly* 12, no. 3 (1975): 281–93; and Day, "Dante, Ibsen, Joyce, Epiphanies, and the Art of Memory."

27. Cf. Giacomo Joyce: "My voice, dying in the echoes of its words. . . . Her eyes have drunk my thoughts: and into the moist warm yielding welcoming darkness of her womanhood my soul, itself dissolving, has streamed and poured and flooded a liquid and abundant seed" (*PSW* 239).

28. Compare Stephen's "*Parable of the Plums*" in "Aeolus," which climaxes with plum seeds spitting from the phallic column of "the onehandled adulterer" (*U* 7.1012–75).

29. Cf. Ezekiel's "vision of the likeness of the glory of the Lord," which he compares to "the appearance of the rainbow when it is in a cloud on a rainy day" (1.28–2.1).

30. These hues, refracted through "the prism of a language manycoloured," are recalled in "Aeolus," where Stephen associates Dante's terza rima with the divine pageant of *Purgatorio* 29, the verses coming "three by three . . . , in green, in rose, in russet" (*U* 7.715–24).

31. This passage is not in Peacock's *English Prose from Mandeville to Ruskin*, which Joyce used to parody Mandeville in "Oxen of the Sun" (*U* 167–272), but Peacock's anthology begins with the *Travels*.

32. Trench's numerous philological works include the widely reprinted *Study of Words* (1851), *English Past and Present* (1855), and *A Select Glossary of English Words* (1859). Trench's seminal role in instigating the *OED* is attested in prefaces to the first and second editions (1915, 1928), as well as the facsicles (1884–1915).

33. Max Muller held similar views about the relationship between language and thought: "Without speech no reason, without reason no speech" (1873, 2.73). He makes the same point about Latin: "in its full reality [Thought] exists nowhere but in Language" (1887, 2.508), for "notio and nomen are two words for the same thing." See Gregory M. Downing, "Diverting Philology: Language and Its Effects in Popularised Philology and Joyce's Work," in *James Joyce: The Study of Languages*, ed. Van Hulle, 121–66 (Bruxelles: P. Lang, 2002), 152–57.

34. With its double alliteration, Miller's line is even more poetic than the line Stephen remembers (Miller's first publication was *Poems, Written in the Leisure Hours of a Journeyman Mason*). Interestingly, Trench also began by writing poetry, before turning to theology.

35. This may explain why the story of "Bous Stephaneferos" (Stephen Ox-soul, 182) begins with a moocow. See Benstock in Thomas Staley, ed., *Approaches to Joyce's Portrait: Ten Essays* (Pittsburgh: University of Pittsburgh Press, 1976), esp. 210–11.

36. Skeat derives it from the Danish *smuk*, meaning pretty, an etymology disputed by the *OED*.

37. Cf. the analogous passage in *Stephen Hero*, where Stephen says, "Words are simply receptacles for human thought" (*SH* 33).

38. It would be nice to know which dictionary Stephen (or Joyce) used, but the source is elusive. The *OED* entry was not published until 1915, after *Portrait*'s serialization in the *Egoist*. The word is not in Skeat, though Joyce could have looked up *tun* and *dish* separately. Other possibilities include *Walker's Pronouncing Dictionary* or the *New Century Dictionary*.

Chapter 6. Permutations of Epiphany in *Ulysses*

1. See *WD* 103 and Beja, "Epiphany and the Epiphanies," in Bowen and Carens, 103. In the quotation, I follow Beja's correction of "washed" to "wasted." Many of the details for her "deadroom" are also drawn from the first entry under "Mother," such as the drawer containing her "secrets," the "birdcage hung in the

sunny window," and the pantomime song from *Turko the Terrible*: "I am the boy / That can enjoy / Invisibility" (*WD* 102; *U* 1.253–62).

2. Stephen's thoughts on Cyril Sargent in "Nestor" weave an equally complex palimpsest from the Trieste notebook passage, "She Comes at Night," and the discussion of *amor matris* in *Portrait* (263): "someone had loved him, borne him in her arms and in her heart. . . . She had loved his weak watery blood drained from her own. Was that then real? The only true thing in life? . . . She was no more: the trembling skeleton of a twig burnt in the fire, an odour of rosewood and wetted ashes" (2.140–46).

3. Yeats's lines read: "And rules the shadows of the wood, / And the white breast of the dim sea" (10–11).

4. Cf. Skeat, who cross-references "mortuary" with "mortal," directing the reader to "deadly" in R. C. Trench's *Select Glossary of English Words*, an entry that has striking affinities with "The Dead."

5. The concision of Bloom's impressions is also achieved by stripping the original epiphany of its anaphoric structure ("The girl / The girl's face / The girl") and by shifting the emphasis from verbs ("push on," "runs," "hurries," etc.) to high-precision noun phrases.

6. The best studies of circulation in *Ulysses* are Mark Osteen's *The Economy of* Ulysses: *Making Both Ends Meet* (Syracuse: Syracuse University Press, 1995), which provides a compelling analysis of monetary circulation and the linguistic or intertextual economies of *Ulysses*, and Maud Ellmann's "*Ulysses:* The Epic of the Human Body," in *A Companion to James Joyce*, ed. Brown (Malden, Mass.: Blackwell, 2008), which shows how "[t]he city in *Ulysses* takes the form of a gigantic body circulating language, commodities, and money, together with the Dubliners whirled round in these economies" (55). However, neither Osteen nor Ellmann attends to Joyce's *breaks* in circulation, which are as significant as the circulating systems.

7. The epiphany is clearly echoed in *Portrait* (70–71), and perhaps also in "Proteus," where Stephen's imagined misrecognition ("We thought you were someone else") by "nuncle Richie" (3.75–76) recalls Eliza's mistake in epiphany #5: "I thought you were Mary Ellen, Jim," although this connection seems to have been overlooked.

8. See "Joyce le symptôme I" in Aubert, ed., *Joyce Avec Lacan* (Paris: Navarin, 1987), 27.

9. In a letter of 1905, Joyce told Stanislaus: "When [Nora] saw me copy Epiphanies into my novel she asked would all that paper be wasted" (*LII* 78).

10. Joyce's intertextuality has received a good deal of attention, from source studies (e.g., Atherton, Helsinger, Moseley, Reynolds, Pelaschiar) to broader, theoretical considerations, such as André Topia's "The Matrix and the Echo" (in

Post-Structuralist Joyce: Essays from the French, ed. Attridge and Ferrer (Cambridge: Cambridge University Press, 1984), Brandon Kershner's "Dialogical and Intertextual Joyce" (in *Palgrave Advances in James Joyce Studies*, ed. Rabaté (Basingstoke, U.K.: Palgrave Macmillan, 2004); and Scarlett Baron's *Strandentwining Cable: Joyce, Flaubert, and Intertextuality* (Oxford: Oxford University Press, 2011).

11. See *P* 24–25, 275, discussed above. The connection to the epiphanies is strengthened by evidence that the first three chapters of *Ulysses* germinated from material left over from *Portrait* (Arthur Walton Litz, *The Art of James Joyce: Method and Design in* Ulysses *and* Finnegans Wake (London: Oxford University Press, 1961); Hans Walter Gabler, "Joyce's Text in Progress," in *The Cambridge Companion to James Joyce*, ed. Attridge (Cambridge: Cambridge University Press, 1990), 213–36.

12. Budgen, who had sailed on schooners like the *Rosevean*, informed Joyce that the correct word for the spars described in "Proteus" is "yards," not "crosstrees." Joyce replied, "There's no sort of criticism I more value than that. But the word 'crosstrees' is essential. It comes in later on and I can't change it" (Frank Budgen, *James Joyce and the Making of* Ulysses, ed. Clive Hart (Oxford: Oxford University Press, 1972), 57.

13. See Rodolphe Gasché, *The Tain of the Mirror: Derrida and the Philosophy of Reflection* (Cambridge: Harvard University Press, 1986), 225–39; and Jacques Derrida, *Dissemination*, trans. Barbara Johnson (Chicago: University of Chicago Press, 1981), 156–236.

14. See Derek Attridge, "Creating" and "The creation of the other" in *The Singularity of Literature* (London: Routledge, 2004), 17–27.

15. Stephen makes full use of his poetic license. Tycho's star, a supernova discovered by the Danish astronomer Tycho Brahe on November 11, 1572, (when Shakespeare was eight), "brightened rapidly until it outshone all the other planets and stars at night and was visible in daylight; it began to fade in December 1572," although the phenomenon lasted until March 1574, causing "considerable imaginative excitement in Elizabethan England as a sort of Star of Bethlehem"; Don Creighton Gifford and Robert J. Seidman, *Notes for Joyce:* Dubliners *and* A Portrait of the Artist as a Young Man (New York: E. P. Dutton, 1967), 244.

16. This hypothesis, still the most widely accepted theory of star formation, shapes Dedalus's theory of language formation from nebulous cloud to shining star in *Portrait* and *Ulysses*, as well as providing a powerful trope in the *Wake*. The nebular hypothesis can be traced back to Swedenborg, but it is more likely that Joyce relied on one of the astronomy books Bloom possesses (17.1373, 1391): either Sir Robert Ball's *The Story of the Heavens* (1885; see chapter 22, "Star Clusters and Distant Suns" [461–68]), or his unidentified *Handbook of Astronomy*. It has been suggested that the latter may be an anachronistic reference to Harold Jacoby's

Astronomy: A Popular Handbook (1913; cf. 360: "how can the spiral nebula, in turn, develop into a sun and planets such as we have in our solar system?"), or a generic reference to popular works such as Amédée Guillemin's *The Heavens: An Illustrated Handbook of Popular Astronomy* (London: Richard Bentley & Son, 1876), which presents the same theory (416–17).

17. "Phenomenon" is derived from the ancient Greek φαινόμενον, usually used in the plural τὰ φαινόμενα: "Things that appear, . . . celestial phenomena" (cf. Aratus's τὰ φαινόμενα, translated by Cicero as *Phenomena*). As a substantive, "φαινόμενος appearing, apparent (to the senses or mind)," derives from the passive present participle of φαίνειν, to show or cause to appear (*OED*).

18. "If only one star [can be seen in the sky] it is yet day; if two stars, it is twilight; three stars, it is night" (M. L. Rockinson, *The Tract Sabbath* 1.61, cited in Gifford and Seidman, *Notes for Joyce*, 399).

19. Fritz Senn points out that Bloom's definition, the "transmigration of souls" (4.342), is identical to *Walker's Pronouncing Dictionary*, the same work Gerty MacDowell uses to look up "halcyon," which is defined substantively as "a bird" and adjectivally as "placid, quiet, still." As the former property of Grandpa Giltrap (from whom the citizen borrows Garryowen), Joyce is perhaps making an oblique comment on the paucity of Walker's dictionary, with its excessive focus on orthography and pronunciation (with few spelling or pronunciation variants, definitions reduced to a single word or short phrase, and no indication of etymology). By contrast, in Skeat, we learn that "halcyon" is derived, via Latin, from the Greek word for kingfisher, for "They lay and sit about midwinter, when daies be shortest; and the time whiles they are broody, is called the *halcyon* daies; for during that season, the sea is calme and nauigable" (Holland's *Pliny* X.32, qtd. in Skeat, *An Etymological Dictionary of the English Language* [Oxford: Clarendon, 1888]). "Metempsychosis," also from the Greek, as Bloom surmises (4.341), and likewise connected to the myth of a winged animal, has an even more interesting etymology: *meta* (with, after, between) + *psyche* (breath, life, soul, spirit, butterfly). While *Walker's Pronouncing Dictionary* provides fixed definitions of form and meaning, Skeat attempts to throw "light on the history of words" (v). Interestingly, Bloom's dream house contains Webster's "New Century Dictionary" (17.1523–24), a work notable for its progressive attitude to language change. Taken together, these reference books give a good guide to Joyce's major linguistic concerns: the materiality of language, its history, and the "remainder."

20. See Stanislaus Joyce, *The Complete Dublin Diary of Stanislaus Joyce* (Ithaca: Cornell University Press, 1971), 43; Morris Beja, *Epiphany in the Modern Novel* (Seattle: University of Washington Press, 1971); Jay B. Losey, "Epiphany in Pater's Portraits," *English Literature in Transition, 1880–1920* 29, no. 3 (1986): 297–308; John McGowan, "From Pater to Wilde to Joyce: Modernist Epiphany and the Soulful Self," *Texas Studies in Literature and Language* 32, no. 3 (1990): 417–45.

21. In fact, as Sam Slote shows in "Epiphanic 'Proteus,'" the earliest draft of "Proteus" consists of sixteen discrete fragments that can be compared to epiphanies, with the last based on epiphany #33. In revising the episode, however, the concept of epiphany is transformed from "a phenomenological event" to "a linguistic event": see http://www.geneticjoycestudies.org/articles/GJS5/GJS5lote.

22. Both episodes begin at 8 a.m.; the lines occur 248 and 218 lines into their respective episodes.

23. The first draft of "Proteus" ended with this passage (Sam Slote, "Epiphanic 'Proteus,'" *Genetic Joyce Studies* 5 [Spring 2005]: http://www.geneticjoycestudies.org/articles/GJS5/GJS5lote). *Giacomo Joyce*, written shortly before "Proteus," echoes the same epiphany (*PSW* 235). On *Giacomo Joyce* and the epiphanies, see Michel Delville, "Epiphanies and Prose Lyrics: James Joyce and the Poetics of the Fragment," in *Giacomo Joyce: Envoys of the Other*, ed. Louis Armand and Clare Wallace, 101–30 (Prague: Litteraria Pragensia, 2006); and John McCourt, "Epiphanies of Language, Longing, Liminality in Giacomo Joyce," in Armand and Wallace, 228–48.

24. A cliché originally referred to "a metal stereotype of a wood-engraving used to print from," and later a photographic negative (see *OED* 1, 2). On clichés in "Eumaeus," see Levine (115–19).

25. See Tim Conley, *Joyces Mistakes: Problems of Intention, Irony and Interpretation* (Toronto: University of Toronto Press, 2003).

26. Cf. *Portrait*: "In the virgin womb of the imagination the word was made flesh" (236) with "Oxen": "In woman's womb word is made flesh but in the spirit of the maker all flesh that passes becomes the word that shall not pass away. This is the postcreation" (14.292–94).

27. Cf. *U* 14.1080–85 with *Giacomo Joyce*: "Twilight . . . Grey eve lowring on wide sagegreen pasturelands, shedding silently dusk and dew. She follows her mother with ungainly grace, the mare leading her filly foal. Grey twilight moulds softly the slim and shapely haunches, the meek supple tendonous neck, the fine-boned skull" (*PSW* 231).

28. As a verb, "wimble" has been in use since the fifteenth century, which Joyce could have found out from Skeat, who quotes Hexham, "to pearce or bore with a wimble." Skeat also defines the adjective as "giddy" or "skittish," which fits neatly with Anne wangling along.

29. See, for example, Hugh Kenner, *Joyce's Voices* (London: Faber and Faber, 1978), 37; Fritz Senn, *Joyce's Dislocutions: Essays on Reading as Translation* (Baltimore, Md.: Johns Hopkins University Press, 1984), 110–11; Derek Attridge, *Joyce Effects: On Language, Theory, and History* (Cambridge: Cambridge University Press, 2001), 172–87.

Chapter 7. The Panepiphanal World of *Finnegans Wake*

1. It is worth recalling that Stanislaus Joyce made at least three copies of epiphany #34 (Cornell 15, 17) and Joyce had already recycled it twice, at crucial moments, in *Ulysses*.

2. For a different reading, see Jay B. Losey, "Dream-Epiphanies in *Finnegans Wake*," *James Joyce Quarterly* 26, no. 4 (1989): 611–17.

3. Mercius's reply also terminates in an eloquent gesture: "He lifts the lifewand and the dumb speak" (195.6), bringing the inanimate to life and drawing speech from silence, like the metamorphosis of stone and tree into (as well as from) two washerwomen gossiping by the banks of the river.

4. Hilary Clark argues that the recognition of these links offers an "experience of insight (epiphany) . . . constitutive of sensitive reading" ("Networking in *Finnegans Wake*," *James Joyce Quarterly* 27, no. 4 (1990): 746).

5. See Dirk van Hulle, "Modernism, Mind, and Manuscripts," in *A Handbook of Modernism Studies*, ed. Jean-Michel Rabaté (Malden, Mass.: Wiley-Blackwell, 2013), 225–38.

6. For transcriptions of the first, second, and fourth drafts, see http://www.ricorso.net/rx/az-data/authors/j/Joyce_JA/apx/sundry/Colloquy.htm; David Hayman reprints the third draft in *A First-Draft Version of Finnegans Wake* (Austin: University of Texas Press, 1963).

7. The missing b is probably a misprint for "roranyellgreeblindigan" (see James Joyce, *Finnegans Wake*, ed. Henkes, Bindervoet and Fordham (Oxford: Oxford University Press, 2012), 646.

8. Joyce also alludes to Kant's *Erscheinung* (appearance, phenomenon) in "Shamwork, be in our scheining!" (613.10), which seems to suggest that Berkeley is, temporarily at least, associated with Shem. The Kantian terms appear several times in *FW*, including "Is dads the thing in such or . . . e'er scheining" (528.15–22), of which more below.

9. The Christian conversion of Ireland is usually dated Easter 433, when Patrick lit the fire at Tara. Presumably Joyce prefers the year "four three two" because of its numerological significance.

10. On the order of composition, see A. Walton Litz, *The Art of James Joyce: Method and Design in* Ulysses *and* Finnegans Wake (London: Oxford University Press, 1961); and Luca Crispi and Sam Slote, eds., *How Joyce Wrote Finnegans Wake: A Chapter-by-Chapter Genetic Guide* (Madison: University of Wisconsin Press, 2007).

11. In the published version, Joyce adds "chinchinjoss" (religious worship), "Lord Joss," "yeh," "noh," "he drink," and "numpa one" to create "pidgin fella" Balkelly's idiolect. As with "Oxen," slang, pidgin, and creole point to Joyce's interest in emergent forms of language.

12. "The range of spoken English becomes oriented toward a new orientalism; one can justly consider this episode as the first step on the royal road that leads the writer toward his universal language."

13. Milesi notes that between sixty-eight and eighty languages have been identified in *Finnegans Wake*, while seventy, the traditional age of man and number of nations on earth, recurs in reference to the text ("you need hardly spell me how every word will be bound over to carry three score and ten toptypsical reading throughout the book of Doublends Jined" [20.13–16]). In Genesis, "the whole earth was of one language, and of one speech," when "the children of men" sought to make a name for themselves by building a tower to heaven, thereby threatening God who confounds them by dividing their language, scattering "the generations of Shem" across the earth (Gen. 11:1–10). In Dante's version, after the fall of Babel, the universal language split into seventy tongues, one for each type of laborer, while according to the Talmud, each of God's commandments on Mount Sinai was divided into seventy languages "so that each people could hear the divine revelation" (Laurent Milesi, "Joyce, Language, and Languages," in *Palgrave Advances in James Joyce Studies*, ed. Rabaté (Basingstoke, U.K.: Palgrave Macmillan, 2004), 153). In this context it may be significant that Joyce's epiphanies are numbered to seventy-one.

14. For instance, he describes Berkeley's tongue as "native Druidic" and ignores the Japanese inflection given to "the Invader Patrick," distorting Joyce's characterization of their (Chinese) "pidgin" and "Nippon" English (*LI* 406).

15. Juva and Muta reprise Butt and Taff from 2.3, who first appeared as Jute and Mutt in 1.1. Both episodes can be read as versions of Buckley shooting the Russian General. For details, see Adaline Glasheen, *Third Census of Finnegans Wake* (Evanston, Ill.: Northwestern University Press, 1977), 42.

16. The Ballast Office Clock was Daedalus's object of epiphany (*SH* 216–18).

17. One of the most interesting variations is "In the beginning was the gest" (468.5), which, as Atherton points out, refers primarily to "Marcel Jousse's theory of the formation of language from gesture, but it is inflected by the German *geist*—'spirit'—which is the word used in some German translations for *logos*" (177).

18. David Spurr argues that 2.4, and "the *Wake* as a whole . . . is a prolonged unveiling of language as the site of convergence between body and spirit. . . . The scripture of this countergospel is the language of *Finnegans Wake*" (Spurr, "Joyce's Countergospel in II.4," in *Joyce's Allmaziful Pluralities: Polyvocal Explorations of Finnegans Wake*, ed. Devlin and Smedley [Gainesville: University Press of Florida, 2015], 2, 22).

19. McHugh notes Joyce's source: the Finnegan family crest, as given in the *Weekly Irish Times*, July 19, 1936: "Out of a cloud a hand erect, holding a book

expanded." There is no doubt Joyce used this source, which was copied by Eugene Jolas, but the biblical echo is prominent.

20. "The stars began to crumble and a cloud of fine stardust fell through space" (*P* 110); "—What is that, Mr Dedalus? . . .—A star by night, Stephen said. A pillar of the cloud by day" (*U* 9.944).

21. Cf., e.g., Exodus 14.19–24, 16.10. Joyce's interpretation is literal in two respects. First, interpreting the pillar of fire as a star, he provides a physical explanation of God's manifestation, alluding to the contemporary hypothesis that the physical elements in the universe, including everything that makes up life on earth, was born in stars and that stars themselves took shape in dark clouds of cold matter we call nebulae. Second, Joyce reinterprets both star and cloud as epiphanies of *language*.

22. It may also allude to The Office of Our Blessed Lady at Matins, with its repeated invocations to the Lord our God ("est Dominus Deus noster").

23. *The Catholic Encyclopedia* inverts the association, making Patrick the bringer of light who banishes the clouds of darkness conjured by pagan spells, as the druids sought to put out Patrick's inextinguishable conflagration.

24. On October 9, 1923, Joyce wrote to Harriet Shaw Weaver, "I am sorry that Patrick and Berkeley are unsuccessful in explaining themselves. The answer, I suppose, is that given by Paddy Dignam's apparition: metempsychosis" (*LI* 204).

25. Jean-Michel Rabaté makes the point more forcefully in "Joyce and Jolas: Late Modernism and Early Babelism," *Journal of Modern Literature* 22, no. 2 (1998): 245–52.

26. "The first men had to create matter by the force of their imagination, and 'poet' means 'creator'" (*OE* 9).

27. See Margot Norris's *Decentered Universe of Finnegans Wake: A Structuralist Analysis* (Baltimore, Md.: Johns Hopkins University Press, 1976) and Derek Attridge's *Peculiar Language: Literature as Difference from the Renaissance to James Joyce* (Ithaca: Cornell University Press, 1988).

28. These dislocutions are not exclusively the property of the author: "It is, of course, the reader who—potentially—executes all the mental shifts" (209).

29. The notebooks also contain reference to "lovers' silence" (VI.B.3.38i; *FW* 280.28–33), priestly gestures of silence (VI.B.3.79b; *FW* 476.6–7), and guilty silence (VI.B.6.84; *FW* 193.11).

30. See Milesi 2018 for an excellent analysis of the "Wakean dynamics of language and silence" (61).

31. Cf. Alan Roughley: "Joyce's text . . . makes the 'seim anew' (215.23), renewing the semes of language" (138).

32. For example, "His logic is that of life and his inventions are organic necessities" (Budgen, *OE* 37); English "is in a constant state of becoming . . . the organic evolution of speech" (Jolas, *OE* 82).

33. See also Crispi and Slote, *How Joyce Wrote* Finnegans Wake; Claude Jacquet and Daniel Ferrer, eds., *Genèse de Babel: Joyce et la Création* (Paris: CNRS, 1985).

34. Interestingly, the first of these is followed by one of the clearest "epiphanoids." See VI.A.271–72; and David Hayman, "Epiphanoiding," in *Genitricksling Joyce*, ed. Slote and Van Mierlo, 27–41 (Amsterdam: Rodopi, 1999).

35. "To look through the mirror is to look at its reverse side, at the dull side doubling the mirror's specular play, in short, at the *tain* of the mirror. It is on this reverse side—on the tinfoil—that dissemination writes itself" (Rodolphe Gasché, *The Tain of the Mirror: Derrida and the Philosophy of Reflection* [Cambridge: Harvard University Press, 1986], 225).

36. See also "The Double Session" in Jacques Derrida, *Dissemination*, trans. Barbara Johnson (Chicago: University of Chicago Press, 1981), 156–236.

37. See Roland McHugh, *The Sigla of* Finnegans Wake (London: Edward Arnold, 1976) 50; and Henkes and Bindervoet, "Oversystematising the Wake: The Quiz Chapter as the Key to a Potential Schema for *Finnegans Wake*," *Genetic Joyce Studies* 4 (2004): §10. Henkes and Bindervoet show that "Isolde split in two for the first time in VI.B.18 (April–May 1927), but a premonition appears already in VI.B.14.216 (August–November 1924), and also on VI.B.14.82 you can see the two Issys when Joyce makes a note sideways on the page" (n.p., §10).

38. As well as linking back to Maggy, recipient of "the letter selfpenned to one's other," these references recall the myths of doubling invoked by the four when they summon Issy. "[L]inkingclass girl" (459.04) alludes to Alice's looking glass, but there were, of course, two Alices (or "Secilas" in reverse); hence "Alicious, twinstreams twinestraines, through alluring glass or alas in jumboland [Wonderland]" and "Secilas through their laughing classes becoming poolermates in laker life" (528.17–18, 526.35–36). (Here "poolermates" echoes Narcissus, or "Nircississies," "as the doaters of inversion," inverting the proverb "necessity is the *mother* of invention," like the inverted reflection in a pool of water that Narcissus doted upon).

39. The litany runs "Mirror of justice . . . Tower of ivory, House of gold, Ark of the covenant!"

40. As well as alluding to *The Book of Kells* and *Hamlet* ("Ay, very like a whale" [3.2.406]), the highly condensed egg stuffed with food for thought recalls "Proteus" ("Remember your epiphanies . . . Ay, very like a whale" [*U* 3.139–44]), calling attention to the central aspects of Joyce's epiphanic language: materiality, self-reflexivity ("that ideal reader suffering from an ideal insomnia"), omissions, repetition.

41. As Attridge points out in *Peculiar Language*, "the consequences of accepting [the *Wake's* portmanteau style] extend to all our reading. Every word in every text is, after all, a portmanteau of sorts, a combination of sounds that echo through

the entire language and through every other language and back through the history of speech" (208).

Chapter 8. Conclusion

1. One could go back further, to Joyce's early poetry, *Moods* (ca. 1896–1897) and *Shine and Dark* (ca. 1900); the narrative sketches he called *Silhouettes* (ca. 1896–1897); or his lost plays, *A Brilliant Career* (1900) and *Dream Stuff* (ca. 1901). However, none of these works has survived intact and the fragments we have are rarely, if ever, reused in the subsequent works. One could also make a case for the early critical writings where Joyce began to formulate his aesthetics, or *Chamber Music*, Joyce's first publication (1907), but I agree with Litz that the epiphanies are Joyce's first major literary works. Ultimately, however, if Joyce's texts form a single oeuvre, they should be taken together, and the choice of origin is irrelevant, because each of them possesses the same properties as every other—silence, repetition, materiality, and self-reflexivity. I have focused on the epiphanies because they bring out these qualities more clearly than any previous work, initiating Joyce's lifelong endeavor to reveal the linguistic epiphany.

2. Indeed, these theoretical approaches are compatible: Lacan's unsymbolizable Real, the object of desire, is equivalent to Kant's noumenon, which phenomenal appearances can never attain; Derrida places Kant's "Analytic of the Sublime" (*Critique of Judgment* §§23–29) at the center of the Kantian system, before deconstructing the oppositions between subject and object, inside and outside, through the "*parergon*" that frames the work of art, a limit concept structurally equivalent to *différance* (1987, 37–118).

3. Cf. Woolf's diary for September 30, 1926: "I wished to add some remarks to this, on the mystical side of this solitude [. . .]: One sees a fin passing far out" (1980, 113) with *The Waves* (Oxford: Oxford University Press, 1992): "I note under F., therefore, 'Fin in a waste of waters'" (145); "silences which are now and again broken by a few words, as if a fin rose in the wastes of silence; and then the fin, the thought, sinks back into the depths" (210).

4. Sam Slote gives a concise and insightful account of silence as the limit of discourse in "Penelope" and *The Unnamable*: "Both texts present us with multiple, incommensurable fragments of ratiocination that asymptotically tend towards a silence that never quite comes within the interval of discourse" ("'Affirmations and Negations Invalidated as Uttered' in *Ulysses* and *How It Is*," in Wawrzycka and Zanotti, 110).

5. I have focused on the Anglophone tradition, but these qualities are also frequent in French modernist literature. For instance, Proust emphasizes that it is material objects, such as the famous madeleine or an uneven paving stone in Paris, that revive Marcel's memory, allowing lost time to be not simply regained

but recreated. Such moments become motifs, woven through the *Recherche* in patterns of silence and repetition, allowing the narrator to gradually come to consciousness of himself through his own self-reflexive narration. The same features are evident in Nathalie Sarraute's *Tropismes*, which have been compared to Joyce's epiphanies (Doris T. Wight, "Ironies Romantic and Naturalistic: James Joyce's Epiphanies and Nathalie Sarraute's Tropisms," *Rackham Journal of the Arts and Humanities* [1987]: 15–45; Morris Beja, *Epiphany in the Modern Novel* [Seattle: University of Washington Press, 1971], 221–22). Sarraute's first "tropism" begins with silent figures gazing at white objects including a doll whose eyes are repeatedly lit up and extinguished, so that their consumer identities are reflected in the commodities they observe. This scene is perhaps recalled in the first of Alain Robbe-Grillet's "Reflected Visions," where a still life containing three objects (including a dressmaker's dummy) is reflected over and over between two mirrors. The scene is then briefly returned to, with signs of human intervention that suggest a self-reflexive move from the photographic snapshot ("instantané") to the objects represented, and from textual representation to the text that represents.

6. Giuseppe Sertoli's interpretation of silence in *Heart of Darkness* offers an illuminating comment on Eliot's change of epigraph: "It is not the forest or the savages who are *formless*. . . . What is *formless* is the silence *of the* langue *in the* language itself" (qtd. in Jolanta Wawrzycka and Serenella Zanotti, *James Joyce's Silences* [London: Bloomsbury Academic, 2018], 240).

BIBLIOGRAPHY

Abrams, Meyer Howard. *Natural Supernaturalism: Tradition and Revolution in Romantic Literature.* London: Oxford University Press, 1971.
Adams, Robert M. *James Joyce: Common Sense and Beyond.* New York: Random House, 1966.
Alighieri, Dante. *La Divina Commedia.* Ed. Umberto Bosco and Giovanni Reggio. 3 vols. Le Monnier: Florence, 2002.
Ansermet, François, and Pierre Magistretti. "Le troisième inconscient." *L'Herne* 110 (2015): 286–92.
Aristotle (pseud.). *Master-Piece Illustrated.* New York: n.p., 1846. Internet Archive.
———. *Works, Illustrated: Containing the Masterpiece.* London: n.p., 1900. Internet Archive.
Atherton, James Stephen. *The Books at the Wake: A Study of Literary Allusions in James Joyce's Finnegans Wake.* Mamaroneck: P. Appel, 1974.
Attridge, Derek, ed. *The Cambridge Companion to James Joyce.* Cambridge: Cambridge University Press, 1990.
———. *Joyce Effects: On Language, Theory, and History.* Cambridge: Cambridge University Press, 2001.
———. *Peculiar Language: Literature as Difference from the Renaissance to James Joyce.* Ithaca: Cornell University Press, 1988.
———. *The Singularity of Literature.* London: Routledge, 2004.
Attridge, Derek, and Daniel Ferrer, eds. *Post-Structuralist Joyce: Essays from the French.* Cambridge: Cambridge University Press, 1984.
Aubert, Jacques. *The Aesthetics of James Joyce.* Baltimore, Md.: Johns Hopkins University Press, 1992.
———, ed. *Joyce Avec Lacan.* Paris: Navarin, 1987.
———, ed. *Joyce et Paris: 1902 . . . 1920–1940 . . . 1975.* Paris: CNRS, 1979.
Auerbach, Erich. *Mimesis: The Representation of Reality in Western Literature.* Princeton: Princeton University Press, 1974.
———. *Scenes from the Drama of European Literature.* Gloucester: P. Smith, 1973.

Augustine. *Confessions*. Oxford: Oxford University Press, 1992.
———. *Sermons for Christmas and Epiphany*. New York: Newman, 1978.
Bakhtin, Mikhail Mikhaïlovich. *The Dialogic Imagination: Four Essays*. Austin: University of Texas Press, 1987.
Ball, Sir Robert Stawell. *The Story of the Heavens*. London: Cassell, 1885.
Baron, Scarlett. *Strandentwining Cable: Joyce, Flaubert, and Intertextuality*. Oxford: Oxford University Press, 2011.
Baudelaire, Charles. *Petits Poèmes en Prose*. Paris: Larousse, 2009.
Bazargan, Susan. "Oxen of the Sun: Maternity, Language, and History." *James Joyce Quarterly* 22, no. 3 (1985): 271–80.
Beare, Francis Wright. *The Gospel According to Matthew*. Oxford: Blackwell, 1981.
Beck, Warren. *Joyce's* Dubliners*: Substance, Vision, and Art*. Durham, N.C.: Duke University Press, 1969.
Beckett, Samuel. *The Complete Dramatic Works*. London: Faber, 2006.
———. *Three Novels: Molloy, Malone Dies, The Unnamable*. New York: Grove, 2009.
Beckett, Samuel, et al. *Our Exagmination Round His Factification for Incamination of "Work in Progress."* London: Faber and Faber, 1972.
Beebe, Maurice. "Joyce and Aquinas: The Theory of Aesthetics." In Connolly 1962, 272–89.
Begnal, Michael. "The Language of *Finnegans Wake*." In Bowen and Carens, 633–46.
Beja, Morris. "Epiphany and the Epiphanies." In Bowen and Carens, 707–25.
———. *Epiphany in the Modern Novel*. Seattle: University of Washington Press, 1971.
———. "The Incertitude of the Void: Epiphany and Indeterminacy." *Joyce, the Artist Manqué, and Indeterminacy: A Lecture and an Essay*. Gerards Cross: Colin Smyth, 1989.
———, ed. *James Joyce:* Dubliners *and* A Portrait of the Artist as a Young Man*: A Casebook*. Basingstoke: Macmillan, 1985.
———. *James Joyce: A Literary Life*. Basingstoke: Macmillan, 1992.
———. "Mau-Mauing the Epiphany Catchers." *Proceedings of the Modern Language Association* 87, no. 5 (1972): 1131–32.
———. "One Good Look at Themselves: Epiphany in *Dubliners*." In *Work in Progress: Joyce Centenary Essays*, ed. Richard F. Peterson, Alan M. Cohn, and Edmund L. Epstein, 3–14. Carbondale: Southern Illinois University Press, 1983.
———. "'Shut Up He Explained': Joyce and 'Scornful Silence.'" In Wawrzycka and Zanotti, 115–22.
Benjamin, Walter. *Illuminations*. London: Pimlico, 1999.

Benstock, Bernard, ed. *Bloomsday 100: Essays on Ulysses*. Gainesville: University Press of Florida, 2009.

———, ed. *Critical Essays on James Joyce's Ulysses*. Boston: G. K. Hall, 1989.

———, ed. *James Joyce: The Augmented Ninth; Proceedings of the Ninth International James Joyce Symposium, Frankfurt 1984*. Syracuse, N.Y.: Syracuse University Press, 1988.

———. "The Kenner Conundrum: Or Who Does What with Which to Whom." *James Joyce Quarterly* 13, no. 4 (1976): 428–35.

Berressem, Hanjo. "The Letter! The Litter! The Defilements of the Signifier in *Finnegans Wake*." In Lernout, 139–64.

Bidney, Martin. *Patterns of Epiphany: From Wordsworth to Tolstoy, Pater, and Barrett Browning*. Carbondale: Southern Illinois University Press, 1997.

Bishop, John. *Joyce's Book of the Dark:* Finnegans Wake. Madison: University of Wisconsin Press, 1986.

Boldrini, Lucia. *Joyce, Dante, and the Poetics of Literary Relations: Language and Meaning in* Finnegans Wake. Cambridge: Cambridge University Press, 2001.

Bollettieri Bosinelli, Rosa Maria, ed. *ReJoycing: New Readings of Dubliners*. Lexington: University Press of Kentucky, 1998.

Bollettieri Bosinelli, Rosa Maria, C. Marengo Vaglio, and Christine van Boheemen, eds. *The Languages of Joyce*. Philadelphia: John Benjamins, 1992.

Booth, Wayne. "The Problem of Distance in *A Portrait of the Artist*." In Wollaeger, 59–72.

Bowen, Zack. "Epiphanies, Stephen's Diary, and the Narrative Perspective of *A Portrait of the Artist as a Young Man*." *James Joyce Quarterly* 16 (1979): 485–88.

———. "Joyce and the Epiphany Concept: A New Approach." *Journal of Modern Literature* 9, no. 1 (1981): 103–14.

Bowen, Zack, and James F. Carens, eds. *A Companion to Joyce Studies*. Westport: Greenwood, 1984.

Boyd, Elizabeth F. "James Joyce's Hell-Fire Sermons." *Modern Language Notes* 75, no. 7 (1960): 561–71.

Boyle, Robert. "Miracle in Black Ink: A Glance at Joyce's Use of His Eucharistic Image." *James Joyce Quarterly* 10, no. 1 (1972): 47–60.

Brady, Philip, and James F. Carens, eds. *Critical Essays on James Joyce's* A Portrait of the Artist as a Young Man. New York: G. K. Hall, 1998.

Brewster, William T. *Representative Essays on the Theory of Style*. New York: Macmillan, 1905.

Brown, Raymond Edward. *The Birth of the Messiah: A Commentary on the Infancy Narratives in the Gospels of Matthew and Luke*. New York: Doubleday, 1993.

Brown, Richard, ed. *A Companion to James Joyce*. Malden, Mass.: Blackwell, 2008.

Budgen, Frank. *James Joyce and the Making of* Ulysses. Ed. Clive Hart. Oxford: Oxford University Press, 1972.

Burke, Kenneth. "Fact, Inference, and Proof in the Analysis of Literary Symbolism." In Joyce, 2007, ed. Riquelme, 311–28.
Cage, John. *Silence: Lectures and Writings*. Middletown, Conn.: Wesleyan University Press, 1961.
Cage, John, and David Tudor. *Indeterminacy: New Aspect of Form in Instrumental and Electronic Music*. New York: Folkways Records, 1959.
Campbell, Joseph, and Henry Morton Robinson. *A Skeleton Key to Finnegans Wake*. London: Faber and Faber, 1959.
Cary, Phillip. *Augustine's Invention of the Inner Self: The Legacy of a Christian Platonist*. Oxford: Oxford University Press, 2000.
Caufield, James Walter. "The Word as Will and Idea: Dedalean Aesthetics and the Influence of Schopenhauer." *James Joyce Quarterly* 35 (1998): 695–714.
Cheng, Vincent J. "'Goddinpotty': James Joyce and the Language of Excrement." In Bollettieri Bosinelli et al., 85–99.
Cixous, Hélène. *The Exile of James Joyce*. Trans. Sally A. J. Purcell. New York: David Lewis, 1972.
Clark, Hilary. "Networking in *Finnegans Wake*." *James Joyce Quarterly* 27, no. 4 (1990): 745–58.
Conley, Tim. *Joyces Mistakes: Problems of Intention, Irony and interpretation*. Toronto: University of Toronto Press, 2003.
Connolly, Thomas Edmund, ed. *Joyce's Portrait: Criticisms & Critiques*. N.p.: Ardent, 1962.
———. *The Personal Library of James Joyce: A Descriptive Bibliography*. Buffalo: State University of New York Press, 1957.
Connor, Stephen. *Samuel Beckett: Repetition, Theory, and Text*. Oxford: Blackwell, 1988.
Conrad, Joseph. *The Nigger of the "Narcissus."* New York: Norton, 1979.
———. *Youth, Heart of Darkness, The End of the Tether*. Ed. Owen Knowles. Cambridge: Cambridge University Press, 2010.
Crispi, Luca, and Sam Slote, eds. *How Joyce Wrote Finnegans Wake: A Chapter-by-Chapter Genetic Guide*. Madison: University of Wisconsin Press, 2007.
Culler, Jonathan. *Theory of the Lyric*. Cambridge: Harvard University Press, 2015.
D'Annunzio, Gabriel. *Il Fuoco*. Milan: Teeves, 1907.
Danow, D. K. "Epiphany in 'Doctor Zhivago.'" *Modern Language Review* 76, no. 4 (1981): 889–903.
Day, Robert Adams. "Dante, Ibsen, Joyce, Epiphanies, and the Art of Memory." *James Joyce Quarterly* 25, no. 3 (1988): 357–62.
Delville, Michel. "Epiphanies and Prose Lyrics: James Joyce and the Poetics of the Fragment." In *Giacomo Joyce: Envoys of the Other*, ed. Louis Armand and Clare Wallace, 101–30. Prague: Litteraria Pragensia, 2006.

De Man, Paul. *The Rhetoric of Romanticism*. New York: Columbia University Press, 1984.
Derrida, Jacques. *Acts of Literature*. Ed. Derek Attridge. New York: Routledge, 1992.
———. *Dissemination*. Trans. Barbara Johnson. Chicago: University of Chicago Press, 1981.
———. *Of Grammatology*. Trans. Gayatri Chakravorty Spivak. Baltimore, Md.: Johns Hopkins University Press, 1976.
———. *Ulysse Gramophone; Deux Mots Pour Joyce*. Paris: Galilée, 1987.
———. *La Vérité En Peinture*. Paris: Flammarion, 1993.
———. *Writing and Difference*. Trans. Alan Bass. Chicago: University of Chicago Press, 1978.
Devlin, Kimberly J., and Christine Smedley, eds. *Joyce's Allmaziful Plurabilities: Polyvocal Explorations of Finnegans Wake*. Gainesville: University Press of Florida, 2015.
Doherty, James. "Joyce and 'Hell Opened to Christians': The Edition He Used for His 'Hell Sermons.'" *Modern Philology* 61, no. 2 (1963): 110–19.
Downing, Gregory M. "Diverting Philology: Language and Its Effects in Popularised Philology and Joyce's Work." In Hulle 2002, 121–66.
Eco, Umberto. *The Middle Ages of James Joyce: The Aesthetics of Chaosmos*. London: Hutchinson Radius, 1989.
Eliade, Mircea. *Le sacré et le profane*. Paris: Gallimard, 1992.
Eliot, T. S. *The Poems*. Ed. Christopher Ricks and Jim McCue. 2 vols. London: Faber, 2015.
———. *The Waste Land: A Facsimile and Transcript of the Original Drafts Including the Annotations of Ezra Pound*. Ed. Valerie Eliot. London: Faber and Faber, 1971.
Ellmann, Maud. "Polytropic Man: Paternity, Identity and Naming in *The Odyssey* and *A Portrait of the Artist as a Young Man*." In Attridge and Ferrer, 73–104.
———. "*Ulysses:* The Epic of the Human Body." In Brown 2008, 54–70.
Emerson, Ralph Waldo. *The Early Lectures of Ralph Waldo Emerson*. 3 vols. Cambridge: Harvard University Press, 1959.
Faulkner, William. *Light in August*. New York: Vintage, 1972.
———. *New Orleans Sketches*. New York: Random House, 1958.
Feshbach, Sidney. "Hunting Epiphany-Hunters." *PMLA* 87, no. 2 (1972): 304–6.
———. "A Slow and Dark Birth: A Study of the Organization of *A Portrait of the Artist as a Young Man*." *James Joyce Quarterly* 4, no. 4 (1967): 289–300.
Fogarty, Anne, and Fran O'Rourke, eds. *Voices on Joyce*. Dublin: University College Dublin, 2015.

Fordham, Finn. *Lots of Fun at* Finnegans Wake*: Unravelling Universals*. Oxford: Oxford University Press, 2007.

———. "The Writing of Growth and the Growths of Writing: A Genetic Exegesis of *Finnegans Wake* 503.30–505.29. *Hypermedia Joyce Studies* 8, no. 2; 9, no. 1 (2007–2008).

Frawley, Oona, ed. *A New & Complex Sensation: Essays on Joyce's Dubliners*. Dublin: Lilliput, 2004.

French, Marilyn. "Missing Pieces in Joyce's *Dubliners*." *Twentieth Century Literature* 24, no. 4 (1978): 443–72.

———. "Women in Joyce's *Dubliners*." In Benstock 1988, 267–72.

Freud, Sigmund. *The Interpretation of Dreams*. Trans. James Strachey. London: Penguin, 1977.

Gabler, Hans Walter. "The Christmas Dinner Scene, Parnell's Death, and the Genesis of *A Portrait of the Artist as a Young Man*." *James Joyce Quarterly* 13, no. 1 (1975): 27–38.

———. "The Genesis of *A Portrait of the Artist as a Young Man*." In Brady and Carens, 83–114.

———. "Joyce's Text in Progress." In Attridge 1990, 213–36.

Gasché, Rodolphe. *The Tain of the Mirror: Derrida and the Philosophy of Reflection*. Cambridge: Harvard University Press, 1986.

Gibson, George Cinclair. *Wake Rites: The Ancient Irish Rituals of Finnegans Wake*. Gainesville: University Press of Florida, 2005.

Gifford, Don Creighton, and Robert J. Seidman. *Notes for Joyce:* Dubliners *and* A Portrait of the Artist as a Young Man. New York: E. P. Dutton, 1967.

———. Ulysses *Annotated*. 2nd ed. Berkeley: University of California Press, 1988.

Gillespie, Gerald. *Proust, Mann, Joyce in the Modernist Context*. 2nd ed. Washington, D.C.: Catholic University of America Press, 2010.

Glasheen, Adaline. "*Finnegans Wake* and the Secret Languages of Ireland." *A Wake Newslitter*, O.S. 10 (February 1963): 1–3.

———. *Third Census of Finnegans Wake*. Evanston, Ill.: Northwestern University Press, 1977.

Gogarty, Oliver St John. *As I Was Going Down Sackville Street: A Phantasy in Fact*. Harmondsworth, U.K.: Penguin, 1954.

Goldberg, Samuel Louis. *The Classical Temper: A Study of James Joyce's Ulysses*. London: Chatto and Windus, 1961.

Gorman, Herbert Sherman. *James Joyce: A Definitive Biography*. London: John Lane, 1941.

Gornat, Tomasz. *"A Chemistry of Stars": Epiphany, Openness and Ambiguity in the Works of James Joyce*. Opole: Wydawnictwo Uniwersytetu Opolskiego, 2006.

Gottfried, Roy. *Joyce's Misbelief*. Gainesville: University Press of Florida, 2008.

Gray, Richard T. *Constructive Destruction: Kafka's Aphorisms*. Tübingen: Niemeyer, 1987.
Guillemin, Amedee. *The Heavens: An Illustrated Handbook of Popular Astronomy*. London: Richard Bentley & Son, 1876.
Harrison, Kate. "The *Portrait* Epiphany." *James Joyce Quarterly* 8 (1971): 142–50.
Hart, Clive. "Note on the Above [Glasheen 1963]." *A Wake Newslitter* O.S. 10 (February 1963): 3.
———. *Structure and Motif in* Finnegans Wake. London: Faber and Faber, 1962.
Hart, Clive, and David Hayman, eds. *James Joyce's* Ulysses*: Critical Essays*. Berkeley: University of California Press, 1974.
Hayman, David. "Epiphanoiding." In Slote and Van Mierlo, 27–41.
———, ed. *A First-Draft Version of Finnegans Wake*. Austin: University of Texas Press, 1963.
———. "From *Finnegans Wake*: A Sentence in Progress." *PMLA* 73, no. 1 (1958): 136–54.
———. "The Purpose and Permanence of the Joycean Epiphany." *James Joyce Quarterly* 35 (1998): 633–56.
Heath, Stephen. "Ambiviolences: Notes for Reading Joyce." In Attridge and Ferrer, 31–68.
Heller, Vivian. *Joyce, Decadence, and Emancipation*. Urbana: University of Illinois Press, 1995.
Heidegger, Martin. *On the Way to Language*. New York: Harper & Row, 1982.
———. *Poetry, Language, Thought*. New York: Harper & Row, 1971.
Hendry, Irene. "Joyce's *Epiphanies*." *Sewanee Review* 54 (1946): 449–67.
Henke, Suzette. "Stephen Dedalus and Women: A Portrait of the Artist as a Young Misogynist." In *Women in Joyce*, ed. Suzette Henke and Elaine Unkeless, 82–107. Urbana: University of Illinois Press, 1982.
———. "Virginia Woolf Reads James Joyce: The *Ulysses* Notebook." In *James Joyce: The Centennial Symposium*, ed. Morris Beja et al., 39–42. Urbana: University of Illinois Press, 1986.
Henkes, Robbert-Jan, and Erik Bindervoet. "Oversystematising the Wake: The Quiz Chapter as the Key to a Potential Schema for *Finnegans Wake*." *Genetic Joyce Studies* 4 (2004): n.p.
Herring, Phillip F. *Joyce's Uncertainty Principle*. Princeton, N.J.: Princeton University Press, 1987.
Homer. *Iliad*. Trans. Robert Fagles. London: Penguin, 1998.
———. *Odyssey*. Trans. Robert Fagles. London: Penguin, 1999.
Hulle, Dirk van, ed. *James Joyce: The Study of Languages*. Brussels: P. Lang, 2002.
———. "Modernism, Mind, and Manuscripts." In *A Handbook of Modernism Studies*, ed. Jean-Michel Rabaté, 225–38. Malden, Mass.: Wiley-Blackwell, 2013.

Jacoby, Felix. *Die Fragmente Der Griechischen Historiker*. Berlin: E. J. Brill, 1968.
Jacoby, Harold. *Astronomy: A Popular Handbook*. New York: Macmillan, 1913.
Jacquet, Claude, and Daniel Ferrer, eds. *Genèse de Babel: Joyce et la Création*. Paris: CNRS, 1985.
Jager, Colin. *The Book of God: Secularization and Design in the Romantic Era*. Philadelphia: Pennsylvania University Press, 2007.
James, Henry. *The Art of the Novel: Critical Prefaces*. New York: C. Scribner's, 1950.
———. *The House of Fiction*. Ed. Leon Edel. London: Mercury, 1962.
Janusko, Robert. *The Sources and Structures of James Joyce's "Oxen."* Ann Arbor: University of Michigan Press, 1983.
Jolas, Eugene, ed. *transition* 21. The Hague: Servire, 1932.
Joyce, James. *Dubliners*. Viking Critical Edition. Ed. Robert Scholes and A. Walton Litz. New York: Viking, 1969.
———. *Dubliners: An Illustrated Edition with Annotations*. Ed. John Wyse Jackson and Bernard McGinley. New York: St. Martin's Griffin, 1995.
———. *Epiphanies*. Ed. O. A. Silverman. Repr. Philadelphia: R. West, 1979.
———. *Poems and Shorter Writings*. Ed. Richard Ellmann, A. Walton Litz, and John Whittier-Ferguson. London: Faber and Faber, 1991.
———. *Finnegans Wake*. Ed. Robbert-Jan Henkes, Erik Bindervoet, and Finn Fordham. Oxford: Oxford University Press, 2012.
———. *A Portrait of the Artist as a Young Man: Authoritative Text, Backgrounds and Contexts, Criticism*. Ed. John Paul Riquelme. New York: Norton, 2007.
Joyce, Stanislaus. *The Complete Dublin Diary of Stanislaus Joyce*. Ithaca: Cornell University Press, 1971.
———. *My Brother's Keeper: James Joyce's Early Years*. New York: Viking, 1958.
Kant, Immanuel. *Critique of Judgement*. Trans. James Creed Meredith. Oxford: Oxford University Press, 2009.
———. *Critique of Pure Reason*. Trans., ed. Paul Guyer. Cambridge: Cambridge University Press, 1998.
Kearney, Richard. "Epiphanies in Joyce." In Fogarty and O'Rourke, 239–59.
Kenner, Hugh. *Dublin's Joyce*. New York: Columbia University Press, 1987.
———. *Joyce's Voices*. London: Faber and Faber, 1978.
———. "The *Portrait* in Perspective." *Kenyon Review* 10, no. 3 (1948): 361–81.
———. *The Pound Era*. London: Faber and Faber, 1972.
———. "The Rhetoric of Silence." *James Joyce Quarterly* 14, no. 4 (1977): 382–94.
———. "Shem the Textman." In Bollettieri Bosinelli et al., 145–61.
———. *Ulysses*. London: Allen and Unwin, 1982.
Kershner, R. B. "The Artist as Text: Dialogism and Incremental Repetition in Joyce's *Portrait*." *ELH* 53, no. 4 (1986): 881–94.
———. "Time and Language in Joyce's *Portrait of the Artist*." *ELH* 43, no. 4 (1976): 604–19.

Kim, Sharon. *Literary Epiphany in the Novel, 1850–1950: Constellations of the Soul*. New York: Palgrave Macmillan, 2012.

Kimball, Jean. "Love and Death in Ulysses: 'Word Known to All Men.'" *James Joyce Quarterly* 24, no. 2 (1987): 143–60.

Lacan, Jacques. *Ecrits*. Paris: Seuil, 1996.

———. *Le Séminaire*. 10 vols. Paris: Seuil, 1975–2001.

Langbaum, Robert. "The Epiphanic Mode in Wordsworth and Modern Literature." *New Literary History* 14, no. 2 (1983): 335–58.

Lecercle, Jean-Jacques. *Philosophy Through the Looking-Glass: Language, Nonsense, Desire*. La Salle: Open Court, 1985.

Leonard, Garry. *Reading* Dubliners *Again: A Lacanian Perspective*. Syracuse: Syracuse University Press, 1993.

Lernout, Geert, ed. *Finnegans Wake: Fifty Years*. Amsterdam: Rodopi, 1990.

Levenson, Michael, ed. *The Cambridge Companion to Modernism*. 2nd ed. Cambridge: Cambridge University Press, 2011.

Levin, Harry. *James Joyce: A Critical Introduction*. Norfolk: New Directions, 1941.

Levina, Jūratė. "The Aesthetics of Phenomena: Joyce's Epiphanies." *Joyce Studies Annual* (2017): 185–219.

Levine, Jennifer Schiffer. "Originality and Repetition in *Finnegans Wake* and *Ulysses*." *PMLA* 94, no. 1 (1979): 106–20.

Litz, Arthur Walton. *The Art of James Joyce: Method and Design in* Ulysses *and* Finnegans Wake. London: Oxford University Press, 1961.

Loevlie, Elisabeth Marie. *Literary Silences in Pascal, Rousseau, and Beckett*. Oxford: Oxford University Press, 2003.

Losey, Jay B. "Dream-Epiphanies in Finnegans Wake." *James Joyce Quarterly* 26, no. 4 (1989): 611–17.

———. "Epiphany in Pater's Portraits." *English Literature in Transition, 1880–1920* 29, no. 3 (1986): 297–308.

MacDuff, Sangam. "Death and the Limits of Epiphany: Wordsworth's 'Spots of Time' and Joyce's Epiphanies of Death." *James Joyce Quarterly* 53, nos. 1–2 (Fall/Winter 2015–16): 61–74.

———. "The Yale Epiphanies: A New Typescript." *Genetic Joyce Studies* 17 (Spring 2017): 1–15. http://www.geneticjoycestudies.org/articles/GJS17/GJS17_Macduff.

Magalaner, Marvin. "Joyce, Nietzsche, and Hauptmann in James Joyce's 'A Painful Case.'" *PMLA* 68, no. 1 (1953): 95–102.

Mahaffey, Vicki. "Joyce's Shorter Works." In Attridge 1990, 185–211.

———. *Reauthorizing Joyce*. Gainesville: University Press of Florida, 1995.

Maltby, Paul. *The Visionary Moment: A Postmodern Critique*. New York: State University of New York Press, 2002.

Mamigonian, Marc A., and John Noel Turner. "A Parallel Paraphrase of the Opening of 'Oxen of the Sun.'" *James Joyce Quarterly* 39, no. 2 (2002): 337–45.
McCabe, Colin, ed. *James Joyce: New Perspectives*. Sussex: Harvester, 1982.
———. *James Joyce and the Revolution of the Word*. London: Macmillan, 1981.
McCarthy, Patrick A. "The Last Epistle of *Finnegans Wake*." *James Joyce Quarterly* 27, no. 4 (1990): 725–33.
———. *The Riddles of* Finnegans Wake. Rutherford: Fairleigh Dickinson University Press, 1980.
McCourt, John. "Epiphanies of Language, Longing, Liminality in *Giacomo Joyce*." In *Giacomo Joyce: Envoys of the Other*, ed. Louis Armand and Clare Wallace, 228–48. Prague: Litteraria Pragensia, 2006.
———, ed. *James Joyce in Context*. Cambridge: Cambridge University Press, 2009.
McFadzean, Angus. "Epiphany and Transgression: From Aesthetics to Narrative in the Novels of James Joyce." Doctoral thesis, University of Oxford, 2010.
McGowan, John. "From Pater to Wilde to Joyce: Modernist Epiphany and the Soulful Self." *Texas Studies in Literature and Language* 32, no. 3 (1990): 417–45.
McHugh, Roland. *Annotations to* Finnegans Wake. 3rd ed. Baltimore, Md.: Johns Hopkins University Press, 2006.
———. *The* Finnegans Wake *Experience*. Dublin: Irish Academic, 1981.
———. *The Sigla of* Finnegans Wake. London: Edward Arnold, 1976.
McLuhan, Eric. *The Role of Thunder in* Finnegans Wake. Toronto: University of Toronto Press, 1997.
McLuhan, Marshall. "Joyce, Mallarmé, and the Press." *Sewanee Review* 62, no. 1 (1954): 38–55.
Melchiori, Giorgio. "The Languages of Joyce." In Bollettieri Bosinelli et al., 1–18.
Mickalites, Carey. "*Dubliners* IOU: The Aesthetics of Exchange in 'After the Race' and 'Two Gallants.'" *Journal of Modern Literature* 30, no. 2 (2007): 121–38.
Mikhail, Edward Halim, ed. *James Joyce: Interviews and Recollections*. Basingstoke: Macmillan, 1990.
Milesi, Laurent. "L'idiome babelien de *Finnegans Wake*: Recherches thématiques dans une perspective génétique." In Jacquet and Ferrer, 155–215.
———. "In the Beginning Was the Nil: The 'Eloquence of Silence' in *Finnegans Wake*." In Wawrzycka and Zanotti, 61–80.
———. "Joyce, Language, and Languages." In Rabaté 2004, 144–61.
———. "Metaphors of the Quest in *Finnegans Wake*." In Lernout, 79–108.
Miller, Hugh. *The Old Red Sandstone; Or, New Walks in an Old Field*. Edinburgh: Johnstone and Hunter, 1841.
———. *Poems, Written in the Leisure Hours of a Journeyman Mason*. Inverness: R. Carruthers, 1829.
———. *The Testimony of the Rocks; Or, Geology in Its Bearings on the Two Theologies, Natural and Revealed*. Edinburgh: Thomas Constable, 1857.

Miller, J. Hillis. *Fiction and Repetition: Seven English Novels*. Oxford: Blackwell, 1982.
Millot, Catherine. "Épiphanies." In *Joyce Avec Lacan*, ed. Jacques Aubert, 87–95. Paris: Navarin, 1987.
Monk, Maria Hoyte. *Awful Disclosures of Maria Monk*. New York: D. M. Bennett, 1878.
Moseley, Virginia. *Joyce and the Bible*. De Kalb: Northern Illinois University Press, 1967.
Natali, Ilaria. "A Portrait of James Joyce's Epiphanies as a Source Text," http://www.humanicus.org/global/issues/humanicus-6–2011/humanicus-6–2011–3.pdf.
Neuhold, Birgit. *Measuring the Sadness: Conrad, Joyce, Woolf and European Epiphany*. Frankfurt am Main: Peter Lang, 2009.
Nichols, Ashton. *The Poetics of Epiphany: Nineteenth-Century Origins of the Modern Literary Moment*. Tuscaloosa: University of Alabama Press, 1987.
Nietzsche, Friedrich Wilhelm. *Thus Spoke Zarathustra: A Book for All and None*. Trans. Walter Kaufmann. New York: Penguin, 1978.
Noël, Lucie. *James Joyce and Paul L. Léon: The Story of a Friendship*. New York: Gotham Book Mart, 1950.
Noon, William T. *Joyce and Aquinas*. New Haven: Yale University Press, 1957.
Norris, Margot. *The Decentered Universe of* Finnegans Wake: *A Structuralist Analysis*. Baltimore, Md.: Johns Hopkins University Press, 1976.
———. *Suspicious Readings of Joyce's Dubliners*. Philadelphia: University of Pennsylvania Press, 2003.
O'Rourke, Fran. "Joyce's Early Aesthetic." *Journal of Modern Literature* 34, no. 2 (2011): 97–120.
O'Sullivan, Michael. *The Incarnation of Language: Joyce, Proust and a Philosophy of the Flesh*. London: Bloomsbury Academic, 2013.
Osteen, Mark. *The Economy of* Ulysses: *Making Both Ends Meet*. Syracuse: Syracuse University Press, 1995.
———. "Serving Two Masters: Economics and Figures of Power in Joyce's 'Grace.'" *Twentieth Century Literature* 37, no. 1 (1991): 76–92.
Pater, Walter. *Appreciations; With an Essay on Style*. London: Macmillan, 1927.
———. *Marius the Epicurean: His Sensations and Ideas*. London: J. Cape, 1931.
———. *The Renaissance: Studies in Art and Poetry*. London: Macmillan, 1873.
Peacock, William. *English Prose from Mandeville to Ruskin*. Oxford: Oxford University Press, 1903.
Perlis, Alan D. "Beyond Epiphany: Pater's Aesthetic Hero in the Works of Joyce." *James Joyce Quarterly* 17 (1980): 272–79.
Pillow, Kirk. *Sublime Understanding: Aesthetic Reflection in Kant and Hegel*. Cambridge, Mass.: MIT Press, 2000.

Plato. *The Last Days of Socrates: Euthyphro, Apology, Crito, Phaedo.* Trans. Hugh Tredennick. London: Penguin, 1993.
Platt, Verity J. *Facing the Gods: Epiphany and Representation in Graeco-Roman Art, Literature and Religion.* Cambridge: Cambridge University Press, 2011.
Pound, Ezra. *The Cantos of Ezra Pound.* New York: New Directions, 1948.
———. *Selected Poems and Translations.* Ed. Richard Sieburth. New York: New Directions, 2010.
Power, Arthur. *Conversations with James Joyce.* London: Millington, 1974.
Power, Mary, ed. *New Perspectives on "Dubliners."* Amsterdam: Rodopi, 1997.
Prescott, Joseph. "James Joyce's Epiphanies." *Modern Language Notes* 64, no. 5 (1949): 346.
Rabaté, Jean-Michel. "Joyce and Jolas: Late Modernism and Early Babelism." *Journal of Modern Literature* 22, no. 2 (1998): 245–52.
———. *Joyce Upon the Void: The Genesis of Doubt.* New York: St. Martin's, 1991.
———, ed. *Palgrave Advances in James Joyce Studies.* Basingstoke: Palgrave Macmillan, 2004.
———. "Silence in *Dubliners.*" In Attridge and Ferrer, 45–72.
Rasula, Jed. "*Finnegans Wake* and the Character of the Letter." *James Joyce Quarterly* 34, no. 4 (1997): 517–30.
Reynolds, Mary T. *Joyce and Dante: The Shaping Imagination.* Princeton: Princeton University Press, 1981.
Rimbaud, Arthur. *Illuminations.* Genève: Droz, 1967.
Rossman, Charles. "Stephen Dedalus' Villanelle." *James Joyce Quarterly* 12, no. 3 (1975): 281–93.
Roughley, Alan. "ALP's 'Sein' und 'Zeit': Questions of *Finnegans Wake*'s Being and Language in a Philosophical Context." In Lernout, 125–38.
Rousseau, Jean Jacques. *Les Confessions.* Paris: H. Champion, 2010.
Saintsbury, George. *A History of English Prose Rhythm.* London: Macmillan, 1912.
Schlauch, Margaret. "The Language of James Joyce." *Science & Society* 3, no. 4 (1939): 482–97.
Scholes, Robert. *The Cornell Joyce Collection, a Catalogue.* Ithaca: Cornell University Press, 1961.
———. "Joyce and the Epiphany: The Key to the Labyrinth?" *Sewanee Review* 72 (1964): 65–77.
Scholes, Robert, and Marlena G. Corcoran. "The Aesthetic Theory and the Critical Writings." In Bowen and Carens, 689–705.
Scholes, Robert, and Richard M. Kain. *The Workshop of Daedalus: James Joyce and the Raw Materials for* A Portrait of the Artist as a Young Man. Evanston, Ill.: Northwestern University Press, 1965.
Scholes, Robert, and Florence L. Walzl. "The Epiphanies of Joyce." *PMLA* 82, no. 1 (1967): 152–54.

Scotto, Robert M. "'Visions' and 'Epiphanies': Fictional Technique in Pater's *Marius* and Joyce's *Portrait*." *James Joyce Quarterly* 11 (1973): 41–49.
Senn, Fritz. "Gnomon Inverted." In Bollettieri Bosinelli et al., 249–57.
———. *Inductive Scrutinies: Focus on Joyce*. Ed. Christine O'Neill. Dublin: Lilliput, 1995.
———. *Joyce's Dislocutions: Essays on Reading as Translation*. Baltimore, Md.: Johns Hopkins University Press, 1984.
Shaw, Bernard. *The Quintessence of Ibsenism*. 3rd ed. London: Constable, 1926.
Shelley, Percy Bysshe. *Poetry and Prose: Authoritative Texts, Criticism*. 2nd ed. New York: W. W. Norton, 2002.
Singer, Thomas C. "Riddles, Silence, and Wonder: Joyce and Wittgenstein Encountering the Limits of Language." *ELH* 57, no. 2 (1990): 459–84.
Skeat, Walter W. *An Etymological Dictionary of the English Language*. Oxford: Clarendon, 1888.
Slepon, Raphael. *Finnegans Wake* Extensible Elucidation Treasury. www.fweet.org.
Slote, Sam. "'Affirmations and Negations Invalidated as Uttered' in *Ulysses* and *How It Is*." In Wawrzycka and Zanotti, 105–14.
———. "Epiphanic 'Proteus.'" *Genetic Joyce Studies* 5 (Spring 2005): http://www.geneticjoycestudies.org/articles/GJS5/GJS5lote.
Slote, Sam, and Wim Van Mierlo, eds. *Genitricksling Joyce*. Amsterdam: Rodopi, 1999.
Splitter, Randolph. "Watery Words: Language, Sexuality, and Motherhood in Joyce's Fiction." *ELH* 49, no. 1 (1982): 190–213.
Spurr, David. "Joyce's Countergospel in II.4." In Devlin and Smedley, 201–19.
———. *Joyce and the Scene of Modernity*. Gainesville: University Press of Florida, 2002.
Staley, Thomas, ed. *Approaches to Joyce's Portrait: Ten Essays*. Pittsburgh: University of Pittsburgh Press, 1976.
Steppe, Wolfhard. "The *Merry Greeks* (With a Farewell to epicleti)." *James Joyce Quarterly* 32, nos. 3–4 (1995): 597–617.
Stroup, Thomas B. "Bottom's Name and His Epiphany." *Shakespeare Quarterly* 29, no. 1 (1978): 79–82.
Synge, John Millington. *Collected Works*. London: Oxford University Press, 1962.
Thornton, Weldon. *Allusions in* Ulysses: *An Annotated List*. Chapel Hill: University of North Carolina Press, 1968.
Thrane, James R. "Joyce's Sermon on Hell: Its Source and Its Backgrounds." *Modern Philology* 57, no. 3 (1960): 172–98.
Tigges, Wim. *Moments of Moment: Aspects of the Literary Epiphany*. Amsterdam: Rodopi, 1999.
Tindall, William York. *A Reader's Guide to* Finnegans Wake. London: Thames and Hudson, 1969.

———. *A Reader's Guide to James Joyce*. London: Thames and Hudson, 1970.
Torchiana, Donald T. *Backgrounds for Joyce's Dubliners*. Boston: Allen & Unwin, 1987.
Trench, C.E.F. "Dermot Chenevix Trench and Haines of *Ulysses*." *James Joyce Quarterly* 13, no. 1 (1975): 39–48.
Trench, Richard Chenevix. *On the Study of Words: Five Lectures*. London: John W. Parker and Son, 1851.
———. *Poems*. Privately printed, 1841.
———. *Proverbs and Their Lessons: Being the Substance of Lectures Delivered to Young Men's Societies*. London: Macmillan, 1869.
———. *The Star of the Wise Men: A Commentary on the Second Chapter of St. Matthew*. Philadelphia: H. Hooker, 1850.
Tucker, Herbert F. "Epiphany and Browning: Character Made Manifest." *PMLA* 107, no. 5 (1992): 1208–21.
Turner, John Noel. "A Commentary on the Closing of 'Oxen of the Sun.'" *James Joyce Quarterly* 35, no. 1 (1997): 83–111.
Vico, Giambattista. *The New Science*. Trans. Thomas Goddard Bergin and Max Harold Fisch. Ithaca: Cornell University Press, 1948.
———. *Principj di scienza nuova*. 3 vols. Milan: Sesta, 1816.
Vitoux, Pierre. "Aristotle, Berkeley, and Newman in 'Proteus' and *Finnegans Wake*." *James Joyce Quarterly* 18, no. 2 (1981): 161–75.
Waisbren, Burton, and Florence Walzl. "Paresis and the Priest: Jame's Joyce's Symbolic Use of Syphilis in 'The Sisters.'" *Annals of Internal Medicine* (1974): 758–62.
Walker's Pronouncing Dictionary of the English Language. London: Frederick Warne, 1866.
Walzl, Florence L. "*Dubliners*." In Bowen and Carens, 157–228.
———. "Gabriel and Michael: The Conclusion of 'The Dead.'" In Joyce 1969, 423–44.
———. "The Liturgy of the Epiphany Season and the Epiphanies of Joyce." *PMLA* 80, no. 4 (1965): 436–50.
———. "Pattern of Paralysis in Joyce's *Dubliners*: A Study of the Original Framework." *College English* 22, no. 4 (1961): 221–28.
Watts, Isaac. *Divine Songs: Attempted in Easy Language for the Use of Children*. London: T. Longman, 1761.
Wawrzycka, Jolanta, and Serenella Zanotti. *James Joyce's Silences*. London: Bloomsbury Academic, 2018.
Weir, Lorraine. "The Choreography of Gesture: Marcel Jousse and *Finnegans Wake*." *James Joyce Quarterly* 14, no. 3 (1977): 313–25.
Wight, Doris T. "Ironies Romantic and Naturalistic: James Joyce's Epiphanies

and Nathalie Sarraute's Tropisms." *Rackham Journal of the Arts and Humanities* (1987): 15–45.
Wildi, Max. "Wordsworth and the Simplon Pass." *English Studies* 40 (1959): 224–32.
Wittgenstein, Ludwig. *Tractatus Logico-Philosophicus*. Trans. D. F. Pears and B. F. McGuinness. London: Routledge & Kegan Paul, 1981.
Wolfe, Thomas. *Of Time and the River: A Legend of Man's Hunger in His Youth*. Harmondsworth: Penguin, 1971.
Wollaeger, Mark A., ed. *James Joyce's* A Portrait of the Artist as a Young Man*: A Casebook*. New York: Oxford University Press, 2003.
Woolf, Virginia. *Between the Acts*. London: Hogarth, 1941.
———. *The Diary of Virginia Woolf.* Vol. 3. Ed. Anne Olivier Bell. London: Hogarth, 1980.
———. *Essays*. Vol. 6. Ed. Stuart N. Clarke. London: Hogarth, 2011.
———. *Moments of Being*. 2nd ed. London: Grafton, 1989.
———. *Mrs. Dalloway*. Oxford: Oxford University Press, 1992.
———. *A Room of One's Own; Three Guineas*. Oxford: Oxford University Press, 1992.
———. *To the Lighthouse*. Oxford: Oxford University Press, 1992.
———. *The Waves*. Oxford: Oxford University Press, 1992.
Wordsworth, William. *Lyrical Ballads*. Ed. R. L. Brett and A. R. Jones. London: Methuen, 1986.
———. *The Prelude: 1798–1799*. Ed. Stephen Parrish. Ithaca: Cornell University Press, 1977.
———. *The Prelude: Or, Growth of a Poet's Mind*. Ed. Ernest de Selincourt. Oxford: Oxford University Press, 1959.
———. *The Prose Works*. Ed. Warwick Jack Burgoyne Owen and Jane Worthington Smyser. Oxford: Clarendon, 1974.
Yeats, William Butler. *The Collected Plays*. London: Macmillan, 1963.
Zaniello, Thomas. "The Epiphany and the Object-Image Distinction." *JJQ* 4 (1967): 286–88.

INDEX

Page numbers followed by *t* indicate tables.

Abrams, M. H., 39–40, 45, 51
Absences: "The Dead," 99; in epiphanies, 12–13, 15–17, 52, 54, 75, 155, 192; and language, 15, 75; and linguistic epiphany, 50, 143–44; *A Portrait of the Artist as a Young Man (P)*, 143–44; in *Ulysses*, 161, 177
Absences, linguistic: in epiphanies, 16–17; in Joyce's work generally, 15; in "She Comes at Night," 16; in "The Hole in Georgie's Stomach," 12–14; in *Ulysses*, 16
Aesthetics, Joyce's: of beauty, 69–71; O'Rourke on, 34–35; reproduction in, 20; revelation and language, 6–7; Romantic roots of, 44. See also Epiphany, Joyce's aesthetics of
Aphorisms, 90
Apocalypse metaphors, 39–40
"The Apocalypse of St. John," 7
"Apologise": chiasmus in, 82; dating of, 57; and *Portrait*, 103–7, 116, 118, 122; repetition and variation in, 103–7; and *Ulysses*, 152
Aquinas, Thomas, 34–35, 69, 71–72
"Araby": beginning-ending mirroring, 84–85; desire in, 79–80, 84; dialogue in, 79; and epiphanies, 79–84; *versus* "fragment of colloquy," 80; gestures and words in, 67; leitmotifs, 80–81; lyricism of, 81–83; perspective changes in, 86–87; *versus* "The Race" epiphany, 81; repetition and variation in, 82; significance, emptying and doubling, 85; speculation, inviting, 80–81, 85
"An Arctic Beast," 185
Aristotle's Masterpiece, 172, 173f
Atherton, James, 174–75, 199, 208–9, 218, 257n17
Attridge, Derek: on *Dubliners*, 77–78, 244n4; on *Finnegans Wake*, 208, 223–24, 259n41; on Lecercle's linguistic theory, 128–29
Augustine, 32–34, 37, 40, 241n12
Aum syllable, 186–87

Bakhtin, Mikhail, 105–6
Beach, Sylvia, 204
Beare, Francis Wright, 29–30
Beauty, phases of apprehension, 69–72
Beck, Warren, 77–78
Beckett, Samuel: epiphany, theatrical, 230; on *Finnegans Wake*, 197, 204–5; Joyce, influence of, 229; repetition, use of, 229; silence, use of, 229–30; *The Unnameable*, 228, 260n4; on Vico, 205, 207
Begnal, Michael, 208
Beja, Morris: on epiphanies, 46, 53, 183, 185–86; on epiphany, 25, 31, 241n11; epiphany definition, 48; on epiphany in Joyce, 48, 70; on epiphany in Joyce studies, 181; mentioned, 37, 51; on modernist fiction, 46; on "The Stars on Joyce's Nose," 59; on *Ulysses*, 153
Bélra na filed, 196
Benjamin, Walter, 102, 106, 112

Benstock, Bernard, 155
the Bible: Exodus, Joyce's interpretation of, 200, 258n21; *Finnegans Wake* allusions to, 198–200, 220–21; Genesis, 199; Gospel of St. John, 68, 199; interpretive methods, 39–40; New Testament epiphanies, 198, 200; *Portrait* allusions to, 117, 132, 248nn15–16, 250n29; *Ulysses* allusions to, 159–60. *See also* Epiphany, biblical; Revelation, book of
Bishop, John, 209
Blake, William, 40
Boehme, Jacob, 40
Boldrini, Lucia, 35–36, 181–82
Booth, Wayne, 250n22
Bowen, Zack, 116
Brown, Raymond Edward, 29
Budgen, Frank, 174, 192
Burke, Kenneth, 102, 125–26

Cage, John, 21, 238n18
Campbell, Joseph, 208, 214
Candlemas, 23, 199–200
Cary, Philip, 33
Caufield, James Walter, 70
Chamber Music, 4, 260n1
Chapter overviews, 18–19
Cheng, Vincent, 216
Chiasmus: in "Apologise," 82; in "The Dead," 89; in *A Portrait of the Artist as a Young Man*, 101, 104, 106, 109, 111, 124–26, 142; in *Ulysses*, 152–53
Christian theology and apocalypse metaphors, 39–40
Cixous, Hélène, 77
Clark, Hilary, 256n4
Clifford, Martha, 18
Color: in *Finnegans Wake*, 190–94, 201; in *Portrait*, 134, 169, 251n30; in *Ulysses*, 169–70, 251n30
Connor, Steven, 228–29
Conrad, Joseph, 46
Corcoran, Marlena G., 70
"Counterparts," 22

The Critical Writings (CW), 4–7
Culler, Jonathan, 230

Dante, 35–36, 191, 193
"The Dead": ending of, 88, 92, 101; epiphany in, 98, 101; gnomonic structure of, 98; indeterminacy in, 99, 101; ironic realism in, 99–100; and "Is That Mary Ellen?," 154–55; and "Ithaca," 154; lacunae of, 99; lyrical symbolism in, 99–100; lyricism of, 83; other stories, connections to, 97–98; repetition and mutation, 101; repetition in, 89, 97–99, 101; snow in, 99–101; and Trench's *Select Glossary*, 252n4; *Ulysses*'s allusions to, 176; uncertainty in, 99
Death, 13–14, 16–17
Derrida, Jacques: *la brisure* term, 125, 218; *différance*, 260n2; on *Finnegans Wake*, 219; iteration, theory of, 19, 227; mentioned, 75, 103, 224; and nothingness, 210; reflection, philosophy of, 218; on repetition, 21, 125
Desire: "Araby," 79–80, 84; *Dubliners*, 79–80, 84, 91; and *FW* linguistic epiphany, 186; Lacanian, 227, 260n2; "A Painful Case," 91; *Portrait*, 20; *Ulysses*, 156
Doubling: in *Finnegans Wake*, 210, 218–22, 218–22, 259n38; originary, 158, 218; and splitting, 184, 210, 218–19
Drama, Joyce's theory of, 5–6
"Drama and Life," 34, 66
Dubliners: "After the Race," 87; "An Encounter," 87; "The Boarding House," 87; breaks in, 86; as circular, 85, 97; "Clay," 244n4; "Counterparts," 22; as doubly epiphanic, 83–84; endings, 78, 88–90, 92–93, 95–97, 101; epiphanic nature of, 99; epiphany in, 47, 76–78; "Eveline," 77, 86–87, 245n7; and gnomons, 95–96, 246n13; "Grace," 88; indeterminacy in, 78, 99, 101, 128; "Ivy Day in the Committee Room," 110; Joyce on, 81–82; lacunae of, 99; light

Index · 281

imagery in, 246n12; "A Little Cloud," 88, 100; lyricism of, 83, 89, 245n6; materiality of, 22; "A Painful Case," 89–93, 245n8; perspective changes in, 86–88; versus *Portrait*, 118–19, 127; as revelation, 9; "Two Gallants," 87–88; uncertainty in, 99; unifying elements, 86. *See also* individual stories

Dubliners, repetition in: "Araby," 82; and characterization, 88–89; "The Dead," 89, 97–99, 101; in dialogue, 89; and endings, 88, 93; and epiphanies, 89, 93; gnomonic, 96, 246n13; and indeterminacy, 99; "A Painful Case," 89, 92–93; "The Sisters," 95–97; ubiquity of, 93; variation in, 89

Dubliners, silence in: as critical approach, 77–78; and epiphanies, 88, 93; as epiphany, 88; functions of, 88, 127; "A Painful Case," 89, 92–93; repeated use of, 96; "The Sisters," 59, 88, 93–97, 245n9; ubiquity of, 93

Dubliners-epiphanies connections: epiphanic, 76–77; ironic realism, 79, 87, 89, 225; lyrical symbolism, 79, 87, 89, 225; repetition, use of, 89; structural, 85–88, 225; stylistic, 79–85; thematic, 85–86

"Ecce Homo," 66
Eco, Umberto, 35, 181
Eliade, Mircea, 240n7
Eliot, T. S., 31, 230–31, 232, 261n6
Ellmann, Maud, 14, 142
Ellmann, Richard, 76, 148, 154, 238n7, 239n3
Emerson, Ralph Waldo, 24
Epicleti neologism, 76
Epiphanic mode in modernism, 227–28
Epiphanies: overviews of, 2, 12, 51; absences and meaning in, 12–13, 15–17, 54, 75, 155, 192; *versus* aphorisms, 90; archival locations of, 52–53, 243n4; Baudelaire's influence on, 46; and Book of Revelation, 8; and circulation breaks, *Ulysses*, 151; commentaries, 3–4; copies of, 12, 238n12; critical dismissals of, 51, 242n1; critiques of, 51; death, theme of, 16–17, 52; description of, 55; drafts in "My Crucible," 11; and etymology, 14–15; *Finnegans Wake*, connections to, 204; as first major work, 260n1; importance to Joyce, 53, 186; indeterminacy of, 52; intentions for, Joyce's, 11–12; interest in, Joyce's, 17–18; lacunae, self-replicating, 155; language, as emphasizing, 52; language-silence paradox in, 21; materiality and reflexivity in, 22; narrative, lack of, 51; and navels, 13–16; number of, 52; ordering of, 53, 111; as origin for later work, 12, 53, 225; and Pater, 46; as *Portrait* material, 76; publications of, 2, 4, 24, 237n3; reuse of, 2–4, 12, 51, 76, 233–35t, 238n12; role in Joyce's work, 18; in "Selections in Prose from Various Authors," 4; and Shelley, 55; and silence and repetition, 227; sound in, 82; and Stephen's theory of epiphany, 54–55; subjectivity and dreams, 62; and the sublime, 227; as textual objects, 72; title of, 237n3; types of, 12, 52; uncertainties regarding, 2–3; uncertainty and signification, 15, 191; unifying elements, 85–86; verbal slips, 57, 61, 77, 113; writing of, 52, 65–66, 243n3. *See also Dubliners*-epiphanies connections; *Finnegans Wake*, epiphanies in; *A Portrait of the Artist as a Young Man* and epiphanies; *Ulysses*, epiphanies in; individual epiphanies

Epiphanies, dramatic: overviews of, 2, 12; authenticity of, 55–57; and *Dubliners*, 79, 87, 89, 225; goals of, 57; Gogarty in, 55–56; ignorance, theme of, 58; interpretations of, 51; Joyce in, 58–59, 61; language and absence in, 52; real speech, techniques for, 57; settings of, 56–57; silences in, 2, 19, 145, 177; in

Epiphanies—*continued*
two-pole model, 18–19; verbal slips and gestures in, 57–58, 61
Epiphanies, elegiac: overview of, 16–17; and limits of language, 149; rupture, moments of, 86; and spots of time, 41, 43–44
Epiphanies, lyrical: overviews of, 2, 12, 62; dreams in, 15–16, 62; harmonies of sound in, 82; meaning from absence in, 16; people appearing in, 62; presence and signification in, 52; repetition in, 63–64, 145, 177; Stanislaus Joyce on, 15–16, 62; techniques used in, 62; in two-pole model, 18–19; variation in, 63–64; writing of, 62. *See also* "She Comes at Night"
Epiphanies, two-pole model of, 18–19, 52. *See also* Ironic realism; Lyrical symbolism
Epiphany: in Christian theology, 23, 27; classical, 23–27, 239n1; in Dante, 35; as divine manifestation, 23–24; Emerson on, 24; etymology of, 23, 25; in fiction generally, 46–47; in Joyce studies, 2, 47–48, 77, 181, 242n25; as literary term, 24; literay, 37, 42, 45–46, 231; modern literary, 31; De Quincy on, 24; and subjective experience, 31–32; *Wakean*, 181–82. *See also Finnegans Wake*, epiphany in
Epiphany, biblical: Acts *versus* Pauline Epistles, 32; Augustine's sermons on, 23, 32–33; *versus* classical, 25; Gospel of Luke, 240n10; Gospel of Matthew, 29–30; Hebrew word used, 240n6; New Testament, 23, 195, 239n1; Old Testament, 27–28, 30, 195; Old Testament *versus* evangelical, 33; Revelation, 28–29; star of the magi, 29; St. Paul's conversion, 32
Epiphany, definitions of: Beja's, 48; contemporary, 24; Eco's, 35; Langbaum's, 48; Nichol's, 48; original, 23–24, 199;

Shelley's, 44; in *Stephen Hero*, 1, 24, 44, 49, 66–67, 160, 181, 192, 239n3; Tigges's, 48–49
Epiphany, Joyce's aesthetics of: and *Dubliners*, 77; in Paris-Pola notebook, 65–66, 70; *versus* Rousseau's, 38; Scholes on, 70; *Stephen Hero*, 65–69, 71–72, 74
Epiphany, linguistic: overviews of, 1, 6, 51; absence in, 50; and absences, 50, 143–44; characteristics of, 183; and Eliot's epiphanies, 231; *Finnegans Wake*, 11, 36, 183, 186, 201, 204, 210, 222, 227; and gaps becoming visible, 178; and gesture, 67; as gnomonic, 96; and irony, 177; and Joyce's theory of language, 11; Lacanian readings of, 49; language, communal nature of, 129, 135; language as epiphany, 72; and materiality, 22, 72; *versus* prior forms, 51; and reflexivity, 22; and Revelation, language of, 49; and Romantic epiphany, 38, 49; roots of, 25, 241n15; and silence, 21–22; and the sublime, 227. *See also A Portrait of the Artist as a Young Man*, linguistic epiphany in; *Ulysses*, linguistic epiphany in
Epiphany, Romantic: overview of, 25; in Augustine, 33; *versus* epiphany of the stars, 160–61; *versus* Joyce's, 1, 6, 18; and linguistic Epiphany, 38; and modernist fiction, 46; and the ordinary, 27; Wordsworth's, 38–39
Epiphany in Joyce: as arbitrary and ever-present, 160; attributes of, 217; centrality of, 48; and drama, 5–6; Ellmann on, 239n3; *versus* Emerson, 24; evolution of, 69; joyous outbursts, 5–6, 160; as ordinary, 27, 72; as problematic, 78; *versus* Rousseau, 38; subjects of, 197–98; and the visible world, 6; whatness, manifestations of, 72; *versus* Wordsworth, 41, 43–44. *See also* Epiphany, Joyce's aesthetics of
The Escaped Nun, 58, 172
Etymology: and epiphanies, 14–15; of

epiphany, 23, 25; of phenomenon, 161, 254n17; and *Portrait*s linguistic epiphany, 134, 139–44; in *Stephen Hero*, 14; in *Ulysses*, 163–64, 254n19; Vico's interest in, 205. *See also* Skeat, Walter
Euripides, 26
Exiles, 12, 17

Feast of Epiphany, 23
Feshbach, Sidney, 48
Finnegans Wake: "the Angel of the Lord" references, 198–200; Augustine's sermons, allusions to, 33–34, 241n12; Aum syllable in, 186–88; authorship, comments on, 221; autobiographical aspects, 184–85; and Babel, 33–34; biblical allusions, 220–21; Book Four, 11, 186, 190, 198, 200, 202, 213; and Book of Revelation, 8; cloud, star and fire motifs, 200–203; cloud-rain-river-water cycle, 201–2, 215; color in, 190–94, 201; as countergospel, 199, 257n18; criticism on, 204–11, 214–15; and Dante, 35–36, 193; doubling in, 210, 218–22, 259n38; dreaming levels and Victorian ages, 186–87; *Electra*, allusions to, 26; epiphanies, connections to, 204, 225; epiphany, linguistic, 11, 36, 183, 186, 201, 204, 210, 222, 227; as epiphany, 47, 181–82; epiphany of language in, 181–82; and Finnegan family crest, 200, 257n19; fraternal relations theme, 183–84; genetic criticism on, 214–15; George Joyce, references to, 184; gestures in, 67; guides to, 208–9; identity and alterity, 184; John Augustine Joyce, references to, 184; Joyce on, 188, 192, 201; Joyce's other works, allusions to, 185; as Joyce's Revelation, 199; and Kant, 191, 221, 256n8; language as light in, 68; language as revelation vehicle, 36; language-silence paradox in, 22; the letter, 216–18, 223, 259n38; light in, 36, 190–95, 201, 220;

linguistic insights of, 222–24; materiality of, 22, 204, 215–18, 222; meaning production in, 175; metatextuality of, 222–24; motif agglomeration, 216; nodality of, 215; original-reproduction connections in, 184; as panepiphanal, 18, 192; purpose of, 199; rainbow motif, 193–94, 202–3, 220; repetition, 19, 22, 204, 209, 212–14, 219; repetition and variation, 214–15, 217; Revelation, allusions to, 10–11; as revelation, 9; *ricorso*, 165, 186, 204–5, 212; silence in, 203–4, 211–12; splendor of truth in, 6; Stanislaus, references to, 184; St. Patrick's passchal fire, 201–2; and the sublime, 74; three-part historical cycle, 186, 205; time in, 70; the Trinity in, 193–94, 202; *Ulysses*, connections to, 179–80, 184, 186, 200, 259n40; uncertainty in, 217; water cycles in, 132–33

—epiphanic passages: Berkeley and St. Patrick vignette, 190–96, 220; biblical allusions, 198–200; Buckley shooting Russian General anecdote, 197–98; clouds in, 201–3; color in, 190–93; epiphanoids, 188–89, 215; "Father Epiphanies," 197; light in, 190–93; method, 188; Mutt and Jeff banter, 201–2, 258n22; real-life revelations, 188–89; sacred-profane conflations, 196–98; sources for, 189; types of, 188; "wolk in the process," 201–2

Finnegans Wake, epiphanies in: "An Arctic Beast," 185; "Fred Leslie's My Brother," 186; "Half-Men, Half-Goats," 185–86; "Is Mabie Your Sweetheart?," 186; reductions of, 186, 189; reuse of, 12, 18, 53, 76, 225, 233–35t; "She Comes at Night," 183–85, 188

Finnegans Wake, epiphany in: burning bush, 203–4; Christian, 194; critics on, 181; feminine and masculine, 202–3; qualities of, 196; and silence, 203–4; thunder, 205–6

284 · Index

Finnegans Wake, language of: Attridge on, 223; and Babelian parable, 206; Beckett on, 204–5; and *Bélra na filed*, 196; and Berkely's color theory, 192; bifurcation, 210; *versus* Carroll's, 208; and Dark Tongue of Ireland, 195–96; Derrida on, 218–19; development of, 195; doubling and splitting, 184, 210, 218–19; epiphanic, 187–88, 256n3; genetic criticism, 214–15; Gibson on, 196, 257n14; Gilbert on, 205–8; Hayman on, 214; languages used in, 36, 195, 256n11, 257n13; McCabe on, 209; McLuhan on, 206; Melichiori on, 210; Milesi on, 218; Paul Léon's theory, 192–93; portmanteaux, 223; repetition in, 212–14; scatological, 215–16; scholarship on, 204–10; Senn on, 210–11, 258n28; and silence, 211–12; Spurr on, 209–10; techniques, 208; thunderwords, 206–7, 231; universality, tendency toward, 195, 257n12

Finnegans Wake, self-reflexivity of: chapter 1.7, 185; and doubling, 218–22, 259n38; and epiphanies, 204; and epiphany, linguistic, 204; and the letter, 217–18, 223; and materiality of language, 218, 222–24; sealed book of life, 10–11

Fordham, Finn, 210, 215
"Forty Thousand Pounds," 61–62
"Fred Leslie's My Brother," 57, 186
French, Marilyn, 77, 174
French modernist literature, 260n5
Freud, Sigmund, 16

Gabler, Hans Walter, 109, 121, 247n4
Gasché, Rodolphe, 21, 158, 218, 221–22, 227, 259n35
Gesture, 57–58, 61, 67, 187–88, 256n3
Giacomo Joyce, 12
Gibson, George Sinclair, 196
Gifford, Creighton, 78, 105
Gilbert, Stuart, 179, 205–6
"The Girls, The Boys," 67, 115
Glasheen, Adaline, 195, 208–9

Gnomons: and "The Dead," 98; definitions of, 246n13; and linguistic epiphany, 96; repetition in *Dubliners*, 96, 246n13; and "The Sisters," 59, 68, 93, 95–97
Gogarty, Oliver St. John, 55–56, 188, 243n9
Gottfried, Roy, 7
Gray, Richard T., 90
Groden, Michael, 7

"Half-Men, Half-Goats," 122, 126, 185–86
Hart, Clive, 186–87, 195, 209, 216
Hayman, David, 149, 189, 214
Heath, Stephen, 77
Heidegger, Martin, 21
Hendry, Irene, 2, 47, 181
Henke, Suzette, 228
Herring, Philip, 15, 52, 59, 61, 78
"His Dancing," 57
Hölderlin, Friedrich, 38
"The Hole in Georgie's Stomach," 12–15, 142, 238n13
"The Holy Office," 34
"Hoofs upon the Dublin Road," 112–13, 187
Hulle, Dirk van, 189

"I lie along the deck," 82
"Images of Fabulous Kings," 112–13, 115–16, 123, 247n9
Indeterminacy: in *Dubliners*, 78, 99, 101, 128; of epiphanies, 52; Herring on, 59, 61, 78; as limit of language, 177; and silence, 177; in *Ulysses*, 150, 226
Ireland, Christian conversion of, 193–94, 256n9
Ironic realism: in *Dubliners*, 79, 87, 89, 99–100, 225; lyrical symbolism, fusion with, 117–21; and silence, 121, 127; in *Ulysses*, 148. *See also* Epiphanies, dramatic
"Is That Mary Ellen?," 112, 114, 154–55, 157, 252n7

Jager, Colin, 231–32, 242n19
James, Henry, 46
"James Clarence Mangan," 5–6, 66
Janusko, Robert, 174–75
Jolas, Eugene, 188, 204
Jolas, Maria, 238n12
Joyce, Georgie, 13–15, 149, 239n15
Joyce, James: Abin's portrait of, 59, 60f, 243nn10–11; Aquinas, influence of, 34–35; as Aristotelian, 34–35; and Beckett, 229; birth of, 199–200; on Blake, 40; and Dante, 35–37; death of, 14; early work of, 260n1; and Georgie's death, 14; on *Heimat,* 4; on his work, 238n6; letters of, 45, 53, 76, 81, 174–75, 192; medieval mind of, 34–36; paper recycling, 157; Renaissance writers, views on, 36–37; and Richard Trench's work, 136–37; and Russian General anecdote, 196–97; and Samuel Trench, 136–37; Stanislaus Joyce on, 3; on Wordsworth, 45; works as single oeuvre, 260n1. *See also My Brother's Keeper*
Joyce, John, 197, 243n12
Joyce, Mary, 13, 15–17, 148
Joyce, Stanislaus: on epiphanies, 55, 57, 62; on Georgie's death, 14; on Joyce's ambition, 46; on Joyce's technique, 13; "My Crucible," 3–4, 7–8, 11, 238n8, 238n10; and "A Painful Case," 245n8; paper recycling, 157; "Selections in Prose and Verse," 52; "Selections in Prose from Various Authors," 4, 111; on "She Comes at Night," 15–16, 145. *See also My Brother's Keeper*
Joyce studies: early, 204; epiphany in, 2, 47–48, 77, 181, 242n25; *Finnegans Wake* in, 204–9; Joyce's friends and acquaintances, 204–5; post-structuralist turn, 209

Kain, Richard M., 7. *See also The Workshop of Daedalus*
Kant, Immanuel: aesthetic as sensory perception, 71, 244n17; aesthetics of, 71; apprehension, 71; beauty, theory of, 73; *Finnegans Wake* and, 191, 221, 256n8; on genius, 74; noumenon, 71–72, 192, 221, 260n2; reproduction, 71–72; the sublime, theory of, 72–75, 227, 260n2; transcendental aesthetic, 71, 74; Wordsworth, influence on, 39, 41, 43, 74
Kenner, Hugh: on *Dubliners,* 77, 245n7; on language and modernism, 214–15; on Latin, 140; on *Portrait,* 104, 124–25, 250n22; on *Ulysses,* 14, 29n17

Lacan, Jacques, 15, 21, 156, 227, 239n16, 260n2
"The Lame Beggar," 157–58
Langbaum, Robert, 28, 37, 45, 51, 227
Language: and absences, 15, 75; epiphanic nature of, 222; as epiphany, 223; general properties of, 230; incertitude, 180; Joyce's theory of, 11, 68, 74–75; Lacan on, 15, 21, 239n16; language-silence paradox, 21–22; Lecercle's theory, 128, 135; and light, 68; limits of, 177; in process of becoming, 139; and revelation, 6–11; ruptures in, 179; as self-reflexive, 222, 226; as sensory experience, 72; and spirit, 11, 27, 66–67, 74, 128–29, 131, 139; as sublime, 74–75; in *Ulysses,* 165, 169–71; and uncertainty, 15–15. *See also* Epiphany, linguistic; Etymology; *Finnegans Wake,* language of; Philology
Language, materiality of: *The Critical Writings* on, 6; in *Finnegans Wake,* 218, 222–24; Joyce's emphasis on, 124–25; and linguistic epiphany, 22, 72, 129, 133–34; philology and, 128; in *Portrait,* 129, 133–34; and silence, 226–27; in "The Sisters," 227; in *Ulysses,* 156, 164, 171
Language-silence paradox, 21–22
"The Last Tram," 112, 114–15, 121, 248n13
Laurence, Patricia, 228
Lecercle, Jean-Jacques, 128, 135

Léon, Lucie, 191
Léon, Paul, 193–94
Leonard, Garry, 78
Levin, Harry, 2, 77–78
Levine, Jennifer, 209
Light: in *Dubliners,* 246n12; in *Finnegans Wake,* 36, 190–93, 190–95, 201, 220; and language, 68; and logos, 195; in "The Sisters," 68
Linguistic embodiment, 129–30
Litz, A. Walton, 4, 18, 52, 183, 225
Llona, Victor, 205
Loevlie, Elisabeth Marie, 250n24
Losey, Jay, 46
Lyrical symbolism: in *Dubliners,* 79, 87, 89, 99–100, 225; *My Brother's Keeper* on, 82; in *Portrait,* 109, 117–21; and repetition, 121; in *Ulysses,* 148, 158. *See also* Epiphanies, lyrical

Macalister, R. A., 195
Magalaner, Marvin, 90–91, 245n8
Maltby, Paul, 51
de Man, Paul, 38, 241n17
Materiality, 22, 204, 215–18, 222. *See also* Language, materiality of
Matthew, 29
McAlmon, Robert, 205
McCabe, Colin, 77, 209
McCarthy, Patrick, 209, 217–18
McGowan, John, 46, 119
McHugh, Roland, 186, 208–9, 211, 257n19
McLuhan, Eric, 206
Melchiori, Giorgio, 182, 210
Milesi, Laurent, 36, 195, 206, 216–18
Miller, Hugh, 133, 137–39, 251n34
Miller, J. Hillis, 20, 106, 228
Modernism, 31, 38, 230
Modernist fiction, 46, 230–32
Moseley, Virginia, 7, 9–10
Muller, Max, 251n33
Murray, Lillie, 61, 243n12
My Brother's Keeper: epiphanies, 51, 55, 57, 61, 62, 77, 113; Georgie's death, 14, 239n15; Joyce's hubris, 4; lyrical symbolism, 82; Mary Joyce's death, 17, 56, 149; "A Painful Case," 245n8; "She Comes at Night," 15, 143, 183; "She Dances with Them in the Round," 56; Stephen's villanelle, 249n14; "The Two Mourners," 56
"My Crucible," 3–4, 7–8, 11, 238n8, 238n10

Navels, 13–16, 148
"Nestor," 5–6
Neuhold, Birgit, 26–27, 32, 37
Nichols, Ashton: on classical epiphany, 25; on Emerson, 24; epiphany definition, 48; mentioned, 37, 51; on Romantic epiphany, 31, 45–46; on Shelley and Joyce, 44–45
Norris, Margot, 78, 186, 208–9

Originary doubling, 158, 218
O'Rourke, Fran, 34–35
O'Sullivan, Michael, 129–30

"A Painful Case," 22, 89–93, 245n8
Pater, Walter, 46, 132, 165, 174
Phenomena, 161, 254n17
Philology, 128, 135–37, 254n19
Pillow, Kirk, 73, 101
Polysemy technique, 17
Pomes Penyeach, 12
"Poor Little Fellow," 56
A Portrait of the Artist as a Young Man: allusions to, in *Ulysses,* 176; and Aquinas, 34; artistic conception terminology, 171, 255n26; beauty, theory of, 68–69; bird-girl passage, 115, 119–20, 124, 127, 130, 249n20; blindness in, 104, 247n3; center of, 124–26; chains of association, 123–24; chapter climaxes, 120–21, 250n22; chiasmus in, 101, 104, 106, 109, 111, 124–26, 142; Cranly motifs, 248n10; as creation myth, 138; Dante in, 105, 107, 112; as dialogical, 105–6; dialogue in, 118–19; diary, Stephen's, 111, 113–18,

121; discontinuity in, 113–14, 117; *versus Dubliners,* 118–19, 127; English language politics, 143; epiphany in, 103, 116, 120; Eucharistic imagery, 121; female figures in, 105; genetive principle of, 102–3; gestures in, 67; heteroglossia in, 106; and Hugh Miller's work, 133, 137–39; internality, farthest point of, 125–26; ironic realism in, 119–20; irony in, 124; language in, 20, 118, 137–40, 227, 249n18; language-silence paradox in, 22; lyrical symbolism-ironic realism fusion, 117–21; meaning generated by, 111; narrative mode of, 119; nationalism of, 110; National Library scene, 129–30, 250n25; opening of, 104, 106, 118; origins of, 53; overtones in, 123–24; overture, 117–18; Parnell in, 107, 109–12; quotations in, 105–6; repetition and silence, 117, 121–27, 250n23; Revelation, allusions to, 9, 200; revelation and language, 7; sexuality in, 130–31; "smugging" term in, 139–40, 251n36; "The spell of arms and voices," 65; splendor of truth in, 5; Stephen's diary, 117; Stephen's identity, 142–43, 162; structure of, 102, 106, 111, 114, 118, 125; themes of, 104; and Trench's theory of language, 136; water imagery, 130–33; and Watts's "Obedience to Parents," 105, 107

—villanelle, Stephen's: and epiphanies, 112, 114–15, 118, 123; and irony, 20; and linguistic epiphany, 130–31; and *Parable of the Plum,* 250n28; and *Stephen Hero,* 248n14; water imagery in, 130–31; writing of, 248n14

A Portrait of the Artist as a Young Man, linguistic epiphany in: overview of, 128; and absences, 143–44; and aesthetic theory, 132; and color, 134, 169, 251n30; in "dewy wet soul" section, 131–32; and embodiment, 129–32; and etymology, 134, 139–44; and Hugh Miller's work, 133, 137–39, 142, 251n34; lamp metaphor,

142–43; language, as communal, 129, 135; language, materiality of, 129, 133–34; language, musicality of, 133–34; language, recycling of, 132–33; language and spirit, 139, 143; and Lecercle's linguistic theory, 128–29; in the process of becoming, 140–41; and sexual language, 129–31, 139; Stephen's identity and name, 141–43; and Stephen's villanelle, 130–31; "tundish" term, 142–44, 251n38; *versus Ulysses*'s, 172

A Portrait of the Artist as a Young Man, repetition and variation in: "Apologise," 103–7; and Benjaminian image, 106, 112; diary segment, 113–14, 117, 248nn15–16; and endless proliferation, 102–3, 102–3; and epiphanic workings of, 107; gaps creating associations, 226; infirmary scene, 107–11, 247n5; and language, 249n17; and language in the process of becoming, 142; overture, 117–18; quotations, 106; Stephen's diary, 117; Stephen's memories, 109–11; Stephen's name, 142

A Portrait of the Artist as a Young Man and epiphanies: "Apologise," 103–7, 116, 118, 122; changes to, 122; and climactic moments, 114–15; in concluding section, 111; "The Girls, The Boys," 115; "Half-Men, Half-Goats," 122, 126; "Her Arm on My Knees," 122–23; "Hoofs upon the Dublin Road," 112–13, 187; "Images of Fabulous Kings," 112–13, 115–16, 123, 247n9; "Is That Mary Ellen?," 112, 114, 154; "The Last Tram," 112, 114–15, 121, 248n13; literary creation, 227; lyrical symbolic, 109, 117; as material for, 76; poles, fusion of, 117, 121, 225–26; repetition and silence, 122–23; reuse of, generally, 12, 53, 65, 76, 102, 103*t,* 116, 225; "She Dances," 115, 248n12; "The Ship," 108–9, 111–13; speech in, 122; "The Spell," 112–13; and Stephen's artistic growth, 115; and Stephen's diary, 111, 113–17; and Stephen's villanelle,

A Portrait of the Artist as a Young Man and epiphanies—*continued*
112, 114–15, 118, 123; as structuring, 102, 112, 114–15, 128; style, impact on, 115; as unremarkable, 114–15; "Upon Me from the Darkness," 122

"A Portrait of the Artist" essay, 102–3

Rabaté, Jean-Michel, 15–16, 52, 77–78, 88, 209

"The Race": lyrical qualities of, 62–63, 80–81; in *Ulysses*, 151–53, 157, 170

Repetition: in Beckett, 229; in "Counterparts," 22; in "The Dead," 89, 97–99, 101; Derrida on, 21; and difference, 19–20; in *Finnegans Wake*, 19, 22, 204, 209, 212–14, 219; in Joyce's work, 22, 35; in lyrical epiphanies, 63–64; and lyrical symbolism, 121; in poetry, 230; in *Portrait*, 121–27, 250n23; and semantic proliferation, 177; in *Ulysses*, 19, 22, 152, 157–58. *See also Dubliners*, repetition in; Silence and repetition

Repetition and variation: in *Dubliners*, 82, 101; in *Finnegans Wake*, 214–15, 217; in *Ulysses*, 145, 147–48, 157–58, 170–71, 174. *See also A Portrait of the Artist as a Young Man*, repetition and variation in

Reproduction, 20

Revelation, book of: allusions to, Joyce's, 9–11, 200; allusions to, Wordsworth's, 39–41; beasts of, 8, 10; epiphany in, 28; Joyce's copy of, 7–8, 41, 199, 238n8, 238n10; Joyce's interpretations of, 8–9; King James Version, 8; structure of, 8

Revelation and language, 6–11

Reynolds, Mary, 35

Riquelme, John Paul, 243n7, 250n22

Robinson, Henry Morton, 208, 214

Romanticism, 38. *See also* Epiphany, Romantic

Rousseau, Jean-Jacques, 37–38

Scholes, Robert: and "The Apocalypse of St. John," 7; on epiphanies, 51, 53; on epiphany in Joyce studies, 47–48, 77; influence of, 2, 47; on "Is Mabie Your Sweetheart?," 155; on "The spell of arms and voices," 65; on *Stephen Hero*, 102; on Stephen's epiphany aesthetics, 70; on *Ulysses*, 145. *See also The Workshop of Daedalus*

The Secret Language of Ireland, 195

Self-reflexivity: of aphorisms, 90; in epiphanies, 22; and irony, 177; of language, 222, 226; and linguistic epiphany, 22, 183; and modernism, 38; of *Stephen Hero*, 74; of text, 223, 227; textuality, as emphasizing, 227; in *Ulysses*, 151, 168–69, 171, 178–79. *See also Finnegans Wake*, self-reflexivity of

Senn, Fritz, 167, 210, 254n19

"She Comes at Night": overview of, 15–17; absences in, 16; in *Finnegans Wake*, 183–85, 188; importance to Joyce, 256n1; Joyce, Stanislaus on, 15–16, 143, 145, 183; and Joyce, Mary, 15–16; in *Ulysses*, 145, 147–48, 151–53, 157

"She Dances with Them in the Round," 56, 115, 248n12

Shelley, Percy Bysshe, 45–55, 132

"The Ship," 108–9, 111–13, 157, 166

Silence: and artistic conception, 20; in Beckett, 229–30; and concealment, 17; in epiphanies, dramatic, 2, 19, 145, 177; in *Finnegans Wake*, 203–4, 211–12; and indeterminacy, 177; and ironic realism, 121, 127; John Cage on, 21, 238n18; and language, 21–22, 127, 158, 226–27; and linguistic epiphany, 21–22; in modernist literature, 230–31; in *Portrait*, 117, 121–27, 250n23; signifying, 21; in "The Sisters," 59, 88, 93–97, 245n9; and "The Stars on Joyce's Nose," 158–59, 161; texts arising from, 158; textual, 125, 226; in theater, 229; thought arising from, 158;

in Woolf's work, 228. *See also Dubliners*, silence in

Silence and repetition: and circulation breaks, 151; and *différance*, 227; in Eliot's poetry, 231; and epiphanies, 227; mutual dependence, 19–21, 226–27; "A Painful Case," 89, 92–93; in *Portrait*, 117, 121–27, 250n23; in *Ulysses*, 226; Woolf's, 228

Silverman, O. A., 77

"The Sisters": dialogue in, 96–97; ending of, 78, 95–97; epiphany in, 59, 78, 97; as gnomonic, 59, 68, 93, 95–97; lacunae of, 97; language and light in, 68; and materiality of language, 227; perspective changes in, 87; the priest's death, 93–95, 245n10; repetition in, 95–97; Silence in, 59, 88, 93–97, 245n9; structure of, 97; suspicious interpretations of, 93–94

Skeat, Walter: body, etymology of, 14; dappled, etymology of, 134; epiphany, etymology of, 25; Etymological dictionary of, 14, 25, 135–36; halcyon, etymology of, 254n19; matter, etymology of, 14; phase, etymology of, 68; smugging, etymology of, 251n36; in *Stephen Hero*, 134; and theology, 136; tundish, etymology of, 143–44

Slepon, Raphael, 209

Slingsby, G.V.L., 205

Slote, Sam, 260n4

"The Spell of Arms and Voices," 64–65, 91, 112–13, 157, 166

Spencer, Theodore, 181–82

Spirit, 11, 27, 66–67, 74, 128–29, 131, 139

Spurr, David, 199, 209–10, 257n18

Stars, 160, 161–63, 177, 253n16

"The Stars on Joyce's Nose," 58–59, 158–59, 158–59, 161

Stephen Hero (SH): affirmation of man, 6; alexia, Stephen's, 134–35; and Aquinas, 34, 72; beauty, aesthetics of, 70–72; chapter numbering, 243n7; epiphanies, reuse of, 12, 53, 57, 65, 76, 102, 225; epiphany, signature, 103; etymology in, 14; fragment of colloquy, 54, 57, 80; Harry Levin on, 2; Kantian aesthetics in, 71–72; philology in, 135; portions surviving, 102, 247n1; publication of, 24; repetition and death, 148–49; revelation, aesthetics of, 7–8; Skeat's dictionary in, 134–35; "The spell of arms and voices" in, 65; and "Two Mourners," 149; Villanelle of the Temptress, 54; words and gestures in, 67

—epiphany in: aesthetics of, 65–69, 71–72, 74; Ballast Office clock example, 69–70, 72; definition of, 1, 24, 44, 49, 66–67, 160, 181, 192, 239n3; and Kantian sublime, 74; and language, 66; linguistic, 135; objects capable of, 72; and Schopenhauer, 70; term use, 182–83; theory of, 33, 54, 70, 72; and vulgarity, 66–67

Steppe, Wolfhard, 76

"The Study of Languages," 11

The sublime: Kantian, 72–75, 227, 260n2; and language, 74–75, 227; Wordsworth's aesthetics of, 41

Sublime reflection, 101

Sudermann, Hermann, 4

"They Pass in Twos and Threes," 168

Tigges, Wim, 46, 48–49, 51

Tindall, William, 47, 208, 225

Torchiana, Donald, 78

Trench, Richard Chenevix, 136–37, 240n8, 251n32, 251n34

Trench, Samuel Chenevix, 136–37

Truth, 5–6, 238n7

"Two Mourners," 56, 149–50, 252n5

Ulysses: authority, breaks from, 153; and *The Awful Disclosures of Maria Monk*, 172; Bloom, 161–63, 166–67, 170, 177; Calypso, 150; center of, 174; chiasmus
—"Aeolus": circulation in, 150–51; color

Ulysses—continued
in, 152–53; circulation trope, 150–51, 178, 252n6; clouds, 165–66; color, use of, 169–70; "Cyclops," 161, 170; divergence in, 177–78; epiphanic structure, *versus* *Portrait*, 158; epiphany, stellar, 159–63, 177, 253n15; errancy, aesthetic of, 171; etymology in, 163–64, 254n19; "Eumaeus," 19, 158, 169–70, 179; *Evening Telegraph* articles, 171; *Finnegans Wake*, connection to, 179–80, 200, 259n40; and fossil poetry, 170; gestures in, 67; "Hades," 146*t*, 149–50, 252n5; Haines, model for, 137; and *Hamlet*, 152, 157, 162, 165–66; hockey players, 5, 136, 151–52; indeterminacy in, 150, 226; irony, 165, 226; "Ithaca," 146*t*, 156, 160–63; *lalangue* in, 156–57; language in, 165, 169–71; language-silence paradox in, 22; linguistic absences in, 16; linguistic world of, 161; *Love's bitter mystery*, 148; lyrical-symbolic method in, 158; man, affirmation of, 6; materiality of language in, 156, 164, 171; meanings, irreducible, 170; Molly, 163–64; "Mother" dream, 145, 147, 251n1; mutation in, 172, 174–76, 226; "Nestor," 5, 136, 146*t*, 151–52, 170, 252n2; and the *Odyssey*, 26; œmissions, 164–65; and the omphalos, 14; originary gaps in, 175, 177, 226; parallax in, 162–63, 166, 176; "Penelope," 146*t*, 158; phenomena motif, 161–62; and *Portrait*, material from, 253n11; repetition and variation in, 145, 147–48, 157–58, 170–71, 174; repetition in, 22, 152, 157–58; revelation, allusions to, 9–10; as revelation, 9; "Rhymes and Reasons," 168–69; "Scylla and Charybdis," 146*t*, 157, 164, 253n12; self-reflexivity in, 151, 168–69, 169, 171, 178–79; signifiers in, 162–64; silence and repetition, 226; splendor of truth in, 6; Stephen-Bloom relationship, 153; Stephen's name, 162, 164; Stephen's poem, 167–69, 177; stradentwining cables, 14, 142, 148, 169; structure of, 177–78; "Telemachus," 145, 146*t*, 147–48, 150, 153; time in, 70; and Trieste notebook, 145, 147; Tycho's star, 159, 162, 253n15; wordplay in, 164, 168, 171; Yeats, allusions to, 148, 166, 252n3

—and *Portrait*, 251n30; epiphanies used in, 146*t*; origins of writing, 68, 240n6; Stephen's poem, 167–69; "wimbles," 179, 255n28

—"Circe": "Apologise," 152; "aum" syllable, 187; chiasmus in, 152–53; end of, 153; epiphanies used in, 146*t*; ironic realism in, 148; lyrical symbolism in, 148; "phenomena" term in, 161; "The Race," 152–53, 170; Rudy, apparition of, 153–54; "She Comes at Night," 145, 147–48, 152–53; "Upon Me from the Darkness," 152

—"Nausicaa": Bloom's sandwriting, 166–67, 177; cloud passage, 166; desire, deferral of, 156; epiphanies used in, 146*t*; "Is Mabie Your Sweetheart?," 155–56; *lalangue* in, 227; and language, as communal, 156; and materiality of language, 156, 171; and "Proteus," 166–67; stellar epiphany in, 162

—"Oxen of the Sun": anachronism in, 175; and *Aristotle's Masterpiece*, 172; "The Dead," allusions to, 176; difficulty of, 175; divergence in, 177; Joyce on, 174–75; and materiality of language, 175; meaning production in, 175–76; mutation and irony in, 172, 174–77; originary gaps in, 175; phantoms in, 176; phenomena motif, 161; *Portrait*, allusions to, 176; postcreation, 171, 255n26; and reproduction, 20; stylistic imitation in, 174–75; uncertainty, tonal, 177

—"Proteus": allusions to epiphanies, 17–18; cloud passage, 165; "crosstrees" term, 253n12; epiphanies passage, 165–66; epiphanies used in, 146*t*; "Is

That Mary Ellen?," 252n7; and Joyce's aesthetics, 165; and "Nausicaa," 166–67; and philology, 14; "The Ship," 157, 166; "The Spell," 157, 166; Stephen's poetry, 167, 177; "They Pass in Twos and Threes," 168
—"Wandering Rocks": *Aristotle's Masterpiece* in, 172; *The Awful Disclosures of Maria Monk* in, 172, 174; central break in, 172, 174, 177; epiphanies used in, 146t; "The Lame Beggar," 157; structure of, 177–78

Ulysses, epiphanies in: "Apologise," 152; as intertextual links, 157–58; as intratextual links, 157–58; "Is Mabie Your Sweetheart?," 155–57; "Is That Mary Ellen?," 154, 157, 252n7; "The Lame Beggar," 157–58; and linguistic innovation, 227; "The Race," 151–52, 157, 170; and repetition, 157–58; reuse in, generally, 12, 53, 76, 146t, 225; reuse in, reasons for, 157; "She Comes at Night," 145, 147–48, 151–52, 157; "The Ship," 157, 166; "The Spell," 157, 166; structure of, 178; "They Pass in Twos and Threes," 168; "Two Mourners," 149–50, 252n5; "Upon Me from the Darkness," 152

Ulysses, linguistic epiphany in: baby Boardman's speech, 156, 171; circulation breaks enabling, 151; climactic, 153–54; evolution of, 178; gaps producing, 163, 178–79; and hockey players, 151–52; and œmissions, 165; versus *Portrait*'s, 172; "wimbles" term, 179, 255n28

Uncertainty: in "The Dead," 99; in epiphanies, 2–3, 15, 191; in *Finnegans Wake*, 217; and Language, Joyce's, 15–16; *and Ulysses*, 171, 177

Uncertainty principle, 44, 59, 61

"Upon Me from the Darkness," 122, 152

Variation. *See* Repetition and variation

Vico, Giambattista, 205–7, 212–13

Vitoux, Pierre, 190

Walker's Pronouncing Dictionary, 254n19

Walzl, Florence, 47–48, 76–77, 101

Watts, Isaac, 105, 107

Weaver, Harriet Shaw, 175, 258n24

Winstanley, Gerrard, 40

Wolfe, Thomas, 46

Woolf, Virginia, 46, 228, 232, 260n3

Wordsworth, William: descent to Gondo, 39; epiphany in, 38–39, 42, 44–45; *The Excursion*, 45; father's death, 42–43; internal divinity themes, 40–41; Joyce, influence on, 45; language and sense perception in, 241n17; and Modernism, 38; phenomenology of, 31; *The Prelude*, 40–42, 242n19; Revelation, allusions to, 40–41; Shelley, influence on, 45; spots of time, 17, 25, 41–43; sublime, aesthetics of, 41

Work in Progress, 33, 190, 193–94, 204, 207, 229. *See also Finnegans Wake*

The Workshop of Daedalus, 2, 76, 111, 237n3, 238n13

Yeats, William Butler, 148, 252n3

"Your Favorite Poet," 58

SANGAM MACDUFF is working on logic and modern literature at Royal Holloway, University of London. He read English at Trinity Hall, Cambridge University, holds a master's degree from the University of Edinburgh, and wrote his doctoral thesis on James Joyce's epiphanies at the University of Geneva. He has published on Joyce and modernism in the *James Joyce Quarterly*, *James Joyce Broadsheet*, *Swiss Proceedings in English Language and Literature*, *Genetic Joyce Studies*, and *European Joyce Studies*.

THE FLORIDA JAMES JOYCE SERIES
Edited by Sebastian D. G. Knowles

The Autobiographical Novel of Co-Consciousness: Goncharov, Woolf, and Joyce, by Galya Diment (1994)
Bloom's Old Sweet Song: Essays on Joyce and Music, by Zack Bowen (1995)
Joyce's Iritis and the Irritated Text: The Dis-lexic "Ulysses," by Roy Gottfried (1995)
Joyce, Milton, and the Theory of Influence, by Patrick Colm Hogan (1995)
Reauthorizing Joyce, by Vicki Mahaffey (paperback edition, 1995)
Shaw and Joyce: "The Last Word in Stolentelling," by Martha Fodaski Black (1995)
Bely, Joyce, and Döblin: Peripatetics in the City Novel, by Peter I. Barta (1996)
Jocoserious Joyce: The Fate of Folly in "Ulysses," by Robert H. Bell (paperback edition, 1996)
Joyce and Popular Culture, edited by R. B. Kershner (1996)
Joyce and the Jews: Culture and Texts, by Ira B. Nadel (paperback edition, 1996)
Narrative Design in "Finnegans Wake": The Wake Lock Picked, by Harry Burrell (1996)
Gender in Joyce, edited by Jolanta W. Wawrzycka and Marlena G. Corcoran (1997)
Latin and Roman Culture in Joyce, by R. J. Schork (1997)
Reading Joyce Politically, by Trevor L. Williams (1997)
Advertising and Commodity Culture in Joyce, by Garry Leonard (1998)
Greek and Hellenic Culture in Joyce, by R. J. Schork (1998)
Joyce, Joyceans, and the Rhetoric of Citation, by Eloise Knowlton (1998)
Joyce's Music and Noise: Theme and Variation in His Writings, by Jack W. Weaver (1998)
Reading Derrida Reading Joyce, by Alan Roughley (1999)
Joyce through the Ages: A Nonlinear View, edited by Michael Patrick Gillespie (1999)
Chaos Theory and James Joyce's Everyman, by Peter Francis Mackey (1999)
Joyce's Comic Portrait, by Roy Gottfried (2000)
Joyce and Hagiography: Saints Above!, by R. J. Schork (2000)
Voices and Values in Joyce's "Ulysses," by Weldon Thornton (2000)
The Dublin Helix: The Life of Language in Joyce's "Ulysses," by Sebastian D. G. Knowles (2001)
Joyce Beyond Marx: History and Desire in "Ulysses" and "Finnegans Wake," by Patrick McGee (2001)
Joyce's Metamorphosis, by Stanley Sultan (2001)
Joycean Temporalities: Debts, Promises, and Countersignatures, by Tony Thwaites (2001)
Joyce and the Victorians, by Tracey Teets Schwarze (2002)
Joyce's "Ulysses" as National Epic: Epic Mimesis and the Political History of the Nation State, by Andras Ungar (2002)
James Joyce's "Fraudstuff," by Kimberly J. Devlin (2002)
Rite of Passage in the Narratives of Dante and Joyce, by Jennifer Margaret Fraser (2002)
Joyce and the Scene of Modernity, by David Spurr (2002)
Joyce and the Early Freudians: A Synchronic Dialogue of Texts, by Jean Kimball (2003)
Twenty-First Joyce, edited by Ellen Carol Jones and Morris Beja (2004)
Joyce on the Threshold, edited by Anne Fogarty and Timothy Martin (2005)
Wake Rites: The Ancient Irish Rituals of "Finnegans Wake," by George Cinclair Gibson (2005)
"Ulysses" in Critical Perspective, edited by Michael Patrick Gillespie and A. Nicholas Fargnoli (2006)
Joyce and the Narrative Structure of Incest, by Jen Shelton (2006)

Joyce, Ireland, Britain, edited by Andrew Gibson and Len Platt (2006)
Joyce in Trieste: An Album of Risky Readings, edited by Sebastian D. G. Knowles, Geert Lernout, and John McCourt (2007)
Joyce's Rare View: The Nature of Things in "Finnegans Wake," by Richard Beckman (2007)
Joyce's Misbelief, by Roy Gottfried (2007)
James Joyce's Painful Case, by Cóilín Owens (2008; first paperback edition, 2017)
Cannibal Joyce, by Thomas Jackson Rice (2008)
Manuscript Genetics, Joyce's Know-How, Beckett's Nohow, by Dirk Van Hulle (2008)
Catholic Nostalgia in Joyce and Company, by Mary Lowe-Evans (2008)
A Guide through "Finnegans Wake," by Edmund Lloyd Epstein (2009)
Bloomsday 100: Essays on Ulysses, edited by Morris Beja and Anne Fogarty (2009)
Joyce, Medicine, and Modernity, by Vike Martina Plock (2010; first paperback edition, 2012)
Who's Afraid of James Joyce?, by Karen R. Lawrence (2010; first paperback edition, 2012)
"Ulysses" in Focus: Genetic, Textual, and Personal Views, by Michael Groden (2010; first paperback edition, 2012)
Foundational Essays in James Joyce Studies, edited by Michael Patrick Gillespie (2011; first paperback edition, 2017)
Empire and Pilgrimage in Conrad and Joyce, by Agata Szczeszak-Brewer (2011; first paperback edition, 2017)
The Poetry of James Joyce Reconsidered, edited by Marc C. Conner (2012; first paperback edition, 2015)
The German Joyce, by Robert K. Weninger (2012; first paperback edition 2016)
Joyce and Militarism, by Greg Winston (2012; first paperback edition, 2015)
Renascent Joyce, edited by Daniel Ferrer, Sam Slote, and André Topia (2013; first paperback edition, 2014)
Before Daybreak: "After the Race" and the Origins of Joyce's Art, by Cóilín Owens (2013; first paperback edition, 2014)
Modernists at Odds: Reconsidering Joyce and Lawrence, edited by Matthew J. Kochis and Heather L. Lusty (2015)
James Joyce and the Exilic Imagination, by Michael Patrick Gillespie (2015)
The Ecology of "Finnegans Wake," by Alison Lacivita (2015)
Joyce's Allmaziful Pluralities: Polyvocal Explorations of "Finnegans Wake," edited by Kimberly J. Devlin and Christine Smedley (2015)
Exiles: A Critical Edition, by James Joyce, edited by A. Nicholas Fargnoli and Michael Patrick Gillespie (2016; first paperback edition, 2019)
Up to Maughty London: Joyce's Cultural Capital in the Imperial Metropolis, by Eleni Loukopoulou (2017)
Joyce and the Law, edited by Jonathan Goldman (2017)
At Fault: Joyce and the Crisis of the Modern University, by Sebastian D. G. Knowles (2018)
"Ulysses" Unbound: A Reader's Companion to James Joyce's "Ulysses," Third Edition, by Terence Killeen (2018)
Joyce and Geometry, by Ciaran McMorran (2020)
Panepiphanal World: James Joyce's Epiphanies, by Sangam MacDuff (2020)

www.ingramcontent.com/pod-product-compliance
Lightning Source LLC
Chambersburg PA
CBHW031758220426
43662CB00007B/455